DEATH Investigators' HANDBOOK

This book is dedicated to the investigator who

Knocks on one more door;
Misses one more hot meal;
Looks at the scene photographs one more time;
Makes one more phone call;
Makes one last try;

Solves one more case.

VOLUME THREE
Scientific Investigations

DEATH
Investigator's
HANDBOOK

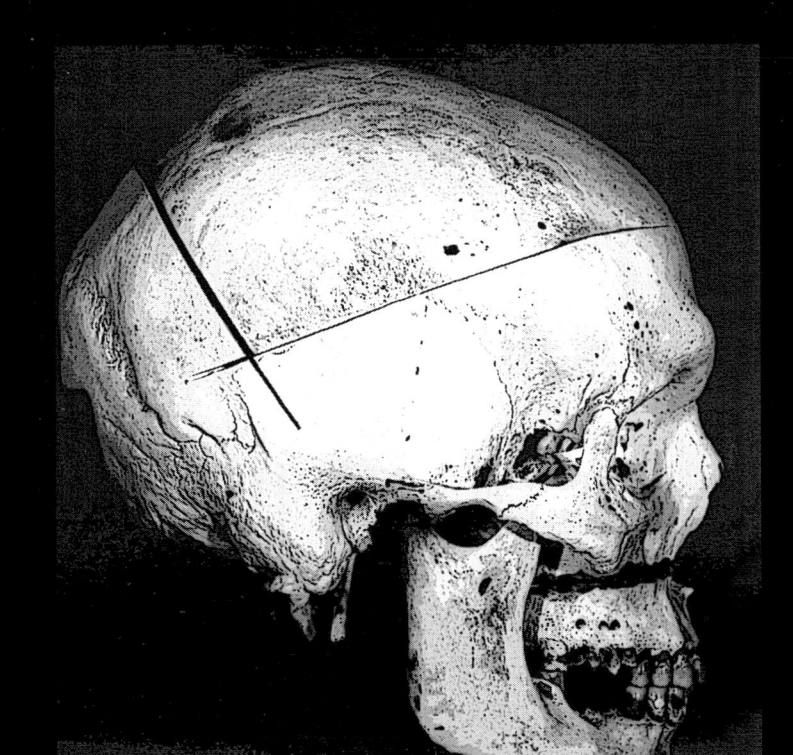

Louis N. Eliopulos
Paladin Press • Boulder, Colorado

Death Investigator's Handbook:
Volume Three: Scientific Investigations
by Louis N. Eliopulos

Copyright © 2003 by Louis N. Eliopulos

ISBN 13: 978-1-58160-498-6
Printed in the United States of America

Published by Paladin Press, a division of
Paladin Enterprises, Inc.
Gunbarrel Tech Center
7077 Winchester Circle
Boulder, Colorado 80301 USA
+1.303.443.7250

Direct inquiries and/or orders to the above address.

PALADIN, PALADIN PRESS, and the "horse head" design
are trademarks belonging to Paladin Enterprises and
registered in United States Patent and Trademark Office.

All rights reserved. Except for use in a review, no
portion of this book may be reproduced in any form
without the express written permission of the publisher.

Neither the author nor the publisher assumes
any responsibility for the use or misuse of
information contained in this book.

Visit our Web site at www.paladin-press.com

TABLE OF CONTENTS

PART III: SCIENTIFIC INVESTIGATIONS • 649

Chapter 62:	Medical Examiner and Coroner Systems	651
Chapter 63:	Requesting a Pathologist at a Death Scene	667
Chapter 64:	The Forensic Autopsy	669
Chapter 65:	The Purpose of an Autopsy in an Apparent Homicide Case	673
Chapter 66:	Autopsy References	675
Chapter 67:	Forensic Odontology	679
Chapter 68:	AFBO Bitemark Methodology Guidelines	695
Chapter 69:	Forensic Anthropology	705
Chapter 70:	Toxicology	711
Chapter 71:	Drugs of Abuse	715
Chapter 72:	Common Prescription Medications	731
Chapter 73:	Fingerprints	765
Chapter 74:	Firearms	817
Chapter 75:	DNA Procedures	839
Chapter 76:	Serology	859
Chapter 77:	Trace Evidence and Other Crime Lab Examinations	863
Conversion Charts		901
Contributors		907
Bibliography		913
Index		937

This card typifies the well wishes and offers for assistance that were prevalent after the horrible events of September 11, 2001. It was given to the author by the Red Cross at the Pentagon crash site. The author carried it with him while he worked with forensic body-recovery teams at the Pentagon.

SEPTEMBER 11, 2001

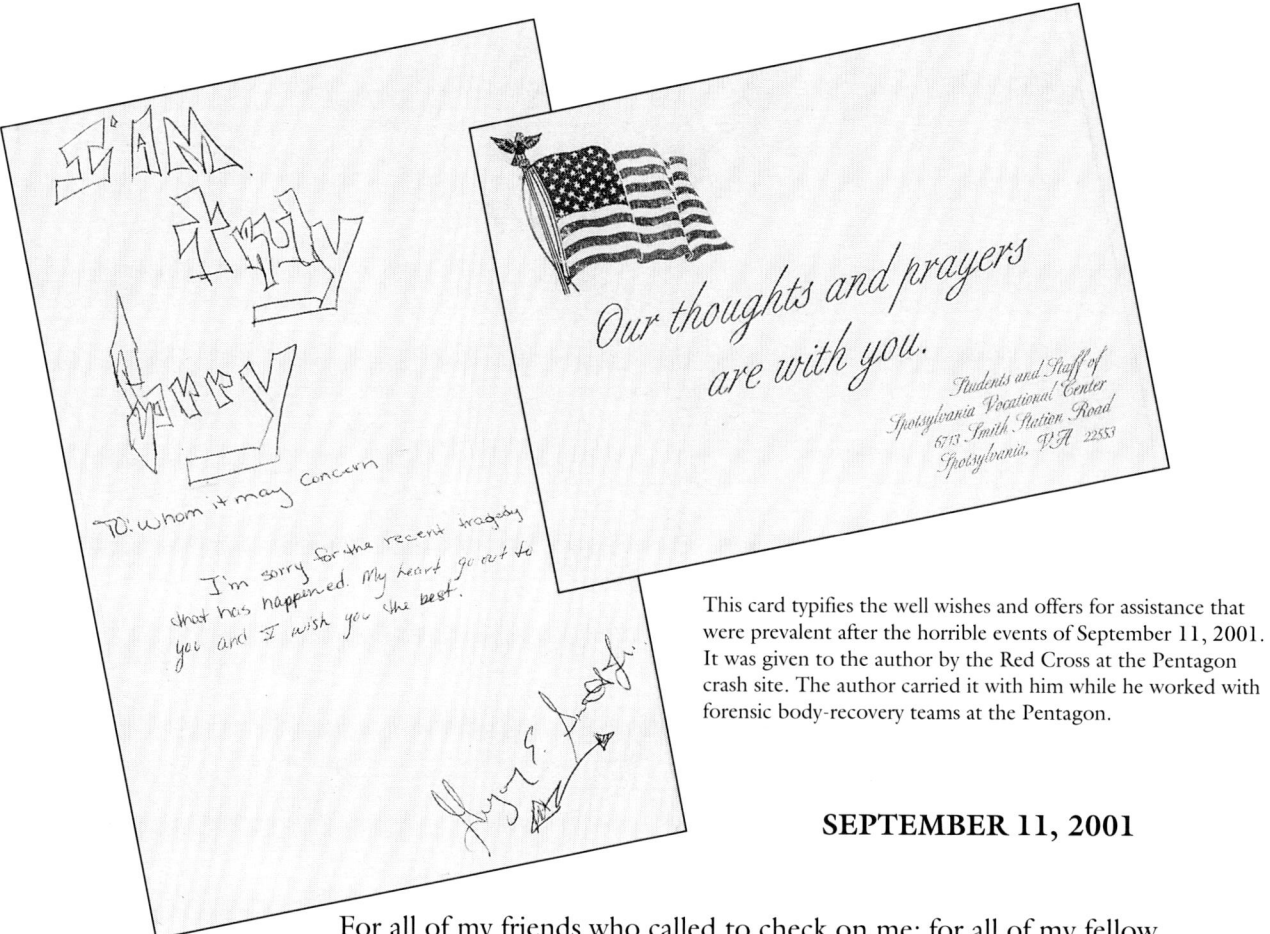

For all of my friends who called to check on me; for all of my fellow professionals who contacted me to volunteer their time and effort; for the homicide detective that called me and told me if it was his son who had died inside the Pentagon, he would want me to be the one to bring him out; for the school children who sent us notes and the people who brought flowers; for the Salvation Army and the Red Cross, which took care of our every want and need; to the church group from North Carolina who slept on the floor so that they could serve us hot meals—I say thank you.

Among the senseless tragedy and horrible carnage that occurred on September 11, 2001, I saw America at its very best. Deeply saddened, we collected our dead and grieved our terrible losses. And then, we moved on. I was never so proud to be an American. Your thoughts and prayers were not only heard but also deeply felt. I was so very proud to represent you.

—Lou Eliopulos
2003

ACKNOWLEDGMENTS

A very special thank-you for the continuous education and opportunity of working with the following true professionals of the forensic sciences:

>Dr. Peter Lipkovic
>Dr. Bonifacio Floro
>Dr. William Maples
>Dr. Arthur Burns
>Dr. Margarita Arruza
>Dr. Anthony Falsetti

Also, my profound appreciation to those individuals with whom I have shared the joy of solved cases and the agony and frustration of having a case remain unresolved:

>Bruce Herring
>William Hagerty
>Dave Early
>Tom Asimos
>Robbie Hinson
>Carol Dean
>Pete Hughes
>Jim Grebas
>Mike Sullivan
>Ralph Blincoe
>Mark Fox
>Sheri Blanton
>Gerry Nance
>Dayle Hinman
>Dr. Jason Byrd
>Brian Stamper

PUBLISHER'S NOTE

The contact information contained in this book was accurate at the time of publication.

PART III
SCIENTIFIC INVESTIGATIONS

CHAPTER 62:
MEDICAL EXAMINER AND CORONER SYSTEMS

CORONER/MEDICAL EXAMINER SYSTEMS IN THE UNITED STATES

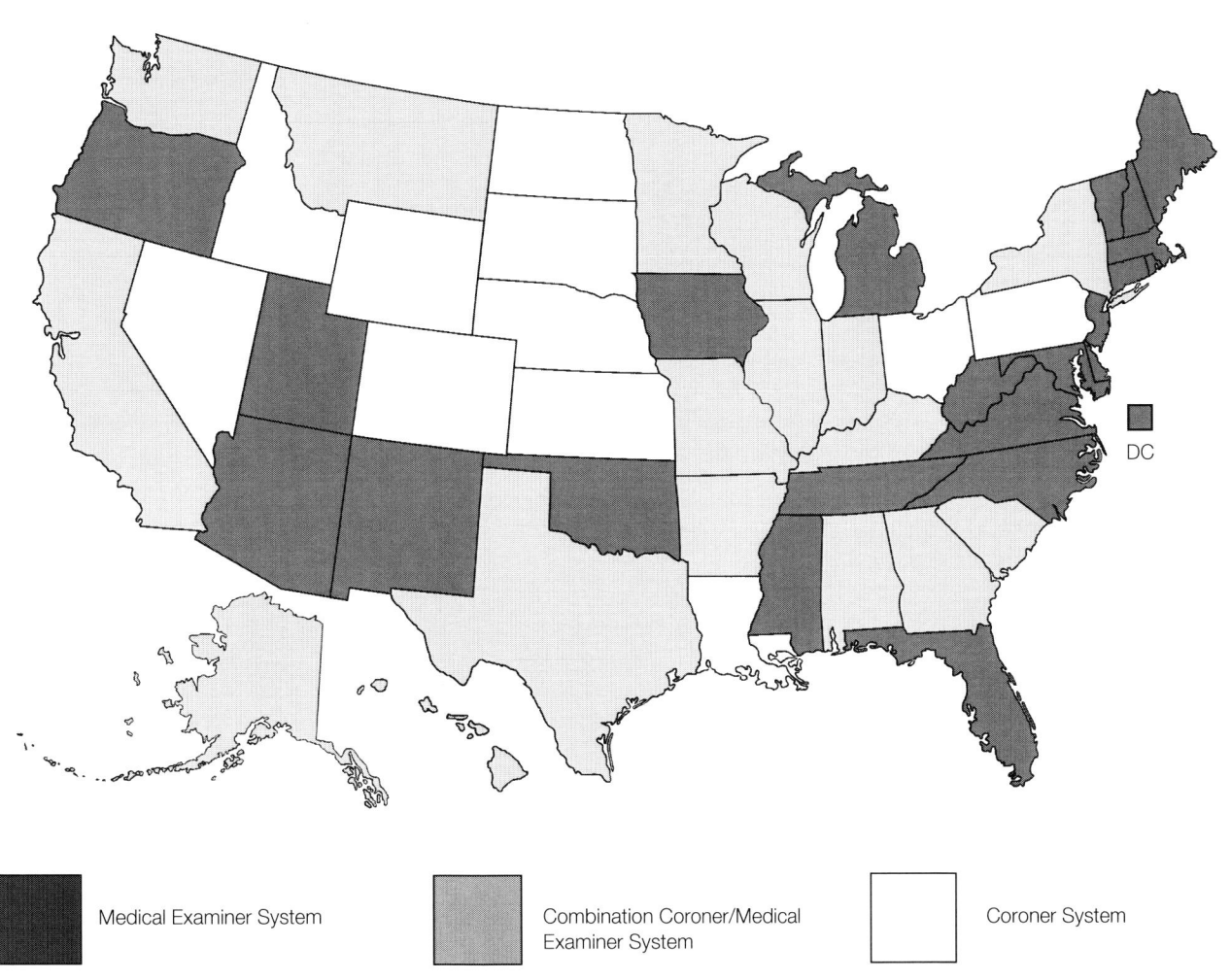

STATE/SYSTEM TYPE	DEATH CASES FALLING UNDER JURISDICTION
Alabama State ME County Coroner	• If the person dies by violence of homicide, suicide, accidental or industrial • Criminal abortion • Sudden death, if in apparent good health • In suspicious circumstances • When there is a public health hazard • If the body is to be cremated
Alaska District Coroner County ME	• Homicide • Suspicion of criminal means • Suicide • With no physician in attendance • When physician is unable to execute death certificate • When cause of death cannot be determined
Arizona County ME	• When not under current care of a physician for a potentially fatal illness • When the attending physician is unavailable to sign the death certificate. • By violence • Of a prisoner or occurring in prison • Occurring suddenly to a person in apparent good health • By occupational disease or accident • Where a public health hazard is presented • Occurring during anesthetic or surgical procedures • Occurring in a suspicious, unusual, or unnatural manner
Arkansas Sate ME County Coroner	• Death appears to be caused by violence, homicide, suicide, or accident. • Death appears to be the result of the presence of drugs or poisons in the body. • Death appears to be the result of a motor vehicle accident, or the body was found in or near a roadway or railroad. • Death appears to be the result of a motor vehicle accident, and there is no obvious trauma to the body.
California County ME County coroner	• Violent, sudden, or unusual • Unattended • Deaths where the deceased has not been attended by a physician in the 20 days before death • Self-induced or criminal abortion • Known or suspected homicide, suicide, or accidental poisoning • By recent or old injury or accident
Colorado Coroner	• From external violence • Unexplained cause • Under suspicious circumstances • Suddenly, when in good health • Where no physician is in attendance or the attending physician is unable to certify the cause of death

	• From thermal, chemical, or radiation injury • From criminal abortion • From disease that may be hazardous or contagious or may constitute a hazard to the public health • While in custody of law enforcement officials or while incarcerated in a public institution • From industrial accident
Connecticut State ME	• Violent, whether apparently homicidal, suicidal, or accidental, including but not limited to deaths due to thermal, chemical, electrical, or radiation injury • Due to criminal abortion, whether apparently self-induced or not • Sudden or unexpected deaths not caused by readily recognizable disease • Under suspicious circumstances
Delaware State ME	• By violence, suicide or casualty • While under anesthesia • By abortion or suspected abortion • By poison or suspicion of poison • Suddenly when in apparent good health • When unattended by a physician • In prison or penal institution or police custody • Resulting from employment • From undiagnosed cause, which may be related to a disease constituting a threat to public health • In any suspicious or unusual manner
District of Columbia ME	• By violence, whether apparently homicidal, suicidal, or accidental, including deaths due to thermal, chemical, electrical, or radiation injury • Due to criminal abortion, whether apparently self-induced or not • Under suspicious circumstances • Of persons whose bodies are to be cremated, dissected, buried at sea, or otherwise disposed of so as to be thereafter unavailable for examination • Sudden deaths not caused by readily recognizable disease • Related to disease resulting from employment or to accident while employed • Related to disease that might constitute a threat to public health
Florida District ME	• By criminal violence • By accident • By suicide • Suddenly, when in apparent good health • Unattended by a physician or other recognized practitioner • In a prison or penal institution • In police custody • In any suspicious or unusual circumstances • By criminal abortion

	- By poison
- By disease constituting a threat to public health
- By disease, injury, or toxic agent exposure resulting from employment
- When a body is brought into the state without proper medical certification
- When the body is to be cremated, dissected, or buried at sea
Georgia State ME County Coroner	- By violence, suicide, or casualty
- Suddenly, when in apparent good health
- When unattended by a physician
- When an inmate of a state hospital or state, county, or city penal institution.
- When ordered by a court having criminal jurisdiction
- After birth but before 7 years of age if the death is unexpected or unexplained
- In any suspicious or unusual manner, with particular attention to those persons 16 years of age and under
- As a result of an execution carried out pursuant to imposition of the death penalty
Hawaii County ME	- As the result of violence
- As the result of any accident
- By suicide
- Suddenly when in apparent good health
- When unattended by a physician
- In prison
- In a suspicious or unusual manner
- Within 24 hours after admission to a hospital or institution
Idaho County Coroner	- As a result of violence whether apparently homicidal, suicidal, or accidental
- Under suspicious or unknown circumstances
- When not attended by a physician during last illness and the cause of death cannot be certified by a physician
Illinois County ME Coroner	- Sudden or violent death, whether apparently suicidal, homicidal, or accidental, including but not limited to deaths apparently caused or contributed to by thermal, traumatic, chemical, electrical, or radiation injury, or a complication of any of them, or by drowning, suffocation, or motor vehicle accident
- Maternal or fetal death due to abortion
- Due to sex crime or crime against nature
- Where the circumstances are suspicious, obscure, mysterious, or otherwise unexplained, and where, in the written opinion of the attending physician, the cause is not determined
- Where addiction to alcohol or to any drug may have been a contributory cause
- Where the decedent was not attended by a licensed physician
- Occurring in state institutions or of wards of the state
- If a child less than 2 years dies suddenly or unexpectedly and circumstances concerning the death are unexplained

	• While being pursued, apprehended, or taken into custody by law enforcement officers or while in custody of any law enforcement agency
Indiana District ME County Coroner	• Has died from violence • Has died by casualty • Has died when apparently in good health • Has died in an apparently suspicious, unusual, or unnatural manner • Has been found dead
Iowa State ME	• Violent, including homicidal, suicidal, or accidental • Caused by thermal, chemical, electrical, or radiation injury • Caused by criminal abortion including those self-induced, or by rape, carnal knowledge, or crimes against nature • Related to disease thought to be virulent or contagious, which might constitute a public hazard • Occurring unexpectedly or from unexplained causes • Of a person confined in jail, prison, or correctional institution • Where a physician was not in attendance at any time at least 36 hours preceding death, with the exception of prediagnosed terminal or bedfast cases for which the time period shall be extended to 20 days • Where the body is not claimed by relatives or friends • Where the identity of the deceased is unknown • Of a child under the age of 2 years when sudden infant death syndrome is suspected or cause of death is unknown
Kansas District Coroner	• Death is suspected to have been the result of violence, caused by unlawful means or suicide • By casualty • Suddenly when the decedent was in apparent good health • When the decedent was not regularly attended by a licensed physician • In any suspicious or unusual manner, or when in police custody, or when in a jail or correctional institution • When the determination of the cause of death is held to be in the public interest
Kentucky State ME County Coroner	• Caused by homicide, violence, suicide, an accident, drugs, poison, motor vehicle, train, fire, explosion, drowning, illegal abortion, or unusual circumstances • By criminal means • Sudden infant death syndrome • Child abuse • Death in a person less than 40 years of age with no past medical history to explain the death • Death occurring at a work site • Death in any mental institution • Death in any prison, jail, or penal institution, or while decedent was in police custody • When the death was sudden and unexplained or the decedent was unattended by a physician by more than 36 hours prior to death

	- When skeletonized or extensively decomposed human remains are found
- When the body is to be cremated
- When circumstances of death result in a request by any responsible citizen for an investigation
Louisiana County Coroner	- When suspicious, unexpected, unusual, or sudden
- By violence
- Due to unknown or obscure causes
- Where the body is found dead
- Without attending physician within 36 hours prior to the hour of death
- When abortion, whether self-induced or otherwise, is suspected
- Due to suspected suicide or homicide
- When poison is suspected
- From natural causes occurring in a hospital within 24 hours of admission unless seen by a physician in the last 36 hours
- Following an injury or accident either old or recent
- Due to drowning, hanging, burns, electrocution gunshot wounds, stabs or cuts, lightning, starvation, radiation, exposure, alcoholism, addiction, tetanus, strangulation, suffocation, or smothering
- Due to trauma from whatever cause
- Stillborn deaths
- Due to criminal means
- If victim of alleged rape, carnal knowledge, or crime against nature
- By casualty
- In prison or while serving a sentence
- Due to virulent contagious disease that might be caused by or cause a public hazard (AIDS cases included)
Maine State ME	- Violence of any kind
- Any cause where the death occurs suddenly while the person is in apparent good health
- Any cause where there is no attending physician capable of certifying the death is due to natural causes
- Poisoning, either chronic or acute
- Diagnostic or therapeutic procedures under circumstances indicating gross negligence or unforeseen clearly traumatic causes
- Any cause while the person is in custody or confinement, unless clearly certifiable by an attending physician as due to natural causes
- Disease or pathological process constituting a threat to public health if the authority of the medical examiner is required to adequately study the death to protect the public health
- Deaths that may have been improperly certified or inadequately examined, including, but not limited to, bodies brought into the state under these circumstances
- In the case of a child under the age of 3, from any cause, including sudden infant death syndrome, unless the death is clearly due to a specific natural cause
- As a result of disease, injury, or toxic agent related to employment

Maryland State ME	- By violence, suicide or casualty - Suddenly when in apparent good health or when unattended by a physician - In any suspicious or unusual manner - Fetuses, regardless of duration of pregnancy, if the mother is not attended by a physician at or after the delivery
Massachusetts State ME	- By violence - By the action of chemical, thermal, or electrical agents - Following abortion - From diseases resulting from injury or infection relating to occupation - Suddenly when not disabled by recognizable disease - From malnutrition - From sexual abuse - Of a child who is determined to be physically dependent on an addictive drug at birth - When any person is found dead - When sudden infant death syndrome is suspected
Michigan County ME	- By violence - When unexpected - Without medical attendance during the 48 hours prior to the hour of death unless the attending physician, if any, is able to determine accurately the cause of death - As the result of an abortion, whether self-induced or otherwise - Of any prisoner in any county or city jail
Minnesota County ME Coroner	- Violent, whether apparently homicidal, suicidal, or accidental, including but not limited to deaths due to thermal, chemical, electrical, or radiation injuries - Due to criminal abortion, whether apparently self-induced or not - Under unusual or mysterious circumstances - Of persons whose bodies are to be cremated, dissected, buried at sea, or otherwise disposed of so as to be thereafter unavailable for examination - Of inmates of public institutions who are not hospitalized therein for organic diseases
Mississippi State ME	- All deaths affecting the public interest, including, but not limited to, the following: - Violent, including homicidal, suicidal, or accidental - Caused by thermal, chemical, electrical, or radiation injury - Caused by criminal abortion, including self-induced, or abortion related to or by sexual abuse - Related to disease thought to be virulent or contagious that may constitute a public health hazard - Unexpected or from an unexplained cause - Of a person confined in a prison, jail, or correction institution (autopsy mandatory if prisoner was in custody of state correctional system) - Of a person where physician was not in attendance within 36 hours

preceding death, or in prediagnosed terminal or bedfast cases within 30 days
- Of a person where the body is not claimed by a relative or friend
- Of a person where the identity of the deceased is unknown
- Of a child under the age of 2 where death results from an unknown cause or where the circumstances surrounding the death indicate that sudden infant death syndrome may be the cause of death (autopsy mandatory)
- Where a body is brought into this state for disposal and there is reason to believe either that the death was not investigated properly or that there is not an adequate certification of death.
- Where a person is admitted to a hospital emergency room unconscious or unresponsive, with cardiopulmonary resuscitative measures being performed, and dies within 24 hours of admission without regaining consciousness or responsiveness, unless a physician was in attendance within 36 hours preceding presentation to the hospital, or in cases in which the decedent had a prediagnosed terminal or bedfast condition, unless a physician was in attendance within 30 days preceding presentation to the hospital
- Of a person found dead on the premises of the state correctional system (investigation by state medical examiner mandatory)

Missouri

- Coroner: In any city of 700,000 or more inhabitants or in any county of the first or second class in which a coroner is required, the coroner must investigate all deaths where there is reason to believe that death was caused by criminal violence or following abortion.
  —By violence by homicide, suicide, or accident.
  —By criminal abortion, including those self-induced
  —By some unforeseen occurrence and the deceased had not been attended by a physician during the 36-hour period preceding death
  —Occurring in any unusual or suspicious manner
- Medical Examiner
  —By violence by homicide, suicide, or accident
  —By criminal abortion, including those self-induced
  —By disease thought to be of a hazardous and contagious nature or which might constitute a threat to public health
  —Suddenly when in apparent good health
  —When unattended by a physician, chiropractor, or accredited Christian Science practitioner during the 36-hour period preceding death
  —While in the custody of the law
  —While an inmate of a public institution
  —Occurring in any unusual or suspicious manner

Montana
State ME
County Coroner

- Coroner
  —Death caused or suspected to have been caused by an injury, either recent or remote in origin.
  —Death caused or suspected to have been caused by the deceased or any other person that was the result of an act or omission, including, but not limited to, a criminal or suspected criminal act; a medically

          suspicious death, unusual death, or death of unknown circumstances, including any fetal death; or an accidental death
        —Death caused or suspected to have been caused by an agent, disease, or medical condition that poses a threat to public health
        —Death occurring while the deceased was incarcerated in a prison or jail or confined to a correctional or detention facility owned and operated by the state or a political subdivision of the state
        —Death occurring while the deceased was in the custody of, or was being taken into the custody of, a law enforcement agency or a peace officer
        —Death occurring during or as a result of the deceased's employment
        —Death occurring less than 24 hours after the deceased was admitted to a medical facility or if the deceased was dead upon arrival at a medical facility
        —Death occurring in a manner that was unattended or unwitnessed and the deceased was not attended by a physician at any time in the 30-day period prior to death
        —If the dead body is to be cremated or shipped into the state and lacks proper medical certification or burial or transmit permits
        —Death that occurred under suspicious circumstances
        —Death that is the result of a judicial order
        —Death where no physician or surgeon licensed in Montana will sign a death certificate

Nebraska County Coroner	• By criminal means or violence • Homicide or suicide • By drowning • If sudden or unusual • If drug related • If sudden infant death syndrome is suspected • When involving the sudden and unexplained death of a child between the ages of 1 week and 3 years, and when neglect, violence, or any unlawful means are possible • When death is not certified by an attending physician • When an individual has died while being apprehended by or while in the custody of a law enforcement officer or detention personnel • Any suspicious, unexplained, or unattended death
Nevada District Coroner	• Unattended deaths • In deaths where the deceased has not been attended by a physician in the 10 days before death, the coroner shall issue the certificate of death following consultation with a physician licensed to practice in the state • Deaths related to or following known or suspected self-induced or criminal abortion • Known or suspected homicide, suicide, or accidental death • Deaths known or suspected to have resulted in whole or in part from or to be related to an accident or injury • Deaths from drowning, fire, hanging, gunshot, stabbing, cutting, exposure, starvation, alcoholism, drug addiction, strangulation, or aspiration

	• Deaths in whole or in part occasioned by criminal means • Deaths in prison • Deaths under such circumstances as to afford reasonable ground to suspect that the death was caused by the criminal act of another, or any deaths reported by physicians or other persons having knowledge of death for inquiry by the coroner
New Hampshire State ME	• By violence or unlawful act • In any suspicious, unusual, or unnatural manner • In prison • When unattended by a physician • Suddenly when in apparent health, including those sudden and unexpected deaths of children under 3 years of age or when sudden infant death syndrome is suspected
New Jersey State ME	• By violence whether apparently homicidal, suicidal, or accidental, including but not limited to deaths from thermal, chemical, electrical, or radiation injury • Deaths due to criminal abortion, whether apparently self-induced or not • Not caused by readily recognizable disease, disability, or infirmity • Under suspicious or unusual circumstances • Within 24 hours after admission to a hospital or institution • Of inmates in prison • Of inmates of institutions maintained in whole or in part at the expense of the state or county where the inmate was not hospitalized therein for organic disease • From causes that might constitute a threat to public health • Related to disease resulting from employment or to accident while employed • Sudden or unexpected deaths of infants and children under 3 years of age • Fetal deaths occurring without medical attendance
New Mexico State ME	• Sudden, violent, or untimely • Found dead and the cause of death is unknown or obscure • If caused by criminal act or omission
New York County ME Coroner	• By violence, whether criminal violence, suicide, or casualty • Caused by unlawful act or criminal neglect • Occurring in a suspicious, unusual, or unexplained manner • Caused by suspected criminal abortion • While unattended by a physician so far as can be discovered or where no physician is able to certify the cause of death as provided in public health law and in form as prescribed by the commissioner of health can be found • Of a person confined in a public institution other than a hospital, infirmary, or nursing home • Death occurring to an inmate of a correctional facility

North Carolina State ME	• Homicide • Suicide • Trauma related • Accidental • Disaster related • Violence related • Unknown, unnatural, unusual, or suspicious circumstances • In police custody, jail, prison, or correctional institution • Poisoning or suspicion of poisoning • Possible public health hazard (such as acute contagious disease or epidemic) • Deaths during surgical or anesthetic procedure • Sudden unexpected deaths that are not reasonably related to known previous disease • Deaths without medical attendance, as defined by statute
North Dakota County Coroner	• As a result of criminal or violent means • By casualty or accident • By suicide • Suddenly when in apparent good health • In a suspicious or unusual manner • Occurring without medical attendance • When the Worker's Compensation Board deems it necessary under the Crime Victims Reparation Act
Ohio County Coroner	• As a result of criminal or other violent means • By casualty • By suicide • Suddenly when in apparent health • In any suspicious or unusual manner • Threat to public health
Oklahoma State ME	• By violence, whether apparently homicidal, suicidal, or accidental, including, but not limited to, death from thermal, chemical, electrical, or radiation injury • Due to criminal abortion, whether apparently self-induced or not • Under suspicious, unusual, or unnatural circumstances • Related to disease that might constitute a threat to public health • Unattended by a licensed medical or osteopathic physician for a fatal or potentially fatal illness • Of persons after unexplained coma • That are medically unexpected and occur in the course of a therapeutic procedure • Of any inmates occurring in any place of penal incarceration • Of persons whose bodies are to be cremated, buried at sea, transported out of state, or otherwise made ultimately unavailable for pathological study
Oregon State ME	• Apparently homicidal, suicidal, or occurring under suspicious or unknown circumstances

	- Resulting from the unlawful use of dangerous or narcotic drugs or the use or abuse of chemicals or toxic agents
- Occurring while incarcerated in any jail, correction facility, or in police custody
- Apparently accidental or following an injury
- By disease, injury, or toxic agent exposure during or arising from employment
- While not under the care of a physician during the period immediately preceding death
- Related to disease that might constitute a threat to the public health
Pennsylvania County Coroner	- Sudden deaths not caused by readily recognizable disease, or wherein the cause of death cannot be properly certified by a physician on the basis of prior (recent) medical attendance
- Deaths occurring under suspicious circumstances, including those where alcohol, drugs, or other toxic substances may have had a direct bearing on the outcome
- Deaths occurring as a result of violence or trauma, whether apparently homicidal, suicidal, or accidental (including, but not limited to, those due to mechanical, thermal, chemical, electrical, or radiation injury, drowning, and cave-ins)
- Any death in which trauma, chemical injury, drug overdose, or reaction to drugs or medication or medical treatment was a primary or secondary, direct or indirect, contributory, aggravating, or precipitating cause of death
- Operative and perioperative deaths in which the death is not readily explainable on the basis of prior disease
- Any death where the body is unidentified or unclaimed
- Deaths known or suspected to have resulted from a contagious disease that constitutes a public hazard
- Deaths occurring in a prison or penal institution or while in the custody of the police
- Deaths of persons whose bodies are to be cremated, buried at sea, or otherwise disposed of so as to be thereafter unavailable for examination
- Sudden infant death syndrome
- Stillbirths
Rhode Island State ME	- By homicide, suicide, or casualty
- Due to a criminal abortion
- Due to an accident involving a lack of due care on the part of a person other than the deceased
- Which is the immediate or remote consequences of any physical or toxic injury incurred while the deceased person was employed
- Due to the use of addictive or unidentifiable chemical agents
- Due to an infectious agent capable of spreading an epidemic within the state
- When unattended by a physician
South Carolina Coroner	- By violence
- By suicide

County ME	• When in apparent good health • When unattended by a physician • In any unusual or suspicious manner • While an inmate in a penal or correctional institution • As a stillbirth, medically unattended
South Dakota County Coroner	• By unnatural means, including all deaths of accidental, homicidal, suicidal, and undetermined manner, regardless of suspected criminal involvement in the death • Identity of victim is unknown or the body is unclaimed • Inmates of any state, county, or municipally operated correctional facility, mental institution, or special school • Those believed to represent a public health hazard • Children under 2 years of age resulting from unknown cause or if circumstances suggest sudden infant death syndrome as the cause • Natural deaths if the decedent is not under the care of a physician or the decedent's physician does not feel qualified to sign the death certificate
Tennessee State ME	• From sudden violence • By casualty • By suicide • Suddenly when in apparent good health • When found dead • In prison • In any suspicious, unusual, or unnatural manner • Where the body is to be cremated • For worker's compensation claims if cause of death is obscure or disputed

Texas
County ME
Coroner
	• Justice of the Peace
	  —In prison or jail
	  —When a person is killed or dies an unnatural death from any cause, except under sentence of the law
	  —In the absence of one or more good witnesses
	  —When decedent found dead, the circumstances of death unknown
	  —When the circumstances lead to suspicion of unlawful means
	  —By suicide or suspected suicide
	  —When unattended by a duly licensed and practicing physician and the local health officer or registrar required to report the cause of death does not know the cause of death
	  —When the attending physician(s) cannot certify the cause of death
	• Medical examiner
	  —Same as above and in addition any death within 24 hours after admission to a hospital or institution

Utah State ME	• By violence, gunshot, suicide, or accident (except highway accidents) • Suddenly when in apparent good health • When unattended (not seen by a physician within 30 days) • Under suspicious or unusual circumstances

	- Resulting from poisoning or overdose of drugs
- Resulting from diseases that may constitute a threat to public health
- Resulting from disease, injury, toxic effect, or unusual exertion incurred within the scope of the deceased's employment
- Due to sudden infant death syndrome
- Resulting when the deceased was in prison, jail, police custody, the state hospital, or a detention or medical facility operated for the treatment of mentally ill or emotionally disturbed or delinquent persons
- Associated with diagnostic and therapeutic procedures
- Involving questions of civil liability, in accordance with provisions of the Workman's Compensation Act
Vermont State ME	- From violence
- Suddenly when in apparent good health
- When unattended by a physician
- By casualty
- By suicide
- As a result of injury
- When in jail, prison, or any mental institution
- In any unusual, unnatural, or suspicious manner
- In circumstances involving a hazard to public health, welfare, or safety
Virginia State ME	- By trauma, injury, violence, poisoning, accident, suicide, or homicide
- Suddenly when in apparent good health
- When unattended by a physician
- In jail, prison, other correctional institution, or police custody
- Suddenly as an apparent result of fire
- In any suspicious, unusual, or unnatural manner
- The sudden death of any infant less than 18 months of age where SIDS is suspected
- When the body shall be cremated or buried at sea
- Fetal death not attended by a physician
Washington County ME	- Those in which the coroner suspects that the death was unnatural, or violent, or resulted from unlawful means, or from suspicious circumstances, or was of such a nature as to indicate the possibility of death by the hand of the deceased or through the instrumentality of some other person
- Those occurring suddenly when the decedent was in apparent good health and without medical attendance within 36 hours preceding death
- Those resulting from unknown or obscure causes
- Those occurring within 1 year following an accident
- Those as a result of any violence whatsoever
- Those resulting from a known or suspected abortion, whether self-induced or otherwise
- Those apparently resulting from drowning, hanging, burns, electrocution, gunshot wounds, stabs or cuts, lightning, starvation, radiation, exposure, alcoholism, narcotics or other addictions, tetanus, strangulation, suffocation, or smothering

	• Those due to premature birth or stillbirth • Those due to virulent or suspected contagious disease that may be a public health hazard • Those resulting from alleged rape, carnal knowledge, or sodomy • Those occurring in a jail or prison • Those in which a body is found dead or is not claimed by relatives or friends • Industrial deaths when cause of death is unknown and investigation is requested by the Department of Labor and Industries
West Virginia State ME	• From violence or suspected violence, or where natural disease cannot be assumed • When unattended by a physician • When during incarceration, protective custody, as a ward of the state, or associated with police intervention • From disease or environmental condition that might constitute a threat to the public health • When in any suspicious, unusual, or unnatural manner • In deaths thought to be due to, or associated with, suspected abuse or neglect
Wisconsin County ME Coroner	• If circumstances are unexplained, unusual, or suspicious • By homicide or manslaughter, including death resulting from reckless conduct, negligent control of a vicious animal, or negligent use of a firearm • By suicide • Following an abortion • By poisoning, whether homicidal, suicidal, or accidental • Following accidents, whether the injury is or is not the primary cause • When a physician or accredited practitioner of a bona fide religious denomination relying upon prayer or spiritual means for healing was not in attendance within 30 days preceding death or if the deceased was not being treated for the condition causing death • When a physician refuses to sign the death certificate • When a physician cannot be obtained to sign the medical certification of death • At the request of the Worker's Compensation Department
Wyoming	The coroner shall conduct an investigation when he is notified that the dead body of any person has been found within the limits of the county or that the death resulted from injury sustained within the county, and he suspects that the death may involve any of the following conditions: • Violent or criminal action • Apparent suicide • Accident • Apparent drug or chemical overdose or toxicity • The deceased was unattended or had not seen a physician within 6 months prior to death • Apparent child abuse • The deceased was a prisoner, trustee, inmate, or patient of any county

	or state corrections facility or state hospital • If the cause is unknown
Armed Forces Institute of Pathology (AFIP)	Medicolegal investigations for determining cause and manner of death under specific circumstances for (1) members of the armed forces on active duty or on active duty for training and (2) civilians, including dependents of military members, where the federal government has exclusive jurisdictional authority, and if the circumstances surrounding the death are suspicious, unexpected, or unexplained, including: • Unnatural or violent deaths, whether due to known or suspected accident, homicide, suicide, or other undetermined means • Deaths directly or apparently related to the occupation or employment of the deceased and deaths of individuals enrolled in the Personnel Reliability Program • Deaths related to vehicular, aircraft, or vessel accidents • Sudden deaths not caused by readily recognizable disease • Deaths possibly related to disease that might constitute a threat to the public health • Deaths occurring in a prison or death of a prisoner • Deaths occurring to individuals assigned as military crewmembers of military aircraft or military vessel

CHAPTER 63: REQUESTING A PATHOLOGIST AT A DEATH SCENE

The following list represents the minimum recommendations involving the circumstances in which a medical examiner, coroner, forensic pathologist, or other person charged with the responsibility of establishing the cause and manner of death should be notified and asked to respond to the scene.

1) Major scenes
    a) High-profile cases where every decision, nondecision, and action are probably going to become heavily scrutinized by some segment of the population or media representatives. This may involve the following:
        i) Deaths involving prominent people
        ii) Sensational activity causing the death of one or more people

2) Multiple deaths

3) Identification of weapon
    a) In cases where it may be extremely critical to identify or eliminate a possible weapon that may have been used to inflict injuries on a decedent.
        i) This initial inspection may have ramifications that relate not only the manner of death, but may implicate or exonerate a particular suspect.
        ii) The weapon may be a common household item that may be easily overlooked.

4) Reconstruction of the scene
    a) In complicated scenes it may be important to analyze and reconstruct the events leading up to the death of the decedent(s), for example:
        i) Identification of the suspect and the victim in a homicide/suicide scene
        ii) The sequence of the events where the incident may have involved a prolonged activity or multiple weapons
        iii) Whether the apparent movement of the injured person, prior to death, was consistent with the evidence present or witness statements concerning the incident
        iv) To assist in distinguishing what version may be closer to the truth in conflicting statements
        v) To assist in determining if a suspect may have been injured and bleeding when he was at a death scene

5) Recovery of skeletal remains
    a) To supervise in the collection of all bones, teeth, and other artifacts necessary in identifying the remains. These items may not be readily identifiable by the technician processing the scene and, therefore, may go uncollected.
    b) The pathologist may be called on to distinguish the following while at the scene:
        i) Whether the bones are human or animal in origin
        ii) Whether the bones are modern
        iii) Race, sex, approximate age, and how long the remains may have been at this location

6) Recovery of remains from a fire scene
    a) To supervise in the collection of all bones, teeth, and other artifacts necessary in

identifying the remains. These items may not be readily identifiable by the technician processing the scene and therefore may go uncollected.

    b) To allow for the immediate collection of fragments of clothing to ensure hydrocarbon preservation for future testing for accelerants

7) Undetermined deaths
   a) The pathologist may be requested at the scene where initial information concerning the manner of death may be extremely important in determining what steps are initiated, or are contemplated being initiated, based on preliminary information which may be supplied by the pathologist at the scene.

8) Establishing time of death
   a) In cases where it may be critical to establish the time of death, the pathologist should be requested at the scene to begin collecting information, which will be used to arrive at a general conclusion.

9) Unusual or educational
   a) On any case in which it appears the activity, method, type of weapon, or circumstances are rare or may serve a purpose in future investigations through the education of others

10) Police or correctional custody deaths
    a) These cases are critical. Any variation in protocol involving the processing of the scene, handling of the decedent, interviewing of witnesses, or handling or processing of evidence is categorized as cover-up activities of the involved investigative agencies by community activist groups and media reporters.

11) Buried remains

12) Airplane crash

13) Identification cases (multiple)
    a) In a case involving multiple decedents where identification could become confused, a pathologistshould be requested. A numbering and organization procedure can be initiated with the processing of the scene and ensure less confusion and proper compliance throughout the entire process.

14) On any scene in which the investigators feel that they would be more comfortable or that they need the support of the pathologist

Simply informing the on-call pathologist that he may be needed at a scene is not adequate unless this manner of notification cannot be helped. Whenever possible, telephone contact should be made, and a description of the circumstances should be related.

If a person dies in any of the circumstances described above, but the investigators feel that a delay in the removal of the body could cause serious problems, injury, or jeopardize evidence while awaiting the arrival of the on-call pathologist, removal should be effected. Notification to the on-call pathologist should then be made with an explanation for the actions that were taken.

CHAPTER 64: THE FORENSIC AUTOPSY

A forensic autopsy is carried out under the laws of the state for the protection of its citizens. As such, the performance of the autopsy presupposes state rather than individual permission.

1) Reasons for performing a forensic autopsy
    a) To determine the cause and manner of death
    b) To approximate time of death
    c) To identify, collect, and preserve physical evidence
    d) To provide factual information to law enforcement agencies, prosecutors, defense attorneys, families, news media, and others who need to know
    e) To protect the innocent as well as to assist in the identification and prosecution of the guilty

2) Requirements
    a) Complete autopsy
    b) Thorough examination
    c) Factual, objective written report without prejudice, advocacy, or theory

3) Preliminary steps
    a) Examine the body before removal of the clothing.
    b) Protect the clothing, body, and hands from contamination.
    c) Note the general state of the body.
    d) Observe the state of rigor mortis and lividity.
    e) Determine any other details necessary to assist in determining a general time frame for death.

4) Autopsy procedure
    a) Notation of time and place of autopsy examination
    b) External examination including apparent age, height and weight, state of nutrition, scars, tattoos, color of eyes and hair, state of dentition, muscular development, abnormalities, deformities, and marks of hospitalization
    c) Detailed examination of injuries including size, shape, location, pattern, and relationship to anatomic landmarks

5) Photographs
    a) To identify deceased
    b) To document injuries and their location (include a scale for comparison)
    c) To show relationship of external and internal injuries
    d) To demonstrate pathologic processes other than those of traumatic origins

6) X-ray examination
    a) To locate bullets or other radiopague objects
    b) To identify victims
    c) To document old and recent fractures, anatomic deformities, metallic foreign bodies, plates, nails, and screws from surgical procedures

7) Internal examination
    a) General examination of the head, neck, spine, thorax, and abdomen

b) Note course and direction of wound tracks within the body.
c) Note relationship and conditions of viscera. (Ante- and postmortem relationships of wounds and viscera may not always be the same.)
d) Preserve evidence. Recover and identify foreign objects. Establish chain of custody.

8) Procedures frequently used in forensic autopsies
   a) Collect specimens.
      i) Recover hair from scalp and pubis.
      ii) Comb pubic hair for recovery of foreign hair.
      iii) Collect specimens of blood, bile, urine, liver, and others.
      iv) Collect specimens for determining the presence or absence of spermatozoa or seminal fluid.
      v) Examine clothing:
         (1) Examine prior to removal.
         (2) Correlate defects with bodily injuries.
         (3) Note areas of blood spatter.
         (4) Remove and air-dry if wet.
         (5) Label and preserve.
   b) Preserve specimens in appropriate containers under appropriate conditions.
   c) Commence or maintain chain of custody for evidence.

9) Observation relating to the general development for the estimation of time of death
   a) Rigor mortis development
   b) Livor mortis development
   c) Temperature of viscera
   d) State of digestion of any food in the stomach
   e) State of decomposition
   f) Presence of insect activity
   g) Presence and state of plant growth involving the remains

10) Postmortem artifacts
    a) Artifacts of decomposition
    b) Third-party artifacts
       i) Animal activity (arthropophagy)
       ii) Insect activity (anthropophagy)
       iii) Medical treatment
       iv) Deliberate mutilation
          (1) Dismemberment
    c) Artifacts of the environment
       i) Postmortem burning
       ii) Postmortem corrosion
       iii) Postmortem maceration
       v) Other artifacts
          (1) Artifacts of storage prior to examination

11) Cautions
    a) Do not assume the cause of death prior to actual completion of the autopsy.
    b) Do not confuse time of death with the time of infliction of the fatal injury.

12) Guidelines for the organization of autopsy protocol

a) External description
b) Evidence of injury
    i) External
    ii) Internal
c) Systems and organs
d) Special dissections and examinations
e) Brain (and other organs) after fixation
f) Microscopic examinations
g) Findings (diagnosis)
h) Opinion as to manner of death
i) Signature

CHAPTER 65:
THE PURPOSE OF AN AUTOPSY IN AN APPARENT HOMICIDE CASE

The investigation of a known or suspected homicide requires that the attending pathologist ask six critical questions:

1) Who are you?
    a) Investigative and prosecutorial reasons
        i) To establish identification
        ii) To trace decedent's whereabouts immediately preceding his death in the hopes of establishing suspects who had opportunity and motive to kill him.
    b) Humanitarian reasons
        i) To ensure prompt burial
        ii) To avoid unnecessary delays for settling the estate, probating wills, paying Social Security and life insurance benefits, and remarrying by surviving spouse

2) When were you hurt? When did you become ill? When did you die?
    a) What is the time interval from the time of the injury or illness until the time of the death?
    b) What is the postmortem interval?
        i) Relevance
            (1) To establish what suspects may have had opportunity to murder the decedent

3) Where did you get hurt? Where did you die?
    a) Did decedent die at the location where the remains were recovered, or could the remains have been dumped at this location?
    b) Was the decedent capable of being mobile after the infliction of the injury?
        i) Relevance
            (1) To develop a link between the suspect and the decedent through the discovery of evidence

4) Why did you die?
    a) What is the cause of your death?

5) How did you die?
    a) What is the manner of your death?
        i) Could your injury be self-inflicted (suicide or accident) or most likely administered at the hands of someone else (homicide)?

6) Who committed the homicide?
    a) What evidence do you bring to the autopsy table that points to, implicates, or identifies the person responsible for your death?

CHAPTER 66: AUTOPSY REFERENCES

The following information involves a collection of various measurements, identifications, and descriptions that the death investigator may find helpful in understanding the medical information he may be exposed to when conducting a death investigation.

AVERAGE WEIGHTS AND SIZES

During autopsy examination, the organs are removed and weighed. Discrepancies in weight may indicate infection, injury, or disease involving the particular organ. Please note that the weight of the organ is also a function of height and weight of the particular individual involved.

ORGAN		WEIGHT
Heart	Male	300–350 grams
	Female	250–300 grams
Brain	Male	1,200–1,360 grams
	Female	1,150–1,320 grams
Lungs	Right	360–570 grams
	Left	325–480 grams
Liver		1,400–1,600 grams
Spleen		150–200 grams
Pancreas		90–120 grams
Kidneys	(each)	120–150 grams
Adrenals	(each)	5–6 grams
Thyroid		25–30 grams
Thymus	Newborn	13 grams
	11–15 years	38 grams
	Adult	Decreasing size
	During pregnancy	0.84–1.06 grams

Unusual discrepancies in the average thickness involving the following vessels' size may indicate a respiratory or circulatory problem.

ORGAN		SIZE
Heart	Atriae	0.1–0.2 cm
(measured as thickness)	Ventricle (left)	1.0–1.3 cm
Ventricle (right)	0.2–0.4 cm	
Valves	Tricuspid	12.0 cm
(measured in	Pulmonic	8.5 cm
circumference)	Mitral	10.0 cm
	Aortic	7.5 cm
Vessels	Pulmonary artery	8.0 cm
	Aorta ascending	7.4 cm
	Descending	4.5–6.0 cm
	Abdominal	3.5–4.5 cm

FACE AND HEAD DESCRIPTIONS

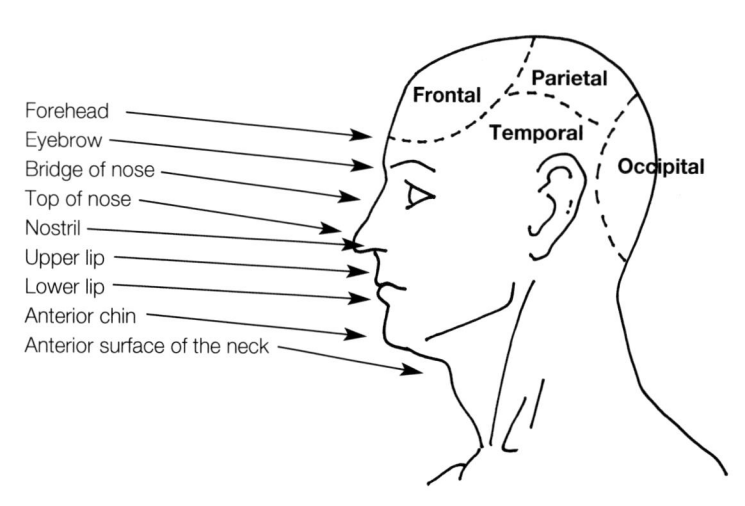

Autopsy references of the head.

ANTERIOR ANATOMY

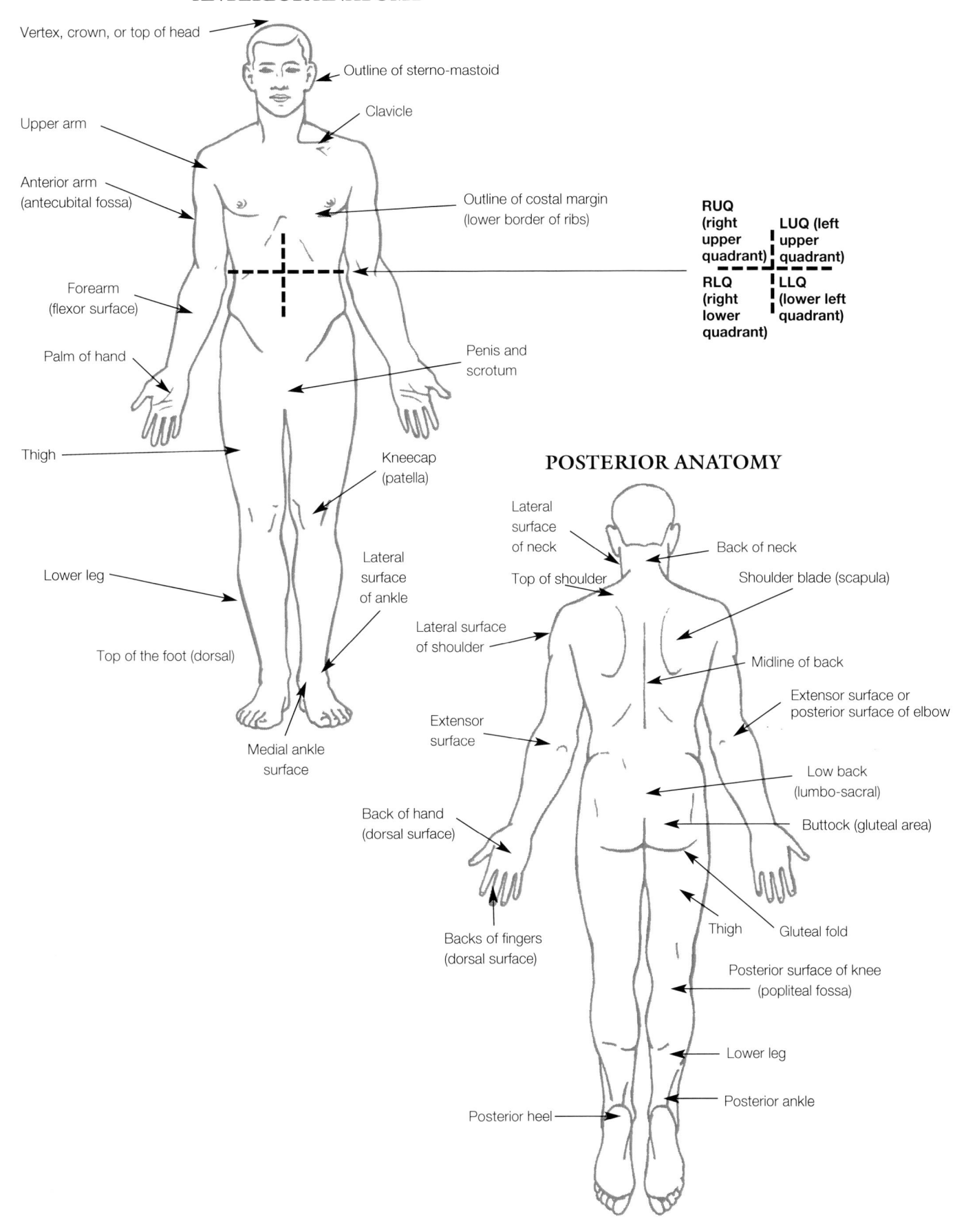

- Vertex, crown, or top of head
- Outline of sterno-mastoid
- Upper arm
- Clavicle
- Anterior arm (antecubital fossa)
- Outline of costal margin (lower border of ribs)
- Forearm (flexor surface)
- Palm of hand
- Penis and scrotum
- Thigh
- Kneecap (patella)
- Lower leg
- Lateral surface of ankle
- Top of the foot (dorsal)
- Medial ankle surface

RUQ (right upper quadrant) | LUQ (left upper quadrant)
RLQ (right lower quadrant) | LLQ (lower left quadrant)

POSTERIOR ANATOMY

- Lateral surface of neck
- Back of neck
- Top of shoulder
- Shoulder blade (scapula)
- Lateral surface of shoulder
- Midline of back
- Extensor surface
- Extensor surface or posterior surface of elbow
- Low back (lumbo-sacral)
- Back of hand (dorsal surface)
- Buttock (gluteal area)
- Backs of fingers (dorsal surface)
- Thigh
- Gluteal fold
- Posterior surface of knee (popliteal fossa)
- Lower leg
- Posterior ankle
- Posterior heel

MAJOR ORGANS

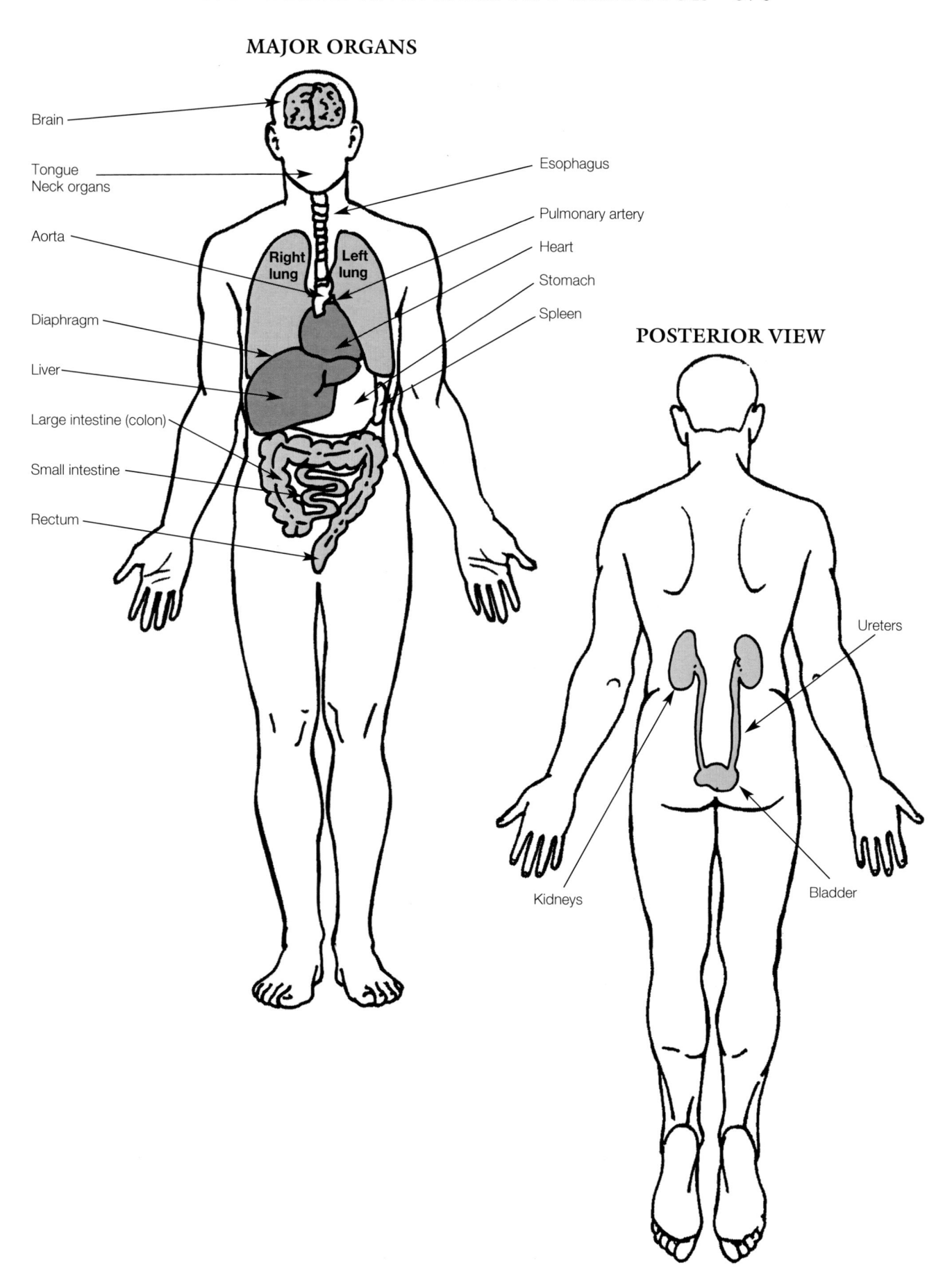

- Brain
- Tongue
- Neck organs
- Aorta
- Diaphragm
- Liver
- Large intestine (colon)
- Small intestine
- Rectum
- Esophagus
- Pulmonary artery
- Heart
- Right lung
- Left lung
- Stomach
- Spleen

POSTERIOR VIEW

- Ureters
- Kidneys
- Bladder

CHAPTER 67: FORENSIC ODONTOLOGY

The American Board of Forensic Odontology (ABFO) suggests the following identification guidelines.

COLLECTION AND PRESERVATION OF POSTMORTEM DENTAL EVIDENCE

1) The postmortem dental examination is conducted by the authority and under the direction of the coroner/medical examiner or his designee, typically a forensic pathologist. Thus, the protocol for the collection of postmortem dental evidence, particularly decisions to incise the facial tissues for access or resect the jaws, is subject to approval by the regional coroner/medical examiner. The actual procedures to be followed in a dental identification case depend in large part on the condition of the remains (as well as other circumstances of the case).

2) Examination procedures
    a) Visually identifiable body
        i) Photographs
        ii) Radiographs
        iii) Dental charting
        iv) Dental impressions, as applicable
        v) Resection by inframandibular dissection
    b) Decomposed/incinerated body
        i) Photographs
        ii) Radiographs
        iii) Dental charting
        iv) Resection and preservation of jaw specimens, if indicated
    c) Skeletonized remains
        i) Photographs
        ii) Radiographs
        iii) Dental charting
        iv) Preservation of jaw specimens, if indicated

3) Photography
    a) Photographic documentation of dental evidence can provide objective data that is often more graphic than the written chart. Photographs (with an accompanying scale) should be taken before and after appropriate cleansing. The ABFO right-angle ruler is recommended. The photographs should be clearly labeled with the case number/name and date. All relevant photographic information should be documented.

4) Recommended equipment
    a) Single-lens reflex 35-mm camera
        i) The Lester Dine instant close-up camera, model IV, has been useful in mass-disaster evidence documentation.
    b) Bellow system and/or lenses for close-up photography
    c) Electronic flash
        i) Preferably point flash or ring light system

5) Film
   a) Color film
      i) Slide or print format
   b) Black and white film, as required
      i) Polaroid film may be of help in special circumstances

6) Cheek retractors
   a) Intraoral front-surface mirrors

7) Views
   a) Full face, lips retracted
   b) Close-up view of anterior teeth
   c) Lateral views of teeth in slightly open position and in occlusion
   d) Occlusal views, upper and lower teeth
   e) Special views, as required

8) Jaw resection
   a) Facial dissection and/or jaw resection, which may be necessary for full access to dental structures, is done only with approval of the coroner/medical examiner. Ordinarily, the circumstances dictating decisions to resect are applicable as follows:
      i) Viewable bodies—restricted opening due to rigor may require the following:
         (1) Intraoral incision of masticatory muscles, with or without fracture of the condyles
         (2) Breaking the rigor with bilateral leverage on the jaws in the retro molar regions
         (3) Waiting until the rigor subsides
         (4) Infra-mandibular dissection with or without mandibular resection
         (5) Removal of the larynx and tongue at autopsy may facilitate the visual examination of the teeth and placement of intraoral films. Again, the removal of these tissues should only be performed after the autopsy and with permission of the pathologist. These tissues should either be retained by the pathologist or replaced with the body.
      ii) Decomposed, incinerated, or fragmented bodies
         (1) Jaw resection in such cases facilitates dental charting and radiographic examination
            (a) Careful dissection of the incinerated head, in particular, is required to preserve fragile tooth structure and jaws in situ.
            (b) Radiographs should be made prior to manipulation of badly burned fragments (mechanical or chemical); stabilization of such tissue should be instituted where necessary.
      iii) Skeletonized remains
         (1) Once the skull and mandible are readily separated from the remainder of the skeleton, resection of the maxilla is not required unless the remains will be buried as an unknown. Storage of the maxilla and mandible will then be required. Resection of the maxilla will then be necessary.

9) Preservation of evidence
   a) Jaw resection may be indicated in these cases:
      i) Body parts are to be transferred, with proper authorization, to other facilities for additional examination and testing
      ii) A homicide victim is to be cremated.

10) Techniques for dissection/resection
    a) Selected techniques include the following:
        i) Facial dissection:
            (1) Bilateral incisions of the face. Beginning at the oral commissures and extending posteriorly to the anterior ramus, permit reflection of the soft tissues for better access.
        ii) Infra-mandibular approach:
            (1) Bilateral incisions are made across the upper anterior neck and extend to points posterior and inferior to the ears. The skin and underlying tissues are then reflected upward over the lower face, thereby exposing the mandible.

11) Jaw resection
    a) Stryker autopsy saw method
        i) The soft tissue and muscle attachments on the lateral aspect of the mandible are dissected away by incisions that extend through the muco-buccal fold to the lower border of the mandible. Lingual attachments are similarly incised to include the internal pterygoid attachments to medial aspect of the rami and the masseter attachments on the lateral aspect. On the maxilla, facial attachments are incised high on the malar processes and superior to the anterior nasal spine. Stryker saw cuts are made high on the rami to avoid possible impacted third molars. Alternatively, the mandible may also be removed by disarticulation at the temporomandibular joints. Bony cuts on the maxilla are made high on the malar processes and above the anterior nasal spine to avoid the apices of the maxillary teeth. A surgical mallet and chisel inserted in the Stryker saw cuts in the malar processes and above the anterior nasal spine are used to complete the separation of the maxilla. Remaining soft tissues in the soft palate and fauces are then dissected free.
    b) Mallet and chisel method
        i) A mallet and chisel can be used to induce a "Le Fort" Type I fracture of the maxilla. The chisel blows are made below the zygomatic arch, high on the maxillary sinus walls bilaterally. Since it is virtually impossible to fracture the mandibular rami with the mallet and chisel, the mandible can be disarticulated at the temporomandibular joint in such cases.
    c) Pruning shears method
        i) An alternative technique for resection of the jaws involves the use of large pruning shears. The small blade of the pruning shears is placed within the nares and forced back into the maxillary sinus. A cut is then made along a plane superior to the apices of the maxillary teeth bilaterally. The mandibular bone cuts are performed by inserting the small blade of the shears high on the lingual aspect of the ramus near the coronoid notch bilaterally.

12) The postmortem dental record
    a) While most morgues will have the standard autopsy equipment, the forensic odontologist may wish to assemble his own forensic kit to include mouth mirrors, explorers, camera equipment, anatomic dental charts, impression materials, etc.
    b) Postmortem dental examinations might use anatomic dental charts, photographs, radiographs, models, tape recordings, or narrative descriptions.
    c) The data collected should be comprehensive in scope since antemortem records are commonly not discovered until days, weeks, or even years later. Accordingly, the postmortem dental record will include all or most of the items listed.

d) Basic data
   i) Case number
   ii) Date/time
   iii) Jurisdiction/authority
   iv) Location
   v) Tentative ID, if any
   vi) Body description, general
   vii) Approximate age
   viii) Race
   ix) Sex
   x) Condition of remains
e) The universal tooth-numbering system should be used. The record should reflect any missing dental structures or jaw fragments, as well as those present and available for evaluation. The chart should illustrate as graphically as possible the following:
   i) Configuration of all dental restorations (including prostheses), caries, fractures, anomalies, abrasions, implants, erosions, or other features for all teeth
   ii) Materials used in dental restorations and prosthetic devices, when known
   iii) Periodontal conditions, calculus, stain
   iv) Occlusal relationships, malposed teeth; anomalous, congenitally missing, and supernumerary teeth.
   v) Intraoral photographs should be used to show anatomic details of teeth restorations, periodontium, occlusion, lesions, etc.
f) Narrative description and nomenclature
   i) The anatomic dental chart may be supplemented by a narrative description of the postmortem findings with particular emphasis on unusual or unique conditions. Standardized dental nomenclature should be used as follows:
      (1) Universal numbering system
         (a) The system of numbering teeth used in the United States. The teeth are numbered from 1 to 32. The upper right third molar is 1, the upper central incisors are 8 and 9, the upper left third molar 16, the lower left third molar is 17, and the lower right third molar is 32. The universal tooth-numbering system plus the actual name of the tooth should be used (e.g., tooth 3, upper right first permanent molar).
g) Dentition type and tooth surfaces
   i) Primary, permanent, and mixed dentition
   ii) Mesial, occlusal, distal, facial, and lingual surfaces
   iii) Prosthetics and other appliances
   iv) Crowns: full-, 3/4-, or 7/8-coverage restorations
   v) Prostheses: partial, full, or fixed
   vi) Orthodontic bands, brackets, space maintainers, and retainers
   vii) Mouth guards and night guards
h) The FDI numbering system
   i) Odontologists should be aware of the FDI system of numbering teeth. This system is used throughout the developed world. Quadrants are numbered from 1 to 4. The upper right quadrant is 1, the upper left 2, the lower left 3, and the lower right 4. Teeth are numbered from the midline to the posterior. Central incisors are 1, canines 3, and third molars 8. Teeth are represented by a two-digit code with the quadrant first and the tooth second. Thus, the upper left first molar is 26.

i) Dental impressions
> i) Impressions should be considered when bitemarks, rugae patterns, or other evidence warrants the procedure.

13) Supplies and equipment
    a) Appropriate trays, plastic or metal, that can be modified to fit the mouth
    b) Alginate or other American Dental Association (ADA)-approved dental impression material
    c) Dental stone is the material of choice for pouring models. Plaster of paris should not be used.

14) Impressions and preparation of models
    a) Two sets of impressions, both maxillary and mandibular, are obtained in the conventional manner.
    b) Models should be trimmed and appropriately labeled with the case number and date.

15) Dental radiology
    a) Postmortem radiographs graphically complement the visual examination/charting of the oral and perioral structures and can provide significant data essential for identification.
    b) In general, radiographs are required in cases where there is no putative ID, antemortem records have not yet been located, or the jaws can not be retained. Postmortem radiographs must be considered the prime method of identification. A comprehensive postmortem radiographic examination might include all or some of the following views, depending on the circumstances of the case.
        i) Intraoral radiographs
            (1) Bitewing and periapical radiographs of anterior and posterior teeth comparable to those taken antemortem ("bitewing" views need not be taken in the conventional manner with the teeth in occlusion; rather, periapical film can be used for separate views of the upper and lower teeth, using a horizontal bitewing angulation).
    c) Dental fragments, dissociated teeth
        i) Appropriate radiographs of all dental fragments, dissociated teeth, bone, and restorations should be obtained. Occlusal or lateral plate film may be used for objects larger than a periapical film.
    d) Edentulous areas
        i) Periapical radiographs of edentulous arches or areas, especially the third molars, which may be impacted or previously extracted
        ii) Periapical radiographs of sockets of teeth lost postmortem should be taken because antemortem radiographs of these same teeth may be the only evidence that becomes available.
    e) Extraoral radiographs
        i) Extraoral radiographs (e.g., lateral jaw, maxillary or frontal sinus, and panoramic radiographs) are often useful.
    f) Disposition of radiographs
        i) Double-pack intraoral film is recommended.
        ii) One set of films should be retained by the forensic odontologist for his case file. The second set may be mounted and forwarded with a written report to the medical examiner/coroner for the master file.
        iii) NOTE: All duplicate films should bear right and left notations.

16) Sources for antemortem data
    a) Antemortem data may include dental radiographs, written records, models, and photographs. Original radiographs should be obtained if possible. The discovery and collection of antemortem records is ordinarily the responsibility of the investigative agency that has access to missing persons reports at the local, state, or national level. However, the forensic odontologist may recognize additional characteristics (e.g., prior orthodontic treatment) that could be helpful in establishing a potential ID. This section lists a variety of resource agencies or individuals who might assist in locating records when the identification of the unidentified decedent is suspected.
        i) Local agencies
        ii) Hospitals, other health care facilities
        iii) Dental schools
        iv) Health care providers
        v) Employer dental insurance carrier
        vi) Public aid insurance administrator
        vii) Federal agencies
            (1) FBI National Crime Information Center (NCIC)
            (2) Military Records Depository, St. Louis
        viii) Other sources
            (1) Family members, friends, co-workers
            (2) Public aid insurance administrator
            (3) Employer (current and former) dental insurance carrier
            (4) Prior military service
            (5) Prior judicial detention in county
            (6) State or federal institutions
            (7) Prior hospitalizations (e.g., chest films, skull films)
            (8) Oral surgeons in the area
            (9) Veterans Administration hospitals
            (10) Any previous areas of residence
            (11) Chiropractic X-rays
            (12) If evidence of ortho treatment, orthodontists in the area
            (13) Checkbook inside decedent's residence.
            (14) Address book of decedent
            (15) Yellow and white pages of telephone directory, determining whether any dogeared pages or notations mark a particular section of dentist listings

17) Comparison of antemortem and postmortem evidence
    a) Most dental identifications are based on restorations, caries, missing teeth, and/or prosthetic devices that may be readily documented in the records.
        i) It should be emphasized that, given adequate records, a nearly infinite number of objective factors have identification value.
    b) Apparent discrepancies between the antemortem and postmortem evidence (e.g., errors in recording, dental treatment subsequent to the available antemortem record) must be resolved.

18) Dental features useful in identification
    a) Teeth
        i) Teeth present
        ii) Erupted, unerupted/impacted

iii) Missing teeth
- (1) Congenitally missing
- (2) Lost antemortem
- (3) Lost perimortem/postmortem

iv) Tooth type
- (1) Permanent
- (2) Mixed dentition
- (3) Retained primary teeth
- (4) Supernumerary teeth

v) Tooth position

b) Malpositions: facial/linguoversion, rotations, supra/infra positions, diastemas, other occlusal discrepancies

c) Crown morphology
- i) Size and shape of crowns
- ii) Enamel thickness
- iii) Location of contact points, cemento-enamel junction

d) Racial variations (e.g., shovel-shaped incisors, Carabelli cusp)

e) Crown pathology

f) Caries

g) Attrition/abrasion/erosion

h) Atypical variations (e.g., peg laterals, fusion/gemination, enamel pearl, multiple cusps)

i) Dens in dente

j) Dentigerous cyst

k) Root morphology
- i) Size, shape, number, dilaceration, divergence of roots
- ii) Root pathology
- iii) Root fracture
- iv) Hypercementosis
- v) External root resorption
- vi) Root hemisections
- vii) Pulp chamber and root canal morphology
  - (1) Size, shape, number
  - (2) Secondary dentin
  - (3) Pulp stones, dystrophic calcification
- viii) Root canal therapy (e.g., gutta percha, silver points, endo paste and retrofill procedures)
  - (1) Internal resorption
- ix) Periapical pathology
- x) Periapical abscess/granuloma/cyst
- xi) Cementoma
- xii) Condensing osteitis

l) Dental restorations
- i) Metallic restorations: amalgams, gold, or nonprecious metal crowns/inlays, endoposts, pins, fixed prostheses, implants
- ii) Nonmetallic restorations: acrylics, silicates, composites, porcelain, etc.

m) Partial and full removal prostheses

n) Periodontium

o) Gingiva: morphology/pathology
- i) Contour: gingival recession, focal/diffuse enlargements, interproximal craters

p) Color: inflammatory changes, physiologic or pathologic pigmentations

q) Plaque and concretions oral hygiene status, stains, calculus
r) Periodontal ligament: morphology/pathology
    i) Thickness
s) Widening (e.g., scleroderma)
t) Lateral periodontal cyst
u) Alveolar process and lamina dura
v) Height/contour/density of crestal bone
w) Thickness of inter-radicular alveolar bone
x) Exostoses, tori
y) Pattern of lamina dura (e.g., loss, increased density)
z) Periodontal bone loss
aa) Trabecular bone pattern osteoporosis, radiodensities
bb) Residual root fragments, metallic fragments
cc) Maxilla and mandible
    i) Maxillary sinuses: size, shape, retention cyst, antrolith, foreign bodies, oral-antral fistula, relationship to adjacent teeth
    ii) Anterior nasal spine, incisive canal, median palatal suture, incisive canal: size, shape, cyst
    iii) Pterygoid hamulus: size, shape, fracture
    iv) Mandibular canal/mental foramen: diameter, anomalous (bifurcated), canal, relationship to adjacent teeth
    v) Coronoid and condylar process: size and shape
    vi) Temporomandibular joint
    vii) Size, shape, hypertrophy/atrophy, ankylosis, fracture, arthritic changes
dd) Other pathologic processes/jaw bones
ee) Developmental/fissural cysts, hemorrhagic (traumatic) bone cyst, salivary gland depression, reactive/neoplastic lesions, metabolic bone disease, other disorders inducing focal or diffuse radiolucencies or radiopacities, evidence of orthognathic surgery, or prior evidence of trauma (e.g., wire sutures, surgical pins)

19) Categories and terminology for body identification

POSITIVE IDENTIFICATION:
- The antemortem and postmortem data match in sufficient detail to establish that they are from the same individual. In addition, there are no irreconcilable discrepancies.

POSSIBLE IDENTIFICATION:
- The antemortem and postmortem data have consistent features, but, due to the quality of either the postmortem remains or the antemortem evidence, it is not possible to positively establish dental identification.

INSUFFICIENT EVIDENCE:
- The available information is insufficient to form the basis for a conclusion.

EXCLUSION:
- The antemortem and postmortem data are clearly inconsistent. However, it should be understood that identification by exclusion is a valid technique in certain circumstances.

NOTE: The forensic dentist is not ordinarily in a position to verify that the antemortem records are correct as to name, date, etc. Therefore, the report should state that the conclusions are based on records that are purported to represent a particular individual.

DENTAL RECORDS ACQUISITION

When it is necessary to obtain antemortem dental records from the decedent's previous dentist, the following recommendations result in rapid and efficient identification efforts.

Call the Dentist

1) Confirm that he is the dentist of record for the decedent.

2) Have the dentist write an antemortem reconstruction containing the latest status of each tooth (1–32) based on his review of the dental chart and X-rays. (NOTE: This can be done over the telephone to facilitate making a tentative identification.)

3) Have the dentist agree to permanently release all of the original X-rays to the medical examiner/coroner's office. If he insists on their return, please note this in the file. If copies of the originals are received, make sure the copies are marked to distinguish left from right and labeled with the patient's name.

4) Make sure all pages of the dental chart are legible. If any question exists, have the dentist clarify the chart entry. The patient's name should be on each page of the chart. The last dated entry of the chart should read, "Records and X-rays released to the MEO/Coroner."

5) Ask the dentist for the names of any other treating dentists.

6) Obtain any other records, such as casts of the jaw on which dentures were made or the name of the dental lab that constructed appliances for the patient.

7) Arrange a mutually convenient time to take possession of the patient's dental records.

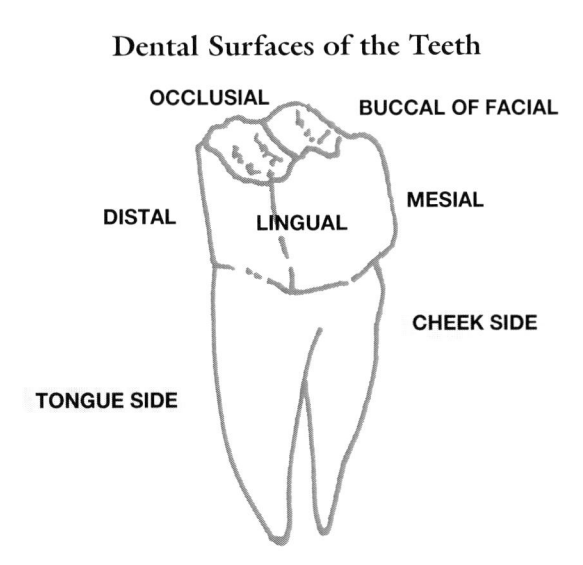

Dental Surfaces of the Teeth

CAPMI* DENTAL CODES

PRIMARY CODE		SECONDARY CODE	
C	Crown	A	Anomaly
D	Distal	B	Deciduous
F	Facial	G	Gold
I	Incisal	N	Nonmetal
L	Lingual	P	Pontic
M	Mesial	Q	3/4 crown
O	Occlusial	R	Root canal
U	Unerupted	S	Silver amalgam
X	Missing	Z	Carious
/	No data		

* Computer-assisted postmortem identification (CAPMI) is used by many agencies in conjunction with NCIC.

WinID3 DENTAL COMPUTER SYSTEM

1) WinID3 is a dental computer system that matches missing persons to the unidentified.

2) WinID3 makes use of dental and anthropometric characteristics to rank possible matches.

3) Information about physical descriptors and pathological and anthropologic findings can be entered into the WinID3 database.

4) WinID3 is used by forensic dentists, forensic odontologists, pathologists, coroners, and medical personnel to identify the unknown.

5) WinID3 has proved useful in mass-disaster situations and in the creation and maintenance of missing person databases.

WinID Codes

WinID codes are an extension of CAPMI codes. Up to five primary and five secondary codes may be specified. A hyphen (-) is placed between the primary and secondary codes. If you are unsure of a secondary code, leave the code out. Most searches in WinID use only the primary codes.

The dental portion of the data entry form should be filled out by a board-certified forensic odontologist. Contact the American Board of Forensic Odontology (phone: 719-636-1100; fax: 719-636-1993; mail: P.O. Box 669, Colorado Springs, CO 80901-0669) for the name of a forensic odontologist in a specific area.

WinID PRIMARY CODES

M -	Mesial surface of tooth is restored.
O -	Occlusal surface of posterior tooth is restored.
D -	Distal surface of tooth is restored.
F -	Facial surface of tooth is restored.
L -	Lingual surface of tooth is restored.
I -	Incisal edge of anterior tooth is restored.
C -	Tooth is fitted with a crown.
U -	Tooth is unerupted.
V -	Tooth is unrestored—virgin.
X -	Tooth is missing—extracted.
J -	Tooth is missing postmortem, or the clinical crown of the tooth is not present for examination. This code also used for avulsed tooth. The root or an open socket is present, but no other information is available.

WinID SECONDARY CODES

A -	An anomaly is associated with this tooth. Specifics of the anomaly may be detailed in the comment section.
B -	Tooth is deciduous.
E -	Resin filling material.
G -	Gold restoration.
H -	Porcelain.
N -	Nonprecious filling or crown material. Includes stainless steel.
P -	Pontic. Primary code must be X to indicate missing tooth.
Q -	Three-quarter crown. Primary code must be C to indicate crown.
R -	Root canal filled.
/ -	No information about tooth is available.
S -	Silver amalgam.

T -	Denture tooth. Primary code must be X to indicate missing tooth.
Z -	Temporary filling material. Also indicates gross caries (used sparingly).

WinID EXAMPLES	
MODFL-S	Mesial occlusal distal facial lingual silver amalgam restoration.
DL	Tooth has distal lingual restoration.
C-G	Gold crown.
C-HR	Endodontically treated tooth with porcelain crown.
MI-E	Mesial incisal resin.
X	Tooth missing.
V-B	Virgin deciduous tooth.
MO-SB	Mesial occlusal silver amalgam in deciduous tooth.
X-PN	Missing tooth replaced with nonprecious pontic.
X-T	Missing tooth replaced with denture tooth.
C-QG	Gold 3/4 crown
J	Missing postmortem
MO-AZ	Mesial occlusal temporary filling (or caries) on tooth with an anomaly.

WinID ANTEMORTEM DENTAL RECORD FORM

Sample of a WinID antemortem (before death) dental chart. The dentist should be contacted and allowed to read the dental chart, starting out with tooth number 1 and continuing through all 32 teeth.

WinID POSTMORTEM CHART

Example of WinID Postmortem Identification form. The listing of teeth (1–32) is intended to mirror the antemortem form so that a tooth-to-tooth comparison may be facilitated.

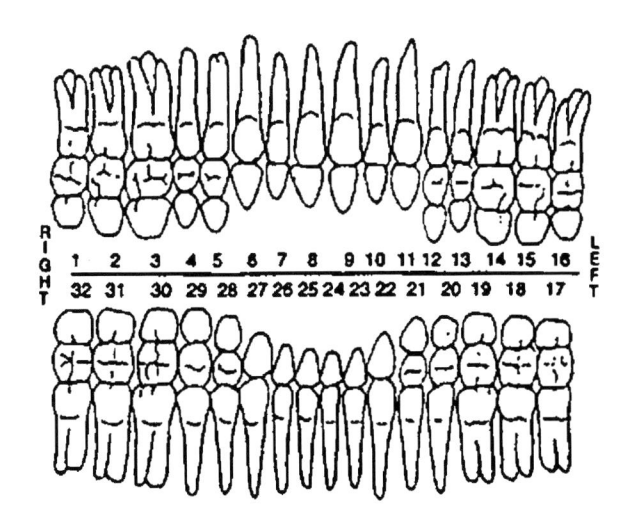

RIGHT			LEFT	
Upper	Lower		Upper	Lower
1	32	Third molars	16	17
2	31	Second molars	15	18
3	30	First molars	14	19
4	29	Second bicuspids	13	20
5	28	First bicuspids	12	21
6	27	Cuspids	11	22
7	26	Lateral incisors	10	23
8	25	Central incisors	09	24

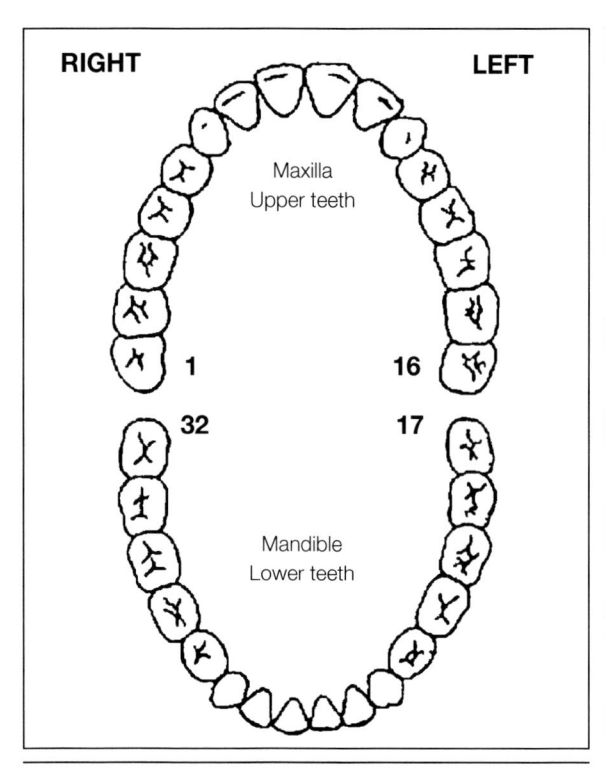

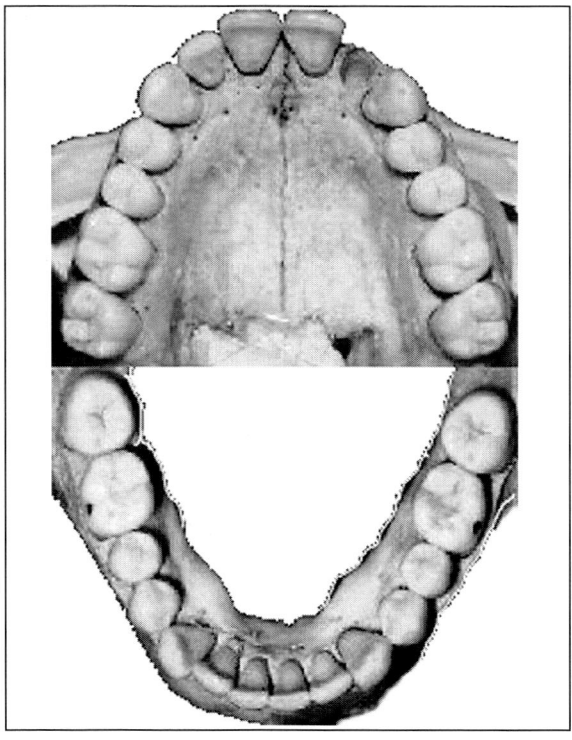

UPPER TEETH	ERUPT
Central incisor	7–8 years
Lateral incisor	8–9 years
Canine (cuspid)	11–12 years
First bicuspid	10–11 years
Second bicuspid	10–12 years
First molar	6–7 years
Second molar	12–13 years
Third molar	17–21 years

LOWER TEETH	ERUPT
Third molar	17–21 years
Second molar	12–13 years
First molar	6–7 years
Second bicuspid	10–12 years
First bicuspid	10–11 years
Cuspid	11–12 years
Lateral incisor	8–9 years
Central incisor	7–8 years

CHILDREN'S TEETH—ERUPTION AND SHEDDING

Upper Teeth	Erupt	Shed
Central incisor	8–12 months	6–7 years
Lateral incisor	9–13 months	7–8 years
Canine (cuspid)	16–22 months	10–12 years
First molar	13–19 months	9–11 years
Second molar	25–33 months	10–12 years

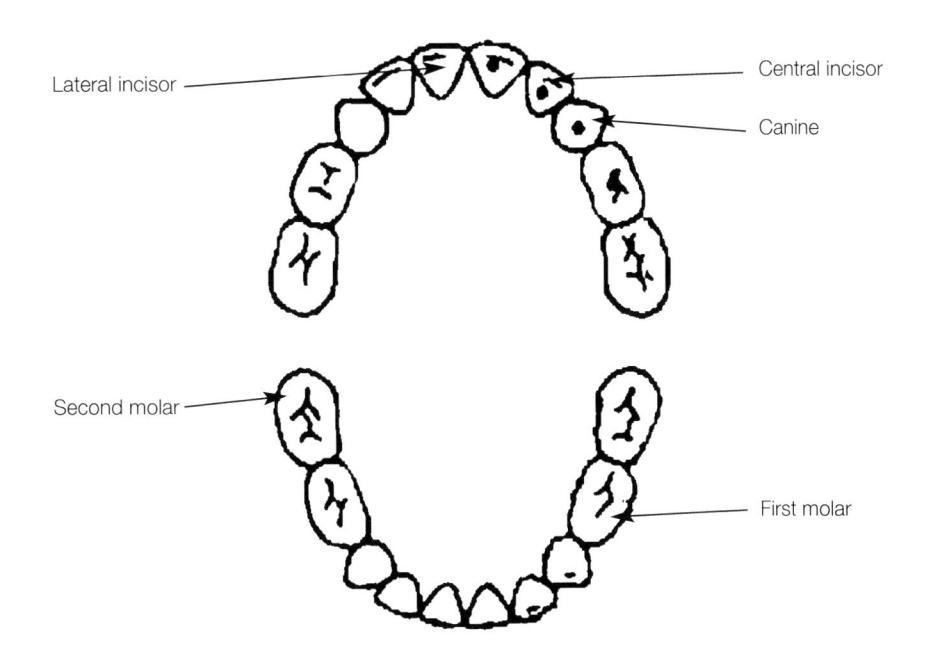

Lower Teeth	Erupt	Shed
Second molar	23–31 months	10–12 years
First molar	14–18 months	9–11 years
Canine (cuspid)	17–23 months	9–12 years
Lateral incisor	10–16 months	7–8 years
Central incisor	6-10 months	6–7 years

CHAPTER 68: ABFO BITEMARK METHODOLOGY GUIDELINES

There is no intention for the American Board of Forensic Odontology to mandate methods but only to provide a list of generally accepted valid methods for this point in the development of our science.

METHODS TO PRESERVE BITEMARK EVIDENCE

1) Bite site evidence
    a) Saliva swabs of bite site
        i) Saliva swabbings of the bite site should be obtained in all cases. Obviously, certain circumstances may preclude the collection of this evidence.
            (1) If swabbing the area would damage or alter the pattern, it should either not be done or accomplished only after all other preservation methods have been employed.
        ii) It is acceptable to use either cotton-tip applicators or cigarette paper to gather this evidence.
        iii) Control swabbings should be taken from other regions or portions of the object or individual that was bitten.
    b) Photographic documentation of the bite site
        i) The bite site should be photographed using conventional photography
        ii) The actual photographic procedures should be performed by the forensic dentist or under the odontologist's direction to ensure accurate and complete documentation of the bite site.
        iii) Color print or slide film and black and white film should be used whenever possible.
        iv) Color or specialty filters may be used to record the bite site in addition to unfiltered photographs.
        v) Alternative methods of illumination may be used.
            (1) Off-angle lighting using a point flash is the most common form of lighting and should be used whenever possible.
            (2) A light source perpendicular to the bite site can be used in addition to off-angle lighting; however, care should be taken to prevent light reflection from obliterating mark details in photographs due to "washout" from light reflection.
            (3) A light source parallel to the bite site can be used, in addition to off-angle lighting.
            (4) A ring flash, natural light, or overhead diffuse lighting can be used to off-angle lighting.
        vi) Video/digital imaging may be used in addition to conventional photography.
        vii) A tripod, focusing rail, bellows, or other devices may be used.
        viii) Scale
            (1) An ABFO number 2 scale should be used whenever possible.
    c) Impressions of bite site
        i) Victim's dental impressions
            (1) When the bite site is accessible to the victim's dentition impressions of the victim's teeth should be obtained.
            (2) This would be useful if victim had bitten the assailant.

ii) Impressions of the bite site
- (1) Impressions of the bite site should be taken when indicated.
- (2) A backing material should be used to maintain the contour of the impression site.

d) Tissue specimens
- i) General considerations
    - (1) The bite site should be preserved when indicated following proper stabilization prior to removal.
    - (2) Tissue fixative
        - (a) Ten-percent formalin is a common fixative.

2) Evidence collection of suspected dentition
   a) Dental records
   b) Photographic documentation of the dentition
      - i) Photographs of the dentition should be taken by the forensic dentist or by the odontologist's direction.
      - ii) A scale such as the ABFO number 2 scale should be used when using a scale in these photographs.
      - iii) Video or digital imaging can be used to document the dentition when used in addition to conventional photography.
      - iv) Tripods or focusing rails can be used at the discretion of the photographer.
      - v) Extraoral photographs
          - (1) A frontal full-face view and a view with the teeth in centric should be taken.
      - vi) Intraoral photographs
          - (1) Maxillary and mandibular occlusal views of the dentition should be taken whenever possible.
          - (2) Lateral views of the dentition may be taken.
   c) Clinical examination
      - i) Extraoral considerations
          - (1) Maximum vertical opening and any deviations should be noted whenever possible.
          - (2) Evidence of surgery, trauma, or facial asymmetry should be noted.
          - (3) TMJ function may be checked in addition to the previous observations.
      - ii) Intraoral considerations
          - (1) Missing and misaligned teeth should be noted.
          - (2) Broken and restored teeth should be noted.
          - (3) The periodontal condition and tooth mobility should be noted whenever possible.
      - iii) Previous dental charts should be reviewed if available.
          - (1) Occlusal disharmonies should be noted whenever possible.
      - iv) The bite classification may be noted in addition to the previous observations.
   d) Dental impressions
      - i) Dental impressions should be taken by the forensic dentist or by the odontologist's direction.
      - ii) Bite exemplars should be obtained in addition to the dental impressions.
   e) Saliva samples
      - i) Saliva swabbings should be obtained.

3) Methods of comparing bitemark evidence
    a) Generation of overlays
        i) Acetate tracing directly from models of the suspect
        ii) Acetate tracing indirect from photocopy of model with scale
        iii) X-ray film overlay created from radiopaque material applied to the wax bite
        iv) Alternative methods
            (1) Life-size photos of model printed on acetate film
            (2) Greater than life-size photos of models on acetate
    b) Test bite media
        i) Wax exemplars (e.g., aluwax, baseplate wax)
        ii) Styrofoam
        iii) Volunteer's skin
        iv) Alternative methods
            (1) Fruits
            (2) Clay
    c) Comparison techniques
        i) Acetate tracings to life-size photos of wound
        ii) Working study model of teeth to life-size photo of wound
        iii) Working study model to impression of wound or to actual victim
        iv) Acetate overlays of teeth compared with greater than life-size photo of wound:
            (1) Five times life size
            (2) Three times life size
            (3) Two times life size
    d) Technical aids employed for analysis
        i) Transillumination of tissue
        ii) Computer enhancement or digitization of mark or teeth
        iii) Stereomicroscopy or macroscopy
        iv) Scanning electron microscopy
        v) Videotape
        vi) Caliper use for measurement

STANDARDS FOR BITEMARK ANALYTICAL METHODS

1) A list of all the evidence analyzed and the specific analytical procedures should be included in the body of the final report. All available evidence associated with the bitemark must be reviewed prior to rendering an expert opinion.

2) Any new analytical methods not listed in the previously described list of analytical methods should be thoroughly explained in the body of the report.

    a) New analytical methods should be scientifically sound and duplicated by other forensic experts.
    b) New analytical methods should, if possible, be backed up with the use of one or more of the accepted techniques listed in these guidelines.

BITEMARK ANALYSIS GUIDELINES

1) Description of bitemark
    a) In the case of a living victim or a deceased individual, the odontologist should determine and record certain vital information.

i) Demographics
> (1) Name of victim
> (2) Case number
> (3) Date of examination
> (4) Referring agency
> (5) Person to contact
> (6) Age of victim
> (7) Race of victim
> (8) Sex of victim
> (9) Name of examiner(s)

ii) Location of bitemark
> (1) Anatomical location
> (2) Surface contour: flat, curved, or irregular
> (3) Tissue characteristics:
>> (a) Underlying structure: bone, cartilage, muscle, fat
>> (b) Skin: relatively fixed or mobile
> (4) Shape
>> (a) Shape of the bitemark (e.g., essentially round, ovoid, crescent, irregular)
> (5) Color
>> (a) Color should be noted (e.g,. red, purple)
> (6) Size
>> (a) Vertical and horizontal dimensions of the bitemark, preferably in using metric system
> (7) Type of injury
>> (a) Petechial hemorrhage
>> (b) Contusion (ecchymosis)
>> (c) Abrasion
>> (d) Laceration
>> (e) Incision
>> (f) Avulsion
>> (g) Artifact
> (8) Other information
>> (a) It should be also be noted whether the skin surface is indented or smooth.
>> (b) At some point, the odontologist will evaluate the evidence to determine such things as position of maxillary and mandibular arches, location and position of individual teeth, intradental characteristics, etc.

COLLECTION OF EVIDENCE FROM VICTIM

1) It should first be determined whether washing, contamination, lividity, embalming, decomposition, change of position, etc., have affected the bitemark.

2) Photography
   a) A variety of types of photographic equipment and films may be used.
   b) Orientation and close-up photographs should be taken.
   c) Photographic resolution should be of high quality.
   d) If color film is used, accuracy of color balance should be ensured.

e) Photographs of the mark should be taken with and without a scale in place.
- i) When the scale is used, it should be on the same plane and adjacent to the bitemark.
    - (1) Include a circular reference in addition to a linear scale.

f) The most critical photographs should be taken in a manner that will eliminate distortion.

g) In the case of a living victim, it may be beneficial to obtain serial photographs of the bitemark.

3) Salivary swabbing
   a) Whenever possible, salivary trace evidence should be collected according to recommendations of the testing laboratory.

4) Impressions
   a) Impressions should be taken of the surface of the bitemark whenever it appears that this may provide useful information.
   b) The impression materials used should meet ADA specifications and be identified by name in the report.
   c) Suitable support should be provided for the impression material to accurately reproduce body contour.
   d) The material used to produce the case should accurately represent the area of impression and should be prepared according to the manufacturer's instructions.

5) Tissue samples
   a) Tissue specimens of the bitemark should be retained whenever it appears this may provide useful information.
      i) It is assumed that evidence gathering from bitemark victims will be done with authorization from the appropriate authorities.

COLLECTION OF EVIDENCE FROM SUSPECT

1) Before collecting evidence from the suspect, the odontologist should ascertain that the necessary search warrant, court order, or legal consent has been obtained, and should make a copy of this document part of his records. The court document or consent should be adequate to permit collection of the evidence listed below.

2) History of any dental treatment subsequent to, or in proximity to, the date of bitemark

3) Photography
   a) Whenever possible, good-quality extraoral photographs should be taken, both full face and profile.
      i) Intraoral photographs preferably would include frontal view, two lateral views, occlusal view of each arch, and any additional photographs that may provide useful information.
      ii) It is also useful to photograph the maximum interincisal opening with scale in place.
      iii) If inanimate materials, such as foodstuffs, are used for test bites, the results should be preserved photographically.

4) Extraoral examination

a) The extraoral examination should include observation and recording of significant soft and hard-tissue factors that may influence biting dynamics, such as temporomandibular joint status, facial asymmetry, muscle tone, and balance.
    i) Measurement of maximal opening of the mouth should be taken, noting any deviations in opening or closing, as well as any significant occlusal disharmonies.
    ii) The presence of facial scars or evidence of surgery should be noted, as well as the presence of facial hair.

5) Intraoral examination
    a) In cases in which saliva evidence has been taken from the victim, it should also be taken from the suspect.
    b) The tongue should be examined for size and function. Any abnormality, such as ankyloglossia, should be noted.
    c) The periodontal condition should be observed with particular reference to mobility and areas of inflammation or hypertrophy.
    d) If anterior teeth are missing or badly broken down, it should be determined how long these conditions have existed.
    e) When feasible, a dental chart of the suspect's teeth should be prepared to encourage thorough study of the dentition.

6) Impressions
    a) Whenever feasible, at least two impressions should be taken of each arch, using materials that meet appropriate ADA specifications.
        i) The interocclusal relationship should be recorded.

7) Sample bites
    a) Whenever feasible, sample bites should be made into an appropriate material, simulating the type of bite under study.

8) Study casts
    a) Master casts should be prepared using ADA-approved Type II stone prepared according to manufacturer's specifications, using accepted dental techniques.
    b) Additional casts may be fabricated in appropriate materials for special studies. When additional models are required, they should be duplicated from master casts using accepted duplication procedures. Labeling should make it clear which master cast was used to produce a duplicate.
    c) The teeth and adjacent soft tissue areas of the master casts should not be altered by carving, trimming, marking, or other alterations.

TERMS INDICATING DEGREE OF CONFIDENCE THAT AN INJURY IS A BITEMARK

1) Possible bitemark
    a) An injury showing a pattern that may or may not be caused by teeth could be caused by other factors, but biting cannot be ruled out.
        i) Criteria
            (1) General shape and size are present, but distinctive features such as tooth marks are missing, incomplete, or distorted or a few marks resembling tooth marks are present but the arch configuration is missing.

2) Probable bitemark
- a) The pattern strongly suggests or supports origin from teeth but could conceivably be caused by something else.
    - i) Criteria
        - (1) Pattern shows (some) (basic) (general) characteristics of teeth arranged around arches.

3) Definite bitemark
- a) There is no reasonable doubt that teeth created the pattern, and other possibilities were considered and excluded.
    - i) Criteria
        - (1) Pattern conclusively illustrates (classic features) (all the characteristics) (typical class characteristics) of dental arches and human teeth in proper arrangement so that it is recognizable as an impression of the human dentition.

DESCRIPTIONS AND TERMS USED TO LINK A BITEMARK TO A SUSPECT

1) Match
- a) Nonspecific term indicating some degree of concordance between a single feature, combination of features, or a whole case
- b) An expression of similarity without stating degree of probability or specificity
    - i) This term *match* or *positive match* should not be used as a definitive expression of an opinion in a bitemark case. The statement "It is a positive match" or "It is my opinion that the bitemark matches the suspect's teeth" will likely be interpreted by juries as tantamount to specific perpetrator identification. In fact, the odontologist may be implying that a poorly defined or nonspecific bitemark was generally similar to the suspect's teeth, as it might be to a large percentage of the population.

2) Consistent (compatible) with
- a) Synonymous with *match*, a similarity is present, but specificity is unstated.
    - i) If used to represent the odontologist's conclusion, the term *consistent with* should be explained in the report or testimony as indicating similarity but implying no degree of specificity to the match.

3) Possible biter
- a) Could have done it; may or may not have done it
    - i) Teeth like the suspect's could be expected to create a mark like the one examined, but so could other dentitions.
        - (1) Criteria
            - (a) There is a nonspecific similarity or a similarity of class characteristics; match points are general or few, and there are no incompatible inconsistencies that would serve to exclude.

4) Probable biter
- a) Suspect most likely made the bite; most people in the population could not leave such a mark.
    - i) Criteria

          (1) Bitemark shows some degree of specificity to the individual suspect's teeth by virtue of a sufficient number of concordant points, including some corresponding individual characteristics.
          (2) There is an absence of any unexplainable discrepancies.

5) Reasonable medical certainty
    a) Highest order of certainty is that the suspect made the bite.
    b) The investigator is confident that the suspect made the mark.
    c) Perpetrator is identified for all practical and reasonable purposes by the bitemark.
    d) Any expert with similar training and experience evaluating the same evidence should come to the same conclusion of certainty.
    e) Any other opinion would be unreasonable.
        i) Criteria
          (1) There is a concordance of sufficient distinctive, individual characteristics to confer (virtual) uniqueness within the population under consideration.
          (2) There is absence of any unexplainable discrepancies.
    f) The term *reasonable medical certainty* conveys the connotation of virtual certainty or beyond reasonable doubt. The term deliberately avoids the message of unconditional certainty only in deference to the scientific maxim that one can never be absolutely positive unless everyone in the world was examined or the expert was an eyewitness. The board considers that a statement of absolute certainty such as "indeed, without a doubt," is unprovable and reckless. Reasonable medical certainty represents the highest order of confidence in a comparison. It is, however, acceptable to state that there is "no doubt in my mind" or "in my opinion, the suspect is the biter" when such statements are prompted in testimony.

PROTOCOL FOR BITEMARKS ON DECEDENTS

1) The bodies of all decedents involved in homicides with sexual overtones should be checked at the scene by the MEO/coroner investigator for the presence of bitemarks, especially in those cases where the breasts and buttocks of the decedent are exposed.

2) If a suspicious area is present on the body, the MEO/coroner investigator or evidence technician should proceed in the following manner:
    a) Do not touch this area.
    b) Notify the homicide detective and the evidence technician to ensure that the area involved will be properly photographed prior to transporting the remains.
    c) Notify the medical examiner pathologist on call.
    d) Notify the forensic odontologist.

3) Do not publicize or give any information to anyone, especially the news media, that a bitemark may be present.
    a) This is to keep the suspect (assailant), even if in custody, from intentionally altering or mutilating the biting edge of his teeth, thus hindering or preventing a possible forensic comparison.

4) Take initial photographs of the bitemark at the scene. The camera is to be placed at a 90-degree angle from the bitemark.

5) Process the bitemark
    a) Depending on the preference of your crime lab serology specialist, a cotton swab or gauze square is used with either sterile water or isotonic saline to pick up saliva traces in the area of the bitemark where the lips and tongue most probably contacted the skin. Do not swab over the teeth marks!
        i) Follow this procedure for each bitemark.
        ii) Using sterile gloves to avoid contamination, work from the periphery toward the center of the bitemark, allowing the swabs to air-dry for a few moments and then placing them in a sterile, sealed, and properly marked test tube (or paper envelope if using gauze).
    b) Note whether blood or other fluids contaminate the area.
    c) For control purposes, it is recommended that unbitten areas of the decedent be swabbed. Forexample, if a bitemark is apparent on the right wrist, a swabbing should be completed on the left wrist. Upon arriving at the MEO or morgue facility, a hold should be placed on the release of the body until specific approval for the release of the body is given by the pathologist handling the case.

PHOTOGRAPHING BITEMARK EVIDENCE

1) Begin with a general orientation photo that clearly shows the location of each bitemark on the body. Place a color scale/ruler containing the necessary information identifying name, case number, and date adjacent to the bitemark.

2) Take another photograph without any adjacent chart or ruler.

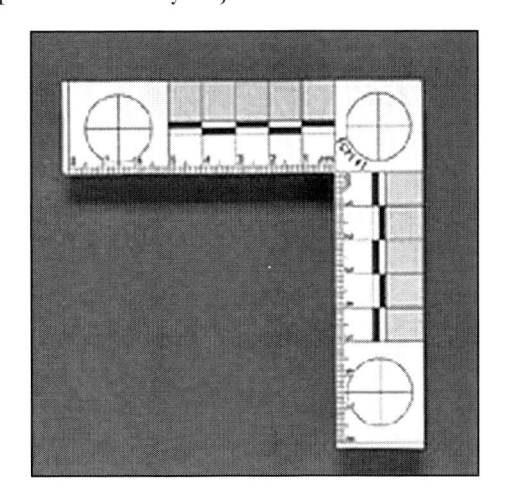

Ruler used in taking photographs of bitemarks.

3) Take close-up color photographs under the following conditions:
    a) The central axis of the lens should be perpendicular to the general view of the desired area to be shown.
    b) An adjacent ruler must be parallel with the film plane.
    c) The light source should be placed at an angle between 30 and 45 degrees to the surface of the bitemark in an effort to highlight the texture of the skin.
    d) Take at least four (bracketed) exposures at 3, 6, 9, and 12 o'clock angles.
        i) Use more exposures for bitemarks on black skin.

e) If both upper and lower teeth curves are apparent, then one to two, or one to one (35mm format) of each of the halves of the bitemark should be photographed in the same manner.

BITEMARKS—POSSIBLE INVESTIGATIVE SIGNIFICANCE

The following information should be used as a general guideline, in consideration of a possible source of the inflicted bites.

LOCATION	SEX	CHARACTERISTIC OF BITEMARK ON VICTIM
Extremities	Male or Female	Nonsexual
Thorax	Male or Female	Nonsexual
Chest	Male or Female	Nonsexual
Breast	Female	Heterosexual
Thigh	Female	Heterosexual
Anterior shoulder	Female	Heterosexual
Pubic area	Female	Heterosexual
Neck	Female	Heterosexual
Arm	Female	Heterosexual
Buttocks	Female	Heterosexual
Abdomen	Male	Heterosexual
Chest	Male	Heterosexual
Arm	Male	Heterosexual
Upper back	Male	Homosexual
Axilla (armpit)	Male	Homosexual
Posterior shoulder	Male	Homosexual
Penis	Male	Homosexual
Scrotum	Male	Homosexual
Breast	Male	Homosexual
Arm	Male	Homosexual

CHAPTER 69: FORENSIC ANTHROPOLOGY

When a bone, partial skeleton, or complete skeleton is found, protocol should require that the specimen be referred to a forensic anthropologist for the following considerations.

1) Is the bone, partial or complete skeleton, or other suspicious specimen human or nonhuman in origin.

2) Are the bones modern?
    a) Modern (how long deposited) considerations:
        i) Presence of soft tissue
        ii) Discernible smell
        iii) Insect activity
        iv) Inherent vegetation
        v) Bleaching and staining status
        vi) Condition of teeth

3) Co-mingling: How many remains are present?

4) What are the cause and manner of death?

5) Age determination. The biological age of a skeleton can be estimated by the following:
    a) Beginning of ossification of cartilage, which is especially prevalent in the ribs.
    b) Pubis synthesis
    c) Closing of suture in the skull
    d) Teeth, including eruptions and wear

6) Determine the race.
    a) This will be very difficult.
    b) The only part of the skeleton from which the origin of race can be accurately determined is the skull.
        i) Through evaluation and comparison of the anatomical and morphological skull feature variations and anthropometric measurements, racial origin (i.e., Caucasoid, Mongoloid, or Negroid) can be determined.
    c) Make eye socket comparisons.
    d) Measure bones, including the femur and tibia.

RACIAL DETERMINATION

SKULL FEATURE	CAUCASOID	MONGOLOID	NEGROID
Nasal bones	Narrow, long, high-bridged	Narrow, low-bridged short	Broad, flat, short
Nasal root	Narrow, high	Narrow, low	Broad, low
Nasal cavity	Narrow	Narrow	Wide
Anterior nasal spine	Long, straight	Short, straight	Short, slanted
Nasal sill	Sharp ridge	Sharp ridge	Guttered, rounded
Zygomatic bones	Curved	Squared	Curved
Profile	Straight	Variable	Prognathic
Maxillary incisors	Smooth	Shoveled	Smooth
Bone feature	Slight bowing	Bowed more	Straight
Zygo-maxillary suture	Curved	Straight	Curved
Transverse palatine suture	Straight	Straight	Curved, forward

7) Determine gender estimation.
    a) The estimation of gender can be determined through analysis of the skull (cranium and mandible) and skeleton.
    b) Examine the pelvis.
        i) The pelvis is considered the best area to determine the sex of a skeleton.

PELVIS EXAMINATION

BONE FEATURE	MALE	FEMALE
Pubic bone	Robust	Delicate
Pubic region	Shorter	Longer
Subpubic angle	Less angle (narrow)	Greater angle (wide)
Subpubic cavity	No ventral arc	Ventral arc
Ilium	Flat sacroiliac articulation	Elevated sacroiliac articulation
Sciatic notch	Narrow	Wide
Obturator foramen	Large, oval shaped	Small, triangular shaped
Pelvic basin	Funnel shaped, less space	Rounder shape, spacious
Pubic symphysis	Young adult: rough	Old adult: smooth

    c) The skull is the next best area. The skull and bone features vary from male to female, and this is based on the generalization that male features are more pronounced and marked than female features.
        i) Skulls of males have a large mastoid process and a prominent ridge over the eyes.

SKULL EXAMINATION

SKULL FEATURE	MALE	FEMALE
Bony superciliary ridges	Prominent	Absent or slight
Frontal bone	Low, slanting	Globular, rounded
Mastoid process	Large	Small
Supraorbital margin	Rounded	Sharp
External occipital protuberance	Generally present	Generally absent
Nuchal crest (occipital bone)	Rugose	Smoother
Zygomatic process	Extends past external	Does not
Symphysis of mandible	Square	Rounded
Ramus of mandible	Straight	Slanting
Mandible gonion (gonion angle)	Flaring	Less so
Total skull	Heavier, larger	More rounded, smaller

8) Determine the pysique of the individual.
    a) Measure stature, weight, and build.
        i) Weight is usually developed through the examination of the clothing found with the remains.

9) Make a personal identification.
    a) Dental records and dental X-ray comparison
    b) Check medical records and conduct medical X-ray comparisons.

10) Examine secondary features.
    a) Make an occupational recording of the bones.
    b) Determine handedness of the individual.
        i) Right-handers make up approximately 85 percent of the population.
    c) Determine pathologies and anomalies of the bone.

LATERAL SKULL VIEW

ANTERIOR SKULL VIEW

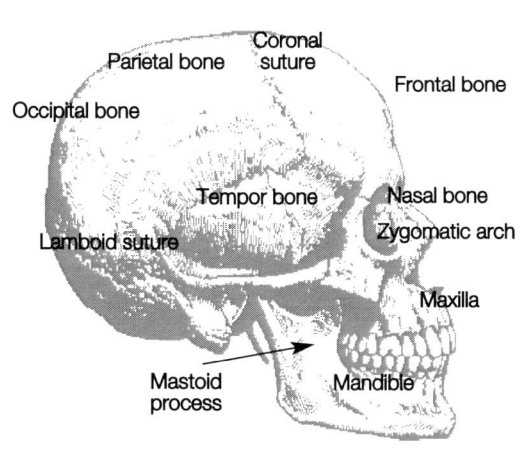

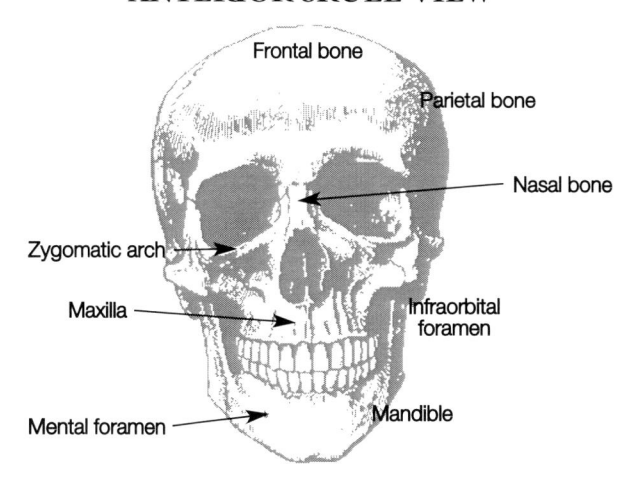

FULL SKELETAL—ANTERIOR

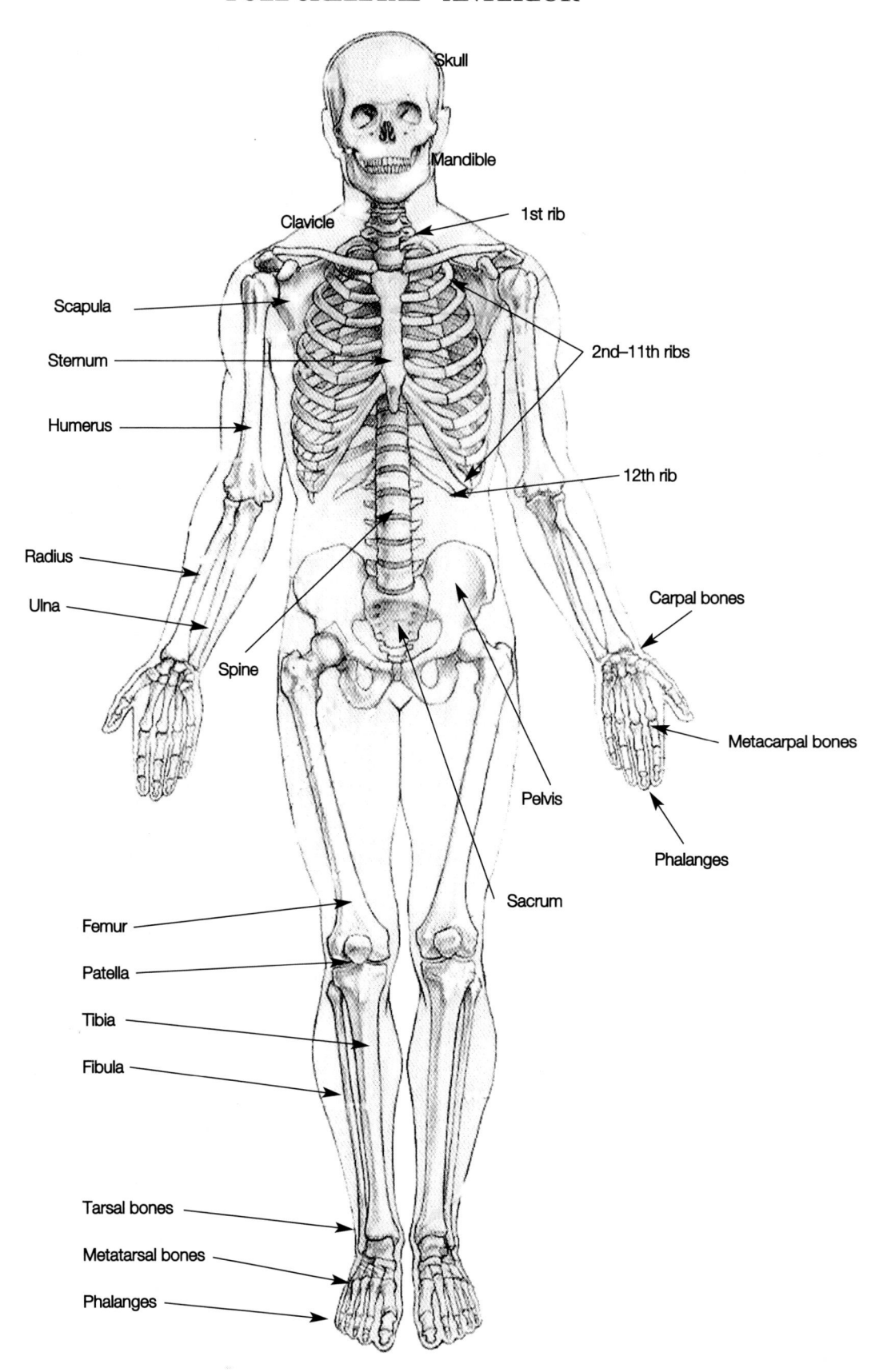

FORENSIC ANTHROPOLOGY

FULL SKELETAL—POSTERIOR VIEW

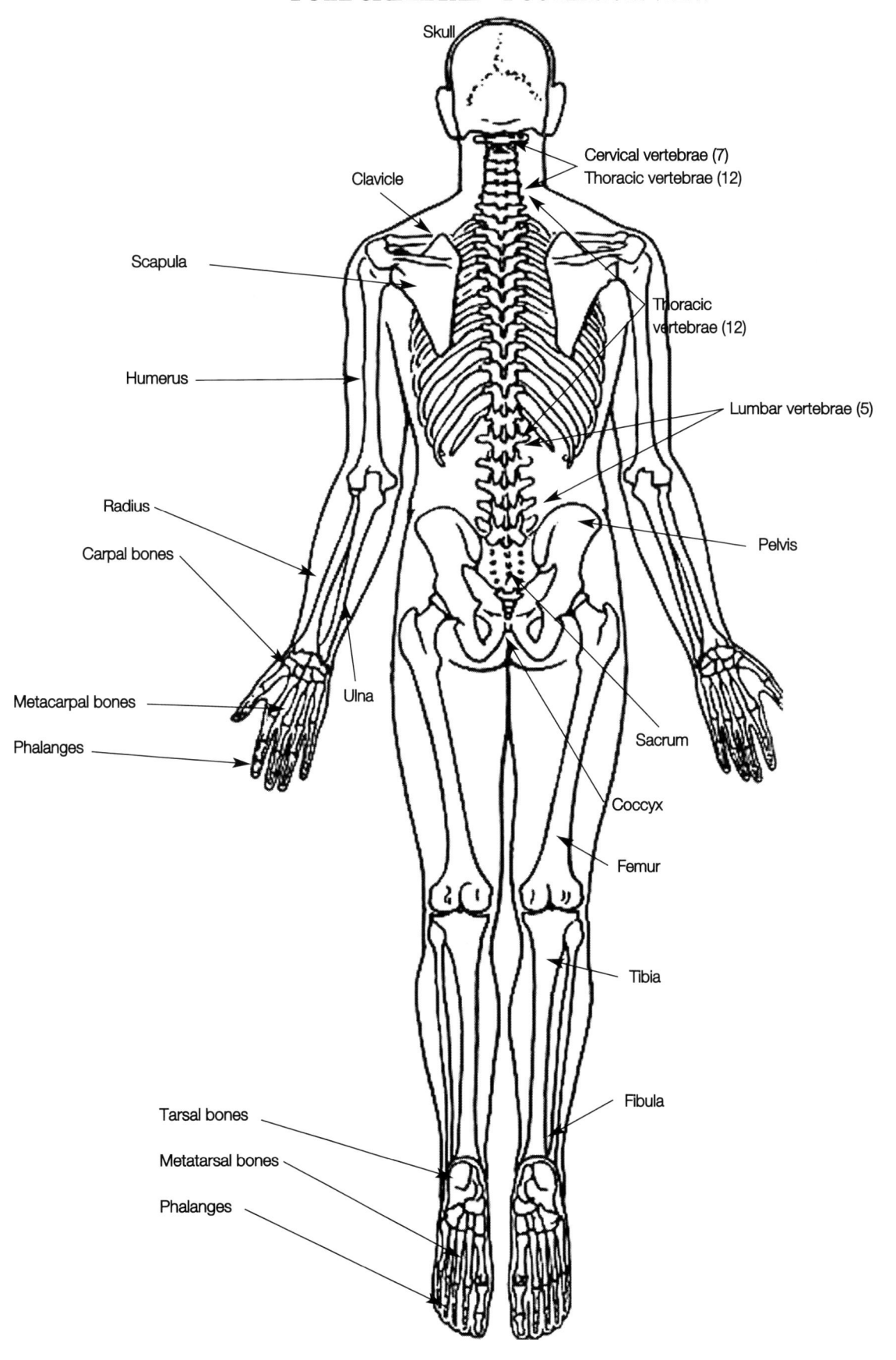

- Skull
- Cervical vertebrae (7)
- Thoracic vertebrae (12)
- Clavicle
- Scapula
- Thoracic vertebrae (12)
- Humerus
- Lumbar vertebrae (5)
- Radius
- Carpal bones
- Pelvis
- Ulna
- Metacarpal bones
- Phalanges
- Sacrum
- Coccyx
- Femur
- Tibia
- Fibula
- Tarsal bones
- Metatarsal bones
- Phalanges

CHAPTER 70: TOXICOLOGY

1) Toxicology is the study of drugs and how they affect the biological system. In the medicolegal investigation of death, toxicology will address the question of whether drugs caused or contributed to the cause of death.

2) Analysis is conducted on the following.
    a) Biological specimens:
        i) Blood
        ii) Urine
        iii) Vitreous
        iv) Bile
        v) Liver tissue
        vi) Brain tissue
        vii) Kidney tissue
        viii) Spleen tissue
    b) Nonbiological specimens, including:
        i) Pills
        ii) Air samples
        iii) Clothing

3) Toxicology checks for the presence or absence of chemical substances.

4) A toxicological examination will not reveal all foreign substances present in the body. Specific substances must be screened during the exam. Consequently, toxicological information should be developed in all cases, regardless of the cause of death, where a drug screen is conducted to determine what influence alcohol, drugs, or other chemical substances may have had in the specific death. For example, investigators may have a case in which it has become fairly obvious that the decedent died as a result of a self-inflicted gunshot wound. However, the investigation may develop concerns about whether or not the decedent had been taking his prescribed medication. Specifically, screening involves the presence (qualitative) of substances and, if present, the amount (quantitative) present.

5) These types of substances are screened:
    a) Alcohol
    b) Antidepressants
    c) Barbiturates
    d) Benzodiazepines (minor tranquilizers)
    e) Carbon monoxide
    f) Chlorinated hydrocarbons
    g) Cocaine
    h) Heavy metals (e.g., arsenic, antimony, bismuth, and mercury)
    i) Insecticides
    j) Lead
    k) Opium alkaloids
    l) Nonbarbiturate sedative hypnotics
    m) Phenothiazines (antiemetic)
    n) Stimulants

6) These are typical samples taken for toxicological analysis.

TYPES	QUANTITY	ANALYSIS
Blood (from heart and femoral artery)	20 ml	Volatiles, drugs
Urine	20 ml	Drugs, heavy metals
Bile	20 ml	Narcotics, other drugs
Kidney	Entire	In absence of urine
Liver	20 gms	Many drugs
Gastric contents	Total	Drugs taken orally
Vitreous humor	Both eyes	Alcohol, glucose, drugs, and electrolytes

7) Some studies have shown that there may be a discrepancy in quantitative amounts present in blood samples of heart versus femoral specimens. The recommendation is to take femoral blood for quantitative analysis when the following drugs have been indicated:

>   Alprazolam   Almantidine   Amitriptyline
>   Amoxapine   Amphetamine   Brompheniramine
>   Caffeine   Chlordiazepoxide   Chlorpheniramine
>   Cocaine   Desipramine   Diphenhydramine
>   Doxepin   Doxylamine   Fluoxetine
>   Imipramine   Maprotoline   Meperidine
>   Methamphetamine   Metoprodol   Nordoxepin
>   Norfluoxetine   Normeperidine   Norpropoxyphene
>   Nortriptyline   Phencyclidine   Propoxyphene
>   Propranolol   Thioridazine   Trimipramine
>   Verapamil

8) These are frequently encountered substances in postmortem cases.
    a) Gases and volatiles, including:
        i) Alcohols, chlorinated hydrocarbons, aromatic hydrocarbons, carbon monoxide, and cyanide
    b) Acids, including:
        i) Barbiturates, salicylates, and acetaminophen
    c) Neutrals, including:
        i) Glutethimide, ethchlorvynol, meprobamate, and carisoprodol
    d) Bases, including:
        i) Cocaine, propoxyphene, opium alkaloids, antidepressants, and benzodiazepines.
    e) Metals, including:
        i) Arsenic and mercury

9) Based on the information obtained during the initial stages of the investigation, the specimen may initially be run through a screening stage to detect the presence or absence of substances. Screening tests are usually performed directly on biological specimens with little or no sample preparation. These tests are rapid and informative but only presumptive. Since many of the screening tests only identify a class of compounds, the examination usually requires further identification of the specific toxicant and confirmation.

SPECIFIC SCREEN	TESTS FOR	SPECIMEN
Volatile	Ethanol	Blood
Drugs of Abuse (DAS)	Amphetamines Barbiturates Benzodiazepines Cocaine Marijuana Methadone Propoxyphene Phencyclidine Opiate alkaloids	Urine
General Drug Screen (GDS)	Various drugs	Urine blood, gastric contents, tissue homogenate
Acidic and Neutral Drug Screen (ANS)	Acidic drugs Neutral drugs Barbiturates Sedative hypnotics (nonbarbiturate such as glutethimide) Muscle relaxants (e.g., meprobamate and carisoprodol)	Blood, urine, tissue homogenate
Basic Drug Screen (BDS)	Many of the basic drugs: Propoxyphene Cocaine Antidepressants Opiates (e.g., codeine, oxycodone, hydromorphone, and meperidine) Calcium channel blockers	Blood, urine tissue homogenate
Colorimetric Screening Test	Phenothiazines Imipramine Desipramine Tripramine Halogenated compounds Salicylates Acetaminophen Ethchlorvynol Heavy metals	

10) Types of testing available include the following:
    a) Spectroscopy
        i) This is based on the principle that substances will gain or lose energy when subjected to electromagnetic radiation. Wavelengths are produced at a particular location where energy changes take place. These changes are indicative of a particular substance and are proportional to the quantity of substance present. As a result, this test can be used in quantitating the substance.
        ii) The common types of spectroscopy may include visible, ultraviolet, fluorometry, atomic absorption, and infrared.
    b) Chromotography
        i) This process uses a separation technique involving a partitioning process. The separation will depend on the polarity of the solvent system and the solubility characteristics of the compounds in the extract. There are three types of chromatography tests.
            (1) Thin-layer chromatography (TLC) is a fairly basic testing system. It is based on the premise that drugs and their metabolites will separate when placed on a plate as a biological specimen and submerged in a solvent.
            (2) Gas-liquid chromatography (GLC) is one of the most widely used techniques for drug analysis. It uses an inert gas, such as nitrogen or helium, as the mobile phase of the testing.
            (3) Gas chromatography/mass spectrometry (GC/MS) combines the separating powers of the gas chromatograph with the discriminating abilities of a mass spectrometer. Currently, this system is recognized as the most definitive method of identification of a drug in a biological specimen.
    c) Immunoassays
        i) Immunoassays are based on a competition between the drug of interest in the specimen and a labeled drug added to the specimen for sites on an antibody for the drug of interest.
        ii) Radioimmunoassay (RIA) is also a competitive reaction for antibody sites between a drug and or its metabolites and a radioactive labeled drug.

11) Interpretation of drug test results requires the responsible individual to evaluate the findings and to determine whether the specific concentration is present in an amount that will be:
    a) Sufficient to cause the death
    b) Sufficient to have affected the actions of the decedent so as to have caused the death
    c) Insufficient to have any involvement in the cause of death
    d) Insufficient to protect the individual from an underlying mechanism of death, such as an epileptic seizure

CHAPTER 71: DRUGS OF ABUSE

DEPRESSANT

Drug Type	Alcohol	Barbiturate	Barbiturate
Classification	Depressant	Depressant	Depressant
Drug	Beer/liquor/wine	Chloral hydrate	Doriden
Source	Grain/grain/fruit	Synthetic	Synthetic
Average amount Consumed	12/1.5/3 ounces	500 milligrams	400 milligrams
Drug form	Liquid	Pill	Pill
Ingestion method	Swallowed	Swallowed	Swallowed
Short-term effects of average consumption	Relaxation, breakdown of inhibitions, euphoria, depression impaired coordination, decreased alertness	Relaxation, euphoria, decreased alertness drowsiness, impaired coordination, sleep	Relaxation, euphoria, decreased alertness, drowsiness, sleep
Duration	Body metabolizes at .02 ounces per hour	4 to 8 hours	4 to 8 hours
Short-term effect of large amounts	Stupor, nausea, unconsciousness hangover, death	Slurred speech, stupor, hangover, death	Slurred speech, stupor, hangover, death
Long-term effects	Obesity, impotence, psychosis, ulcers, malnutrition, liver damage, brain damage, delirium tremens, death	Excessive sleepiness, confusion, irritability, severe withdrawal sickness	Excessive sleepiness, confusion, irritability, severe withdrawal sickness
Addiction potential	Moderate	High	High

Tolerance	Increasing	Increasing	Increasing
Medical Uses	None	Insomnia, tension, epileptic seizures	Insomnia, tension epileptic seizures

DEPRESSANT

Drug	Nembutal	Phenobarbital	Seconal
Classification	Depressant	Depressant	Depressant
Drug type	Barbiturate	Barbiturate	Barbiturate
Source	Synthetic	Synthetic	Synthetic
Average amount consumed	400 milligrams	50–100 milligrams	50–100 milligrams
Drug form	Pill	Pill	Pill
Ingestion method	Swallowed	Swallowed	Swallowed
Short-term effects of average consumption	Relaxation, euphoria, decreased alertness, drowsiness, impaired coordination, sleep	Relaxation, euphoria, decreased alertness, drowsiness, impaired coordination, sleep	Relaxation, euphoria, decreased alertness, drowsiness, impaired coordination, sleep
Duration	4 to 8 hours	4 to 8 hours	4 to 8 hours
Short-term effect of large amounts	Slurred speech, stupor, hangover, death		
Long-term effects	Excessive sleepiness, confusion, irritability, severe withdrawal sickness		
Addiction potential	High	High	High
Tolerance	Increasing	Increasing	Increasing
Medical uses	Insomnia, tension epileptic seizures	Insomnia, tension epileptic seizures	Insomnia, tension epileptic seizures
Lethal levels	50–500 milligrams	80–250 milligrams	50–500 milligrams

DEPRESSANT

Drug	Aerosols (freon)	Amyl nitrite	Model glue
Classification	Depressant	Depressant	Depressant
Drug type	Inhalant	Inhalant	Inhalant
Source	Synthetic	Synthetic	Synthetic
Average amount consumed	Varies	Varies	Varies
Drug form	Gas	Gas	Gas
Ingestion method	Inhaled	Inhaled	Inhaled
Short-term effects of average consumption	Relaxation, euphoria, impaired coordination	Relaxation, euphoria, impaired coordination	Relaxation, euphoria, impaired coordination
Duration	1 to 3 hours	1 to 3 hours	1 to 3 hours
Short-term effect of large amounts	Stupor, death	Stupor, death	Stupor, death
Long-term effects	Hallucinations, liver damage, kidney damage, bone marrow damage, brain damage, death	Hallucinations, liver damage, kidney damage, bone marrow damage, brain damage, death	Hallucinations, liver damage, kidney damage, bone marrow damage, brain damage, death
Addiction potential	Small	Small	Small
Tolerance	Possibly	Possibly	Possibly
Medical uses	None	Dilation of blood vessels	None
Lethal levels	Varies	Varies	Varies

DEPRESSANT

Drug	Nitrous oxide	Codeine	Demerol
Classification	Depressant	Depressant	Depressant
Drug type	Inhalant	Narcotic	Narcotic
Source	Synthetic	Opium poppy	Synthetic
Average amount consumed	Varies	15–30 milligrams	50–150 milligrams
Drug form	Gas	Pill, liquid	Pill
Ingestion method	Inhaled	Swallowed	Swallowed, injected
Short-term effects of average consumption	Relaxation, euphoria impaired coordination	Relaxation, relief of pain, relief of anxiety, decreased alertness euphoria hallucinations	Relaxation, relief of pain, relief of anxiety, decreased alertness euphoria hallucinations
Duration	1 to 3 hours	4 hours	4 hours
Short-term effect of large amounts	Stupor, death	Stupor, death	Stupor, death
Long-term effects	Hallucinations, liver damage, kidney damage, bone marrow damage, brain damage death	Lethargy, constipation, weight loss, temporary sterility, impotence, withdrawal sickness	Lethargy, constipation, weight loss, temporary sterility, impotence withdrawal sickness
Addiction potential	Small	High	High
Tolerance	Possibly	Increasing	Increasing
Medical uses	Light anesthetic	Cough treatment	Painkiller
Lethal levels	Varies	1–10 milligrams	Varies

DEPRESSANT

Drug	Heroin	Methadone	Morphine
Classification	Depressant	Depressant	Depressant
Drug type	Narcotic	Narcotic	Narcotic
Source	Opium poppy	Synthetic	Opium poppy
Average amount consumed	Varies	5–15 milligrams	10 milligrams
Drug form	White powder or clear liquid	Pill, liquid	White powder or clear liquid
Ingestion method	Smoked, swallowed injected	Swallowed	Injected
Short-term effects of average consumption	Relaxation, relief of pain, decreased alertness, euphoria, hallucinations	Relaxation, relief of pain, decreased alertness, euphoria, hallucinations	Relaxation, relief of pain, decreased alertness, euphoria, hallucinations
Duration	4 hours	4 hours	4 hours
Short-term effect of large amounts	Stupor, death	Stupor, death	Stupor, death
Long-term effects	Lethargy, constipation, weight loss, temporary sterility, impotence, withdrawal sickness	Lethargy, constipation, weight loss, temporary sterility, impotence, withdrawal sickness	Lethargy, constipation, weight loss, temporary sterility, impotence, withdrawal sickness
Addiction potential	High	High	High
Tolerance	Increasing	Increasing	Increasing
Medical uses	None	Heroin withdrawal treatment	Painkiller
Lethal levels	0.01–1 milligram	0.5–2 milligrams	0.01–1 milligram

DEPRESSANT

Drug	Opium	Percodan	Librium
Classification	Depressant	Depressant	Depressant
Drug Type	Narcotic	Narcotic	Tranquilizer
Source	Opium poppy	Synthetic	Synthetic
Average amount consumed	Varies	15–50 milligrams	5–25 milligrams
Drug form	White powder or clear liquid	Pill	Pill
Ingestion method	Smoked, swallowed, injected	Swallowed	Swallowed
Short-term effects of average consumption	Relaxation, relief of pain, relief of anxiety, decreased alertness, euphoria, hallucinations	Relaxation, relief of pain, relief of anxiety, decreased alertness, euphoria, hallucinations	Relief of anxiety, relief of tension, suppression of hallucinations, suppression of aggression, sleep
Duration	4 hours	4 hours	12–24 hours
Short-term effect of large amounts	Stupor, death	Stupor, death	Drowsiness, blurred vision
Long-term effects	Lethargy, constipation, weight loss, temporary impotence, withdrawal sickness	Lethargy, constipation, weight loss, temporary impotence, withdrawal sickness	Destruction of blood cells, jaundice, coma, death
Addiction potential	High	High	High
Tolerance	Increasing	Increasing	None
Medical uses	Diarrhea treatment	Painkiller	Tension treatment
Lethal levels	Varies	Varies	2 milligrams

DEPRESSANT

Drug	Miltown, Equanil	Thorazine
Classification	Depressant	Depressant
Drug type	Tranquilizer	Tranquilizer
Source	Synthetic	Synthetic
Average amount consumed	300–400 milligrams	5–25 milligrams
Drug form	Pill	Pill
Ingestion method	Swallowed	Swallowed
Short-term effects of average consumption	Relief of anxiety, relief of tension, suppression of hallucinations, suppression of aggression, sleep	Relief of anxiety, relief of tension, suppression of hallucinations, suppression of aggression, sleep
Duration	12–24 hours	12–24 hours
Short-term effect of large amounts	Drowsiness, blurred vision, dizziness, slurred speech, allergic reaction, stupor	Drowsiness, blurred vision, dizziness, slurred speech, allergic reaction, stupor
Long-term effects	Destruction of blood cells, jaundice, coma, death	Destruction of blood cells, jaundice, coma, death
Addiction potential	Moderate	Moderate
Tolerance	None	None
Medical uses	Tension treatment, anxiety, psychosis, alcoholism	Tension treatment, anxiety, psychosis, alcoholism
Lethal levels	Varies	0.3–1.2 milligrams

PSYCHEDELIC

Drug	THC	DMT	LSD
Classification	Psychedelic	Psychedelic	Psychedelic
Drug type	Cannabis	Hallucinogen	Hallucinogen
Source	Synthetic	Synthetic	Synthetic
Average amount consumed	Varies	Varies	150–200 micrograms
Drug form	Plastic baggies, roach clips, cigarette rolling papers, pipes	Powder	Plastic, paper wrappers capsule, sugar cube, animal designs or stars on a sheet of paper
Ingestion method	Smoked or swallowed	Inhaled	Swallowed or injected
Short-term effects of average consumption	Relaxation, breakdown of inhibitions, alteration of perception, euphoria, increased appetite	Perceptual changes, especially visual; increased energy; hallucinations; panic	Perceptual changes, especially visual; increased energy; hallucinations; panic
Duration	2–4 hours	30 minutes	10–12 hours
Short-term effect of large amounts	Panic, stupor	Anxiety, hallucinations, psychosis, exhaustion, tremors, vomiting, panic	Anxiety, hallucinations, psychosis exhaustion, tremors, vomiting, panic
Long-term effects	Fatigue, psychosis	Increased delusions and panic psychosis	Increased delusions and panic psychosis
Addiction potential	None	None	None
Tolerance	None	Increasing	Increasing
Medical uses	Tension, depression,	None	None

	headache, poor appetite, antinausea for chemotherapy patients		
Lethal levels	Varies	Varies	Varies

PSYCHEDELIC

Drug	Mescaline	Nutmeg	Psilocybin
Classification	Psychedelic	Psychedelic	Psychedelic
Drug type	Hallucinogen	Hallucinogen	Hallucinogen
Source	Cactus	Nutmeg tree	Mushroom
Average amount consumed	350 milligrams	1/3 ounce	25 milligrams
Drug form	Buttons, powder	Powder	Powder
Ingestion method	Swallowed	Swallowed or sniffed	Swallowed
Short-term effects of average consumption	Perceptual changes, especially visual; increased energy; hallucinations; panic	Perceptual changes, especially visual; increased energy; hallucinations; panic	Perceptual changes, especially visual; increased energy; hallucinations; panic
Duration	12–14 hours	Varies	6–8 hours
Short-term effect of large amounts	Anxiety, hallucinations, psychosis, exhaustion, tremors, vomiting, panic	Anxiety, hallucinations, psychosis, exhaustion, tremors, vomiting, panic	Anxiety, hallucinations, psychosis, exhaustion, tremors, vomiting, panic
Long-term effects	Increased delusions and panic psychosis	Increased delusions and panic psychosis	Increased delusions and panic psychosis
Addiction potential	None	None	None
Tolerance	Increasing	Increasing	Increasing
Medical uses	None	None	None
Lethal levels	Varies	Varies	Varies

PSYCHEDELIC

Drug	Scopolamine	STP	Hashish Marijuana
Classification	Psychedelic	Psychedelic	Psychedelic
Drug type	Hallucinogen	Hallucinogen	Cannabis
Source	Henbane plant, synthetic	Synthetic	Cannabis plant
Average amount consumed	.5 milligram	5 milligrams	Varies
Drug form	Powder	Powder	Varies
Ingestion method	Swallowed	Swallowed	Swallowed
Short-term effects of average consumption	Perceptual changes, especially visual; increased energy; hallucinations	Perceptual changes, especially visual; increased energy; hallucinations	Relaxation, breakdown of inhibitions, alteration of perception, euphoria, increased appetite
Duration	Varies	12–14 hours	2–4 hours
Short-term effect of large amounts	Anxiety, hallucinations, psychosis, exhaustion, tremors, vomiting, panic	Anxiety, hallucinations, psychosis, exhaustion, tremors, vomiting, panic	Panic, stupor
Long-term effects	Increased delusions and psychosis	Increased delusions and psychosis	Fatigue, psychosis
Addiction potential	None	None	None
Tolerance	Increasing	Increasing	None
Medical uses	None	None	Tension treatment depression, headache
Lethal levels	Varies	Varies	0.002–0.02 milligram

STIMULANTS

Drug	Elavil, Ritalin, Tofranil	Coffee	Cola
Classification	Stimulant	Stimulant	Stimulant
Drug type	Antidepressant	Caffeine	Caffeine
Source	Synthetic		
Average amount consumed	10–25 milligrams	1 to 2 cups	12 ounces
Drug form	Tablets	Liquid	Liquid
Ingestion method	Swallowed, injected	Swallowed	Swallowed
Short-term effects of average consumption	Relief of anxiety and depression, temporary impotence	Increased alertness	Increased alertness
Duration	12–24 hours	2–4 hours	2–4 hours
Short-term effect of large amounts	Nausea, hypertension, weight loss, insomnia	Restlessness, insomnia, upset stomach	Restlessness, insomnia, upset stomach
Long-term effects	Stupor, convulsions, coma, congestive heart failure, damage to liver and white blood cells, death	Restlessness, irritability, insomnia, stomach disorders	Restlessness, irritability, insomnia, stomach disorders
Addiction potential	None	None	None
Tolerance	Increasing	Increasing	Increasing
Medical uses	Anxiety, oversedation children's behavioral disorders	Oversedation, headache	Oversedation, headache
Lethal levels	Varies	50 to 500 milligrams	50 to 500 milligrams

STIMULANT

Drug	No-Doz	Benzedrine Dexedrine Methedrine Preludin	Cocaine
Drug type	Caffeine	Amphetamines	Cocaine
Source	Synthetic	Synthetic	Coca leaves
Average amount consumed	5 milligrams	2.5–5 milligrams	Varies
Drug form	Tablets	Pill/capsule	Powder, rock
Ingestion method	Swallowed	Swallowed, injected	Snorted, injected, smoked
Short-term effects of average consumption	Increased alertness	Increased alertness, excitation, euphoria, decreased appetite	Feeling of self-confidence and power, intense exhilaration
Duration	2–4 hours	4–8 hours	Varies
Short-term effect of large amounts	Restlessness, insomnia, upset stomach	Restlessness, rapid speech, irritability, insomnia, stomach disorders, convulsions	Irritability, depression, psychosis
Long-term effects	Restlessness, irritability, insomnia, stomach disorders	Insomnia, excitability, skin disorders, malnutrition, delusions, hallucinations, psychosis	Damage to nasal septum and blood vessels psychosis
Addiction potential	None	High	High
Tolerance	Increasing	Increasing	Increasing
Medical Uses	Oversedation, headache	Obesity, depression, fatigue, narcolepsy, children's behavioral disorders	Local anesthetic
Lethal levels	50–500 milligrams	Varies, 5 to 50 mgs.	0.2–10 milligrams

CLUB DRUGS

Club drugs are being used by young adults at such all-night dance parties as "raves" or "trances," as well as dance clubs and bars. MDMA (ecstasy), GHB, Rohypnol, ketamine, methamphetamine, and LSD are some of the popular club or party drugs. When used in combination with alcohol, these drugs are even more dangerous.

Because some club drugs are colorless, tasteless, and odorless, they can be added unobtrusively to beverages by individuals who want to intoxicate or sedate others. No club drug is benign.

Ecstasy

MDMA, called "Adam," "ecstasy," or "XTC" on the street, is a synthetic, psychoactive (mind-altering) drug with hallucinogenic and amphetamine-like properties.

Health Hazards

Many of the problems users encounter with MDMA are similar to those found with the use of amphetamines and cocaine. These include both psychological and physical symptoms. Psychological difficulties include confusion, depression, sleep problems, drug craving, severe anxiety, and paranoia during and sometimes weeks after taking MDMA (in some cases, psychotic episodes have been reported). Physical symptoms include muscle tension, involuntary teeth clenching, nausea, blurred vision, rapid eye movement, faintness, and chills or sweating. Increases in heart rate and blood pressure are a special risk for people with circulatory or heart disease.

Long-Term Effects

Recent research findings also link MDMA use to long-term damage to those parts of the brain critical to thought and memory. It is believed that the drug causes damage to the neurons that use the chemical serotonin to communicate with other neurons.

MDMA is also related in structure and effects to methamphetamine, which has been shown to cause degeneration of neurons containing the neurotransmitter dopamine. Damage to dopamine-containing neurons is the underlying cause of the motor disturbances seen in Parkinson's disease. Symptoms of this disease begin with lack of coordination and tremors, and can eventually result in a form of paralysis.

GHB

Gamma-hydroxybutyric acid (GHB) is a compound that was initially used by body builders to stimulate muscle growth. In recent years it has become popular as a recreational drug among club party-goers.

This "designer" drug is often used in combination with other drugs, such as ecstasy. GHB is synthesized from a chemical used to clean electrical circuit boards and is available in clear liquid, white powder, tablet, and capsule form.

GHB is odorless and nearly tasteless. Users report that it induces a state of relaxation. The effects can be felt within 5 to 20 minutes after ingestion and the high can last up to 4 hours.

The Food and Drug Administration (FDA) banned GHB in 1990 after 57 cases of GHB-induced illnesses (ranging from nausea and vomiting to respiratory problems, seizures, and comas) were reported to poison control centers and emergency rooms. The drug has been implicated in several deaths and was subsequently added to the Schedule I list of drugs in the Controlled Substance Act.

GHB users risk many negative physical effects, including vomiting, liver failure, potentially fatal respiratory problems, and tremors and seizures, which can result in comas.

GHB has reportedly been used in cases of date rape. Because GHB is odorless and tasteless, it can be slipped into someone's drink without detection.

Rohypnol

Rohypnol use began in the United States in the early 1990s, where it became known as "rophies," "roofies," "roach," "rope," and the "date rape" drug. It is a concern because people may unknowingly be given the drug, which, when mixed with alcohol, can incapacitate and prevent a victim from resisting sexual assault.

Rohypnol may be lethal when mixed with alcohol or other depressants. It produces sedative-hypnotic effects, including muscle relaxation and amnesia.

Rohypnol is not approved for use in the United States, and its importation is banned.

Ketamine

Ketamine hydrochloride, or "Special K," is a powerful hallucinogen widely used as an animal tranquilizer by veterinarians. Liquid ketamine was developed in the early 1960s as an anesthetic for surgeries and was used on the battlefields of Vietnam as an anesthetic. Powdered ketamine emerged as a recreational drug in the 1970s and was known as "Vitamin K" in the 1980s. It resurfaced in the 1990s rave scene as "Special K."

Users sometimes call the high caused by Special K, "K hole," and describe profound hallucinations that include visual distortions and a lost sense of time, sense, and identity. The high can last from 1/2 hour to 2 hours.

The Drug Enforcement Administration (DEA) reports that overt effects can last an hour, but the drug can still affect the body for up to 24 hours. Use of Special K can result in profound physical and mental problems, including delirium, amnesia, impaired motor function, and potentially fatal respiratory problems.

Special K is a powder. The drug is usually snorted, but is sometimes sprinkled on tobacco or marijuana and smoked. Special K is frequently used in combination with other drugs, such as ecstasy, heroin, or cocaine.

Methamphetamine

Methamphetamine is an addictive stimulant drug that strongly activates certain systems in the brain. Methamphetamine is closely related chemically to amphetamine, but the central nervous system (CNS) effects of methamphetamine are greater. Both drugs have some medical uses, primarily in the treatment of obesity, but their therapeutic use is limited.

Street methamphetamine is referred to by many names, such as "speed," "meth," and "chalk."

Methamphetamine hydrochloride, clear chunky crystals resembling ice, which can be inhaled by smoking, is referred to as "ice," "crystal," and "glass."

Health Hazards

Methamphetamine releases high levels of the neurotransmitter dopamine, which stimulates brain cells, enhancing mood and body movement. Over time, methamphetamine appears to cause reduced levels of dopamine, which can result in symptoms like those of Parkinson's disease, a severe movement disorder.

Addiction

Methamphetamine is taken orally or intranasally (snorting the powder), by intravenous injection, and by smoking. Immediately after smoking or intravenous injection, the methamphetamine user experiences an intense sensation, called a "rush" or "flash," that lasts only a few minutes and is described as extremely pleasurable. Oral or intranasal use produces euphoria—a high, but not a rush. Users may become addicted quickly, and use it with increasing frequency and in increasing doses.

Short-Term Effects

The CNS effects that result from taking even small amounts of methamphetamine include increased wakefulness, increased physical activity, decreased appetite, increased respiration, hyperthermia, and euphoria. Other CNS effects include irritability, insomnia, confusion, tremors, convulsions, anxiety, paranoia, and aggressiveness. Hyperthermia and convulsions can result in death.

Long-Term Effects

Methamphetamine causes increased heart rate and blood pressure and can cause irreversible damage to blood vessels in the brain, producing strokes. Other effects of methamphetamine include respiratory problems, irregular heartbeat, and extreme anorexia. Its use can result in cardiovascular collapse and death.

LSD

LSD, also known as "acid," is odorless, colorless, and has a slightly bitter taste and is usually taken by mouth. Often LSD is added to absorbent paper, such as blotter paper, and divided into small, decorated squares, with each square representing one dose.

Health Hazards

The effects of LSD are unpredictable. They depend on the amount taken; the user's personality, mood, and expectations; and the surroundings in which the drug are used. Usually, the user feels the first effects of the drug 30 to 90 minutes after taking it. The physical effects include dilated pupils, higher body temperature, increased heart rate and blood pressure, sweating, loss of appetite, sleeplessness, dry mouth, and tremors.

If taken in a large enough dose, the drug produces delusions and visual hallucinations. The user's sense of time and self changes. Sensations may seem to "cross over," giving the user the feeling of hearing colors and seeing sounds. These changes can be frightening and can cause panic.

LSD trips are long—typically they begin to clear after about 12 hours. Some users experience severe, terrifying thoughts and feelings, fear of losing control, fear of insanity and death, and despair while using LSD. In some cases, fatal accidents have occurred during states of LSD intoxication.

Flashbacks

Many LSD users experience flashbacks, recurrence of certain aspects of a person's experience, without having taken the drug again. LSD users may manifest relatively long-lasting psychoses, such as schizophrenia or severe depression.

DOSE EQUIVALENT IN HOUSEHOLD MEASURES

Less than 5 mg/kg	Less than 7 drops
5 to 50 mg/kg	Between 7 drops and 1 teaspoon
50 to 500 mg/kg	Between 1 teaspoon and 1 ounce
500 to 5,000 (5 gm) mg/kg	Between 1 ounce and 1 pint
5,000 to 15,000 (5 to 15 gm) mg/kg	Between 1 pint and 1 quart
Greater than 15,000 mg (15 gm) mg/kg	Greater than 1 quart

CHAPTER 72:
COMMON PRESCRIPTION MEDICATIONS

GENERAL TERMINOLOGY

acne—An inflammation of the skin resulting in pus formation.
alcoholism—Abuse of alcoholic drink.
anorexiant—A medication used to diminish appetite.
antacid—Medication used to counteract or neutralize the acidity usually associated with the stomach's acid.
antibiotic—Medications used to combat bacterial infections.
anticoagulant—Medication used to prevent blood clotting.
antidepressants—Antidepressant, tricyclic. One of a class of medications used to treat depression. The tricyclic antidepressants are also used for some forms of anxiety, fibromyalgia, and the control of chronic pain.
antidiarrheal—Medication used to prevent or control the effects of diarrhea.
antiemetic—Medication used to prevent vomiting.
antiepileptics—When nerve cells in the brain fire electrical impulses at a rate of up to four times higher than normal, this causes an electrical storm in the brain, known as a seizure. A pattern of repeated seizures is referred to as epilepsy. Known causes include head injuries, brain tumors, lead poisoning, maldevelopment of the brain, and genetic and infectious illnesses. Medication controls seizures for the majority of patients.
antipsychotics—Antipsychotic medication is used to treat a psychosis, a mental illness that markedly interferes with a person's capacity to meet life's everyday demands. In a specific sense, it refers to a thought disorder in which reality testing is grossly impaired. Symptoms can include seeing, hearing, smelling, or tasting things that are not there; paranoia; and delusional thoughts. Depending on the condition underlying the psychotic symptoms, symptoms may be constant or they may come and go. Psychosis can occur as a result of brain injury or disease and is seen particularly in schizophrenia and bipolar disorders.
antispasmodic—A medication that lowers the incidence of or prevents seizures. It may also be a medication that lowers the incidence of or prevents muscle spasms.
antivertigo—Medication used to relieve dizziness and vertigo.
arthritis/anti-inflammatory—Arthritis means "inflamed joints. Arthritis includes more than 100 different forms of this joint disease. The most common therapy for treating arthritis is an analgesic (e.g., aspirin or acetaminophen) or a member of a group of medications called nonsteroidal anti-inflammatory drugs (NSAIDs). Strong anti-inflammatory medications such as corticosteroids or immunosuppressive drugs may also be used.
asthma/respiratory aids—Asthma causes the airways of the lungs to swell and become narrower. As a result, breathing is made more difficult. Wheezing may result during efforts to breathe in and out. Asthma cannot be cured, but it can be relieved with medicine.
cancer medication—Used in the treatment of cancer-related problems.
cholesterol reducer—Medication used in the reduction of harmful buildup of cholesterol. High levels of cholesterol may result in heart disease and strokes.
contraceptive—Medication used in the prevention of pregnancy.
cough and cold (antihistamines and decongestants)—An infection of the upper respiratory system resulting in the inflammation of the mucous membranes. This may produce a cough.
cystic fibrosis—Cystic fibrosis (CF) affects the exocrine glands and is characterized by the production of abnormal secretions, leading to mucous buildup. Accumulation of mucus can impair the pancreas

and the intestine. Mucous buildup in the lungs will ultimately impair respiration. Without treatment, CF results in death for 95 percent of affected children before the age of 5.

diabetes—A chronic disease associated with the body's inability to burn up the sugars (carbohydrates) ingested. This is the result of insufficient insulin being produced by the pancreas.

diuretic—Anything that promotes the formation of urine by the kidney. Diuresis may be due to a huge number of causes, including metabolic conditions such as diabetes mellitus (in which the increased glucose level in the blood causes water to be lost in the urine); substances in food and drink (such as coffee, tea, and alcoholic beverages); and specific diuretic drugs. All diuretic drugs—usually called, more simply, diuretics—cause a person to "lose water," but they do so by diverse means.

female hormone—A hormone that may have been synthesized in an effort to augment glandular deficiencies.

gastrointestinal medication—Used to treat disorders involving the various organs associated with the gastrointestinal tract (esophagus, stomach, duodenum, small intestine, large intestine [colon], appendix, and rectum).

gout—Gout is a condition characterized by abnormally elevated levels of uric acid in the blood, recurring attacks of joint inflammation (arthritis), deposits of hard lumps of uric acid in and around the joints, and decreased kidney function and kidney stones. Gout can be promoted by obesity, weight gain, alcohol intake, high blood pressure, abnormal kidney function, and drugs.

heart drugs (cardiac)—Medication used in to treat not just disorders of the heart itself but a variety of conditions that affect the body's circulatory system, including cardiovascular disease, coronary artery disease, myocardial infarction, heart failure, etc.

high blood pressure (antihypertensive) medication—Given to reduce and control chronic high blood pressure. Blood pressure is a measure of the force the blood puts on the walls of veins, arteries, and the heart. There are two parts to a blood pressure reading: systolic, the first number, and diastolic, the second number. For example, in the reading of 120/80, 120 is the systolic number, and 80 is the diastolic number. The systolic number tells you how hard the blood is pushing against the walls of the arteries, veins, and heart when the heart is pumping blood (during a heartbeat). The diastolic number gives the pressure when the heart is resting between beats. If the systolic number is higher than 140 or the diastolic number is higher than 90, you are said to have high blood pressure. Only one of the numbers needs to be high.

hypoglycemic—An abnormally low level of the sugar glucose in the blood, usually a complication of diabetes, in which the body does not produce enough insulin to fully metabolize glucose. Hypoglycemic symptoms include tiredness, dizziness, confusion, increased heart rate, and a cold, clammy feeling.

immunosuppressant—A suppressor of immunological responses, often after organ transplant.

laxative—Medication given to relieve constipation.

male hormone—A hormone that may have been synthesized in an effort to augment glandular deficiencies.

malaria medication—Used to treat an infectious disease caused by protozoan parasites that can be transmitted by the sting of the anopheles mosquito or by a contaminated needle or transfusion. Falciparum malaria is the most deadly type. The symptoms of malaria include cycles of chills, fever, sweats, muscle aches, and headache that recur every few days. There can also be vomiting, diarrhea, coughing, and yellowing (jaundice) of the skin and eyes. Persons with severe falciparum malaria can develop bleeding problems, shock, kidney and liver failure, central nervous system problems, resulting in a coma or death.

mineral supplement—Mineral substances used to supplement depleted or diminished minerals naturally occurring within the body.

muscle relaxants—A group of drugs used to produce muscle relaxation (not including neuromuscular blocking agents). Their primary therapeutic use is in the treatment of muscle spasm and immobility associated with strains, sprains, and injuries of the back and, less infrequently, injuries of the neck.

narcotic withdrawal medication—Used in the treatment of a patient's attempt to withdraw from the use/abuse of narcotics.
painkiller (analgesic)—Medication used to relieve pain without causing loss of consciousness.
Parkinson's disease—A nerve disorder causing rhythmic tremors, mask-like appearance of the face, rigidity of muscle action, and slowing of all body motion.
senile/mental changes—Medication used in the treatment of the deterioration brought about by old age or Alzheimer's disease.
steroid—Hormonal drugs used in the treatment of various disease states.
stimulants—Any drug whose action promotes stimulation.
thyroid medication—Used in supplementing the hormone produced by the thyroid gland used to control the body's metabolism.
tranquilizers, sedatives, and hypnotics—A large group of medications used in providing a tranquilizing effect. It may be used to promote sleep. An overdose can lead to respiratory depression.
tuberculosis medication—Used in treating any infection caused by the mycobacterium tuberculosis.
vitamins—Organic compounds or chemicals found in various foods that are necessary for the maintenance of normal life. Deficiencies may lead to certain types of diseases.

A

Aarane—asthma/respiratory aid

Abacavir, Lamivudine, Zidovudine (Trizivir)—HIV
Abacavir sulfate (Ziagen)—HIV
Acarbose (Precose)—diabetes
Accolate (Zafirlukast)—asthma/respiratory aid
AccuNeb (Proventil)—asthma/respiratory aid
Accupril (Quinapril hydrochloride)—antihypertensive
Accurbron—asthma/respiratory aid
Accuretic (Quinapril)—antihypertensive
Accutane (Isotretinoin)—acne
Acebutolol (Sectral)—cardiac drug
Aceon (Perindopril erbumine)—antihypertensive
Aceta—painkiller
Acetaminophen (Tylenol)—painkiller
Acetazolamide—diuretic
Acetohexamide—diabetes
Achrocidin—antibiotic
Achromycin—antibiotic
AcipHex (Rabeprazole)—gastrointestinal
Aclovate (Alclometasone)—anti-inflammatory, arthritis
Acrivastine with Pseudoephedrine (Semprex-D)—cough/cold antihistamine or decongestant
Actamin—painkiller
Actamin—cough/cold antihistamine or decongestant
Actidil—cough/cold antihistamine or decongestant

Actifed—cough/cold antihistamine or decongestant
Actigall (Ursodiol) (Urso)—gallstones
Activella (Femhrt)—female hormone
Actonel (Risedronate)—mineral supplement
Actos (Pioglitazone hydrochloride)—diabetes
Actrapid—diabetes
Actron (Orudis)—anti-inflammatory, arthritis
Acyclovir (Zovirax)—herpes
Adalat—cardiac drug
Adapalene (Differin)—acne
Adapin (Doxepin)—antidepressant
Adderall—attention deficit disorder
Adipex—anorexiant
Adphen—anorexiant
Advair Diskus (Fluticasone)—asthma/respiratory aid
Advil—painkiller
Aerobid inhaler (Flunisolide) (Nasalide)—asthma/respiratory aid
Aerolate—asthma/respiratory aid
Afrin—cough/cold antihistamine or decongestant
Afrinol—asthma/respiratory aid
Agenerase (Amprenavir)—HIV
Aggrenox—antihypertensive
Aktob (Tobrex)—antibiotic
Ak-zol—diuretic
Alamast (Pemirolast)—cough/cold antihistamine or decongestant
Albuterol—asthma/respiratory aid
Alclometasone (Aclovate)—anti-inflammatory, arthritis
Aldactazide (Spironolactone)—antihypertensive
Aldactone—diuretic
Aldoment—antihypertensive
Aldomet (Methyldopa)—antihypertensive
Aldoril—antihypertensive
Alendronate (Fosamax)—mineral supplement
Alermine—cough/cold antihistamine or decongestant
Alesse—contraceptive
Aleve (Anaprox)—anti-inflammatory, arthritis
Algenic algimate—antacid
Algitab—antacid
Alka—antacid
Alkabutzone—anti-inflammatory, arthritis
Alka-med—antacid
Alka-Seltzer—antacid
Allegra (Fexofenadrine)—cough/cold antihistamine or decongestant
Allopurinol—anti-inflammatory, arthritis
Almacone—antacid
Almotriptan (Axert)—migraine
Alophen—laxative
Alora—female hormone
Alprazolam (Xanax)—tranquilizer, sedative, hypnotic, or antianxiety
Alprostadil (Caverject)—male impotence
Altace (Ramipril)—antihypertensive
Alterna gel—antacid
Alu-cap—antacid
Aludrox—antacid
Alumid—antacid
Alupent—asthma/respiratory aid
Alurate—tranquilizer, sedative, hypnotic, or antianxiety
Alurex—antacid
Aluscop—antacid
Alusil—antacid
Alu-tab—antacid
Amantidine—Parkinson's Disease
Amaryl (Glimepiride)—diabetes
Ambien (Zolpidem)—tranquilizer, sedative, hypnotic, or antianxiety
Amcil—antibiotic
Amcinonide (Cyclocort)—Skin itch
Amen—female hormone
Amerge (Naratriptan)—migraine
Ameri-ezp—antibiotic
Amersol—anti-inflammatory, arthritis
Amesec—asthma/respiratory aid
Amikin—antibiotic
Amiloride—antihypertensive
Aminophylline—asthma/respiratory aid
Amiodarone—cardiac drug
Amitone—antacid
Amitril—antidepressant
Amitriptyline (Elavil) (Triavil)—antidepressant
Amlodipine (Norvasc)—antihypertensive
Amobarbital—tranquilizer, sedative, hypnotic, or antianxiety
Amoxapine (Asendin)—antidepressant
Amoxicillin—antibiotic
Amoxil—antibiotic
Amphenol—painkiller
Amphetamine—stimulants
Amphojel—antacid
Ampicillin—antibiotic
Ampico—antibiotic

Amprenavir (Agenerase)—HIV
Amrinone—cardiac drug
Amylozine—tranquilizer, sedative, hypnotic, or antianxiety
Amytal—tranquilizer, sedative, hypnotic, or antianxiety
Anacin—painkiller
Anafranil (Clomipramine)—antidepressant
Anamid—antibiotic
Anaprox (Aleve) (Naprelan)—anti-inflammatory, arthritis
Anaspaz—antispasmodic
Anastrozole (Arimidex)—cancer
Anavar—steroid
Android—male hormone
Anexsia—painkiller
Ang-o-span—cardiac drug
Anhydron—antihypertensive
Anolor 300 (Fioricet)—painkiller
Anorex—anorexiant
Ansaid (Flurbiprofen)—anti-inflammatory, arthritis
Antabuse—alcoholism
Antacids—antacid
Antalgesic—painkiller
Antar—antacid
Antipress—antidepressant
Antipyrine (Auralgan)—ear problems
Antistine—cough/cold antihistamine or decongestant
Antivert—antivertigo
Antrenyl—antispasmodic
Anturane—anti-inflammatory, arthritis
Anuphen—painkiller
Apo-flurazepam—tranquilizer sedative hypnotic or antianxiety
Apo-furosemide—diuretic
Apo-naproxen—painkiller
Apresazide—antihypertensive
Apresoline—antihypertensive
Aptrol—anorexiant
Aquamox—antihypertensive
Aquaphyllin—asthma/respiratory aid
Aquatensen—antihypertensive
Arava (Leflunomide)—anti-inflammatory, arthritis
Aricept (Donepezil)—senile/mental changes
Arimidex (Anastrozole)—cancer
Aristocort—steroid
Armour Thyroid—thyroid
Artane—Parkinson's disease
Arthrotec (Diclofenac)—anti-inflammatory, arthritis
Asa—painkiller
Asacol (Rowasa)—gastrointestinal
Asbron—asthma/respiratory aid
Ascorbic acid—vitamin
Ascriptin—painkiller
Asendin (amoxapine)—antidepressant
Asmalix—asthma/respiratory aid
Asperbuf—painkiller
Aspirin (salicyclate)—painkiller
Astelin (Azelastine)—cough/cold antihistamine or decongestant
Atacand (Candesartan cilexetil)—antihypertensive
Atarax—cough/cold antihistamine or decongestant
Atasol—painkiller
Atenolol (Tenormin)—cardiac drug
Athrombin-K—anticoagulant
Ativan (lorazepam)—tranquilizer, sedative, hypnotic, or antianxiety
Atorvastatin (Lipitor)—cholesterol reducer
Atretol (Tegretol)—antiepileptic
Atrovent (Ipratropium bromide)—asthma/respiratory aid
A/T/S (Erythromycin)—acne
Augmentin—antibiotic
Auralgan (Antipyrine)—ear problems
Auranofin (Ridaura)—anti-inflammatory, arthritis
Auroto Otic (Auralgan)—ear problems
Avalide (Irbesartan)—antihypertensive
Avandia (Rosiglitazone maleate)—diabetes
Avapro (Irbesartan)—antihypertensive
Avelox (Moxifloxicin)—antibiotic
Aventyl—antidepressant
Avita (Retin A)—acne
Axert (Almotriptan)—migraine
Axid (Nizatidine)—gastrointestinal
Axotal—painkiller
Azatadine with pseudoephedrine (Trinalin repetabs)—asthma/respiratory aid
Azathioprine—immuno-suppressant
Azelaic acid (Azelex)—acne
Azelastine (Astelin)—cough/cold antihistamine or decongestant
Azelex (Azelaic acid) (Finevin)—acne
Azene—tranquilizer, sedative, hypnotic, or antianxiety

Azithromycin (Zithromax)—antibiotic
Azmacort (Nasacort) (Triamcinolone)—asthma/respiratory aid
Azo gantrisi—antibiotic
Azodine—painkiller
Azolid—anti-inflammatory, arthritis
Azotrex—antibiotic
Azulfidine (Sulfasalazine)—anti-inflammatory, arthritis

B

B.A.C.—tranquilizer sedative hypnotic or antianxiety
Bacarate—anorexiant
Bacitracin—antibiotic
Baclofen—muscle relaxant
Bactocil—antibiotic
Bactopen—antibiotic
Bactrim (Cotrim)—antibiotic
Bactroban (Mupirocin)—antibiotic
Bamate—tranquilizer, sedative, hypnotic, or antianxiety
Banthine—antibiotic
Barbipil—tranquilizer sedative hypnotic or antianxiety
Barbita—tranquilizer, sedative, hypnotic, or antianxiety
Barbiturates—tranquilizer, sedative, hypnotic, or antianxiety
Basajel—antacid
Balsalazide isodium (Colazal)—gastrointestinal
Beclomethasone (Beconase) (Qvar Inhalation Aerosol) (Vancenase)—asthma/respiratory aid
Beclovent—asthma/respiratory aid
Beconase (Beclomethasone)—asthma/respiratory aid
Beepen-vk—antibiotic
Belladenal—tranquilizer sedative hypnotic or antianxiety
Bellatal (Donnatal)—antispasmodic
Bellergal—tranquilizer sedative hypnotic or antianxiety
Benachlor—cough/cold antihistamine or decongestant
Benadryl—cough/cold antihistamine or decongestant
Benazepril (Lotensin)—antihypertensive

Bendopa—Parkinson's disease
Bendylate—cough/cold antihistamine or decongestant
Benedectin—antiemetic
Benemid—gout
Bensylate—Parkinson's disease
Bentyl—laxative
Benzac W (Desquam-E)—acne
BenzaClin (Benzoyl peroxide)—acne
Benzagel (Desquam-E)—acne
Benzamycin (Erythromycin)—acne
BenzaShave—acne
Benzedrine—stimulants
Benzodiazepines—tranquilizer, sedative, hypnotic, or antianxiety
Benzonatate (Tessalon)—cough/cold antihistamine or decongestant
Benzoyl peroxide (BenzaClin)—acne
Benzphetamine—anorexiant
Benztropine (Cogentin)—Parkinson's disease
Berocca—vitamin
Berotec—asthma/respiratory aid
Betagan (Levobunolol hydrochloride)—Glaucoma
Betaine (Cystadane)—mineral supplement
Betaloc—antihypertensive
Betamethasone (Diprolene)—steroid
Betaxolol (Betoptic)—glaucoma
Bethiodyl—asthma/respiratory aid
Betimol (Timoptic)—glaucoma
Betoptic (Betaxolol)—glaucoma
Biaxin (Clarithromycin)—antibiotic
Bilron—laxative
Bimatoprost (Lumigan)—glaucoma
Biocaine—antibiotic
Biphetamine (amphetamine)—stimulants
Biquin durules—cardiac drug
Bisacodyl—laxative
Biscodyl—laxative
Bisodol—antacid
Bleph-10 (Sodium Sulamyd)—eye infection
Blocadren—cardiac drug
Bonine—antivertigo
Bontril—anorexiant
Bontril PDM—anorexiant
Brethaire (Brethine)—asthma/respiratory aid
Brethine (Brethaire)—asthma/respiratory aid
Brevicon—contraceptive
Bricanyl—asthma/respiratory aid
Bristacycline—antibiotic

Bristamycin—antibiotic
Bromamine—cough/cold antihistamine or decongestant
Bromatane—cough/cold antihistamine or decongestant
Bromocriptine—Parkinson's disease
Bromophen—cough/cold antihistamine or decongestant
Bromphen—cough/cold antihistamine or decongestant
Bronkaid mist (Ephedrine)—asthma/respiratory aid
Bronkodyl—asthma/respiratory aid
Bronkometer—asthma/respiratory aid
Brontex (Tussi-Organidin NR)—cough/cold antihistamine or decongestant
Budesonide (Rhinocort)—cough/cold antihistamine or decongestant
Bu-lax plus—laxative
Buffaprin—painkiller
Buffazone—antacid
Bumetanide (Bumex)—diuretic
Bumex (Bumetanide)—diuretic
Buprenex—painkiller
Bupropion (Wellbutrin) (Zyban)—antidepressant
Buspar (Buspirone)—tranquilizer, sedative, hypnotic, or antianxiety
Buspirone (BuSpar)—tranquilizer, sedative, hypnotic, or antianxiety
Busulfan—cancer
Butabarbital—tranquilizer, sedative, hypnotic, or antianxiety
Butal—tranquilizer, sedative, hypnotic, or antianxiety
Butalan—tranquilizer, sedative, hypnotic, or antianxiety
Butabital—tranquilizer, sedative, hypnotic, or antianxiety
Butalbital (Fioricet)—muscle relaxant
Butatran—tranquilizer, sedative, hypnotic, or antianxiety
Butazen—tranquilizer, sedative, hypnotic, or antianxiety
Butazolidin—anti-inflammatory, arthritis
Buticaps—tranquilizer, sedative, hypnotic, or antianxiety
Butisol—tranquilizer, sedative, hypnotic, or antianxiety
Butane—anti-inflammatory, arthritis
Butoconazole nitrate (mycelex-3)—vaginal infection

C

Cafergot (Ergotamine with caffeine)—migraine
Calan (Covera-HS) (Verapamil) (Verelan)—cardiac drug
Calcilac—antacid
Calcilean—anticoagulant
Calcimar (Miacalcin)—thyroid
Calcitonin-salmon (Miacalcin)—thyroid
Calcitriol (Rocaltrol)—mineral supplement
Calcium carbonate (Caltrate 600)—mineral supplement
Calglycine—antacid
Caltrate (Calcium carbonate)—mineral supplement
Cam-ap-es—antihypertensive
Camalox—antacid
Campain—painkiller
Canasa (Rowasa)—gastrointestinal
Candesartan cilexetil (Atacand)—antihypertensive
Cantil—hypoglycemia
Capastat—antibiotic
Capoten—antihypertensive
Capozide—antihypertensive
Captopril—gastrointestinal
Carac (Efudex)—cancer
Carafate (Sucralfate)—gastrointestinal
Carbamazepine (Tegretol)—antiepileptic
Carbatrol (Tegretol)—antiepileptic
Carbidopa—Parkinson's disease
Carbrital—tranquilizer, sedative, hypnotic, or antianxiety
Cardene (Nicardipine)—antihypertensive
Cardilate—cardiac drug
Cardioquin—cardiac drug
Cardizem (Diltiazem) (Dilacor XR) (Tiazac)—cardiac drug
Cardura (Doxazosin mesylate)—prostate
Carisoprodol (Soma)—muscle relaxant
Carvedilol (Coreg)—antihypertensive
Cataflam (Voltaren)—anti-inflammatory, arthritis
Catapres (Clonidine)—antihypertensive
Caverject (Alprostadil) (Edex) (Muse)—Male impotence

Ceclor—antibiotic
Cedax (Ceftibuten)—antibiotic
Cee nu—cancer
Cefaclor—antibiotic
Cefadroxil—antibiotic
Cefdinir (Omnicef)—antibiotic
Cefixime (Suprax)—antibiotic
Cefol—vitamin
Cefprozil (Cefzil)—antibiotic
Cefracycline—antibiotic
Ceftibuten (Cedax)—antibiotic
Ceftin (Cefuroxime axetil)—antibiotic
Cefuroxime (Ceftin)—antibiotic
Cefzil (Cefprozil)—antibiotic
Celebrex (Celecoxib)—anti-inflammatory, arthritis
Celecoxib (Celebrex)—anti-inflammatory, arthritis
Celestone—steroid
Celexa (Citalopram hydrobromide)—antidepressant
Celontin—antiepileptic
Cenafed—asthma/respiratory aid
Cenestin (Premarin)—female hormone
Centet-250—antibiotic
Centrax—tranquilizer sedative hypnotic or antianxiety
Centrum—vitamin
Cephalexin—antibiotic
Cephalosporins—antibiotic
Cephadrine—antibiotic
Ceposex—antibiotic
Cerespan—asthma/respiratory aid
Cesamet—antiemetic
Cetacort (Hydrocortisone)—skin itch
Cetirizine (Zyrtec)—cough/cold antihistamine or decongestant
Chlo-amine—cough/cold antihistamine or decongestant
Chlor-mal—cough/cold antihistamine or decongestant
Chlor-niramine—cough/cold antihistamine or decongestant
Chlorpromazine (Thorazine)—antipsychotic
Chlor-tripolon—cough/cold antihistamine or decongestant
Chloral-hydrate—tranquilizer, sedative, hypnotic, or antianxiety
Chlorambucil—cancer
Chloramead—tranquilizer, sedative, hypnotic, or antianxiety
Chloramphenicol—antibiotic
Chlordiazachel—tranquilizer, sedative, hypnotic, or antianxiety
Chlordiazpoxide (Librium)—tranquilizer, sedative, hypnotic, or antianxiety
Chlorhexidine (Peridex)—gingivitis
Chlorofon—muscle relaxant
Chloronase—hypoglycemia
Chlorophen—cough/cold antihistamine or decongestant
Chlorothiazide—diuretic
Chlorpheniramine (Deconamine)—cough/cold antihistamine or decongestant
Chlorphentermin—anorexiant
Chlorpromazine—tranquilizer sedative hypnotic or antianxiety
Chlorpropamide—diabetes
Chlorspan—cough/cold antihistamine or decongestant
Chlortab—cough/cold antihistamine or decongestant
Chlorthalidone—antihypertensive
Chlorthiazide—antihypertensive
Chlorzide—diuretic
Chlorzone forte—muscle relaxant
Chlorzoxazone (Parafon Forte DSC)—antispasmodic
Choledyl—asthma/respiratory aid
Cholestyramine (Questran)—cholesterol reducer
Choline magnesium trisalicylate (Trilisate)—anti-inflammatory, arthritis
Chooz—antacid
Chronulac Syrup (Lactulose)—laxative
Cibalith—antipsychotic
Ciclopirox (Loprox)—athlete's foot
Cimetidine (Tagamet)—gastrointestinal
Cin-quin—cardiac drug
Cipro (Ciprofloxacin)—antibiotic
Ciprofloxacin (Cipro)—antibiotic
Ciramine—cough/cold antihistamine or decongestant
Citalopram (Celexa)—antidepressant
Citrocarbonate—antacid
Clarithromycin (Biaxin)—antibiotic
Claritin (Loratadine)—cough/cold antihistamine or decongestant
Cleocin—antibiotic
Climara—female hormone

Clinac BPO (Desquam-E)—acne
Clindamycin—antibiotic
Clinoril—anti-inflammatory, arthritis
Clistin—cough/cold antihistamine or decongestant
Clobetasol (Temovate)—skin itch
Clomid (Clomiphene Citrate)—female fertility
Clomiphene Citrate (Clomid) (Serophene)—female fertility
Clomipramine (Anafranil)—antidepressant
Clonazepam (Klonopin)—antiepileptic
Clonidine (Catapres)—antihypertensive
Clonopin—antiepileptic
Clopidogrel (Plavix)—anticoagulant
Clorazepate (Traxene)—tranquilizer, sedative, hypnotic, or antianxiety
Clorazine—tranquilizer, sedative, hypnotic, or antianxiety
Clotrimazole (Gyne-Lotrimin) (Lotrisone)—athlete's foot
Clozapine (Clozaril)—antipsychotic
Clozaril (Clozapine)—antipsychotic
Coastaldyne—painkiller-narcotic
Cocillin-V-K—antibiotic
Codalon—painkiller-narcotic
Codap—painkiller-narcotic
Codeine—painkiller-narcotic
Co-gel—antacid
Co-gesic—painkiller-narcotic
Cogentin (Benztropine)—Parkinson's disease
Cognex (Tacrine hydrochloride)—senile/mental changes
Cohidrate—tranquilizer, sedative, hypnotic, or antianxiety
Colace (Phillips' Liqui-Gels) (Sof-Lax)—laxative
Colazal (Balsalazide disodium)—gastrointestinal
Colbenemid—gout
Colchicine—gout
Colesevelam (WelChol)—cholesterol reducer
Colestid (Colestipol hydrochloride)—cholesterol reducer
Colonaid—antidiarrheal
Combid—antispasmodic
Colestipol (Colestid)—cholesterol reducer
Combipress—antihypertensive
Combivir (Lamivudine)—HIV
Comfolax-plus—laxative
Compal—painkiller-narcotic
Compazine (Prochlorperazine)—antipsychotic

Comtan (Entacapone)—Parkinson's disease
Concerta (Ritalin)—stimulant (attention deficit disorder)
Constant-t—asthma/respiratory aid
Constiban—laxative
Coprobate—tranquilizer sedative hypnotic or antianxiety
Cordarone—cardiac drug
Coreg (Carvedilol)—antihypertensive
Corgard—antihypertensive
Coricidin—cough/cold antihistamine or decongestant
Cormax (Temovate)—skin itch
Coronex—cardiac drug
Cortan—steroid
Cortef—steroid
Cortisporin-TC Otic—ear infection
Corzide—antihypertensive
Cotrim (Bactrim)—antibiotic
Coumadin—anticoagulant
Covera-HS (Calan)—cardiac drug
Cozaar (Losartan potassium)—antihypertensive
Creamalin—antacid
Creon (*Pancrease*)—cystic fibrosis
Crixivan (Indinavir sulfate)—HIV
Crolom (Cromolyn sodium)—cough/cold antihistamine or decongestant
Cromolyn (Crolom)—cough/cold antihistamine or decongestant
Crystodigin—cardiac drug
Cuprimine—anti-inflammatory, arthritis
Curretab—female hormone
Cyclandelate—cardiac drug
Cycline-250—antibiotic
Cyclizine—antiemetic
Cyclobenzaprine (Flexeril)—muscle relaxant
Cyclocort (Amcinonide)—skin itch
Cyclopar 500—antibiotic
Cyclopho-spahmide—cancer
Cyclospasmol—antihypertensive
Cyclosporine (Sandimmune)—immunosuppressant
Cycrin (Provera)—female hormone
Cydel—antihypertensive
Cylert—stimulants
Cyprodine—cough/cold antihistamine or decongestant
Cyproheptadine (Periactin)—cough/cold antihistamine or decongestant
Cystadane (Betaine)—mineral supplement

Cytomel—thyroid
Cytotec (Misoprostol)—gastrointestinal
Cytoxan—cancer
Cyvaso—antihypertensive

D

Dactil—antispasmodic
Dalacin C—antibiotic
Dalmane (Flurazepam)—tranquilizer sedative hypnotic or antianxiety
Damason-P—painkiller-narcotic
Danilone—anticoagulant
Dantrum—muscle relaxant
Dapa—painkiller
Darbid—antispasmodic
Dartal—antipsychotic
Darvocet-N—painkiller
Darvon (Propoxyphene)—painkiller-narcotic
Darvon-N—painkiller-narcotic
Datril—painkiller
Day-barb—tranquilizer sedative hypnotic or antianxiety
Daypro (Oxaprozin)—anti-inflammatory, arthritis
DDAVP (Desmopressin acetate) (Stimate)—diabetes
De-tone—cardiac drug
Deaner-100—stimulants
Debilline "H"—antispasmodic
Decadron—steroid
Declinax—antihypertensive
Declomycin—antibiotic
Decohist—cough/cold antihistamine or decongestant
Deconamine (Chlorpheniramine maleate)—cough/cold antihistamine or decongestant
Delapav—antihypertensive
Delaxin—muscle relaxant
Delcid—antacid
Delcophen—anorexiant
Delsym—cough/cold antihistamine or decongestant
Delta-E—antibiotic
Deltamycin—antibiotic
Deltapen-VK—antibiotic
Deltasone—steroid
Demazin—cough/cold antihistamine or decongestant

Demeclocycline—antibiotic
Demerol (Meperidine)—painkiller-narcotic
Demi-regroton—antihypertensive
Demulen—contraceptive
Denavir (Penciclovir)—herpes
Depakene (Valproic acid)—antiepileptic
Deparkene—antiepileptic
Depakote (Divalproex)—antiepileptic
Depen—anti-inflammatory, arthritis
Depletite—anorexiant
Deprol—antidepressant
Dermacort—skin itch
Des—female hormone
Desipramine (Norpramin)—antidepressant
Desmopressin (DDAVP)—diabetes
Desogen—contraceptive
Desonide (Tridesilon)—skin itch
DesOwen (Tridesilon)—skin itch
Desoximetasone (Topicort)—skin itch
Desquam-E (Benzac W) (Benzagel) (Triaz)—acne
Desyrel (Trazodone)—painkiller
Detensol—cardiac drug
Detrol (Tolterodine tartrate)—overactive bladder
Dexamethasone—steroid
Dexasone—steroid
Dexedrine—stimulants
Dexone—steroid
Dextroamphet-amine—stimulants
Dextromethorphan—cough/cold antihistamine or decongestant
Dezone—steroid
Di-ap-trol—anorexiant
Di-azo—painkiller
Dia-gesic—painkiller-narcotic
Diabeta—diabetes
Diabinese—diabetes
Diaction—antidiarrheal
Diahist—cough/cold antihistamine or decongestant
Dialose—laxative
Dialume—antacid
Diamox—diuretic
Diaqua—diuretic
Diazepam (Valium)—tranquilizer sedative hypnotic or antianxiety
Diaban—antidiarrheal
Dicarbosil—antacid
Diclectin—antiemetic

Diclofenac (Arthrotec)—anti-inflammatory, arthritis
Diclophen—antispasmodic
Dicloxacillin—antibiotic
Dicumarol—anticoagulant
Dicyclomine—antiemetic
Didanosine (Videx)—HIV
Dietaps—anorexiant
Diethylpropon HCL—anorexiant
Differin (Adapalene)—acne
Diflorasone (Psorcon)—skin itch
Diflucan (Fluconazole)—antibiotic
Diflunisal—painkiller
Digel—antacid
Digitoxin—cardiac drug
Digoxin—cardiac drug
Dihydrocodeine—painkiller-narcotic
Dihydroergot-amine (Migranal)—migraine
Dilacor XR (Cardizem)—cardiac drug
Dilantin (Phenytoin)—antiepileptic
Dilantin with phenobarbital—antiepileptic
Dilart—antihypertensive
Dilatrate—cardiac drug
Dilaudid (Hydromorphone)—painkiller
Diltiazem (Cardizem)—cardiac drug
Dimelor—hypoglycemia
Dimenhydrinate—antiemetic
Dimetane—cough/cold antihistamine or decongestant
Dimetapp—cough/cold antihistamine or decongestant
Diminul—antacid
Diothron—laxative
Dioval—antacid
Diovan (Valsartan)—antihypertensive
Dipav—antihypertensive
Dipentum (Olsalazine sodium)—gastrointestinal
Diphen—cough/cold antihistamine or decongestant
Diphenadril—cough/cold antihistamine or decongestant
Diphenhydramine—cough/cold antihistamine or decongestant
Diphenoxylate (Lomotil)—antidiarrheal-narcotic
Diphenylan—antiepileptic
Dipivefrin (Propine)—glaucoma
Diprolene (Betamethasone)—steroid
Dipyridamole—cardiac drug
Dirithromycin (Dynabac)—antibiotic

Disalcid (Salsalate)—anti-inflammatory, arthritis
Disanthrol—laxative
Disipal—Parkinson's disease
Disophrol chronotabs—cough/cold antihistamine or decongestant
Disopyramide—cardiac drug
Disulfiram—alcoholism
Ditan—antiepileptic
Ditropan (Oxybutynin chloride)—bladder spasms
Diu-scrip—diuretic
Diucardin—antihypertensive
Diuchlor—antihypertensive
Diulo—antihypertensive
Diupres—antihypertensive
Diuril—antihypertensive
Divalproex (Depakote)—antiepileptic
Dizmis—antivertigo
Docusate (Colace)—laxative
Dolanex—painkiller
Dolene—painkiller
Dolobid—anti-inflammatory, arthritis
Dolophine—narcotic withdrawal
Donepezil (Aricept)—senile/mental changes
Donnatol (Bellatal)—antispasmodic
Donnazyme—tranquilizer, sedative, hypnotic, or antianxiety
Dopamet—antihypertensive
Dopar—Parkinson's disease
Doral (Quazepam)—tranquilizer, sedative, hypnotic, or antianxiety
Dorbane—laxative
Dorbanex—laxative
Doriden—tranquilizer, sedative, hypnotic, or antianxiety
Dormtabs—tranquilizer, sedative, hypnotic, or antianxiety
Doryx—antibiotic
Doss—laxative
Doxazosin (Cardura)—prostate
Doxepin (Adapin), (Sinequan)—antidepressant
Doxidan—laxative
Doxy-C—antibiotic
Doxychel—antibiotic
Doxycycline—antibiotic
Doxylamine succinate—antiemetic
Dralzine—antihypertensive
Dramamine—antiemetic
Drixoral—cough/cold antihistamine or decongestant

Drixoral-Drixtab—cough/cold antihistamine or decongestant
Dulcodos—laxative
Dulcolax—laxative
Duphalac (Chronulac syrup)—laxative
Duraquin—cardiac drug
Duration—cough/cold antihistamine or decongestant
Duretic—diuretic
Dureticy—diuretic
Duricef—antibiotic
Dyazide (Triamterene)—antihypertensive
Dycill—antibiotic
Dymelor—diabetes
Dynabac (Dirithromycin)—antibiotic
Dynacin (Minocin)—antibiotic
DynaCirc (Isradipine)—antihypertensive
Dynapen—antibiotic
Dyrenium—diuretic

E

Echothiophate (Phospholine iodide)—glaucoma
EC-Naprosyn (Naprosyn)—anti-inflammatory, arthritis
Econazole (Spectazole cream)—athlete's foot
Ecotrin—painkiller
Edecrin—diuretic
Edex (Caverject)—male impotence
Ees 200–400—antibiotic
Efavirenz (Sustiva)—HIV
Efed II—stimulants
Effexor (Venlafaxine)—antidepressant
Efudex (Carac) (Fluorouracil)—cancer
Elavil (Amitriptyline)—antidepressant
El-da-mint—antacid
Eldafed tablets—cough/cold antihistamine or decongestant
Eldatapp—cough/cold antihistamine or decongestant
Eldec—vitamin
Eldepryl (Selegiline hydrochloride)—Parkinson's disease
Elder—painkiller-narcotic
Elixicon—asthma/respiratory aid
Elixophylcin—asthma/respiratory aid
Elixophyllin—asthma/respiratory aid
Elocon (Mometasone furoate)—skin itch
Eltar stimulants—asthma/respiratory aid
Eltroxin—thyroid
E-mycin—antibiotic
Empracet—painkiller-narcotic
Empirin—painkiller
Enalapril (Lexxel) (Vasotec)—antihypertensive
Enbrel (Etanercept)—anti inflammatory, arthritis
Endep—antidepressant
Enduron—antihypertensive
Enduronyl—antihypertensive
Eno—antacid
Enovid—contraceptive
Enoxa—antidiarrheal
Enoxacin (Penetrex)—antibiotic
Entacapone (Comtan)—Parkinson's disease
Entair—asthma/respiratory aid
Entex LA—cough/cold antihistamine or decongestant
Entozyme—gastrointestinal
Entrophen—anti-inflammatory, arthritis
Enzymacol—gastrointestinal
E-pam (Valium)—tranquilizer, sedative, hypnotic, or antianxiety
Ephedrine (Bronkaid mist)—asthma/respiratory aid
Epitol (Tegretol)—antiepileptic
Epivir (Lamivudine)—HIV
Eprosartan mesylate (Teveten)—antihypertensive
Equagesic—muscle relaxant
Equanil—tranquilizer, sedative, hypnotic, or antianxiety
Equilet—antacid
Eramycin—antibiotic
Ergodryl—painkiller
Ergoloid mesylates (Hydergine)—senile/mental changes
Ergomar—painkiller
Ergostat—painkiller
Ergot alkaloids—painkiller
Ergotamine with Caffeine (Cafergot)—migraine
Ery-Tab (Erythromycin)—antibiotic
ERYC (Erythromycin)—antibiotic
Eryc21 erypar—antibiotic
Erycette (Erythromycin)—antibiotic
Erythrocin (Benzamycin)—acne
Erythromid—antibiotic
Erythromycin (A/T/S) (Ery-Tab) (ERYC)

(Erycette) (PCE) (T-Stat)—antibiotic
Eryzole (Pediazole)—middle ear infection
Esclim (Estrogen)—female hormone
Esgic—painkiller
Esidrix—antihypertensive
Esimil—antihypertensive
Eskalith (Lithium)—antipsychotic
Esomeprazole magnesium (Nexium)—antacid
Estazolam (ProSom)—tranquilizer sedative hypnotic or antianxiety
Estomul-M—antacid
Estraderm (Estrogen)—female hormone
Estradiol (CombiPatch)—female hormone
Estring (Estrogen)—female hormone
Estroate—female hormone
Estrogen—female hormone
Estropipate (Ogen)—female hormone
Etanercept (Enbrel)—anti-inflammatory, arthritis
Ethacrynic acid—diuretic
Ethambutol—tuberculosis
Ethchloruynol (Placidyl)—tranquilizer, sedative, hypnotic, or antianxiety
Ethosuximide—antiepileptic
Ethril—antibiotic
Etodolac (Lodine)—anti-inflammatory, arthritis
Etrafon—antidepressant
Eugel—antacid
Eulexin (Flutamide)—cancer
Euthroid—thyroid
Eutonyl—antihypertensive
Evenol—tranquilizer, sedative, hypnotic, or antianxiety
Evestrone—female hormone
Evista (Raloxifene hydrochloride)—mineral supplement
Ex-obese—anorexiant
Exdol—painkiller
Exelon (Rivastigmine tartrate)—senile/mental changes
Exna—diuretic

F

Famciclovir (Famvir)—herpes
Famotidine (Pepcid)—gastrointestinal
Famvir (Famciclovir)—herpes
Fastin (Phentermine)—stimulants
Febrigesic—painkiller

Felbamate (Felbatol)—antiepileptic
Felbatol (Felbamate)—antiepileptic
Feldene—anti-inflammatory, arthritis
Felodipine (Plendil)—antihypertensive
Femhrt (Activella)—female hormone
FemPatch—female hormone
Fenoprofen—anti-inflammatory, arthritis
Fenylhist—cough/cold antihistamine or decongestant
Feosol—mineral supplement
Fergon—mineral supplement
Fendex—stimulants
Fenofibrate (Tricor)—cholesterol reducer
Fernison—steroid
Fersamal—mineral supplement
Festal—gastrointestinal
Fexofenadine (Allegra)—cough/cold antihistamine or decongestant
Finevin (Azelex)—acne
Fioricet (Anolor 300) (Butalbital)—painkiller
Fiorinal—painkiller
First sign—asthma/respiratory aid
Flacid—antacid
Flagyl (Protostat)—antibiotic
Flavoxate (Urispas)—bladder spasms
Flecainide—cardiac drug
Flexeril (Cyclobenzaprine)—muscle relaxant
Flomax (Tamsulosin hydrochloride)—enlarged prostate
Flonase (Fluticasone)—asthma/respiratory aid
Florinal—tranquilizer, sedative, hypnotic, or antianxiety
Flovent (Fluticasone propionate)—asthma/respiratory aid
Floxin (Ofloxacin)—antibiotic
Fluanxol—antipsychotic
Fluclox—antibiotic
Fluconazole (Diflucan)—antibiotic
Flunisolide (AeroBid)—asthma/respiratory aid
Fluocinonide (Lidex)—skin itch
Fluorometholone (FML)—eye inflammation
Fluorouracil (Efudex)—cancer
Fluoxetine (Prozac)—antidepressant
Fluoxymesterone—male hormone
Fluphenazine (Prolixin)—tranquilizer, sedative, hypnotic, or antianxiety
Fluphenazine HCL—antipsychotic
Flurazepam (Dalmane)—tranquilizer, sedative, hypnotic, or antianxiety
Flurbiprofen (Ansaid)—anti-inflammatory, arthritis

Flutamide (Eulexin)—cancer
Fluticasone Proponate (Advair Diskus) (Flonase) (Flovent)—asthma/respiratory aid
Fluvastatin (Lescol)—cholesterol reducer
Fluvoxamine (Luvox)—antipsychotic
FML (Fluorometholone)—eye inflammation
Folic acid—vitamin
Foradil (Formoterol)—asthma/respiratory aid
Forbaxin—muscle relaxant
Forhistal—cough/cold antihistamine or decongestant
Formoterol (Foradil)—asthma/respiratory aid
Formulex—antispasmodic
Fortovase (Saquinavir)—HIV
Fosamax (Alendronate)—mineral supplement
Fosfomycin (Monurol)—antibiotic
Fosinopril (Monopril)—antihypertensive
Foypromazine—tranquilizer, sedative, hypnotic, or antianxiety
Franol—cough/cold antihistamine or decongestant
Fucidin—antibiotic
Fulvicin—antibiotic
Furadantin—antibiotic
Furalan—antibiotic
Furan—antibiotic
Furatoin—antibiotic
Furosemide (Lasix)—diuretic

G

G-1 tablets—painkiller
Gabapentin (Neurontin)—antiepileptic
Galantamine (Reminyl)—senile/mental changes
Gantanol—antibiotic
Gantrisin—antibiotic
Garamycin Ophthalmic (Gentamicin sulfate)—eye infection
Gardenal—antiepileptic
Gatifloxacin (Tequin)—antibiotic
Gaviscon—antacid
Gelusil—antacid
Gelusil-M—antacid
Gemfibrozil (Lopid)—anorexiant
Gemonil—antiepileptic
Genora—contraceptive
Gentamicin (Garamycin Ophthalmic)—eye infection
Geocillin—antibiotic

Geodon (Ziprasidone hydrochloride)—antipsychotic
Gitalgin—cardiac drug
Glimepiride (Amaryl)—diabetes
Glipizide (Glucotrol)—diabetes
Glucagon—hypoglycemia
Glucaloids—mineral supplement
Glucophage (Metformin)—hypoglycemia
Glucotrol (Glipizide)—diabetes
Glucovance—diabetes
Glutethimide—tranquilizer, sedative, hypnotic, or antianxiety
Glyburide—diabetes
Glycogel—antacid
Gycopyrrolate—gastrointestinal
Glynase (Micronase)—diabetes
Glysennid—laxative
Gramcal—mineral supplement
Gravergol—painkiller
Gravol—anorexiant
Grisactin—gastrointestinal
Griseofulvin (Gris-PEG)—athlete's foot
Grisovin—antibiotic
Gris-PEG (Griseofulvin)—athlete's foot
Guaifenesin with Codeine (Tussi-Organidin NR)—cough/cold antihistamine or decongestant
Guanabenz (Wytensin)—antihypertensive
Guanethidine—antihypertensive
Guanfacine (Tenex)—antihypertensive
Gustalac—antacid
Gyne-Lotrimin (Clotrimazole) (Lotrimin)—fungal infection
Gynergen—painkiller

H

Habitrol—nicotine patches
Hal-chlor—cough/cold antihistamine or decongestant
Halzepam—tranquilizer, sedative, hypnotic, or antianxiety
Halcion (Triazolan)—tranquilizer, sedative, hypnotic, or antianxiety
Haldol (Haloperidol)—antipsychotic
Halfprin—painkiller
Haloperidol (Haldol)—antipsychotic
Halopherido—antipsychotic
Halotestin—male hormone

Harmonyl—antihypertensive
Hctz—antihypertensive
Henotal—tranquilizer, sedative, hypnotic, or antianxiety
Hepamig—antispasmodic
Hexadrol—steroid
Hhr tablets—antihypertensive
Hip-rex—antibiotic
Hipprurate—antibiotic
Hispril—cough/cold antihistamine or decongestant
Histarall—cough/cold antihistamine or decongestant
Histaspan—cough/cold antihistamine or decongestant
Histatapp—cough/cold antihistamine or decongestant
Histex—cough/cold antihistamine or decongestant
Histrey—cough/cold antihistamine or decongestant
Hivid (Zalcitabine)—HIV
Homachol—antispasmodic
Hrh tablets—antihypertensive
Humalog (Insulin)—diabetes
Humulin—diabetes
Hycodan—cough/cold antihistamine or decongestant
Hydergine (Ergoloid mesylates)—senile/mental changes
Hydralazine—antihypertensive
Hydrocet—painkiller-narcotic
Hydrochlorothi-azide—antihypertensive
Hydrocodone—painkiller-narcotic
Hydrocortisone (Cetacort) (Hytone) (Nutracort)—skin itch
Hydrodiuril—antihypertensive
Hydrordiuril—antihypertensive
Hydromal—diuretic
Hydromorphone (Dilaudid)—painkiller-narcotic
Hydromax—diuretic
Hydropres—antihypertensive
Hydrosarpan—cardiac drug
Hydro-schlor—diuretic
Hydroxychloro-quine (Plaquenil)—malaria
Hydroxyzine HCL (Vistaril)—cough/cold antihistamine or decongestant
Hydro-z—diuretic
Hygroton—antihypertensive
Hylorel—antihypertensive

Hyoscyamine—antispasmodic
Hyperetic—diuretic
Hy-phen—painkiller-narcotic
Hypnophytol—tranquilizer, sedative, hypnotic, or antianxiety
Hyoscyamine (Levsin)—antispasmodic
Hyserp—antihypertensive
Hytone (Hydrocortisone)—skin itch
Hytrin (Terazosin hydrochloride)—antihypertensive
Hyzaar (Losartan potassium) (Losartan with Hydrochlorothi-azide)—antihypertensive

I

Ibuprofen (Motrin)—anti-inflammatory, arthritis
Idarac—painkiller
Idenal—painkiller
Ihn—tuberculosis
Iletin (Insulin)—diabetes
Ilosone—antibiotic
Ilotycin—antibiotic
Imavate—antidepressant
Imdur (Isosorbide mononitrate) (Ismo) (Monoket)—cardiac drug
Imipramine (Tofranil)—antidepressant
Imitrex (Sumatriptan succinate)—migraine
Imodium—antidiarrheal
Impril—antidepressant
Imuran—anti-inflammatory, arthritis
Indapamide (Lozol)—antihypertensive
Inderal (Propranolol)—cardiac drug
Inderide—antihypertensive
Indinavir (Crixivan)—HIV
Indocin—painkiller
Indomethacin—painkiller
Infibran—laxative
Insulin (Humalog) (Iletin) (Novolin)—diabetes
Insominal—tranquilizer, sedative, hypnotic, or antianxiety
Insomnex—tranquilizer, sedative, hypnotic, or antianxiety
Intal (Nasalcrom)—asthma/respiratory aid
Intrabutazone—anti-inflammatory, arthritis
Inversine—antihypertensive
Iodaminal—thyroid
Ionamin (Phentermine)—stimulants
Ipratropium Bromide (Atrovent)—asthma/respiratory aid

Irbesartan (Avalide) (Avapro)—antihypertensive
Ismelin—antihypertensive
Ismo (Imdur)—cardiac drug
Iso-bid—cardiac drug
Isobutal—painkiller
Isoclor—cough/cold antihistamine or decongestant
Isogard—cardiac drug
Isollyl—painkiller
Isoniazid—tuberculosis
Isoptin (Verapamil)—cardiac drug
Isopto Carpine (Pilocar)—glaucoma
Isordil—cardiac drug
Isosorbide (Imdur)—cardiac drug
Isotamine—tuberculosis
Isotrate—cardiac drug
Isotretinoin (Accutane)—acne
Isoxsuprine—cardiac drug
Isradipine (DynaCirc)—antihypertensive
Isuprel mistometer—asthma/respiratory aid
Itraconazole (Sporanox)—fungal infection

J

Janimine—antidepressant
Jen-diril—diuretic

K

Kadian (MS Contin)—painkiller-narcotic
Kaletra (Lopinavir with Ritonavir)—HIV
Katrex—antibiotic
Kaon—mineral supplement
Kavrin—cardiac drug
K-Dur (Micro-K)—mineral supplement
Keflex (Keftab)—antibiotic
Keftab (Keflex)—antibiotic
Kemadrin—Parkinson's disease
Kenacort—steroid
Keppra (Levetiracetam)—antiepileptic
Ketoconazole (Nizoral)—fungal infection
Ketoprofen (Orudis)—anti-inflammatory, arthritis
Ketorolac (Toradol)—anti-inflammatory, arthritis
Ketotifen fumarate (Zaditor)—cough/cold antihistamine or decongestant
Kinesed—antispasmodic

K-long—mineral supplement
K-lor—mineral supplement
K-lyte—mineral supplement
K-tab—mineral supplement
Klavikordal—cardiac drug
Klonopin (Clonazepam)—antiepileptic
Klor-Con (Micro-K)—mineral supplement
Klotrix—mineral supplement
Kolantyl—antacid
Krem—antacid
Kudrox—antacid

L

Labetalol (Trandate)—antihypertensive
Labid—asthma/respiratory aid
Lactulose (Chronulac Syrup)—laxative
Lamictal (Lamotrigine)—antiepileptic
Lamisil (Terbinafine hydrochloride)—fungal infection
Lamivudine (Combivir) (Epivir)—HIV
Lamotrigine (Lamictal)—antiepileptic
Lanophyllin—asthma/respiratory aid
Lanorinal—painkiller
Lanoxin—cardiac drug
Lanvis—cancer
Lapav—cardiac drug
Lardet—cough/cold antihistamine or decongestant
Largon—tranquilizer sedative hypnotic or antianxiety
Larotid—antibiotic
Larodopa—Parkinson's disease
Lasix (Furosemide)—antihypertensive
Lansoprazole (Prevacid)—gastrointestinal
Latan—mineral supplement
Latanoprost (Xalatan)—glaucoma
Lavadopa—Parkinson's disease
Laxagel—laxative
Lectopam—tranquilizer, sedative, hypnotic, or antianxiety
Leder–BP—cough/cold antihistamine or decongestant
Ledercillin—antibiotic
Leflunomide (Arava)—anti-inflammatory, arthritis
Lente-iletin—diabetes
Lescol (Fluvastatin)—cholesterol reducer

Leukeran—cancer
Levalbuterol hydrochloride (Betagan) (Xopenex)—asthma/respiratory aid
Levaquin (Levofloxacin)—antibiotic
Levate—antidepressant
Levazine—antipsychotic
Levbid (Levsin)—antispasmodic
Levetiracetam (Keppra)—antiepileptic
Levlen—antipsychotic
Levlite—antipsychotic
Levobunolol (Betagan)—glaucoma
Levodopa—Parkinson's disease
Levo-dromoran—painkiller-narcotic
Levofloxacin (Levaquin)—antibiotic
Levoid—thyroid
Levorphanol—painkiller-narcotic
Levothroid—thyroid
Levothyroxine—thyroid
Levoxyl (Synthroid)—thyroid
Levsin (Hyoscyamine) (Levbid) (NuLev)—antispasmodic
Levsinex (Levsin)—antispasmodic
Lexxel (Enalapril maleate)—antihypertensive
Lexo—diuretic
Librax—antispasmodic
Libritabs—tranquilizer, sedative, hypnotic, or antianxiety
Librium (Chlordiaze-poxide)—tranquilizer, sedative, hypnotic, or antianxiety
Lidex (Fluocinonide)—skin itch
Limbitrol—antidepressant
Limit—anorexiant
Lincocin—antibiotic
Linezolid (Zyvox)—antibiotic
Linodil—cardiac drug
Lioresal—muscle relaxant
Lipitor (Atorvastatin)—cholesterol reducer
Liquiprin—painkiller
Liquix-C—painkiller-narcotic
Liquophyllin—asthma/respiratory aid
Lisinopril (Zestril)—antihypertensive
Lithane—antipsychotic
Lithium (Eskalith)—antipsychotic
Lithobid—antipsychotic
Lithonate—antipsychotic
Lithotabs—antipsychotic
Lobac—muscle relaxant
Lodine (Etodolac)—anti-inflammatory, arthritis
Loestrin—contraceptive
Lofene—antidiarrheal

Loflo—antidiarrheal
Loftran—tranquilizer, sedative, hypnotic, or antianxiety
Lomanate—antidiarrheal
Lomefloxacin (Maxaquin)—antibiotic
Lomine—antispasmodic
Lomotil (Diphenoxylate)—antidiarrheal-narcotic
Lomoxat—antidiarrheal
Loniten—antihypertensive
Lonox—antidiarrheal
Loperamide—antidiarrheal
Lopid (Gemfibrozil)—anorexiant
Lopinavir with Ritonavir (Kaletra)—HIV
Lopresor (Metoprolol) (Toprol-XL)—antihypertensive
Loprox (Ciclopirox)—athlete's foot
Lopurin—gout
Lorabid (Loracarbef)—antibiotic
Loracarbef (Lorabid)—antibiotic
Loratadine (Claritin)—cough/cold antihistamine or decongestant
Lorazepam (Ativan)—tranquilizer, sedative, hypnotic, or antianxiety
Lorcet (Vicodin)—painkiller-narcotic
Lorelco—cholesterol reducer
Lortab (Vicodan)—painkiller-narcotic
Losartan (Cozaar) (Hyzaar)—antihypertensive
Losartan with Hydrochlorothia-zide (Hyzaar)—antihypertensive
Lotensin (Benazepril)—antihypertensive
Lotrel—antihypertensive
Lotrimin (Gyne-Lotrimin)—fungal infection
Lotrisone (Clotrimazole)—athlete's foot
Lovastatin (Mevacor)—cholesterol reducer
Low-Ogestre—contraceptive
Low-quel—antidiarrheal
Loxapac—antipsychotic
Loxapine (Loxitane)—antidepressant
Loxitane (Loxapine)—antidepressant
Lozide—antihypertensive
Lozol (Indapamide)—antihypertensive
Ludiomil—antidepressant
Lufyllin—asthma/respiratory aid
Lumigan (Bimatoprost)—glaucoma
Luminal—tranquilizer, sedative, hypnotic, or antianxiety
Luride (Sodium fluoride)—tooth decay prevention
Luvox (Fluvoxamine)—antipsychotic
LV penicillin—antibiotic

M

Maalox—antacid
Macalbis—antacid
Macrobid (Macrodantin)—antibiotic
Macrodantin (Macrobid)—antibiotic
Magmalin—antacid
Magnagel—antacid
Magnalum—antacid
Magnatril—antacid
Magnesium carbonate—antacid
Magnesium oxide—antacid
Magnesium trisilicate—antacid
Mag-ox400—antacid
Malgesic—anti-inflammatory, arthritis
Mallamint—antacid
Mandelamine—antibiotic
Mandrax—tranquilizer, sedative, hypnotic, or antianxiety
Maolate—muscle relaxant
Maox—antacid
Maprotiline—antidepressant
Marax—asthma/respiratory aid
Marbaxin—muscle relaxant
Marezine—antiemetic
Margesic compound 65—painkiller-narcotic
Marnal—painkiller
Marplan—antidepressant
Materna (Stuartnatal Plus)—mineral supplement
Mavik (Trandolapril)—antihypertensive
Maxalt (Rizatriptan benzoate)—migraine
Maxamag—antacid
Maxaquin (Lomefloxacin)—antibiotic
Maxidone (Vicodin)—painkiller-narcotic
Maxzide—antihypertensive
Mazepine—antiepileptic
Mebaral—tranquilizer, sedative, hypnotic, or antianxiety
Mebroin—antiepileptic
Meclizine—antiemetic
Meclomen—anti-inflammatory, arthritis
Medicycine—antibiotic
Medilium—tranquilizer, sedative, hypnotic, or antianxiety
Medimet—antihypertensive
Medipren—painkiller
Meditran—tranquilizer, sedative, hypnotic, or antianxiety
Medomin—tranquilizer, sedative, hypnotic, or antianxiety
Medrol—steroid
Medroxine—asthma/respiratory aid
Medroxyprogesterone—female hormone
Mefenamic acid (Ponstel)—painkiller
Megace—cancer
Megacillin—antibiotic
Megral—painkiller
Melfiat—anorexiant
Mellaril (Thioridazine)—antipsychotic
Melopa—antihypertensive
Meloxicam (Mobic)—anti-inflammatory, arthritis
Mepergan—painkiller-narcotic
Meperidine (Demerol)—painkiller-narcotic
Meprobamate—tranquilizer, sedative, hypnotic, or antianxiety
Meprosan—tranquilizer, sedative, hypnotic, or antianxiety
Mequin—tranquilizer, sedative, hypnotic, or antianxiety
Meravil—antidepressant
Meridia (Sibutramine hydrochloride)—anorexiant
Merital—antidepressant
Mesalamine (Rowasa)—gastrointestinal
Mesantoin—antiepileptic
Mesoridazine—antipsychotic
Metadate (Ritalin)—stimulants
Metandren tablets—male hormone
Metaprel—asthma/respiratory aid
Metaproteranol—asthma/respiratory aid
Metformin (Glucophage)—diabetes
Methadone—narcotic withdrawal
Methamphetamine—stimulants
Methaqualone HCL—tranquilizer, sedative, hypnotic, or antianxiety
Methazolamide (Neptazane)—glaucoma
Methenamine—antibiotic
Methergine (Methylergon-ovine maleate)—blood vessel constrictor
Methimazole—thyroid
Metho—muscle relaxant
Methocarbamol (Robaxin)—muscle relaxant
Methotrexate (Rheumatrex)—cancer
Methoxal—antibiotic
Methoxanol—antibiotic
Methylclothiazide—antihypertensive
Methyldopa (Aldomet)—antihypertensive
Methylergonovin (Methergine)—blood vessel constrictor

Methylin (Ritalin)—stimulants
Methylphenidate—stimulants
Methylpredisolone—steroid
Methyltestos-terone—steroid
Methylprylon—tranquilizer, sedative, hypnotic, or antianxiety
Meticorten—steroid
Metoclopramide (Reglan)—stimulants
Metolazone—antihypertensive
Metoprolol (Lopressor)—antihypertensive
Metra—anorexiant
Metroniadazole—antibiotic
Mevacor (Lovastatin)—cholesterol reducer
Meval—tranquilizer, sedative, hypnotic, or antianxiety
Mexiletine (Mexitil)—cardiac drug
Mexitil (Mexiletine)—cardiac drug
Miacalcin (Calcimar)—thyroid
Micainin—painkiller
Micardis (Telmisartan)—antihypertensive
Miconazole (Monistat)—vaginal yeast infection
Micro-K (K-Dur) (Klor-Con)—mineral supplement
Micronase (Glynase)—diabetes
Micronor—contraceptive
Microsul—antibiotic
Midatane—cough/cold antihistamine or decongestant
Midatap—cough/cold antihistamine or decongestant
Midrin—painkiller
Migranal (Dihydroergot-amine)—migraine
Milk of magnesia—antacid
Milontin—antiepileptic
Milpath—antispasmodic
Miltown—tranquilizer, sedative, hypnotic, or antianxiety
Minipress (Prazosin)—antihypertensive
Minizide—antihypertensive
Minocin (Dynacin)—antibiotic
Minocycline—antibiotic
Minoxidil—antihypertensive
Minto-o-mag—antacid
Mirapex (Pramipexole dihydrochloride)—Parkinson's disease
Mirtazapine (Remeron)—antidepressant
Misoprostol (Cytotec)—gastrointestinal
Moban—tranquilizer, sedative, hypnotic, or antianxiety
Mobenol—hypoglycemia

Mobic (Meloxicam)—anti-inflammatory, arthritis
Modafinil (Provigil)—stimulants
Moderil—antihypertensive
Modicon—contraceptive
Moditen—antipsychotic
Moduret—antihypertensive
Moduretic—antihypertensive
Moexipril (Univasc)—antihypertensive
Mogadon—tranquilizer, sedative, hypnotic, or antianxiety
Mometasone (Elocon)—skin itch
Monacet w/ codeine—painkiller-narcotic
Monistat (Miconazole)—vaginal yeast infection
Monoket (Imdur)—cardiac drug
Monopril (Fosinopril)—antihypertensive
Monpril-HCT—antihypertensive
Montelukast (Singulair)—asthma/respiratory aid
Monurol (Fosfomycin)—antibiotic
Morphine (Roxanol)—painkiller-narcotic
Motion cure—antiemetic
Motrin (Ibuprofen)—painkiller
Moxifloxacin hydrochloride (Avelox)—antibiotic
Ms Contin (Morphine) (Kadian)—painkiller-narcotic
Mupirocin (Bactroban)—antibiotic
Murcil—tranquilizer, sedative, hypnotic, or antianxiety
Muse (Caverject)—male impotence
Myadec—vitamin
Myambutol—tuberculosis
Mycelex (Butoconazole nitrate)—vaginal infection
Mycifradin—antibiotic
Myco-Triacet II (Mycolog-II)—fungal infection
Mycolog-II (Myco-Triacet II)—fungal infection
Mykrox (Zaroxolyn)—diuretic
Mylanta—antacid
Myleran—cancer
Myobid—cardiac drug
Mysoline—antiepileptic
Mytrex (Mycolog-II)—fungal infection

N

Nabumetone (Relafen)—anti-inflammatory, arthritis
Nadolol—antihypertensive

Nadopen-V—antibiotic
Nadozone—anti-inflammatory, arthritis
Nalbuphine—painkiller-narcotic
Naldecon—cough/cold antihistamine or decongestant
Nalfon—painkiller
Naltrexone (ReVia)—narcotic withdrawal
Naphazoline with Pheniramine (Naphcon-A)—cough/cold antihistamine or decongestant
Naphcon-A (Naphazoline with Pheniramine) (Opcon-A)—cough/cold antihistamine or decongestant
Naprelan (Anaprox)—anti-inflammatory, arthritis
Naprosyn (EC-Naprosyn)—anti-inflammatory, arthritis
Naproxen—painkiller
Naqua—diuretic
Naratriptan (Amerge)—migraine
Nardil (Phenelzine)—antidepressant
Nasacort (Azmacort)—asthma/respiratory aid
Nasalcrom (Intal)—asthma/respiratory aid
Nasalide (AeroBid)—asthma/respiratory aid
Natalins (Stuartnatal Plus)—mineral supplement
Nateglinide (Starlix)—diabetes
Natisedine—cardiac drug
Natrimax—antihypertensive
Naturetin—antihypertensive
Navane—tranquilizer, sedative, hypnotic, or antianxiety
Necon—contraceptive
Nedocromil (Tilade)—asthma/respiratory aid
Nefazodone (Serzone)—antidepressant
Nefrol—antihypertensive
Neggram—antibiotic
Nelfinavir (Viracept)—HIV
Nembutal (Pentobarbital)—tranquilizer, sedative, hypnotic, or antianxiety
Neo-barb—tranquilizer, sedative, hypnotic, or antianxiety
Neo-calme—tranquilizer, sedative, hypnotic, or antianxiety
Neo-codema—antihypertensive
Neofed—asthma/respiratory aid
Neo-H.S.—tranquilizer, sedative, hypnotic, or antianxiety
Neopap supprettes—painkiller
Neoral (Sandimmune)—organ transplant rejection
Neo-renal—diuretic
Neo-spasmylstrong—tranquilizer, sedative, hypnotic, or antianxiety
Neo-tetrine—antibiotic
Neo-tran—tranquilizer, sedative, hypnotic, or antianxiety
Neo-tropine—tranquilizer, sedative, hypnotic, or antianxiety
Neo-zoline—cardiac drug
Nephrox—antacid
Neptazane (Methazolamide)—glaucoma
Neuleptil—antipsychotic
Neuramate—tranquilizer, sedative, hypnotic, or antianxiety
Neurontin (Gabapentin)—antiepileptic
Neuro-spasex—tranquilizer, sedative, hypnotic, or antianxiety
Neuro-transentin—tranquilizer, sedative, hypnotic, or antianxiety
Neutracomp—antacid
Neutralca—antacid
Neutralox—antacid
Nevirapine (Viramune)—HIV
Nexium (Esomeprazole magnesium)—antacid
Nicardipine (Cardene)—antihypertensive
NicoDerm CQ—nicotine patches
Nicotrol—nicotine patches
Nifedipine (Procardia)—cardiac drug
Nilandron (Nilutamide)—cancer
Nilutamide (Nilandron)—cancer
Niong—cardiac drug
Nisoldipine (Sular)—antihypertensive
Nitrex—antibiotic
Nitro-bid—cardiac drug
Nitrocap-T.D.—cardiac drug
Nitrodan—antibiotic
Nitrodisc—cardiac drug
Nitro-dur-nitro—cardiac drug
Nitro-dur patches—cardiac drug
Nitrofurantoin—antibiotic
Nitroglycerine—cardiac drug
Nitrol—cardiac drug
Nitrolin—cardiac drug
Nitrolingual Spray (Nitroglycerin)—cardiac drug
Nitrol K-U—cardiac drug
Nitronet—cardiac drug
Nitrong—cardiac drug
Nitrospan—cardiac drug
Nitrostabilin—cardiac drug

Nitrostat—cardiac drug
Nizatidine (Axid)—gastrointestinal
Nizoral (Ketoconazole)—Fungal infection
Noctec—tranquilizer sedative hypnotic or antianxiety
Noludar—tranquilizer, sedative, hypnotic, or antianxiety
Nolvadex (Tamoxifen citrate)—cancer
Norco (Vicodin)—painkiller
Nordette—contraceptive
Nordryl—tranquilizer, sedative, hypnotic, or antianxiety
Norethin—contraceptive
Norflex (Orphenadrine)—muscle relaxant
Norfloxacin (Noroxin)—antibiotic
Norgesic—muscle relaxant
Norgesic forte—muscle relaxant
Norinyl—contraceptive
Norlestrin—contraceptive
Normatane—cough/cold antihistamine or decongestant
Nor-mil—antidiarrheal
Normodyne—antihypertensive
Noroxin (Norfloxacin)—antibiotic
Norpace—cardiac drug
Norpramin (Desipramine)—antidepressant
Nor-tet—antibiotic
Nortriptyline (Pamelor)—antidepressant
Norvasc (Amlodipine)—antihypertensive
Norvir (Ritonavir)—HIV
Noscapine—cough/cold antihistamine or decongestant
Novabutamide—hypoglycemia
Novabutazone—anti-inflammatory, arthritis
Novadipam—tranquilizer, sedative, hypnotic, or antianxiety
Novafed—asthma/respiratory aid
Novahistine LP—cough/cold antihistamine or decongestant
Novamoxin—antibiotic
Novocain—painkiller
Novocloxin—antibiotic
Novodoparil—antihypertensive
Novoflurazine—antipsychotic
Novohydrazide—antihypertensive
Novolexin—antibiotic
Novolin (Insulin)—diabetes
Novomedopa—antihypertensive
Novomethacin—anti-inflammatory, arthritis
Novonaprox—anti-inflammatory, arthritis
Novophenytoin—antiepileptic
Novopoxide—tranquilizer sedative hypnotic or antianxiety
Novopramine—antidepressant
Novopropamide—hypoglycemia
Novoridazine—antipsychotic
Novorythro—antibiotic
Novosemide—diuretic
Novotetra—antibiotic
Novothalidone—antihypertensive
Novotriamzide—antihypertensive
Novotriphyl—asthma/respiratory aid
Novotriptyn—antidepressant
Nozinan—antipsychotic
NPH—diabetes
Nubain—painkiller-narcotic
NuLev (Levsin)—antispasmodic
Numorphan—painkiller-narcotic
Nuprin—painkiller
Nutracort (Hydrocortisone)—skin itch
Nydrazid—tuberculosis
Nystatin—antibiotic

O

Obala—anorexiant
Obepal—anorexiant
Obepar—anorexiant
Obephen—anorexiant
Obetrol—anorexiant
Obezine—anorexiant
Ofloxacin (Floxin)—antibiotic
Ogen (Estropipate) (Ortho-Est)—female hormone
Ogestrel—contraceptive
Olanzapine (Zyprexa)—antipsychotic
Olsalazine (Dipentum)—gastrointestinal
Omeprazole (Prilosec)—gastrointestinal
Omnibese—anorexiant
Omnicef (Cefdinir)—antibiotic
Omnipen—antibiotic
Ondansetron (Zofran)—cancer
Opcon-A (Naphcon-A)—cough/cold antihistamine or decongestant
Optimine—cough/cold antihistamine or decongestant
Oradrate—tranquilizer, sedative, hypnotic, or antianxiety
Oralphyllin—antipsychotic

Orap—antipsychotic
Orapav timecelles—cardiac drug
Oraphen-pd—painkiller
Orasone—steroid
Oretic—antihypertensive
Oreton—male hormone
Organidin—cystic fibrosis
Orinase—diabetes
Orlistat (Xenical)—anorexiant
Ormazine—tranquilizer, sedative, hypnotic, or antianxiety
Ornade—cough/cold antihistamine or decongestant
Orphenadrine (Norflex)—muscle relaxant
Ortho-Cept—contraceptive
Ortho-Cyclen—contraceptive
Ortho-Est (Ogen)—female hormone
Ortho-novum—contraceptive
Ortho Tri-Cyclen—contraceptive
Orudis (Actron) (Ketoprofen) (Oruvail)—anti-inflammatory, arthritis
Oruvail (Orudis)—anti-inflammatory, arthritis
Os-cal—mineral supplement
Oseltamivir (Tamiflu)—antiviral
Ovcon—contraceptive
Ovral—contraceptive
Ovulen—contraceptive
Oxabid—antacid
Oxacillin sodium—antibiotic
Oxalid—anti-inflammatory, arthritis
Oxaprozin (Daypro)—anti-inflammatory, arthritis
Oxazepam—antidepressant, tranquilizer, sedative, hypnotic, or antianxiety
Oxcarbazepine (Trileptal)—antiepileptic
Oxiconazole nitrate (Oxistat)—fungal infection
Oxistat (Oxiconazole nitrate)—Fungal infection
Oxpam—tranquilizer, sedative, hypnotic, or antianxiety
Oxtriphylline—asthma/respiratory aid
Oxybutazone—anti-inflammatory, arthritis
Oxybutynin (Ditropan)—bladder spasms
Oxycodone (Percodan)—painkiller-narcotic
Oxymetazoline HCL—asthma/respiratory aid
Oxymorphone—painkiller-narcotic
Oxyphenbutazoneanti—anti-inflammatory arthritis
Oxyprenolol—antihypertensive
Oxytetracycline—antibiotic

P

P-A-C compound—cough/cold antihistamine or decongestant-narcotic
Paltet—antibiotic
Pama—antacid
Pamelor (Nortriptyline)—antidepressant
Pamine—antispasmodic
Panadol—painkiller
Panahist—cough/cold antihistamine or decongestant
Panasol—steroid
Pancrease (Creon) (Pancrelipase) (Ultrase)—cystic fibrosis
Pancrelipase (Pancrease)—cystic fibrosis
Panelex—painkiller-narcotic
Panex—painkiller
Panmycin—antibiotic
Pantoprazole sodium (Protonix)—gastrointestinal
Panwarfin—anticoagulant
Papa-deine—painkiller-narcotic
Papaverine—cardiac drug
Parachlor—muscle relaxant
Paradione—antiepileptic
Paraflex—muscle relaxant
Parafon Forte (Chlorzoxazone)—antispasmodic
Paregoric—antidiarrheal
Parest—tranquilizer sedative hypnotic or antianxiety
Pargesic 65—painkiller-narcotic
Pargyline—antihypertensive
Parlodel—Parkinson's Disease
Par-mag—antacid
Parmine—anorexiant
Parnate—antidepressant
Paroxetine (Paxil)—antidepressant
Parsidol—Parkinson's Disease
Parsitan—Parkinson's Disease
Partrex—antibiotic
Pas—tuberculosis
Pathocil—antibiotic
Pavabid—cardiac drug
Pavacap unicelles—cardiac drug
Pavacen cenules—cardiac drug
Pavadon elixir—painkiller-narcotic
Pavadur—cardiac drug
Pavadyl—cardiac drug
Pavagen—cardiac drug

Pavakey—cardiac drug
Pava-mead—cardiac drug
Pava-RX—cardiac drug
Pavased—cardiac drug
Pavasule—cardiac drug
Pavatym—cardiac drug
Paverine-spancaps—cardiac drug
Paverolan—cardiac drug
Paxil (Paroxetine)—antidepressant
Paxipam—tranquilizer, sedative, hypnotic, or antianxiety
Pbr/12—tranquilizer, sedative, hypnotic, or antianxiety
Pbz—cough/cold antihistamine or decongestant
PCE (Erythromycin)—antibiotic
PDM—anorexiant
Pe-de-em—anorexiant
Pediamycin—antibiotic
Pediapred (Prednisolone sodium)—anti-inflammatory, arthritis
Pediazole (Eryzole)—middle ear infection
Pedric wafers—painkiller
Peganone—antiepileptic
Pemirolast (Alamast)—cough/cold antihistamine or decongestant
Pemoline—tranquilizer sedative hypnotic or antianxiety
Penapar vk—antibiotic
Penbritin—antibiotic
Penciclovir (Denavir)—herpes
Penetrex (Enoxacin)—antibiotic
Penicillamine—anti-inflammatory, arthritis
Penicillin—antibiotic
Penicillin G—antibiotic
Pensyn—antibiotic
Penta-3b—alcoholism
Pentasa (Rowasa)—gastrointestinal
Pentazocine—painkiller
Pentids—antibiotic
Pentobarbital (Nembutal)—tranquilizer, sedative, hypnotic, or antianxiety
Pentothal—tranquilizer, sedative, hypnotic, or antianxiety
Pentoxifylline (Trental)—diuretic
Pentrium—cardiac drug
Pen-Vee K—antibiotic
Pepcid (Famotidine)—gastrointestinal
Peptol—antacid
Percocet (Roxicet)—painkiller-narcotic
Percodan (Oxycodone)—painkiller-narcotic

Periactin (Cyproheptadine)—cough/cold antihistamine or decongestant
Peri-colace—laxative
Peridex (Chlorhexidine)—gingivitis
Peridol—antipsychotic
Perindopril erbumine (Aceon)—antihypertensive
Peritrate—cardiac drug
Permitil—antipsychotic
Perphenazine—tranquilizer, sedative, hypnotic, or antianxiety
Persantine—cardiac drug
Pertofrane—antidepressant
Pervadil—cardiac drug
Pethidine—painkiller
Pfizer-e—antibiotic
Pfizerpen a—antibiotic
Pfizerpen g—antibiotic
Pfizerpen vk—antibiotic
Phazyme—gastrointestinal
Phedral—cough/cold antihistamine or decongestant
Phenaphen—painkiller-narcotic
Phenaphen with codeine—painkiller-narcotic
Phenat—tranquilizer, sedative, hypnotic, or antianxiety
Phenazine—antipsychotic
Phenazo—painkiller
Phenazodine—antibiotic
Phenazopyridine HCL—antibiotic
Phenbuff—antacid
Phendimead—anorexiant
Phendimetrazine—anorexiant
Phenelzine (Nardil)—antidepressant
Phenergan—tranquilizer, sedative, hypnotic, or antianxiety
Phenetron—cough/cold antihistamine or decongestant
Phenobarbital—tranquilizer, sedative, hypnotic, or antianxiety
Pheno-squar—tranquilizer, sedative, hypnotic, or antianxiety
Phenothiazines—antiemetic
Phensuximide—antiepileptic
Phentermine HCL (Fastin) (Ionamin)—anorexiant
Phentrol—anorexiant
Phenurone—antiepileptic
Phenylbutazone—anti-inflammatory, arthritis
Phenylpropanola-mine—stimulants

Phenytoin (Dilantin)—antiepileptic
Phenzine—anorexiant
Phillips' Liqui-Gels (Colace)—laxative
Phosphaljel—antacid
Phospholine Iodide (Echothiophate)—glaucoma
Phyllocontin—asthma/respiratory aid
Physpan—asthma/respiratory aid
Pilocar (Isopto Carpine) (Pilocarpine)—glaucoma
Pilocarpine (Pilocar)—glaucoma
Pilopine HS Gel (Pilocar)—glaucoma
Pindolol—antihypertensive
Pioglitazone hydrochloride (Actos)—diabetes
Piroxicam—anti-inflammatory, arthritis
Placidyl (Ethchloruynol)—tranquilizer, sedative, hypnotic, or antianxiety
Plaquenil (Hydroxychloroquine)—malaria
Plavix (Clopidogrel)—anticoagulant
Plegine—anorexiant
Plendil (Felodipine)—antihypertensive
Plexonal—tranquilizer, sedative, hypnotic, or antianxiety
PMB—female hormone
Polaramine—cough/cold antihistamine or decongestant
Polycillin—antibiotic
Polymox—antibiotic
Poly-Vi-Flor—vitamin
Ponstan—painkiller
Ponstel (Mefenamic acid)—painkiller
Potassium CL—mineral supplement
Potassium chloride—mineral supplement
Pramet—vitamin
Pramipexole (Mirapex)—Parkinson's disease
Prandin (Repaglinide)—diabetes
Pravachol (Pravastatin sodium)—cholesterol reducer
Pravastatin (Pravachol)—cholesterol reducer
Prazepam—tranquilizer, sedative, hypnotic, or antianxiety
Prazosin (minipress)—antihypertensive
Precose (Acarbose)—diabetes
Pred Forte (Prednisolone acetate)—eye inflammation
Prednicen-m—steroid
Prednisolone acetate (Pediapred) (Pred Forte)—eye inflammation
Prednisone—steroid
Prelu-2—anorexiant

Preludin—anorexiant
Premarin (Cenestin) (Prempro)—female hormone
Premphase—female hormone
Prempro (Premarin)—female hormone
Presamine—antidepressant
Prevacid (Lansoprazole)—gastrointestinal
Prevpac—ulcers
Prilosec (Omeprazole)—gastrointestinal
Primaquine—malaria
Primatene—asthma/respiratory aid
Primaxin—antibiotic
Primidone—antiepileptic
Principen—antibiotic
Prinivil (Zestril)—antihypertensive
Prinzide (Zestoretic)—antihypertensive
Priscoline—cardiac drug
Proavil—antidepressant
Pro-banthine—gastrointestinal
Probenecid—gout
Procainamide (Procanbid)—cardiac drug
Procan—cardiac drug
Procanbid (Procainamide hydrochloride)—cardiac drug
Procarbazine—cancer
Procardia (Nifedipine)—cardiac drug
Prochlorperazine (Compazine)—antipsychotic
Procyclidine—Parkinson's disease
Progesic compound-65—painkiller-narcotic
Proklar—antibiotic
Prolixin (Fluphenazine)—antipsychotic
Proloid—thyroid
Proloprim—antibiotic
Promapar—tranquilizer, sedative, hypnotic, or antianxiety
Promaz—tranquilizer, sedative, hypnotic, or antianxiety
Promethazine—tranquilizer, sedative, hypnotic, or antianxiety
Pronestyl—cardiac drug
Propafenone (Rythmol)—cardiac drug
Propantheline—gastrointestinal
Propecia (Finasteride)—baldness
Propine (Dipivefrin)—glaucoma
Propoxyphene HCL (Darvon)—painkiller-narcotic
Propranolol (Inderal)—antihypertensive
Propylthiouracil—thyroid
Proscar (Finasteride)—prostate enlargement
Prosedyl—tranquilizer, sedative, hypnotic, or antianxiety

ProSom (Estazolam)—tranquilizer, sedative, hypnotic, or antianxiety
Prostaphlin—antibiotic
ProStep—nicotine patches
Protonix (Pantoprazole sodium)—gastrointestinal
Protophylline—asthma/respiratory aid
Protostat (Flagyl)—antibiotic
Protran—tranquilizer, sedative, hypnotic, or antianxiety
Protrin—antibiotic
Protriptyline—antidepressant
Proval—painkiller-narcotic
Proventil (AccuNeb) (Volmax)—asthma/respiratory aid
Provera—female hormone
Provigil (Modafinil)—stimulants
Proxagesic—painkiller-narcotic
Proxagesic compound-65—painkiller-narcotic
Proxene—painkiller
Prozac (Fluoxetine) (Sarafem)—antidepressant
Pruodigin—cardiac drug
Pseudophedrine—cough/cold antihistamine or decongestant
Psorcon (Diflorasone)—skin itch
Psychozine—tranquilizer, sedative, hypnotic, or antianxiety
Puretane—cough/cold antihistamine or decongestant
Puretapp—cough/cold antihistamine or decongestant
Pvf—antibiotic
Pyrazinamide—tuberculosis
Pyridate—painkiller
Pyridium—painkiller
Pyridoxine—vitamin
Pyrodine—painkiller

Q

Quaalude—tranquilizer, sedative, hypnotic, or antianxiety
Quadrinal—asthma/respiratory aid
Quarzan—antispasmodic
Quazepam (Doral)—tranquilizer, sedative, hypnotic, or antianxiety
Questran (Cholestyramine)—cholesterol reducer
Quetiapine (Seroquel)—antipsychotic
Quibron—asthma/respiratory aid
Quide—antipsychotic
Quinaglute (Quinidine)—cardiac drug
Quinapril (Accupril)—antihypertensive
Quinate—cardiac drug
Quinidex—cardiac drug
Quinidine (Quinaglute)—cardiac drug
Quinidine sulfate—cardiac drug
Quinine—malaria
Quinobarb—cardiac drug
Quinora—cardiac drug
Qvar Inhalation Aerosol (Beclomethasone)—asthma/respiratory aid

R

Rabeprazole sodium (AcipHex)—gastrointestinal
Raloxifene (Evista)—mineral supplement
Ramipril (Altace)—antihypertensive
Ranitidine (Zantac)—gastrointestinal
Ratio—antacid
Raudixin—antihypertensive
Rautractyl—antihypertensive
Rauzide—antihypertensive
Regitine—antihypertensive
Reglan (Metoclopramide)—gastrointestinal
Regrotion—antihypertensive
Regulex—laxative
Regutal—laxative
Rela—muscle relaxant
Relafen (Nabumetone)—anti-inflammatory, arthritis
Relenza (Zanamivir)—influenza
Remeron (Mirtazapine)—antidepressant
Reminyl (Galantamine)—senile/mental changes
Renese—antihypertensive
Renova (Tretinoin)—acne
Repaglinide (Prandin)—diabetes
Repen-vk—antibiotic
Requip (Ropinirole hydrochloride)—Parkinson's disease
Reserpine—antihypertensive
Resbid—asthma/respiratory aid
Respirol—cough/cold antihistamine or decongestant
Resteclin—antibiotic
Restoril—tranquilizer, sedative, hypnotic, or antianxiety

Retet—antibiotic
Retin-A (Avita)—acne
Reton—anorexiant
Retrovir (Zidovudine)—HIV
ReVia (Naltrexone hydrochloride)—narcotic withdrawal
Rheumatrex (Methotrexate)—cancer
Rhinocort (Budesonide)—cough/cold antihistamine or decongestant
Riboflavin—vitamin
Ridaura (Auranofin)—anti-inflammatory, arthritis
Rifadin—tuberculosis
Rifampin—tuberculosis
Rifater—antibiotic
Rimactane—antibiotic
Riopan—antacid
Riphen-10—painkiller
Risedronate (Actonel)—mineral supplement
Risperdal (Risperidone)—antipsychotic
Risperidone (Risperdal)—antipsychotic
Ritalin (Concerta) (Metadate) (Methylin)—stimulants
Ritodrine—tranquilizer, sedative, hypnotic, or antianxiety
Ritonavir (Norvir)—HIV
Rivastigmine tartrate (Exelon)—senile/mental changes
Rivotril—antiepileptic
Rizatriptan (Maxalt)—migraine
Robalate—antacid
Robamol—muscle relaxant
Robamox—antibiotic
Robaxin (Methocarbamol)—muscle relaxant
Robaxisal (Codeine)—muscle relaxant
Robicillin-vk—antibiotic
Robimycin—antibiotic
Robinul—gastrointestinal
Robitet—antibiotic
Rocaltrol (Calcitriol)—mineral supplement
Rochephin—antibiotic
Rofecoxib (Vioxx)—anti-inflammatory, arthritis
Rolaids—antacid
Rolox—antacid
Rondec—cough/cold antihistamine or decongestant
Roniacol—cardiac drug
Ropinirole (Requip)—Parkinson's disease
Rosiglitazone maleate (Avandia)—diabetes
Roubac—antibiotic

Rounox—painkiller
Rovamycine—antibiotic
Rowasa (Asacol) (Mesalamine) (Pentasa)—gastrointestinal
Roxanol (Morphine)—painkiller-narcotic
Roxicet (Percocet)—painkiller-narcotic
Roydan—laxative
Rp-mycin—antibiotic
Rufen—anti-inflammatory, arthritis
Rulox—antacid
Ru-tuss—cough/cold antihistamine or decongestant
Rynatan (Trinalin)—cough/cold antihistamine or decongestant
Rythmodan—cardiac drug
Rythmol (Propafenone)—cardiac drug

S

Salatin with codeine—cough/cold antihistamine or decongestant-narcotic
Salazopyrin—gastrointestinal
Salicylate (aspirin)—painkiller
Salmeterol (Serevent)—asthma/respiratory aid
Salsalate (Disalcid)—anti-inflammatory, arthritis
Saluron—antihypertensive
Salutensin—antihypertensive
Sandimmune (Neoral)—organ transplant rejection
Sandril—antihypertensive
Sansert—painkiller
Saquinavir (Fortovase)—HIV
Sarafem (Prozac)—antidepressant
Sarisol—tranquilizer, sedative, hypnotic, or antianxiety
Scopolamine—antiemetic
Scrip-dyne—painkiller-narcotic
Secobarbital (Seconal)—tranquilizer, sedative, hypnotic, or antianxiety
Seconal (Secobarbital)—tranquilizer, sedative, hypnotic, or antianxiety
Sectral (Acebutolol)—cardiac drug
Sedabamate—tranquilizer, sedative, hypnotic, or antianxiety
Sedadrops—tranquilizer, sedative, hypnotic, or antianxiety
Sedapep—tranquilizer, sedative, hypnotic, or antianxiety
Segontin—cardiac drug

Selacryn—antihypertensive
Seldane—cough/cold antihistamine or decongestant
Selegiline (Eldepryl)—Parkinson's disease
Semprex-D (Acrivastine with Pseudoephedrine)—cough/cold antihistamine or decongestant
Septra—antibiotic
Sequels—cough/cold antihistamine or decongestant
Ser-a-gen—antihypertensive
Seralazide—antihypertensive
Ser-ap-es—antihypertensive
Serax—tranquilizer, sedative, hypnotic, or antianxiety
Serc—cardiac drug
Sereen—tranquilizer, sedative, hypnotic, or antianxiety
Serentil—tranquilizer, sedative, hypnotic, or antianxiety
Serevent (Salmeterol)—asthma/respiratory aid
Ser hydrazine—antihypertensive
Seromycin—tuberculosis
Serophene (Clomiphene Citrate)—female fertility
Seroquel (Quetiapine)—antipsychotic
Serpasil—antihypertensive
Sertan—antiepileptic
Sertraline (Zoloft)—antidepressant
Serzone (Nefazodone hydrochloride)—antidepressant
Sibutramine (Meridia)—anorexiant
Silain gel—antacid
Sildenafil (Viagra)—male impotence
Silvadene Cream 1% (Silver sulfadiazine)—burn ointment
Silver sulfadiazine (Silvadene Cream 1%)—burn ointment
Simaal—antacid
Simeco—antacid
Simvastatin (Zocor)—cholesterol reducer
Sinemet—Parkinson's disease
Sinequan (Doxepin)—antidepressant
Singlet tablets—cough/cold antihistamine or decongestant
Singulair (Montelukast)—asthma/respiratory aid
Sintrom—anticoagulant
Sinubid—cough/cold antihistamine or decongestant
Sinufed—asthma/respiratory aid
Sk amitriptyline—antidepressant
Sk ampicillin—antibiotic
Sk-apap—painkiller
Sk-apap w/codeine—painkiller-narcotic
Sk-chlorothiazide—diuretic
Skelaxin—muscle relaxant
Sk-lygen—tranquilizer, sedative, hypnotic, or antianxiety
Sk-65—painkiller-narcotic
Sk-pramine—antidepressant
Slo-bid—asthma/respiratory aid
Slo-phyllin (Theophylline)—asthma/respiratory aid
Slow-k—mineral supplement
Soda mint—antacid
Sodestrin-H—female hormone
Sodium amyta—tranquilizer, sedative, hypnotic, or antianxiety
Sodium fluoride (Luride)—tooth decay prevention
Sodium Sulamyd (Bleph-10) (Sulfacetamide)—eye infection
Soduben—tranquilizer, sedative, hypnotic, or antianxiety
Sof-Lax (Colace)—laxative
Solazine—antipsychotic
Solfotion—tranquilizer, sedative, hypnotic, or antianxiety
Soma (Carisoprodol)—muscle relaxant
Somnol—tranquilizer, sedative, hypnotic, or antianxiety
Somophyllin—asthma/respiratory aid
Somophyllin-T—asthma/respiratory aid
Som-pam—tranquilizer, sedative, hypnotic, or antianxiety
Sonata (Zaleplon)—tranquilizer, sedative, hypnotic, or antianxiety
Soneryl—tranquilizer, sedative, hypnotic, or antianxiety
Sorate—cardiac drug
Sorbide T.D.—cardiac drug
Sorbitrate—cardiac drug
Spancap—stimulants
Sparine—antipsychotic
Spastosed—antacid
Spectazole Cream (Econazole)—athlete's foot
Spenaxin—muscle relaxant
Spengine—senile/mental changes
Spenox—antacid

Spentane—cough/cold antihistamine or decongestant
Sperx—anorexiant
Spiractazide—diuretic
Spiractone—diuretic
Spironazide—diuretic
Spironolactone (Aldactazide)—diuretic
Sporanox (Itraconazole)—fungal infection
Stabinol—hypoglycemia
Starlix (Nateglinide)—diabetes
Statobex—anorexiant
Stavudine (Zerit)—HIV
Stelabid—antipsychotic
Stelazine (Trifluoperazine)—antipsychotic
Stemetil—antipsychotic
Sterapred—steroid
Sterazolidin—cardiac drug
Stilbestrol—female hormone
Stim-35—anorexiant
Stimate (DDAVP)—diabetes
Streptomycin—antibiotic
Stress-pam (Valium)—tranquilizer, sedative, hypnotic, or antianxiety
Stuartnatal Plus (Materna) (Natalins)—mineral supplement
Sublimaze—painkiller-narcotic
Sub-quin—cardiac drug
Sucralfate (Carafate)—gastrointestinal
Sudafed—cough/cold antihistamine or decongestant
Sudoprin—painkiller
Sudrin—asthma/respiratory aid
Suhist tablets—cough/cold antihistamine or decongestant
Sular (Nisoldipine)—antihypertensive
Suldiazo—antibiotic
Sulfacetamide (Sodium Sulamyd)—eye infection
Sulfamethizole—antibiotic
Sulfamethoxazole—antibiotic
Sulfasalazine (Azulfidine)—anti-inflammatory, arthritis
Sulfasox—antibiotic
Sulfinpurazone—gout
Sulfisoxazole—antibiotic
Sulfizin—antibiotic
Sulfonamides—antibiotic
Sulindac—anti-inflammatory, arthritis
Sumatriptan (Imitrex)—migraine
Sumox—antibiotic

Sumycin—antibiotic
Supen—antibiotic
Suprax (Cefixime)—antibiotic
Supres—antihypertensive
Suprol—painkiller
Suprofen—painkiller
Surfak—laxative
Surmontil—antidepressant
Susadrin—cardiac drug
Suspen—antibiotic
Sustaire—asthma/respiratory aid
Sustiva (Efavirenz)—HIV
Symmetrel—Parkinson's disease
Symptom 2—asthma/respiratory aid
Symptom 3—cough/cold antihistamine or decongestant
Synalgos–DC—painkiller-narcotic
Synophylate—asthma/respiratory aid
Synthroid (Levoxyl) (Unithroid)—thyroid
Syntrogel—antacid

T

Tabloid APC—cough/cold antihistamine or decongestant-narcotic
Tacaryl—cough/cold antihistamine or decongestant
Tacrine (Cognex)—senile/mental changes
Tagamet (Cimetidine)—gastrointestinal
Tagatap—cough/cold antihistamine or decongestant
Talacen—painkiller
Talwin—painkiller
Tambocor—cardiac drug
Tamiflu (Oseltamivir)—antiviral
Tamoxifen—cancer
Tamsulosin (Flomax)—enlarged prostate
Tandearil—anti-inflammatory, arthritis
Tapar—painkiller
Tapazole—thyroid
Taractan—antipsychotic
Tarasan—antipsychotic
Tarka—antihypertensive
Tasmar (Tolcapone)—Parkinson's disease
Tavist—cough/cold antihistamine or decongestant
Tazarotene (Tazorac)—acne
Tazorac (Tazarotene)—acne
Teczem—antihypertensive

Tedral—cough/cold antihistamine or decongestant
Tedrol—asthma/respiratory aid
Tegretol (Atretol)—antiepileptic
Teldrin—cough/cold antihistamine or decongestant
Tedrol—asthma/respiratory aid
Tegretol (Carbamazepine) (Carbatrol) (Epitol)—antiepileptic
Teldrin—cough/cold antihistamine or decongestant
Teldrin spansules—cough/cold antihistamine or decongestant
Telmisartan (Micardis)—antihypertensive
Temazepam—tranquilizer, sedative, hypnotic, or antianxiety
Temovate (Clobetasol) (Cormax)—skin itch
Temposil—alcoholism
Tempra—painkiller
Tenax—tranquilizer, sedative, hypnotic, or antianxiety
Tenex (Guanfacine)—antihypertensive
Tenol—painkiller
Tenoretic—antihypertensive
Tenormin (Atenolol)—antihypertensive
Ten-shun—painkiller
Tenuvate—anorexiant
Tepanil—anorexiant
Tequin (Gatifloxacin)—antibiotic
Terazol (Terconazole)—fungal infection
Terazosin (Hytrin)—antihypertensive
Terbinafine hydrochloride (Lamisil)—fungal infection
Terbutaline—asthma/respiratory aid
Terconazole (Terazol)—fungal infection
Terpin hydrate—cough/cold antihistamine or decongestant
Terramycin—antibiotic
Terrastatin—antibiotic
Tertroxin—thyroid
Tessalon (Benzonatate)—cough/cold antihistamine or decongestant
Testolactone—cancer
Testopel (Testosterone pellets)—male hormone
Testred—male hormone
Tet-250—antibiotic
Tetra-bid—antibiotic
Tetra-c—antibiotic
Tetra-co—antibiotic
Tetracap—antibiotic

Tetrachel—antibiotic
Tetracycline—antibiotic
Tetracyn—antibiotic
Tetralan-250—antibiotic
Tetralean—antibiotic
Tetram—antibiotic
Tetrex—antibiotic
Teveten (Eprosartan mesylate)—antihypertensive
Thalitone—antihypertensive
Theo-steroid (Theo-Dur)—asthma/respiratory aid
Theobid—asthma/respiratory aid
Theocap—asthma/respiratory aid
Theochron (Theo-Dur)—asthma/respiratory aid
Theoclear—asthma/respiratory aid
Theodrine—cough/cold antihistamine or decongestant
Theo-dur (Theophylline) (Theo-steroid) (Theochron) (T-Phyl) (Uni-Dur)—asthma/respiratory aid
Theofedral—cough/cold antihistamine or decongestant
Theofenal—cough/cold antihistamine or decongestant
Theolair—asthma/respiratory aid
Theolixir—asthma/respiratory aid
Theon—asthma/respiratory aid
Theophenylln—cough/cold antihistamine or decongestant
Theophyl—asthma/respiratory aid
Theophylline (Slo-phyllin) (Theo-dur)—asthma/respiratory aid
Theoral—cough/cold antihistamine or decongestant
Theospan—asthma/respiratory aid
Theostat—asthma/respiratory aid
Theovent—asthma/respiratory aid
Theragran—vitamin
Therapan—cardiac drug
Therapav—cardiac drug
Thermoloid—thyroid
Thiamine—vitamin
Thiazides—diuretic
Thioguanine—cancer
Thioridazine (Mellaril)—tranquilizer, sedative, hypnotic, or antianxiety
Thioridazine HCL—antipsychotic
Thioril—antipsychotic
Thiosulfil—antibiotic

Thiothixene—antipsychotic
Thorazine (Chlorpromazine)—antipsychotic
Thyrocrine—thyroid
Thyroglobulin—thyroid
Thyroid—thyroid
Thyrolar—thyroid
Tiazac (Cardizem)—cardiac drug
Tigan—antiemetic
Tilade (Nedocromil)—asthma/respiratory aid
Timentin—antibiotic
Timolide—antihypertensive
Timolol—antihypertensive
Timoptic (Betimol)—glaucoma
Tindal—tranquilizer, sedative, hypnotic, or antianxiety
Titralac—antacid
Tobramycin (Tobrex)—antibiotic
Tobrex (Aktob) (Tobramycin)—antibiotic
Tocainide—cardiac drug
Tofranil (Imipramine)—antidepressant
Tolazamide—diabetes
Tolbutamide—hypoglycemia
Tolcapone (Tasmar)—Parkinson's disease
Tolectin—anti-inflammatory, arthritis
Tolinase—diabetes
Tolmetin—anti-inflammatory, arthritis
Tolterodine tartrate (Detrol)—overactive bladder
Tonocard—cardiac drug
Topamax (Topiramate)—antiepileptic
Topicort (Desoximetasone)—skin itch
Topiramate (Topamax)—antiepileptic
Toprol-XL (Lopressor)—antihypertensive
Tora—anorexiant
Toradol (Ketorolac)—anti-inflammatory, arthritis
Torecan—antivertigo
Tornalate—asthma/respiratory aid
Totacillin—antibiotic
T-Phyl (Theo-Dur)—asthma/respiratory aid
Tralmag—antacid
Tramadol (Ultram)—painkiller
Trancopal—tranquilizer, sedative, hypnotic, or antianxiety
Trandate (labetalol)—cardiac drug
Trandolapril (Mavik)—antihypertensive
Tranmep—tranquilizer, sedative, hypnotic, or antianxiety
Transderm nitro—cardiac drug
Transderm scop—antiemetic

Tranxene (Clorazepate)—tranquilizer, sedative, hypnotic, or antianxiety
Trasicor—antihypertensive
Trates granucaps—cardiac drug
Travatan (Travoprost)—glaucoma
Travoprost (Travatan)—glaucoma
Trazodone (Desyrel)—painkiller
Trental (Pentoxifylline)—cardiac drug
Tretinoin (Renova)—acne
Trexan—narcotic withdrawal
Trialka liquid—antacid
Trialka tablets—antacid
Triamcinolone (Azmacort)—asthma/respiratory aid
Triamed—tranquilizer, sedative, hypnotic, or antianxiety
Triamterene (Dyazide)—antihypertensive
Triaphen-10—anti-inflammatory, arthritis
Triavil (Amitriptyline)—antidepressant
Triaz (Desquam-E)—antibiotic
Triazolam (Halcion)—tranquilizer, sedative, hypnotic, or antianxiety
Trichlormethi-azide—diuretic
Tricor (Fenofibrate)—cholesterol reducer
Tridesilon (Desonide)—skin itch
Tridione—antiepileptic
Trifluoperazine (Stelazine)—antipsychotic
Trihexyphenidyl—Parkinson's disease
Trihydroserpine—antihypertensive
Trilafon—tranquilizer, sedative, hypnotic, or antianxiety
Trileptal (Oxcarbazepine)—antiepileptic
Trilisate (Choline magnesium trisalicylate)—anti-inflammatory, arthritis
Trimagel—antacid
Trimethadione—antiepileptic
Trimethobenz-amide—antiemetic
Trimethoprim—antibiotic
Trimipramine—antidepressant
Trimox—antibiotic
Trimpex—antibiotic
Trimstat—anorexiant
Trimtabs—anorexiant
Trinalin (Azatadine with pseudoephedrine) (Rynatan)—cough/cold antihistamine or decongestant
Tri-Norinyl—contraceptive
Tri-pavasule—cardiac drug
Tripelennamine—cough/cold antihistamine or decongestant

Triphasil—contraceptive
Tripolidine—cough/cold antihistamine or decongestant
Triptil—antidepressant
Trisogel—antacid
Trisulfaminic—antibiotic
Trivora—contraceptive
Trizivir (Abacavir, Lamivudine, Zidovudine)—HIV
Trymegen—cough/cold antihistamine or decongestant
T-Stat (Erythromycin)—antibiotic
Tuinal—tranquilizer, sedative, hypnotic, or antianxiety
Tuloidin—thyroid
Tumol—muscle relaxant
Tums—antacid
Tusscapine—cough/cold antihistamine or decongestant
Tussi-Organidin NR (Brontex) (Guaifenesin with Codeine)—cough/cold antihistamine or decongestant-narcotic
Tussionex—cough/cold antihistamine or decongestant
Tuss-ornade—cough/cold antihistamine or decongestant
Tuzon—muscle relaxant
Twinbarbital—tranquilizer, sedative, hypnotic, or antianxiety
Tylenol (Acetaminophen)—painkiller
Tylenol with codeine—painkiller-narcotic
Tylox—painkiller-narcotic

U

Ultracet—antibiotic
Ultram (Tramadol)—painkiller
Ultrase (Pancrease)—cystic fibrosis
Unicap—vitamin
Uni-Dur (Theo-Dur)—asthma/respiratory aid
Unipen—antibiotic
Uniphyl—asthma/respiratory aid
Unipres—antihypertensive
Uniretic—antihypertensive
Unitensen—antihypertensive
Unithroid (Synthroid)—thyroid
Univasc (Moexipril)—antihypertensive
Urecholine—gastrointestinal
Urex—antibiotic
Uridon—antihypertensive
Urifon—antibiotic
Urised—antibiotic
Urispas (Flavoxate)—bladder spasms
Uritol—diuretic
Uro gantanol—antibiotic
Uro-mag—antacid
Urotoin—antibiotic
Urso (Actigall)—gallstones
Ursodiol (Actigall)—gastrointestinal
Uticillin VK—antibiotic

V

Valacyclovir (Valtrex)—herpes
Valadol—painkiller
Valcyte (Valganciclovir)—retinitis
Valdrene—cough/cold antihistamine or decongestant
Valganciclovir (Valcyte)—retinitis
Valium (Diazepam)—tranquilizer, sedative, hypnotic, or antianxiety
Valorin—painkiller
Valpin—gastrointestinal
Valproic acid (Depakene)—antiepileptic
Valrelease—tranquilizer, sedative, hypnotic, or antianxiety
Valsartan (Diovan)—antihypertensive
Valtrex (Valacyclovir)—herpes
Vancenase (Beclomethasone)—asthma/respiratory aid
Vanceril—steroid
Vasal granucaps—cardiac drug
Vaseretic—antihypertensive
Vasocap—cardiac drug
Vasodilan—cardiac drug
Vasoprine—cardiac drug
Vasospan—cardiac drug
Vasotec (Enalapril)—antihypertensive
V-cillin—antibiotic
V-cillin K—antibiotic
Vc-k 500—antibiotic
Veetids—antibiotic
Veganin—painkiller
Velosef—antibiotic
Velosulin—diabetes
Veltane—cough/cold antihistamine or decongestant
Venlafaxine (Effexor)—antidepressant

Ventolin—asthma/respiratory aid
Veracillin—antibiotic
Verapamil (Isoptin)—cardiac drug
Verelan (Calan)—cardiac drug
Verstran—tranquilizer, sedative, hypnotic, or antianxiety
Vesprin—antipsychotic
Vi-Daylin—multivitamin
Viagra (Sildenafil citrate)—male impotence
Vibramycin—antibiotic
Vicodin (Lorcet) (Lortab) (Maxidone) (Norco)—painkiller-narcotic
Vicon—vitamin
Vicoprofen—painkiller
Videx (Didanosine)—HIV
Viokase—gastrointestinal
Vioxx (Rofecoxib)—anti-inflammatory, arthritis
Viracept (Nelfinavir)—HIV
Viramune (Nevirapine)—HIV
Virlin—male hormone
Viskazide—antihypertensive
Visken—antihypertensive
Vistaril (Hydroxyzine)—tranquilizer, sedative, hypnotic, or antianxiety
Vistrax—antispasmodic
Vivactil—antidepressant
Vivelle—female hormone
Vivol (Valium)—tranquilizer, sedative, hypnotic, or antianxiety
Vivox—antibiotic
Volmax (Proventil)—asthma/respiratory aid
Voltaren (Cataflam)—anti-inflammatory, arthritis
Vontrol—antivertigo

W

Wans—antiemetic
Warfarin—anticoagulant
Warfilone—anticoagulant
Warnerin—anticoagulant
Weh-less—anorexiant
Wehvert—antiemetic
Weightrol—anorexiant
WelChol (Colesevelam)—cholesterol reducer
Wellbutrin (Bupropion)—antidepressant
Wel-k—mineral supplement
Wigraine—painkiller
Wigrettes—painkiller
Wilpowr—anorexiant
Wingel—antacid
Wyamycin—antibiotic
Wygesic—painkiller-narcotic
Wymox—antibiotic
Wytensin (Guanabenz)—antihypertensive

X

Xalatan (Latanoprost)—glaucoma
Xanax (Alprazolam)—tranquilizer, sedative, hypnotic, or antianxiety
Xenical (Orlistat)—anorexiant
Xopenex (Levalbuterol hydrochloride)—asthma/respiratory aid

Y

Yasmin—contraceptive
Yocon (Yohimbine hydrochloride)—male impotence
Yohimbine (Yocon) (Yohimex)—male impotence
Yohimex (Yocon)—male impotence
Yutopar—gastrointestinal

Z

Zaditor (Ketotifen fumarate)—cough/cold antihistamine or decongestant
Zafirlukast (Accolate)—asthma/respiratory aid
Zalcitabine (HIVid)—HIV
Zaleplon (Sonata)—tranquilizer, sedative, hypnotic, or antianxiety
Zanamivir (Relenza)—influenza
Zantac (Ranitidine)—gastrointestinal
Zapex—tranquilizer, sedative, hypnotic, or antianxiety
Zarontin—antiepileptic
Zaroxolyn (Mykrox)—diuretic
Zerit (Stavudine)—HIV
Zestoretic (Prinzide)—antihypertensive
Zestril (Lisinopril) (Prinivil)—antihypertensive
Zetran—tranquilizer, sedative, hypnotic, or antianxiety
Ziagen (Abacavir sulfate)—HIV
Zide—diuretic

Zidovudine (Retrovir)—HIV
Zileuton (Zyflo)—asthma/respiratory aid
Ziprasidone (Geodon)—antipsychotic
Zithromax (Azithromycin)—antibiotic
Zocor (Simvastatin)—cholesterol reducer
Zofran (Ondansetron)—cancer
Zolmitriptan (Zomig)—migraine
Zoloft (Sertraline)—antidepressant
Zolpidem (Ambien)—tranquilizer, sedative, hypnotic, or antianxiety
Zomax—painkiller
Zomepirac—painkiller
Zomig (Zolmitriptan)—Migraine
Zonegran (Zonisamide)—antiepileptic
Zonisamide (Zonegran)—antiepileptic
Zovirax (Acyclovir)—herpes
Zyban (Bupropion hydrochloride)—quit smoking aid
Zydone—painkiller-narcotic
Zyflo (Zileuton)—asthma/respiratory aid
Zyloprim—gout
Zynol—gout
Zyprexa (Olanzapine)—antipsychotic
Zyrtec (Cetirizine)—cough/cold antihistamine or decongestant
Zyrtec-D—cough/cold antihistamine or decongestant
Zyvox (Linezolid)—antibiotic

CHAPTER 73: FINGERPRINTS

The following list can be used as a quick-reference guide by death investigators in determining the method to use in obtaining latent prints from various types of materials.

\	QUICK-REFERENCE FINGERPRINT GUIDE
ITEM	**METHOD**
Amino acid techniques	Cyanoacrylate ester DFO 1, 2 Indanedione 5-MTN Ninhydrin
Sebaceous techniques	Gentian violet Iodine fuming Physical developer Small-particle reagent
Eccrine techniques	Cyanoacrylate ester DFO 1, 2 Indanedione 5-MTN Ninhydrin Silver nitrate
Blood techniques	Amido black—methanol Coomassie blue Crowle's double stain DAB Leucocrystal violet
Fluorescent techniques	Ardrox Basic yellow 40 DFO 1, 2 Indanedione Liqui-Drox M.B.D. MRM RAM R.A.Y. Rhodamine 6G Safranin O Thenoyl Europium Chelate
Nondestructive	Iodine fuming Fluorescent light Electrostatic lifting Ultraviolet (UV) lamp Visual examination

Porous surfaces	DFO Iodine fuming 1, 2 Indanedione 5-MTN Ninhydrin Physical developer Zinc chloride
Nonporous surfaces	Cyanoacrylate ester Gentian violet Small-particle reagent
Glass surfaces	Basic yellow 40 Cyanoacrylate ester M.B.D. dye Small particle reagent
Plastic surfaces	Basic yellow 40 Cyanoacrylate ester M.B.D. dye Small-particle reagent
Wet surfaces	Physical developer Small-particle reagent Sudan Black
Postcyanoacrylate	Ardrox Basic red 28 Basic yellow 40 DFO Liqui-Drox M.B.D. M.R.M. 10 RAM R.A.Y. Rhodamine 6G Sudan black Thenoyl europium chelate
Metal surfaces	Cyanoacrylate ester Small-particle reagent M.B.D. dye Basic yellow 40
Adhesive tape surfaces	Gentian violet Liqui-Drox Liqui-Nox Sticky-side powder

Glossy paper surfaces	Cyanoacrylate ester Small-particle reagent M.B.D. dye Basic yellow 40
Cartridge cases	Basic yellow 40 Cyanoacrylate ester Gun bluing
Raw wood surfaces	DFO Iodine fuming 1, 2 Indanedione Ninhydrin 5-MTN Physical developer Silver nitrate
Postninhydrin	Nickel nitrate Physical developer Silver nitrate Small-particle reagent Zinc chloride
Ultraviolet induced	Ardrox Basic yellow 40 Liqui-Drox Silver nitrate Thenoyl europium chelate UV lamp

CHEMICALS USED FOR DEVELOPING AND ENHANCING FINGERPRINTS

Amido Black Formula (Methanol Based)

A dye staining and rinse process used to enhance detail in faint bloody impressions. It is sensitive to the protein in blood.

Surface:	Bloodstained nonporous surfaces (has been successfully used on porous surfaces)	Visual examination ⬇ Forensic light ⬇ Ultraviolet light ⬇ Amido black ⬇ Forensic light
Ridge detail visualization:	Visible chemical/stain reaction	
Development color:	Deep blue	
Shelf life:	Indefinite	

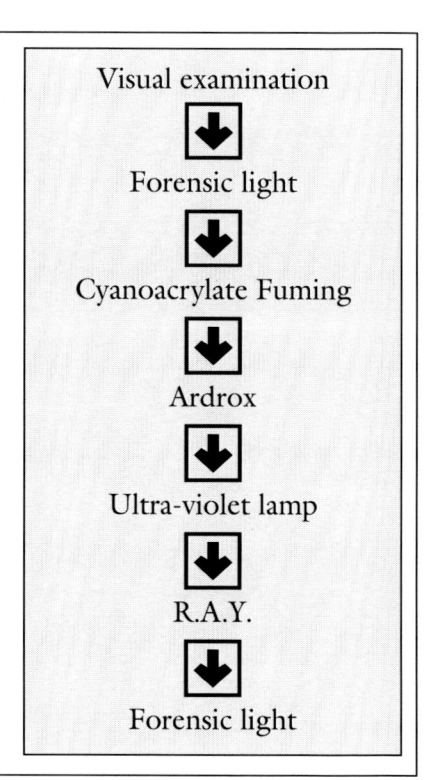

Developer solution:	2 grams amido black dye 100 milliliters glacial acetic acid 900 milliliters methanol Combine and mix with a stirring device for 30 minutes.
Rinse solution:	100 milliliters glacial acetic acid 900 milliliters methanol
Final rinse:	1 liter of distilled water
Application:	• Blood must be dry before application.
Squeegee bottle application:	• Apply for 30 to 90 seconds. • Apply rinse with a squeegee bottle.
Tray immersion:	• Immerse in dye solution for • 30 to 90 seconds. • Immerse in a tray of rinse solution for one minute. • Apply the final water rinse. • Allow item to air-dry.

Ardrox

Ardrox is a fluorescent dye-stain that is commonly used to make cyanoacrylate-developed prints more visible.

Surface:	Nonporous
Development color:	Yellow fluorescence
Ridge detail visualization:	UV light induced; forensic light source induced
Shelf life:	6 months

Visual examination
↓
Forensic light
↓
Cyanoacrylate Fuming
↓
Ardrox
↓
Ultra-violet lamp
↓
R.A.Y.
↓
Forensic light

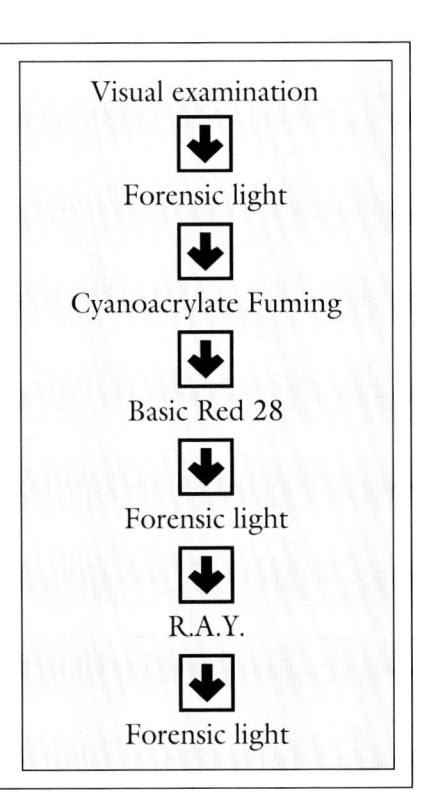

Developer solution: 2 milliliters ardrox P-133D
10 milliliters acetone
25 milliliters Methanol
10 milliliters isopropanol
8 milliliters acetonitrile
945 milliliters petroleum ether

Premeasured vials are designed to make a 2-percent working solution when added to 1 liter of water or methanol. Also available in premixed solutions.

Application:
- The recommended procedure is to soak the item in a tray of the dye. A rinse using petroleum ether may be necessary to avoid excessive dye-staining.
- View under a UV lamp in the 280- to 365-nanometer range. Use UV protection goggles.
- View under a forensic light source in the 435- to 480-nanometer range. Use yellow colored goggles.
- Photograph results using a 2-A haze, yellow-colored or 515 (BP 35) bandpass filter.

Use concerns:
- Items that inherently fluoresce in the 500-nanometer range will interfere with the dye-stain fluorescence.

Basic Red 28

A red-colored dye used with a forensic light source or UV lamp after cyanoacrylate development of latent prints.

Surface:	Nonporous	Visual examination
Development color:	Orange fluorescence	↓
		Forensic light
Ridge detail visualization:	Forensic light source induced	↓
		Cyanoacrylate Fuming
Shelf life:	6 months	↓
		Basic Red 28
		↓
		Forensic light
		↓
		R.A.Y.
		↓
		Forensic light

Developer solution:
- *Stock solution:*
  - —0.2 gram basic red 28 dye dissolved in 60 milliliters propanol, then add
  - —40 milliliters Acetonitrile
- *Working solution:*
  - —5 milliliters stock solution
  - —95 milliliters petroleum ether

Application:
- Immerse or use a squirt bottle to apply the reagent.
- Examine under a forensic light source at 470 to 550 nanometers. Use orange-colored goggles.
- Photograph results using an orange or bandpass 550 (BP35) barrier filter.

Use concerns:
- Items that inherently fluoresce in the 585-nanometer range will interfere with the dye-stain fluorescence.

Basic Yellow 40

A yellow-colored dye used with a forensic light source or UV lamp after cyanoacrylate development of latent prints.

Surface:	Nonporous	Visual examination ↓ Forensic light ↓ Cyanoacrylate Fuming ↓ Basic Yellow 40 ↓ Forensic light ↓ R.A.Y. ↓ Forensic light
Development color:	Yellow fluorescence	
Ridge detail visualization:	Forensic light source induced Ultraviolet induced	
Shelf life:	6 months	

Developer solution:
- *Working solution:*
  - —1 gram basic yellow 40 dye dissolved in 500 milliliters methanol

Application:
- Tray immersion or aerosol sprayer for 5 seconds
- Water rinse by squirt bottle application or gently running stream of water for 10 seconds

	• View under an ultraviolet lamp around 365 nanometers. Use UV protection goggles.
	• Photograph results using a yellow-colored or 515 (BP35) bandpass filter.
Use concerns:	• Items that inherently fluoresce in the 490-nanometer range will interfere with the dye-stain fluorescence.

Coomassie Blue

A dye-staining process that is followed by a rinse procedure used in enhancing detail in a faint bloody impression. The contrast is not as distinct as amido black.

Surface:	Bloodstained porous and nonporous surfaces
Development color:	Deep blue
Ridge detail visualization:	Visible chemical/stain reaction
Shelf life:	Indefinite

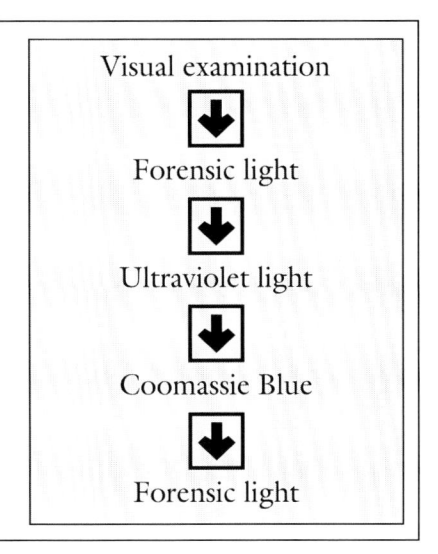

Visual examination
↓
Forensic light
↓
Ultraviolet light
↓
Coomassie Blue
↓
Forensic light

Developer solution:	• *Dye solution:* —Coomassie blue, 4 grams —Methanol, 200 milliliters —Distilled water, 200 milliliters —Glacial acetic acid, 40 milliliters
Rinse solution:	Methanol 450ml Distilled water 450ml Glacial acetic acid 100ml
Application:	• The blood should be fixed to the surface material. • Squeegee bottle application for 30 to 90 seconds. Apply rinse with squeegee bottle. • Can be used with tray immersion into dye solution for 30 to 90 seconds. • Place into tray immersion rinse solution for 1 minute. • Development time may be shortened if the evidence surface readily absorbs the dye-stain.
Use concerns:	• The process is detrimental to some biological examinations.

- This process is not good for porous surfaces that strongly absorb the dye.
- Yields poor results on concrete surfaces.
- The process does not work well with excessively bloody surfaces.

Crowle's Double Stain Formula

A stain used to enhance bloody fingerprint impressions that are visible.

Surface:	Nonporous surfaces	Visual examination ↓ Forensic light ↓ Ultraviolet light ↓ Crowle's Double Stain ↓ Forensic light ↓ Amido black
Development color:	Blue	
Ridge detail visualization:	Visible chemical/stain reaction	
Shelf life:	Indefinite	

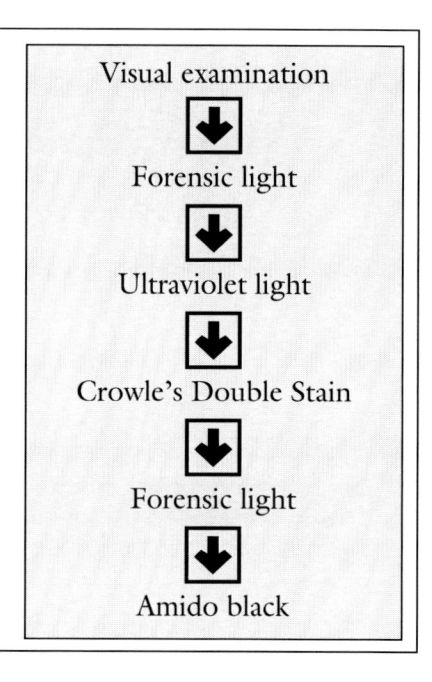

Developer solution:
2.5 grams Crocein scarlet 7B
150 milligrams Coomassie Brilliant Blue
50 milliliters glacial acetic acid
30 milliliters trichloroacetic acid
Dilute above mixture into:
— Liter of distilled water
— Use a stirring device until all the dye is dissolved

Rinse solution:
30 milliliters glacial ascetic acid
970 milliliters distilled water

Application:
- Spray, immerse or use a squirt bottle to apply the developer solution to the item.
- Wait 30 to 90 seconds.
- Repeat these steps until the maximum contrast is achieved.
- Photograph the final result.

Use concerns:
- Porous surfaces that strongly absorb the dye
- Excessive bloodstained items
- Blood impression must be completely dry before processing begins.

Crystal Violet

This chemical is used in developing latent prints on the sticky side of tape.

Cyanoacrylate Ester Formula

A possible evidentiary item is placed in an enclosed chamber in an effort to develop latent prints. Fumes from the active ingredient of cyanoacrylate ester work to create a white ridge impressions. Dye stains may be added to the polymer print for enhancement purposes.

Surface:	Nonporous surfaces	Visual examination ⬇ Forensic light ⬇ Cyanoacrylate fuming ⬇ Dye Stain ⬇ Forensic light
Development color:	White	
Ridge detail visualization:	Visible chemical/stain reaction	
Shelf life:	Indefinite	

Developer solution: Use either liquid glue (approximately 20 millimetres in diameter) into a small porcelain plate or open a commercially available Gel-pac to release the fumes.

Application:
- Place items into the designed chamber.
- Add the cycloacrylate.
- Add a humidity/warm source.
- Fume at least 10 minutes. Be careful to monitor development.
- Evaluate development using a forensic light source.
- Photograph the developed detail.
- Process with dye-stain. (It is recommended to let the developed detail sit overnight before treating the print with dye).

Use concerns:
- Moisture-laden surfaces are not conducive to this process.
- Careful consideration must be given to items that may have to be submitted for firearms and biological testing.
- Light-colored surfaces may not present significant contrast for the developed detail.
- Results that are exposed to direct sunlight should be photographed immediately.
- Very porous items may strongly absorb the dye.
- May not be suitable for excessively bloodstained items.

Diaminobenzidine (D.A.B.) Formula

A colorless liquid that becomes strongly visible when blood is contacted. Can be used in conjunction with amido black.

Surface:	Bloodstained porous and nonporous surfaces	Visual examination ⬇ Forensic light ⬇ Ultraviolet light ⬇ D.A.B. ⬇ Forensic light ⬇ Amido black
Development color:	Brown	
Ridge detail visualization:	Visible chemical/ stain reaction	
Shelf life:	48 hours, if refrigerated	

Developer solution:
- *Solution A:*
  —20 grams 5-sulfosalicyclic acid dissolved in 1 liter of distilled water
- *Solution B:*
  —100 milliliters 1N phosphate buffer (pH 7.4) mixed in 800ml of distilled water
- *Solution C:*
  —1 gram D.A.B. dissolved in 100 milliliters of distilled water
- *Working solution:*
  —180 milliliters of Solution B
  —20 milliliters of Solution C
  —1 milliliter 30-percent hydrogen peroxide.

Application:
- Fix item in Solution A for 2 to 3 minutes, or:
- Immerse item in working solution for 3 or 4 minutes, or:
- Saturate item with a paper towel soaked with the working solution for 3 minutes.
- Rinse area with distilled water.

Use concerns:
- Cyanoacrylate fuming is detrimental to D.A.B. processing.
- Good results have been achieved on paper products. D.A.B. has no effect on ninhydrin processing.

DFO

Prior to the use of ninhydrin, this is a process used because of the chemical's sensitivity and reaction to the amino acids present in latent print residue on porous surfaces. DFO is considered more sensitive to amino acid detection than ninhydrin.

Surface:	Dry paper documents	Visual examination ⬇ Forensic light ⬇ D.F.O. ⬇ Ninhydrin ⬇ Physical developer
Development color:	Yellow fluorescence	
Ridge detail visualization:	Forensic light source induced	
Shelf life:	6 months	

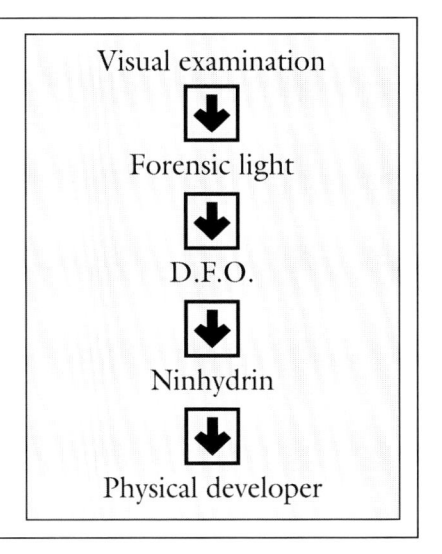

Developer solution:
- *Stock solution:*
  - —1 gram DFO crystals
  - —200 milliliters methanol
  - —200 millilitersl ethyl acetate
  - —40 milliliters glacial acetic acid
  - —Combine and stir wit a magnetic stirring device until all of the ingredients are dissolved.

- *Working solution:*
  - —Add petroleum ether to the stock solution until the total volume is 2 liters.

Application:
- Use prior to ninhydrin in the processing sequence.
- Dip or spray the item.
- Air-dry the item.
- Process and dry a second time.
- Oven bake (or hair dry) at 100°C for 10 or 20 minutes.
- Examine under a forensic light source at 450 to 550 nanometers. Use orange-colored goggles.
- Photograph results using an orange-colored or 550 (BP 35) bandpass filter.

Use concerns:
- Not useful on items that cannot be baked in an oven
- Not useful for nonporous surfaces and items that have been wet

Electrostatic Lifting

A nondestructive process utilizing electric current through a sheet of lifting film that attracts dust particles to the film.

Surface: Dry porous and nonporous surfaces

Ridge detail visual: Electrostatic recovered impressions

Application:
- Place the lifting film over the surface containing the dust impression.
- Place the grounding device adjacent to the lifting film.
- Charge the lifting film with the charger unit.
- Transfer the dust impression to the lifting film by the electrostatic charge.
- View the lifted result using white oblique lighting in a darkened room.
- Photograph opaque lifting films using white oblique light.
- Photograph transparent lifting films using transmitted light or darkfield lighting methods.

Use concerns:
- Cannot be used in extremely dusty surfaces
- Cannot be used in wet or moist conditions

Fluorescence Examination

This is a nondestructive technique used to identify the presence of visible ridge detail. Various types of forensic light sources are available, but the preferred model usually involves one that provides an excitation wavelength range from 350 to 600 nanometers.

The goal of fluorescent examinations is to achieve the maximum fluorescence of the ridge detail with the minimum amount of background fluorescence/reflection. Viewing of the ridge detail is accomplished by examining it through an absorption mode (making the image darker) or by causing its fluorescence. The latter is accomplished by exposing the suspected area to light or causing the image to fluoresce through the application of specific chemicals. Orange, red, or yellow goggles may be worn. Lenses or goggles are used to enhance the detail for viewing or for photographic purposes.

Used for:
- Luminescence of natural components in latent print residue
- Fluorescent fingerprint powders
- Fluorescent dye-stains
- Darkening blood impressions
- Fluorescing fluids for refrigerants, transmissions, fuels, and coolants
- Fluorescent physiological fluids
- Luminesces backgrounds for contrast improvement

Centered wavelengths:
- 300 to 400 nanometers
- Fluorescing UV-sensitive powders or dyes
- Fluorescing physiological fluids
- Ardrox excitation
- 400 to 450 nanometers
- R.A.Y. excitation
- Absorbing blood\bitemark detail
- Fluorescing physiological fluids

- 455 to 515 nnometers
- Searching on nonfluorescent backgrounds
- Basic yellow 40 excitation
- Zinc chloride excitation
- 550 to 590 nanometers
- Searching on highly fluorescent backgrounds
- DFO excitation

Application:
- Reduce ambient light
- Aim the light from the forensic light source
- View the item using yellow-, red-, or orange-colored goggles.
- Photograph detail using colored filters similar to the viewing goggles

Use concerns:
- Items that naturally luminesce may cause the ridge detail to become indistinctive.

Gentian Violet

This process is especially useful in working with surfaces that are contaminated with oils and grease. It is a dye-staining process where the evidence is repeatedly stained and rinsed until optimal development

Surface:	Nonporous surfaces, especially the adhesive side of tape	Visual examination ↓ Forensic light ↓ Gentian Violet ↓ Liqui-Drox ↓ Forensic light
Development color:	Purple	
Ridge detail visualization:	Visible chemical/stain reaction; forensic light source induced	
Shelf life:	Indefinite	

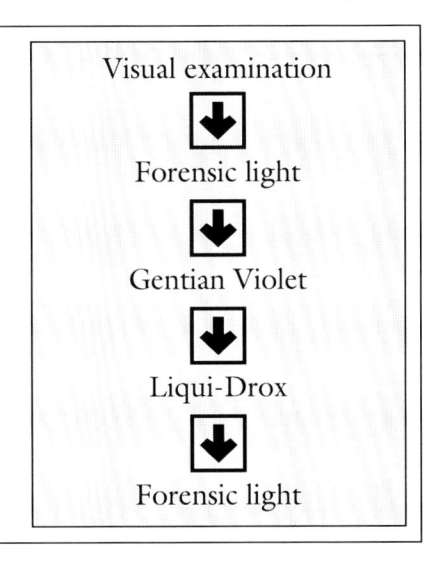

occurs.

Developer solution:
- *Formula A:*
  —1 milliliter gentian violet solution
  —1,000 milliliters distilled water

- *Formula B:*
  —1 gram gentian violet crystals
  —1,000 milliliters distilled water

Clearing solution:

100 milliliters hydrochloric acid in 90 milliliters of tap water (10-percent solution)

Application:	• Pass the item through a tray containing the reagent solution for 1 to 2 minutes. • With cold tap water rinse 30 seconds. • View visually or with a forensic light source between 505 and 570 nanometers with red goggles.
Use concerns:	• Most effective on recently deposited latents on tape • Some surfaces may be too porous because they may absorb too much of the dye. • Tapes containing adhesives that are water soluble should be avoided. • Improved contrast of fingerprint detail may be achieved through the use of a forensic light source.

Gun Bluing

This is used in a diluted solution to develop ridge detail on cartridge surfaces. Cartridges are first fumed with cyanoacrylate ester, then immersed into the gun-bluing solution.

Surface:	Brass or nickel cartridge surfaces
Development color:	Black
Ridge detail visualization:	Visible chemical/stain reaction.
Developer solution:	• *Formula 44/40 (Instant Gun Blue)*: —1 part reagent to 80 parts distilled water • *Outer's Gun Blue:* —1 part reagent to 40 parts distilled water
Application:	• Briefly fume cartridges with cyanoacrylate ester. • Immerse cartridges in gun blue reagent. • Monitor for development. • Halt development by immersing in distilled water.
Use concerns:	• Cannot be used on lacquered-steel cartridges

Hungarian Red

This dye-stain is used to stain prints and patterns in blood. Used with an ALS and white gel lifters, it works as an enhancer for faint prints in blood.

1, 2 Indanedione

An amino-acid-sensitive reagent that is comparable with D.F.O. processing.

Surface:	Dry porous items	Visual examination ⬇ Forensic light ⬇ 1,2 Indanedione ⬇ Forensic light ⬇ Zinc Chloride/P.D.
Development color:	Yellow fluorescence	
Ridge detail visualization:	Forensic light source induced	

Developer solution:
1 gram 1, 2-Indanedione
10 milliliters glacial acetic acid
90 milliliters ethyl acetate
900 milliliters petroleum ether

Application:
- Dip or spray the item.
- Air-dry.
- Oven bake at 100°C for 10 to 20 minutes at 60-percent relative humidity or with no added humidity.
- View under a forensic light source around 530 nanometers. Use orange-colored goggles.
- Post-treatment can be performed with zinc chloride to improve the visualization of the ridge detail

Use concerns:
- Does not work well with such low-quality papers as cardboard, newspaper, or recycled papers
- Should not be used with surfaces that have been exposed to moisture.

Iodine Fuming

This nondestructive fuming technique can be used on porous and nonporous surfaces. The developed ridge detail dissipates quickly, so it is necessary to set up the photography that will be used to record any developed detail in advance.

Surface:	Porous and nonporous surfaces	Visual examination ⬇ Forensic light ⬇ Iodine ⬇ Ninhydrin ⬇ Physical developer
Development color:	Yellow	
Ridge detail visualization:	Visible chemical/stain reaction	
Shelf life:	Indefinite	

Developer solution:	• Obtain commercial model of iodine fuming kit and chamber. • Pack about 1/2 teaspoon of iodine crystals into the fuming kit/chamber. • Follow the manufacturer's instructions.
Application:	• Prepare the photographic setup by presetting camera lighting, aperture, and shutter speed. • Low heat is required to sublimate the iodine crystals into fumes. Pass the fumes over the surface to be examined. • Photograph any developed detail immediately.
Use concerns:	• Items cannot be processed with cyanoacrylate prior to iodine fuming. • Some metal items may corrode upon exposure to iodine fumes. • It may be difficult to distinguish ridge detail on dark surfaces using this process.

Leucocrystal Violet

A process used to enhance blood through the catalytic oxidation of the dye, while simultaneously fixing and enhancing the blood impression. Other blood enhancement techniques, such as amido black, may be applied after this technique.

Surface:	Bloodstained surfaces	Visual examination ↓ Forensic light ↓ Ultraviolet light ↓ Leucocrystal Violet ↓ Forensic light ↓ Amido black
Development color:	Purple	
Ridge detail visualization:	Visible chemical/stain reaction	
Shelf life:	1 month	

Developer solution:
- *Formula "A"*
  - (Solution A)
    10 grams 5-sulfosalicylic acid dissolved in 100 milliliters distilled water
  - (Solution B)
    Add Solution A to 400 milliliters 3-percent hydrogen peroxide.
  - (Working solution)
    — Add .75 gram leucocrystal violet dye to Solution B, stirring the mixture vigorously.
- *Formula "B"*:
  - 10 grams 5-sulfosalicylic acid dissolved in 500 ml 3-percent hydrogen peroxide
  - Add 3.7 grams sodium acetate add 1.0 gram leucocrystal violet dye, stirring the mixture vigorously.

Application:
- Spray the blood impression using a fine-mist sprayer.
- Development should occur in 30 seconds.

Use concerns:
- May not work well with porous items that absorb an exceedingly large amount of dye or on surfaces that are excessively bloody.
- Cyanoacrylate fuming can be detrimental to this particular process.

Liqui-Drox

Effective for dark-colored adhesive tapes, the Liqui-Drox method is a postcyanoacrylate process involving brushing the reagent unto tape, rinsing, then viewing the result under dye-stain long-wave UV light.

Surface:	Dark-colored tapes, adhesive and nonadhesive sides
Development color:	Yellow fluorescent
Ridge detail visualized:	UV light induced
Shelf life:	6 months

Visual examination
⬇
Forensic light
⬇
Cyanoacrylate fuming
⬇
Liqui-Drox
⬇
Ultraviolet lamp
⬇
R.A.M.
⬇
Forensic light

Developer solution:	200 milliliters Ardrox P-133D 400 milliliters Liqui-Nox 400 milliliters distilled water • Combine and stir the chemicals thoroughly. A thick, milky yellow solution should form.
Application:	• Using a camel hair brush, apply the reagent onto both sides of the tape until a lather is produced. • Wait approximately 10 seconds. • Rinse under a gentle stream of cold tap water. • Allow the tape to air-dry. • View under a forensic light source or UV lamp able to produce a long-wave UV light output. Use UV protection, yellow- or orange-colored goggles. • Photograph results using an ultraviolet blocking 2A filter.
Use concerns:	• Items that inherently fluoresce in the dye-stain long-wave UV range will interfere with the dye-stain fluorescence.

Liqui-Nox

Liqui-Nox is a laboratory glassware soap that is used to create a soap/powder foam that is painted onto adhesive tape surfaces.

Surface:	Adhesive tape surfaces	Visual examination ⬇ Forensic light ⬇ Gentian Violet ⬇ Liqui-Nox ⬇ Liqui-Drox ⬇ Forensic light
Development color:	Dark gray	
Ridge detail visualization:	Visible chemical/stain reaction	
Shelf life:	Prepared as needed	

Developer solution: In a shallow bowl mix:
20 drops tap water
20 drops Liqui-Nox
.5 gram black fingerprint powder

Application:
- Mix the ingredients to create a foam with bubbles.
- Use a camel hair brush to paint the tape surface with the mixture.
- Wait 30 to 60 seconds.
- Rinse tape under a gentle stream of tap water. Allow the tape to air-dry.
- Photograph any developed detail.

Use concerns:
- Dark-colored tapes should be processed using gray fingerprint powder in the reagent mixture instead of black fingerprint powder.

Luminol

This highly sensitive chemical technique is commonly used to locate very dilute blood areas. It may be used to locate footprints in blood not seen to the naked eye, as well as to discern "blood trails." It may also be used in identifying areas in which attempts have been made to wash away the blood.

Luminol can be obtained in a premeasured vial that, when mixed with the correct amount of water, is ready for use while at the scene.

M.B.D.

This is a fluorescent dye-stain used to enhance cyanoacrylate-developed latent prints. A fluorescent light source that will output light between 435 and 535 nanometers is required for this process.

Surface:	Nonporous surfaces
Development color:	Orange fluorescence
Ridge detail visualization:	Forensic light source induced
Shelf life:	6 months

Visual examination
⬇
Forensic light
⬇
Cyanoacrylate fuming
⬇
M.B.D.
⬇
Forensic Light
⬇
M.R.M. 10
⬇
Forensic light

Developer solution:
- *M.B.D. stock solution:*
  —1 gram M.B.D. powder dissolved in 1 liter acetone
- *M.B.D. working solution (combine in the order listed):*
  —10 milliliters M.B.D. stock solution
  —30 milliliters methanol
  —10 milliliters isopropanol
  —950 milliliters petroleum ether

Application:
- Spray, immerse, or use a squirt bottle to apply the M.B.D. solution to the item.
- View under a forensic light source in the 435 to 535-nanometer range. Use orange-colored goggles.
- Photograph results using orange barrier filter.

Use concerns:
- Items that fluoresce in the 515-nanometer range may interfere with the dye-stain fluorescence.

5-MTN

Similar to ninhydrin, 5-MTN is used in processing paper evidence. Ridge detail is exhibited as a deeper purple color than with ninhydrin. 5-MTN prints post-treated with zinc chloride become strongly fluorescent.

Surface:	Porous surfaces, especially paper and cardboard	Visual examination ⬇ Forensic light ⬇ D.F.O. ⬇ 5-MTN ⬇ Zinc chloride ⬇ Forensic light
Development color:	Purple	
Ridge detail visualization:	Visible chemical/ stain reaction	
Shelf life:	12 months	

Developer solution:	3 grams 5-MTN crystals 1,000 milliliters petroleum ether
Application:	• Tray immersion of item for 5 seconds • Brush solution on to the item until coated. • Spray solution on to the item until coated. • Heat up to 80°C with humidity exposure of 60 to 70-percent relative humidity (or use a steam iron). Monitor for development. • Photograph the developed detail using a green-colored filter. • View under forensic light source at 530 nanometers (no barrier filter). • Item may be treated with zinc chloride.
Use concerns:	• Not suited for nonporous surfaces or for items that have been water soaked. • Surfaces that have high animal or plant protein content, such as leather and currency, are likely to produce extensive background development.

M.R.M.

This mixture of fluorescent dye-stains is used to enhance cyanoacrylate-developed latent prints. This process requires a fluorescent light source that will output light between 430 and 530 nanometers.

Surface:	Nonporous surfaces
Development color:	Orange fluorescence
Ridge detail visualization:	Forensic light source induced
Shelf life:	6 months

Visual examination
↓
Forensic light
↓
Cyanoacrylate fuming
↓
Rhodamine 6G
↓
Forensic light
↓
M.R.M. 10
↓
Forensic light

Developer solution:
- *Stock solution A:*
  —1 gram rhodamine 6G powder dissolved in 1 liter of methanol
- *Stock solution B:*
  —2 grams basic yellow 40 dissolved in 1 liter of methanol
- *Stock solution C:*
  —1 gram M.B.D. powder dissolved in 1 liter of acetone.
- *M.R.M. 10 Working solution:* (Combine in the order listed.)
  —3 milliliters stock solution A
  —3 milliliters stock solution B
  —7 milliliters stock solution C
  —20 milliliters methanol
  —10 milliliters isopropanol
  —8 milliliters acetonitrile
  —950 milliliters petroleum ether

Application:
- Spray, immerse or use a squirt bottle to apply the M.R.M. 10 solution to the item.

	• Examination under a laser or forensic light source at 430 to 530 nanometers. Use orange-colored goggles.
	• Photograph results using an orange-colored or 550 (BP 35) bandpass filter.
Use concerns:	• Items that inherently fluoresce in the 490 to 555 nanometers range will interfere with the dye-stain fluorescence.

Nickel Nitrate

Nickel nitrate is applied as post-ninhydrin treatment in order to improve the contrast of the ridge detail for viewing and photography. Two methods may be applied: the background may be made to fluoresce, or the treated ridge detail may be made to absorb green-colored light around 530 nanometers.

Surface:	Porous surfaces	Visual examination
Development color:	Orange-red	⬇
		Forensic light
Ridge detail visualization:	Visible chemical/stain reaction.	⬇
	Forensic light source induced.	Ninhydrin
		⬇
		Nickel nitrate
		⬇
		Forensic Light

Developer solution:	3 grams nickel nitrate dissolved in 300 milliliters ethyl ether. Use magnetic stirrer until completely dissolved.
Application:	• Spray the item lightly.
	• Air-dry the item.
	• Process and dry a second time.
	• Oven bake at 80-100°C at 65-percent humidity for 20 minutes.
Ninhydrin treated items:	• View under a forensic light source around 530 nanometers. A fluorescent color is not produced, but the absorbed light may yield better detail.

Nile Red (Lipid Stain)

Nile red stain reagent reacts to the fats and oils (lipids) present in the sebaceous components of latent prints. This can be fluoresced with an ALS.

Ninhydrin

Ninhydrin is an amino acid–developing reagent that is applied by dipping, brushing, or spraying. It may also be used as a blood enhancement technique.

Surface:	Porous surfaces, especially paper and cardboard	Visual examination ⬇ Forensic light ⬇ D.F.O. ⬇ Ninhydrin ⬇ Forensic Light ⬇ Zinc chloride/ physical developer
Development color:	Purple	
Ridge detail visualization:	Visible chemical/ stain reaction	
Shelf life:	12 months	

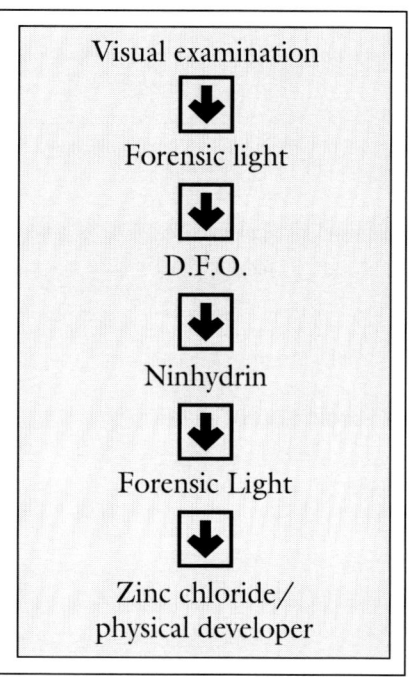

Developer solution:
- *Formula 1:*
  - —12.5 grams ninhydrin crystals dissolved in 1 liter of alcohol solvent
- *Formula 2 (Use a magnetic stirring device):*
  - —5 grams ninhydrin crystals dissolved in 30 milliliters methanol
  - —Add 40 milliliters 2-propanol
  - —Add 930 milliliters petroleum ether
- Or use any commercial spray unit.

Application:
- Tray immersion of item for 5 seconds.
- Brush solution onto item until coated.
- Spray solution on to the item until coated.
- Heat up to 80°C with a humidity exposure 60- to 70- percent relative humidity (or use a steam iron). Monitor for development.
- Photograph the developed detail using a green-colored filter.
- View under forensic light source.
- 530 to 555 nanometers (no filter)
- 490 to 505 nanometers (orange filter)
- 590 nanometers (red filter)

Use concerns:
- Not suited for nonporous surfaces or for items that have been water soaked.
- Surfaces with high animal or plant protein content, (e.g., leather, currency) produce extensive background development.

Phloxine B

A stain used to develop latents on dark or multicolored backgrounds.

Physical Developer

Physical developer is a silver nitrate–based reagent that reacts with the lipids in fingerprint residue. This is a multisolution, multistep process that can be used as a follow-up to ninhydrin cases. This is the technique of choice for paper currency items and porous items that may have been wet.

Surface:	Porous surfaces, especially currency and paper; effective on wet items	Visual examination ⬇ Forensic light ⬇ D.F.O. ⬇ Ninhydrin ⬇ Physical developer ⬇ Sodium hypochlorite
Development color:	Black	
Ridge detail visualization: reaction	Visible chemical/stain	
Shelf life:	Prepare as needed	

Developer solution:	Available as a single-stage premix for easy use and application
Maleic acid pre-wash:	50 grams maleic acid powder dissolved in 2 liters of distilled water
Commercial working solution:	1 part Solution A (5 milliliters/10 milliliters/15 milliliters) to 18 parts Solution B (90milliliters/180milliliters/270milliliters)
Application:	• Prewash (10 minutes) • Working solution (20 minutes) • Rinse (5 minutes)
Use concerns:	• Items that disintegrate in water solutions • Thermal fax papers, blueprints, and photostats with an alkalinity factor above pH 7 will become completely stained. • Items that cannot be effectively rinsed of the working solution • Do not process items that need to be submitted for questioned-document examination. • Use nonmetal tongs on examined items.

"RAM" Mixture

This fluorescent stain mixture of rhodamine 6 grams, ardrox, and M.B.D. is used with an ALS to enhance the cyanoacrylate development of latent prints.

Surface:	Nonporous surfaces
Development color:	Orange fluorescence
Ridge detail visualization:	Forensic light source induced
Shelf life:	1 month

Visual examination
⬇
Forensic light
⬇
Cyanoacrylate fuming
⬇
RAM
⬇
Forensic Light

Developer solution:
- *Rhodamine 6G stock solution:*
  —1 gram rhodamine 6G dissolved in 1 liter methanol
- *M.B.D. stock solution*
  —1 gra M.B.D. dissolved in 1 liter acetone
- *RAM working solution (combine in the order listed):*
  —3 millilers rhodamine stock solution
  —2 millilers ardrox P133D
  —7 millilers M.B.D. stock solution
  —20 millilers methanol
  —10 millilers isopropanol
  —8 millilers acetonitrile
  —950 millilers petroleum ether

Application:
- Spray, dip, or use a squirt bottle to apply RAM to the item.
- Examination under a laser or forensic light source at 415 to 530 nanometers. Absorption max is 460 nanometers. Use orange-colored goggles.
- Photograph results using orange barrier filter

Use concerns:
- Items that inherently fluoresce in the 555-nanometer range will interfere with the dye-stain fluorescence.
- A fluorescent light source that will output light between 415 and 530 nanometers is required for this process.

"R.A.Y." Mixture

This is a mixture consisting of basic red 28, ardrox, and basic yellow 40. It is used to fluoresce cyanoacrylate developed latents.

Surface:	Nonporous surfaces	Visual examination ↓ Forensic light ↓ Cyanoacrylate ↓ Rhodamine 6G ↓ Forensic light ↓ R.A.Y. ↓ Forensic light
Development color:	Orange fluorescence	
Ridge detail visualization:	Forensic light source induced	
Shelf life:	6 months	

Developer solution:
- *R.A.Y. working solution (combine in the order listed)*:
  —.5 gram basic yellow 40 dye
  —10 milliliters glacial acetic acid
  —.05 gram rhodamine 6 dye
  —4 milliliters ardrox P133D
  —450 milliliters isopropanol or denatured ethanol
  —40 milliliters acetonitrile

Application:
- Spray, dip, or use a squirt bottle to apply R.A.Y.
- Examination under a laser or forensic light source at 450 to 550 nanometers. Use orange- or red-colored goggles.
- Photograph results using orange or red barrier filter.

Use concerns:
- Items that inherently fluoresce in the 490- to 555-nanometer range will interfere with the dye-stain fluorescence.
- A fluorescent light source that will output light between 365 and 550 nanometers is required for this process.

Red-Yellow Mixture

This mixture of basic red 28 and basic yellow 40 provides a wide range of fluorescence with cyanoacrylate-developed latents.

Rhodamine 6G

One of the most popular and successful dyes used with cyanoacrylate-developed latents and a laser or forensic light source.

Surface:	Nonporous surfaces
Development color:	Orange fluorescence
Ridge detail visualization:	Forensic light source induced
Shelf life:	6 months

Visual examination
↓
Forensic light
↓
Cyanoacrylate
↓
Rhodamine 6G
↓
Forensic light
↓
RAM
↓
Forensic light

Developer solution:
- *Rhodamine 6G stock solution:*
  —1 gram rhodamine 6G dissolved in 1 liter methanol
- *Rhodamine working solution (combine in the order listed):*
  —3 milliliters rhodamine stock solution
  —15 milliliters acetone
  —10 milliliters acetonitrile
  —15 milliliters methanol
  —32 milliliters isopropanol
  —925 milliliters petroleum ether

Application:
- Spray, dip, or use a squirt bottle to apply the rhodamine solution to the item.
- Examination under a laser or forensic light source at 495 to 540 nanometers. Absorption max is at 525 nm. Use orange- or red-colored goggles.
- Allow the item to air-dry.
- Photograph results using an orange or bandpass 550 (BP35) barrier filter.

Use concerns:
- Items that inherently fluoresce in the 555-nanometer range will interfere with the dye-stain fluorescence.
- A fluorescent light source that will output light between 495 and 530 nanometers is required for this process.

Safranin O

A fluorescent dye-stain used to enhance cyanoacrylate-developed latent prints.

Surface:	Nonporous surfaces
Development color:	Yellow fluorescence
Ridge detail visualization:	Forensic light source induced
Shelf life:	Indefinite

Visual examination
⬇
Forensic light
⬇
Cyanoacrylate
⬇
Safranin O
⬇
Forensic light
⬇
RAM
⬇
Forensic light

Developer solution:
1 gram safranin O powder
1,000 millilitersl methanol
Combine the above and stir using a magnetic stirring device.

Application:
- Spray, immerse, or use a squirt bottle to apply the Safranin O solution to the item.
- Allow the item to air-dry.
- Examination under a laser or forensic light source around the 500-nanometer region. Use orange-colored goggles.
- Photograph results using an orange or bandpass 550 (BP35) barrier filter.

Use concerns:
- Items that inherently fluoresce around the 500-nanometer range will interfere with the dye-stain fluorescence.
- A fluorescent light source that will output light around 500 nanometers is required for this process.

Silver Nitrate

The technique works on wood surfaces that have not been treated with wax or varnish finishes. This process uses sunlight to develop the ridge detail treated with the working solution. Because background staining may be a problem with this process, this technique is not in wide use.

Surface:	Porous surfaces (wood) that have not been wet	Visual examination ⬇ Forensic light ⬇ Ninhydrin ⬇ Silver nitrate ⬇ Ultraviolet light
Development color:	Brown	
Ridge detail visualization:	Visible chemical reaction	
Shelf life:	12 months	

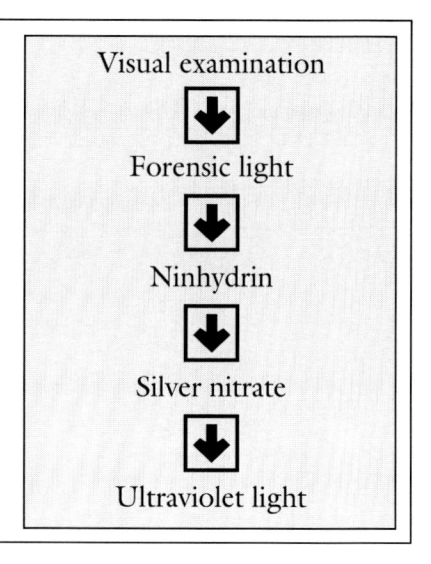

Developer solution:
- *Formula "A" (1.0-percent solution):*
  —1 gram silver nitrate
  —100 milliliters distilled water
- *Formula "B" (3.0-percent solution):*
  —30 grams silver nitrate
  —1,000 milliliters distilled water
- *Formula "C" (alcohol-based solution):*
  —30 grams silver nitrate
  —100 milliliters distilled water
  —1,000 milliliters ethanol

Application:
- Tray immersion of item for 5 seconds
- Reagent solution brushed on to item until coated
- Air-dry for 20 minutes
- Sunlight or ultraviolet light exposure at 366 nanometers for 10 to 60 minutes. Continuously monitor for development.

Use concerns:
- Items that have been wetted may be leached of their chloride and salt impressions.
- Surfaces that have high chloride or salt compounds coating their surfaces or imbedded in them will produce unacceptable background staining.

Small-Particle Reagent

Small-particle reagent is a technique used in developing fingerprints on wet, oily, and textured surfaces. This process is used on items where latent print powders have been proven to be ineffective. This reagent can effectively work on items that have been soaked in liquid accelerants.

Surface:	Nonporous surfaces; effective on wet items	Visual examination ⬇ Forensic light ⬇ Sudan black ⬇ SPR ⬇ Forensic light ⬇ Physical developer
Development color:	Dark gray	
Ridge detail visualization:	Visible chemical stain reaction	
Shelf life:	Indefinite.	

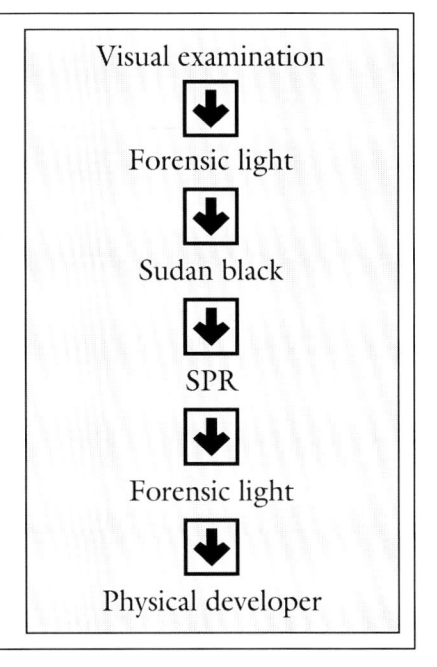

Developer solution:
- *Solution 1:*
  - —4 grams choline chloride
  - —8 milliliters tergitol 7
  - —500 milliliters distilled water and stir
- *Solution 2:*
  - —10 grams molybdenum disulfide
  - —50 milliliters of Solution 1 and stir
- *Solution 3:*
  - —Add 900 milliliters distilled water to Solution 2 and stir.
- Or combine the following into a suspension:
  - —0.4 milliliters tergitol (detergent)
  - —5 grams molybdenum disulfide
  - —50 milliliters distilled water
- Also available in white or black in 10-vial packs or as a premixed solution.

Application: The contents of the vial are mixed in a spray bottle with 6 ounces of water. The mixture is shaken and sprayed as a gentle mist over the area that is being processed. After the print is seen developing, the area should be rinsed with plain water to clean away the excess.

- *Tray immersion:*
  - —Keep stationary for 1 minute.
- *Squeegee bottle application:*
  - —Shake well and apply. Repeat for 1 minute.
  - —Tray rinse excess reagent in tap water for 15 seconds or

rinse under running tap water for 15 seconds.
—Allow the item to dry at room temperature.
—Photograph any developed detail and then try lifting the dried print.

Use concerns:
- Porous surfaces and items that disintegrate in water solutions.
- Items that cannot be effectively rinsed of the working solution.
- This technique requires a large work area that will be subject to messy conditions.

Sticky-Side Powder

The reagent is prepared as a paste and then is brushed on to the adhesive sides of tape surfaces. This reagent is considered to be a more economical alternative to other adhesive-tape processing methods. Cyanoacrylate fuming does not inhibit the use of this reagent.

Surface:	Tape surfaces
Development color:	Gray
Ridge detail visualization:	Visible chemical/stain reaction
Shelf life:	Prepare as needed.

Visual examination
⬇
Forensic light
⬇
Gentian violet
⬇
Sticky-side powder
⬇
Forensic light

Developer solution:
- Place 1 teaspoon of powder in a shallow jar or mixing bowl.
- Equal parts of Photo-Flo and water are mixed with the powder to form a paste.

Application:
- Brush this mixture with a camel hair brush onto the tape's adhesive surface.
- Wait 30 to 60 seconds.
- Rinse under a gentle stream of cold tap water.
- Allow tape to air-dry.
- Photograph any developed ridge detail.

Use concerns:
- Some tapes and adhesive labels absorb the paste too readily and cannot be rinsed of excess paste.

Sudan Black

A dye-stain technique for use on wet items, Sudan black is considered less sensitive than other wet-item techniques in use. Sudan black is considered useful for those wetted items whose surfaces are contaminated with substances such as grease, beverages, and foodstuffs.

Surface:	Wet, nonporous, and grease-contaminated surfaces
Development color:	Dark blue
Ridge detail visualization:	Visible chemical/stain reaction
Shelf life:	Indefinite

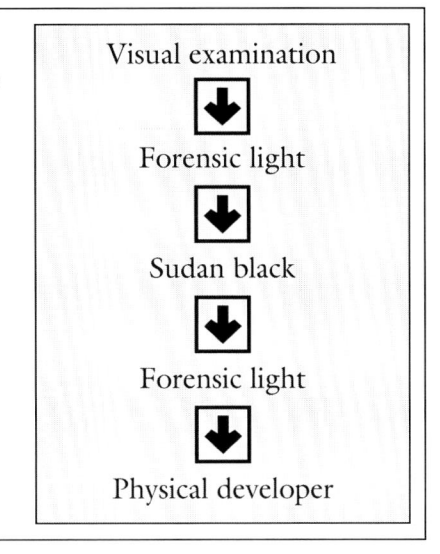

Visual examination
⬇
Forensic light
⬇
Sudan black
⬇
Forensic light
⬇
Physical developer

Developer solution:	• Add 15 grams Sudan black powder dissolved in 1,000 milliliters ethanol and then stir with 500 milliliters distilled water. • Also available as a ready-to-use premixed liquid
Application:	• Immerse in working solution for 2 minutes. • Cold tap water rinse—remove excess dye • Dry item at room temperature
Use concerns:	• Porous items and dark-colored items do not process well with this technique.

Tetramethylbenzidine (TMB)

TMB is used in enhancing ridge detail in blood on porous surfaces.

Developer solution:	• *Acetate buffer:* —Dissolve 10 grams of sodium acetate with 86 milliliters glacial acetic acid. —Add 100 milliliters distilled water. • *Tetrylmethylbenzidine:* —Dissolve 1 gram TMB 3, 3', 5.5' into 50 milliliter acetate buffer. —Thoroughly mix for 5 minutes and then filter solution to remove undissolved particles. • *Collodian-ethanol-ether solution:* —Mix 150 milliliters collodian with 75 milliliters methanol. —Let stand for 5 minutes. —Add slowly while stirring constantly with 600 milliliters ethyl ether.

- *TMB spray reagent:*
  —Mix 1 gram sodium perborate with 12 milliliters TMB/acetate buffer solution.
  —Add 240 milliliters collodian-ethanol-ether solution.
  —Mix well.
  —Spray is ready for use.

Thenoyle Europium Chelate (TEC)

TEC is a fluorescent dye-stain used to enhance cyanoacrylate-developed latent prints. It is used because it produces a brighter fluorescence of ridge detail with less interfering background luminescence.

Surface:	Nonporous surfaces
Development color:	Yellow fluorescence
Ridge detail visualization:	Ultraviolet light induced
Shelf life:	3 months

Visual examination
⬇
Forensic light
⬇
Cyanoacrylate fuming
⬇
TEC
⬇
Ultraviolet lamp
⬇
R.A.Y.
⬇
Forensic light

Developer solution:
- *Stock Solution A:*
  —1 gram thenoyltrifluoroacetone dissolved in 200 milliliters of methyl ethyl ketone
- *Stock Solution B:*
  —0.5 gram europium chloride hexahydrate dissolved in 800 milliliters of distilled water
- *Thenoyl europium chelate working solution (combine in the order listed):*
  —Combine stock Solutions A and B.
  —Mix:
    100 milliliters combined stock solutions
    180 milliliters methyl ethyl ketone
    720 milliliters distilled water

Application:	• Immerse or use a squirt bottle to apply the reagent for about 2 minutes. • Allow the item to air-dry. • Examine under a laser or forensic light source at the long-wave UV region around 350 nanometers. View using UV protection goggles. • Photograph results using a red-colored or 600 (BP 35) bandpass filter.
Use concerns:	• A fluorescent light source that will output light in the long-wave UV region (around 350 nanometers) is required for this process.

Ultraviolet Examination

A nondestructive technique to identify the presence of ridge detail on surface material. Several models of UV light sources are available that produce short-wave and long-wave (or both) lights.

Surface:	All surface types (nondestructive)
Ridge detail visualization:	UV light induced
Uses:	• Fluorescing fingerprint powders • UV-sensitive dye-stains • Skin tissue examination • Darkens blood impressions • Fluorescing fluids for refrigerants, transmissions, fuels, and coolants • Luminesces backgrounds for contrast improvement

Centered wavelengths:	• Short-wave
	  —180 to 280 nanometers viewing
	  —Oily, sweaty, and contaminated ridge detail viewing
	  —Luminol excitation
	• Medium-wave
	  —280 to 320 nm viewing
	  —Bruises, bitemarks, and wounds viewing
	• Long-wave
	  —320 to 400 nanometers viewing
	  —Used for excitation of dye-stains (ardrox, basic yellow 40, and TEC)
	  —Fluoresces many natural and man-made substances

Application:	• Wear UV-absorbing protective eye wear. • Reduce ambient light. • Aim the UV light. • Photograph detail using yellow or 2-A haze barrier filters.
Use concerns:	• Items that inherently luminesce in the UV region may interfere with dye-stain contrast.

Visual Examination

A nondestructive technique to note the presence of visible detail. Natural and artificial sources of light, as well as angles of light may be used in order to visualize any detail that is present.

Surface: Nondestructive for all surfaces

Ridge detail visualized: Visible stain

Application:
- Simple ambient light
- Absorbed light (filter out background color)
- Reflected light
- For greasy impressions
- Directed light
- To subdue surface texture
- Oblique light
- For dust impressions and enhancing texture
- Transmitted light
- On transparent surfaces

Zinc Chloride

Zinc chloride is applied as post-ninhydrin and post-1, 2-Indandione treatments to improve the strength of the fluorescence of the ridge detail for viewing and photography.

Surface: Porous surfaces

Development color: Orange fluorescence

Ridge detail visualization: Forensic light source induced

Shelf life: 6 months

```
Visual examination
      ↓
 Forensic light
      ↓
     DFO
      ↓
Ninhydrin/ 5-MTN
      ↓
 Zinc chloride
      ↓
 Forensic light
```

Developer solution:
- 30 grams zinc chloride dissolved in 500 milliliters methyl-tert-butylether (MTBE)
- 20 milliliters of anhydrous ethanol
- Use magnetic stirrer until completely dissolved.
- Dissolution may be slow.
- Add 10 milliliters glacial acetic acid.
- Dilute with 500 milliliters petroleum ether.

Application:
- Spray the item lightly.
- Air-dry the item.
- Process and dry a second time.
- Oven bake at 80 to 100°C at 65-percent humidity for 20 minutes.

Ninhydrin- and 5-MTN-treated items:
- View under a forensic light source 450 to 530 nanometers.
- Use orange- or red-colored goggles.
- Photograph results using a orange-colored or 550 (BP 35) bandpass filter.

1.2-Indanedione-treated items:
- View under a forensic light source around 530 nanometers. Use orange-colored goggles.
- Photograph results using a red-colored or 600 (BP 35) bandpass filter.

FINGERPRINT DEFINITION

1) A fingerprint is an impression of the ridge detail of the underside of the fingers, palms of hands, toes, or soles of the feet.

2) There are two types of fingerprints:
   a) Direct or inked fingerprint
      i) An impression made of the ridge detail by using ink, powder, or some other material.
   b) Latent print
      i) An impression of a portion of the ridge detail left on an object. The impression is caused by perspiration being deposited onto the ridges through the sweat pores of the fingers.
      ii) Latents can also result when the ridges become soiled through contact with such materials as blood, oil, dirt, grease, etc.

FINGERPRINTS AS PHYSICAL EVIDENCE

1) Fingerprints are probably the most valuable form of physical evidence.

2) Fingerprints can positively prove an individual was present at a particular location.
   a) Identification by fingerprints works on the premise that no two fingerprints are exactly alike even among the fingers of the same person or involving identical twins.
   b) An individual's fingerprint has never been known to change. This premise is interpreted to mean that an individual's prints are a permanent record of an individual that will last a lifetime. Based on this information, identification systems involving the interpretation of fingerprints can be established categorizing fingerprints based on fingerprint characteristics.

3) Fingerprints are filed based on a system of common characteristics. This allows fingerprints to be accessed for comparison purposes.
   a) During the past few years, computer-assisted accessing of prints through the

Automated Fingerprint Identification Systems (AFIS) has completely revolutionized crime-scene investigation and identification and has underlined the importance of crime-scene preservation, crime-scene processing, and improved technology relative to the processing of articles for the development of latent prints.

FINGERPRINT PROCESSING CHEMISTRY

1) Previous processing of prints usually involved using white powder on dark surfaces and dark powder on light surfaces.

2) The first technological breakthrough in fingerprint processing began with the use of superglue fuming.

3) The first forensic light source involved the use of laser light technology. The first fingerprint lasers were expensive and cumbersome, so it was not usually possible to bring them to the scene.

4) The development of ALS allowed for portable light sources to be brought to crime scenes. The ALS was also much cheaper than a laser light source and permitted examination of a scene or evidence related to a scene using different wave-length sources.

5) The convenience of ALS and the added capabilities of locating latent prints on items at the scene through this improved technology were brought about largely through the development and use of AFIS. With the ability to identify the depositor of a print found at a crime scene through a search of a database system, forensic specialists have been searching for more improved and consistent methods of recovering latent prints.
    a) Such stains as rhodamine were used to further enhance the latent print.
    b) Powders that luminesce under various forensic light sourcesare now catalogued by major crime-scene-equipment suppliers. Magnetic powders are available as well as brush powders. A variety of colors allows the technician to select the best powder, producing the maximum amount of contrast.
        i) There is currently a bichromatic powder available that will appear light on a dark surface and dark on a light surface.
    c) Innovative technicians have used silicone rubber, dental material, and even Silly Putty to recover prints from curved surfaces.

TYPES OF PRINTS

1) Visible (patent) prints. There are two different types of prints that are considered visible and may not require further development.
    a) A transfer print created when the subject's prints have come into contact with items such as blood, ink, paint, etc., and is deposited onto a surface
        i) Although the print is visible, processing techniques may be employed to further enhance the visibility of the print. Process as follows:
            (1) The print should be photographed prior to any attempt at enhancing it. A photograph should be made with and without a ruler present.
            (2) On a notepad, indicate the case number, date, and location from which the print was photographed. Write sufficient information to assist you in remembering in court (e.g., front

of dresser drawer, outside of window entry).
- (3) If feasible, cut out or otherwise remove the section containing the print. Package, preserve, and send this item to the crime lab for further processing.
- (4) Bloody prints may be further enhanced through the use of the following chemicals:
    - (a) Luminol
    - (b) Ninhydrin
    - (c) Benzidine
    - (d) Tetra methyl benzidine
    - (e) Ortho tolidine
    - (f) Leuconalachite green
    - (g) Phenolphthalein
    - (h) Amido black 10b. This is the recommended process for the following reasons:
        - (i) It does not destroy or damage the print.
        - (ii) It can be used on cloth, paper, or a nonporous surface.
        - (iii) It remains stable after treatment.

b) Impression type (plastic) prints made when the suspect has come in contact with a soft, impressionable object, such as putty, mud, fresh paint, or clay
  i) Processing techniques
   - (1) Photograph the impression with and without a ruler present.
   - (2) If possible, cut out or otherwise remove the section containing the impression involving a print.
       - (a) If transporting the object containing the imprint is not possible, prepare a cast of the object using dental silicone.

2) Nonvisible (latent) prints are fingerprints left on a surface of an item touched or walked on by an individual. The print is a result of perspiration being deposited onto the ridges of the fingers or palms of the hands or soles and toes of the feet.
  a) Latent fingerprint-lifting techniques involving objects
    i) Powder processing involving dry surfaces
     - (1) Barely insert the ends of the brush into the powder, applying the powder to the brush using a rotary motion. Shake or tap off the excess powder into the powder container.
     - (2) Gently apply the brush to the suspected surface until the fingerprint begins to develop. Work the brush in the same direction as the surface grain.
     - (3) As the fingerprint pattern appears, follow the contour of the ridges. Rid the fingerprint of excess powder by gently brushing or blowing. Too much pressure with the brush can erase the fingerprint.
     - (4) Carefully apply a strip of lifting tape over the developed fingerprint using an index finger or a roller. Put the tape down over the fingerprint from one side to the other, making sure no bubbles or creases appear.
     - (5) One end of the tape should be folded under to minimize the risk of placing your own fingerprints on the adhesive side of the tape.

(6) When applying tape to a print involving a large area of print (palm or entire hand), apply several strips of tape, overlapping them slightly as you lay them down on top of the print. Keep the size of the intended backing card in mind. Also, run your fingernail along the overlaps to get all of the fingerprint detail. To facilitate lifting several side-by-side strips of tape, place a strip of tape at one end and perpendicular to the other strips. This will help hold the strips of tape together during lifting.

(7) As you lift the folded-under end of the tape, be careful not to let the adhesive surface of the tape roll together from the sides or the ends. To help in preventing this from happening, as you lift the tape, push your thumb down on the tape and push up on the tape with the index and middle fingers of your hand.

(8) Place the tape down on the shiny side of the backing card, working the tape from one side to the other. Once again, you have to apply pressure with your index finger, being careful not to crease the tape or allow bubbles to get under the tape.

(9) Tear off the folded end of the tape and check that the edges of the tape are secure on the backing. The result will be similar to a photograph.

(10) On the reverse (dull) side of the backing card, print the departmental case number, date, initials, and location from which the latent was lifted. Give enough information to assist you in recalling (if the lift is to be used in court) the location from which the lift was recovered (e.g., front of dresser, outside of entry window, inside rear-view mirror). Indicating whether the latent was on the outside or inside of a scene or object may be critical to the case.

    (a) In some cases it is advisable to indicate with an arrow the direction of the print as you observed it. You may be able to determine if it appeared that the hand, palm, or fingers were going up or down a wall or in an entry or exit direction.

    (b) It is acceptable to indicate the direction of the print as observed, but never indicate one latent as being from a particular finger unless you are a qualified fingerprint examiner.

(11) If the dusted surface is not flat and is less than desirable (e.g., a round doorknob, a wood-grained rough surface), then photograph the developed latent print prior to attempting to lift it with tape. Place a small ruler next to the print indicating case number, date, and initials. Consider using a silicone cast of the area, since the fingerprint powder will adhere to the silicone material.

(12) Paper products should be taken to the crime lab for spraying with a ninhydrin.

ii) LASER processing of evidence

  (1) Depending on the portability of the involved laser unit and the experience of the technicians, items can be examined at the scene or transported to the crime laboratory. In addition,

decedents may be examined for latent fingerprints prior to autopsy examination while at the morgue.
- (2) Laser processing is possible as a result of certain chemical compounds present in sweat and having a natural fluorescent ability. The argon-ion laser light has the ability to emit light at the wavelength that causes fingerprint residue to luminesce.
- (3) This is used as a complement to regular processing techniques, and normally used to process prints that go undetectable through conventional processing, for example:
  - (a) Latents on the inside of a glove
  - (b) Styrofoam cup
  - (c) Metal surfaces (painted and unpainted)
  - (d) Plastic bags
  - (e) Vinyl
  - (f) Tapes, including duct, black electrical, and Scotch
  - (g) Human skin
  - (h) Paper towel
- (4) Advantages to laser processing of latent prints include:
  - (a) Laser detection is a nondestructive method. other development procedures can still be used if laser detection is unsuccessful.
  - (b) Fingerprints exposed to extremes in temperature and moisture, at least on certain surfaces, remain amenable to laser detection.
  - (c) Processing by other methods does not necessarily preclude the use of laser detection.
  - (d) Fingerprint age does not preclude the applicability of the laser detection procedures.

iii) Superglue fuming
- (1) Vapors of glue containing cyanoacrylate ester produce a white polymer on ridges of latent fingerprints.
- (2) This fuming is generally used on smooth surfaces.

iv) Iodide fuming
- (1) Iodine crystals are heated, slightly producing violet fumes, which are absorbed by the fatty or oily matter that may be present on latent prints.
- (2) This fuming is used to develop latent prints on paper, cardboard, unpainted wood, or other absorbent surfaces.

v) Silver nitrate treatment
- (1) Works through the reaction of silver nitrate with sodium chloride (common table salt) present in the perspiration that forms the ridges of latent prints.
- (2) This fuming is used to develop latent prints on paper, cardboard, unpainted wood, or other absorbent surfaces.

vi) Ninhydrin method
- (1) This method works because ninhydrin reacts to amino acids present in perspiration.
- (2) It is very effective on porous surfaces, such as paper

vii) Dye-staining
- (1) The dye stains epithelial cells present in latent fingerprints.

(2) Dye-staining is used to develop latent prints on the sticky surfaces of almost any kind of adhesive tapes, plastics, cans, etc.
viii) Vacuum metal deposition (VMD)
(1) This is often considered the superior technology in the recovery of latent prints. It may develop prints on objects where no other technology can.
(a) The prints are often higher in quality with greater definition when compared to other techniques.
(b) The process is effective with aqueous and sebaceous materials normally found in prints. This makes the VMD process preferred on old evidence or new evidence.
(2) It is an expensive system, and there are very few crime labs that offer this service to law enforcement agencies.
(a) The amount of gold used in a constantly run system amounts to only about $10 a year.
(3) VMD is a process in which several metals are evaporated onto the evidence while under vacuum. Only a small amount of metal is necessary, and the results are quick with no resulting damage to the rest of the evidence.
(a) Disturbances in the physical and chemical nature of the surface are revealed by different rates of growth of the zinc metal film.
(b) Fingerprints appear either as a positive or negative image in a gray film of metallic zinc.
(c) The process itself only takes about 15 minutes to run the evidence.
(d) System operation is mostly automated, making it easy to use and ensuring high-quality results.
(i) Everything needed to operate the system can be learned in just a few hours.
(4) Larger items, too big to fit within the chamber can be folded, disassembled, or cut into smaller pieces if necessary.
(5) The process is very sensitive and can detect monolayers of fats on smooth surfaces.
(6) It is most commonly used on plastic packaging films, particularly polythene (e.g., trash and sandwich bags), but it is also effective on many other types of smooth, nonporous surfaces.
(a) It has also been successfully used with evidence that is multicolored, such as orange juice or milk cartons.
(b) It works on the following surfaces:
(i) Fine-weave (smooth) fabrics, such as synthetic panties, windbreaker fabric, etc.
(ii) Smooth leather surfaces
(iii) Photographic negatives and prints
(iv) Plastic moldings
(v) Glass
(vi) Smooth paper
(c) It will work on surfaces that were wet or may have been previously processed using some other technique.

(7) In tests conducted by the Royal Canadian Mounted Police, VMD was compared to other fingerprint-developing processes with the following results:
- (a) It developed 100 percent more fingerprints than humidity-controlled Superglue
- (b) It developed 12 percent more marks than Superglue, dye-staining, and fluorescence.
- (c) It developed 15 percent more marks than vacuum superglue, dye-staining, and fluorescence on 7-day-old evidence.
- (d) It developed 70 percent more marks than vacuum superglue, dye-staining, and fluorescence in 1-month-old evidence.
- (e) It developed 100 percent more marks than small-particle reagent (SPR).
- (f) It developed identifiable marks on 60 percent of articles processed.

LOCATING FINGERPRINTS

1) At the indoor scene
   a) Before processing, the technician should meet with all responsible investigating agencies to develop an initial, rough formation of a theory of what may have happened at the scene. An initial walk-through, if it can be done without contaminating the scene, may be most beneficial to the group if handled by the person responsible for the processing of the scene.
   b) Begin with the outdoor location. Are there any indications of the suspect's watching this location from afar? Are there any discarded bottles, cans, bags, etc., at this location? Are there any areas in which the suspect may have come in contact with from this vantage point?
   c) Point of entry. Process thoroughly the area where the suspect entered the facility.
      i) Process any item the suspect may have had to move in gaining access to this area. For example, if the suspect entered the residence through a bathroom window, were items such as shampoo or deodorant cans moved from his path?
      ii) Consider any areas the suspect may have had to grab hold of in an effort to gain access. Process these areas.
      iii) Process any other areas where the suspect may have tried to enter but had his efforts cut short.
   d) Follow the path the suspect appeared to have taken as he traveled through the facility.
      i) Process any article obviously displaced, such as overturned furniture, papers, dropped articles, etc.
   e) Determine the initial location of contact between the suspect and the victim. Follow this area to the location of the decedent. Consider what may have been touched, especially if a struggle took place.
      i) If bloodletting has occurred, be especially diligent in looking for prints made after contact with the blood, especially in surrounding objects.
   f) Examine the body. Look for any prints that may have been left on the body by someone with soiled hands, especially where bloodletting occurred.

i) If the decedent appears to have been dragged or carried, examine the body carefully for latent prints. (The generally accepted time frame for recovering latent prints from bodies is up to 12 to 14 hours from death.)

g) Any articles on or around the body should be evaluated for potential patent or latent prints.
    i) Check eyeglasses, purse, watch, and other personal items of the involved parties that may have been touched during the event.

h) Continue tracing the suspect's possible activities after the homicide was committed.
    i) If ransacking or other indications of theft occurred, process the items, articles, and areas associated with this particular activity.
    ii) If cleanup has occurred, process the items, articles, and areas associated with this activity.
        (1) Such articles as paper towels have the potential to harbor latent prints, and processing may be possible.
        (2) All faucet knobs
        (3) Underside of toilet seat
        (4) Side of bathtub, side and top of vanity, and area of the wall adjacent to the toilet

i) Determine the point of exit for the subject and process this area thoroughly, including:
    (1) Knobs
    (2) Handles
    (3) A djacent glass areas and frames

2) In vehicles
    a) All vehicles should be completely processed.
    b) There may be occasions where it would be advantageous to have the vehicle towed to the crime lab for complete processing.
    c) The vehicle should be completely dry before processing commences.
    d) Gloves should be worn at all times during the handling and processing of the vehicle.
    e) When possible, photograph all latent prints before lifting them.
    f) Record the exact time, date, and location of the vehicle's discovery, as well as who conducted the examination.
        i) Record the license number, vehicle identification number, type, model, year, and color of vehicle.
    g) Examine initially the door handles for latent prints.
        i) Visible latent prints on a shiny door handle should be photographed before they are powdered. Use light from an oblique angle to highlight the ridge detail of the latent. After photographing, powder and lift the prints.
    h) After door handles have been examined and processed, open the doors to the vehicle and check for service station stickers. This may provide a clue as to whether the car was stolen and the owner is unknown and where the vehicle may have originated.
    i) Photograph the interior of the vehicle from each side. Record mileage.
    j) Process the exterior nonporous surfaces for latents:
        i) Side-view mirror

ii) All outside glass areas
iii) License plates
iv) All exterior painted surfaces of the car, including the roof, trunk, doors, hood and hood release, etc.
v) Check the engine. If it has been tampered with, the air cleaner and other areas may have been touched. Be observant for visible prints in grease or oil in the engine area.

k) Process the interior nonporous surfaces:
i) Front and back of rear-view mirror and any visor mirror (detach the rear-view mirror before processing)
ii) Seat adjustment and seat belt buckles
iii) Bottom of armrest
iv) Steering wheel and gear shift handle
v) All interior glass areas
vi) Push buttons on radio (note station set of radio)
vii) Door and window handles
viii) Dash, including light knob, cigarette lighter knob, ashtray, and glove compartment button
ix) Tape deck, ham or citizen's band radio

l) Continue processing by searching the exterior and interior of the vehicle for any items located in the following areas. (NOTE: Maintain a search log to indicate what was found, who found the items, and where they were recovered.)
i) Above the sun visor
ii) Under the seats
iii) Trunk of vehicle
iv) Glove compartment and the shelf under the dash
v) Engine area (under the battery)
vi) Inside the hubcaps
vii) Cigarette butts from ashtray
viii) Seat belt holder
ix) Hollow windshield wiper area in front of and below windshield
x) Magnetic box attached to the frame of the vehicle
xi) Inside the heater hose
xii) Under floor mats
xiii) Under the horn, button, or steering wheel column
xiv) Be observant for any road maps, envelopes, and other paper specimens strewn inside the vehicle.

3) On the decedent's body (see Chapter 2)
a) Magna Brush technique
i) Do not handle exposed areas of skin on the decedent.
ii) Do not refrigerate the body.
iii) Examine the body using a very bright light source and a magnifying glass.
iv) On suspected areas, apply the Magna Brush technique using MacDonell Magna Jet Black Powder.
v) If ridge details develop, it is necessary to photograph the latent. The most consuming problem is finding the correct angle to set the light source to bring out the ridge detail of the latent print.

(1) The light source should be placed at an oblique angle relative to the print.
(2) A tungsten light source should be used.
(3) Because tonal separation is critical to having a photographic reproduction of the latent that is readable, color film, not black and white, must be used.
(4) Standard fingerprint lifting tape should then be applied, and the latent lifted and placed on a white backing card.

b) Argon-ion laser technique
   i) Do not handle exposed areas of the body.
   ii) Ideally, the body can be examined at the scene with a portable unit prior to transporting the remains.
   iii) Examine the body with the laser light. Concentrate on areas where the suspect may have found it necessary to handle the decedent.

FINGERPRINT PRECAUTIONS

1) The use of powders and chemicals may interfere with physical and chemical analysis, particularly in the case of blood, hairs, fibers, and documents. Therefore, fingerprint processing on items that have materials adhering to their surfaces or that require further examinations should not be done at the scene. These items should be forwarded to the crime laboratory.

2) Cotton or cloth should never be placed in direct contact with any nonporous surfaces bearing latent prints.

3) Crime-scene fingerprints are delicate. Examination and processing should take place as quickly as possible.

FINGERPRINTING THE DECEDENT

1) Identification of the decedent
   a) All decedents brought into a medical examiner facility should be fingerprinted. This will become a permanent record for this individual regardless of the disposition of the remains.
      i) An extra copy of the print should be completed and submitted to the local law enforcement agency, which should complete a records check at the local, state, and national level. Forwarding this print may be required for processing purposes. Correct handling ensures that outstanding capiases and warrants will be canceled and proper notification will made of all involved agencies.
   b) If decedent is unidentified and recently dead:
      i) Prepare four sets of fingerprints. Place one set of fingerprints in the file and submit a set to the local law enforcement agency, the state law enforcement agency, and the FBI's Identification Section for classification and search purposes.
   c) If the decedent is decomposing and it is believed that acquiring his prints may pose a challenge, do the following:
      i) Glove formation
         (1) Peel gloves. Be extremely cautious in placing the correct gloves of the fingers in the carefully marked individual plastic or glass containers. Submit them to the crime lab before the gloves begin to dry.

ii) Dried-out digits
- (1) If the case is one in which major case prints need to be collected because of the nature of the homicide, the hands should be severed and transferred to the crime lab.
- (2) If the case is not a homicide and is strictly a matter of identification, the fingers of the hand should be amputated and placed in individual plastic or glass containers properly marked for each individual finger.

2) Proper taking of fingerprints for fingerprint cards involving decedents
- a) Fill out the fingerprint card in detail.
    - i) Under the signature of the person fingerprinted enter "Deceased."
    - ii) Final disposition should be completed with "Deceased."
    - iii) If identifying information is not known when completing the card, note this. If the date of birth is not known, indicate an approximate age, if possible, but be sure to note that this is an approximation.
- b) After the pathologist has examined the hands of the decedent, the hands and fingers should be thoroughly cleaned in preparation for obtaining the prints.
- c) Make a test impression on a scrap of paper to obtain the proper ink density.
- d) If the decedent is in rigor mortis, rigor must be broken. Bending the hand at the wrist should flex open the hand, allowing access to the fingers.
- e) A self-adhesive print strip involving fingers 1 through 5 and a second strip involving fingers 6 through 10 will facilitate obtaining the prints. A spoon can be used to obtain the prints on the strips before placing them on the card. The print should include the ridge detail from one edge of the fingernail to the other side of the fingernail. Please keep in mind that if a spoon is used to obtain the print, the finger must be large enough to not only touch the face of the spoon but must also make contact with the sides of the spoon. If a spoon cannot be used, the finger being printed must be rolled exactly as a suspect print is taken.

3) Major case prints
- a) Often, latent prints found at the scene or developed on articles removed from the scene involve areas of the palms, second and third joints of the fingers, and the extreme finger sides and tip that are not present on the average set of fingerprints taken for routine purposes.
- b) The recording of all friction ridges present on the fingers and palms is referred to as "major case prints." They are obtained on major cases.
- c) The taking of major case prints should not be restricted to suspects only. For elimination purposes major case prints should be obtained from all persons who may have legitimately or inadvertently touched areas or items associated with the scene.
- d) Major case prints can be obtained with regular ink or with fingerprint powder, tape, and a sheet of acetate. If powder is used, a conscious effort must be made to place the tape containing the ridge detail on the underside of the acetate.
- e) Start the process by thoroughly cleaning the subject's hands. The prints should be recorded in the same sequence as the fingers appear on the fingerprint card.
- f) Beginning with the right thumb, completely powder the entire ridge area of the thumb. Take the tape and wrap the tape around the finger. Remove the tape and place it on the underside of the acetate sheet. Do this procedure with each finger.

g) Powder the entire ridge detail of the palm, including the side. Place the tape over this area of the hand and lift. Place this tape on the underside of the acetate sheet. Repeat this process on the other hand.

h) On the outer facing of the acetate sheet, label all fingers and left and right palm, and enter the same information that appears on a fingerprint card.

LIMITATION OF FINGERPRINTS

1) It is not possible to determine how long the latent print has been deposited on a particular surface.

   NOTE: It may be possible, from an investigative standpoint, to develop the age of a print relative to when an incident, such as cleaning, took place.

2) It is not possible to distinguish the age, race, or sex of the person who has left the latent print.

3) Conclusions about the occupation of the person leaving the print are purely conjecture.

BASIS OF FINGERPRINT IDENTIFICATION

1) Fingerprint classification
    a) There are three major classifications of fingerprints, each with subclassifications:
        i) Arch (does not contain any deltas)
            (1) Plain arch
            (2) Tented arch

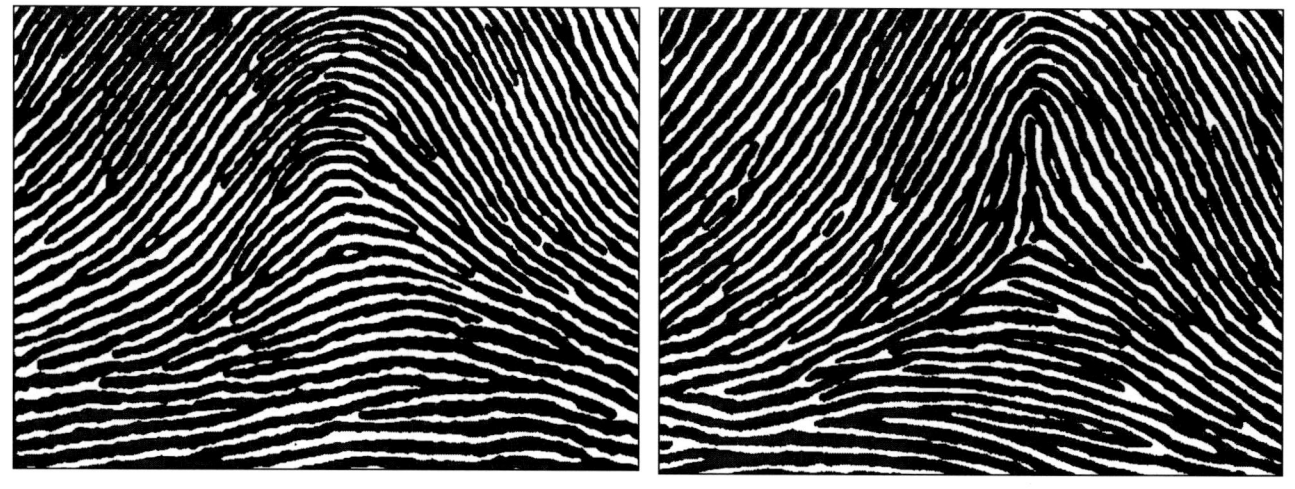

Plain arch.

Tented arch.

ii) Loop (contains a delta)
    (1) Ulnar loop (toward the baby finger)
    (2) Radial loop (toward the thumb)
iii) Whorl (contains two deltas with a recurve in front of each)

Radial loop.

Ulnar loop.

(1) Plain whorl
    (a) At least one ridge must make a complete circuit.
    (b) An imaginary line drawn between the two deltas must touch or cross at least one of the recurving ridges within the inner pattern area.

Central pocket loop

Plain whorl

(2) Central pocket loop
    (a) At least one ridge that makes or tends to make a complete circuit
    (b) An imaginary line drawn between the two deltas must not touch or cross any of the recurring ridges in the inner pattern area.
(3) Double loop
    (a) The double loop consists of two separate loop formations, with two separate and distinct sets of shoulders.
(4) Accidental whorl
    (a) The accidental whorl is a pattern consisting of a

Double loop.   Accidental.

                 combination of two different types of pattern, with the exception of the plain arch.
               (b) A pattern that possesses some of the requirements for two or more different types.
               (c) A pattern that conforms to none of the definitions.

2)   Identification by fingerprints
        a) Comparing the ridge detail of fingerprints is the basis for fingerprint identification. Specifically:
             i) Ridge details include ends of ridges, ridge separations, and the relationship of one ridge with another.
        b) Most experts require between 10 and 12 points of similarity, although there is no set number.
        c) Positive identification is not a consideration if even one unexplainable discrepancy is found.

3)   Other areas of identification
        a) There is a common but incorrect assumption about the identification of fingerprints. Points of comparison are not limited to the pattern area of the finger; they can also be found on the following areas:
             i) The first and second joints of the finger
             ii) The entire palm of the hand
             iii) Ridge surfaces, involving the toes
             iv) The entire soles of the feet

4)   Print size requirement
        a) Positive identification of a fingerprint is not contingent on any preset requirement for the size of the recovered print.
             i) The latent must contain enough detail to include 10 or 12 points of comparison.
        b) As a general rule, if the latent print appears to have several ridges visible, regardless of the size of the print, the investigator or technician should make an effort to lift the print.

AUTOMATED FINGERPRINT IDENTIFICATION SYSTEMS

1) AFIS makes blind searches. It has no idea of whom you may be looking to identify when a latent is entered.

IDENTIFICATION BY FINGERPRINTS

1) The first step in the identification of fingerprints involves classifying the particular pattern of the print. This is accomplished by attempting to locate a delta within the print. If no delta is present, the print is classified as an arch. If two deltas are present, the print becomes a whorl. If one delta is present, the print is classified as a loop.

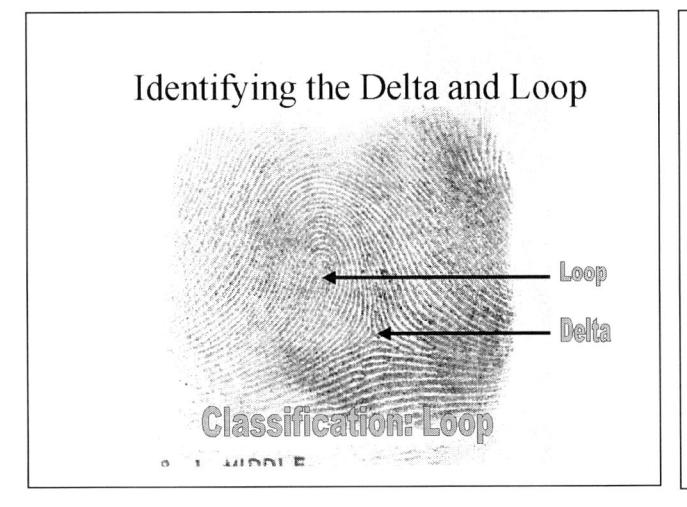

Identifying the delta and loop.

Ridge count in fingerprint identification.

2) An imaginary line is drawn from the delta to the core of the inner loop. Each ridge which crosses or touches the imaginary line, not including the delta or the core, is then counted. The total is known as the ridge count of the bridge.

3) Ridge details are identified for comparison purposes.

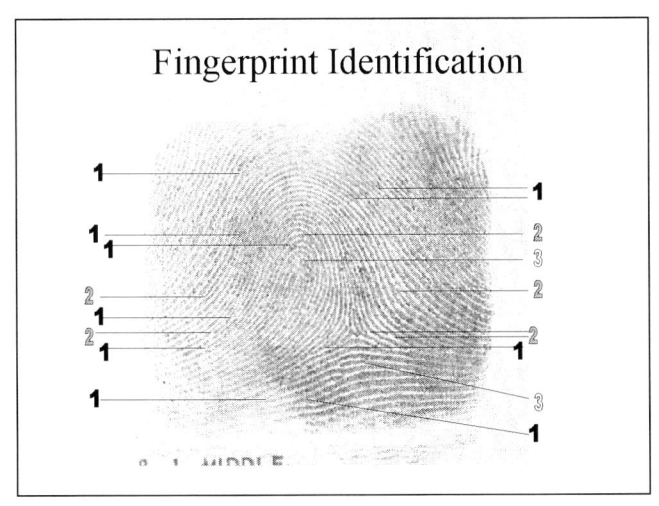

Fingerprint identification.

CHAPTER 74: FIREARMS

DEFINITION

1) A firearm is a device that fires a projectile or projectiles as a result of an explosive or propellant charge.

2) Firearm identification is a discipline of forensic science that determines whether a bullet, cartridge case, or other ammunition component was fired by a particular firearm. This determination is made by scientific examination and a comparison of the firearm and ammunition.

TYPES OF FIREARMS

1) Rifled weapons. The weapon can be a centerfire or rimfire weapon, based on where the firing pin strikes the primer on the cartridge to detonate the primer.
    a) Handguns
        i) Pistol (semiautomatic)
        ii) Revolvers
            (1) Single-action (hammer has to be pulled back and cocked manually before firing the weapon)
            (2) Double-action (pulling the trigger causes the hammer to cock and fire)
    b) Shoulder arms or long guns
        i) Rifle
            (1) A rifle is a long gun with a rifled barrel usually described by the way in which the weapon is loaded. It performs much like a handgun except the bullets fired from a rifle travel much farther and with much greater velocity.
            (2) Examples of rifled long guns include:

(a) Semiautomatic action

(b) Pump or slide action (left)

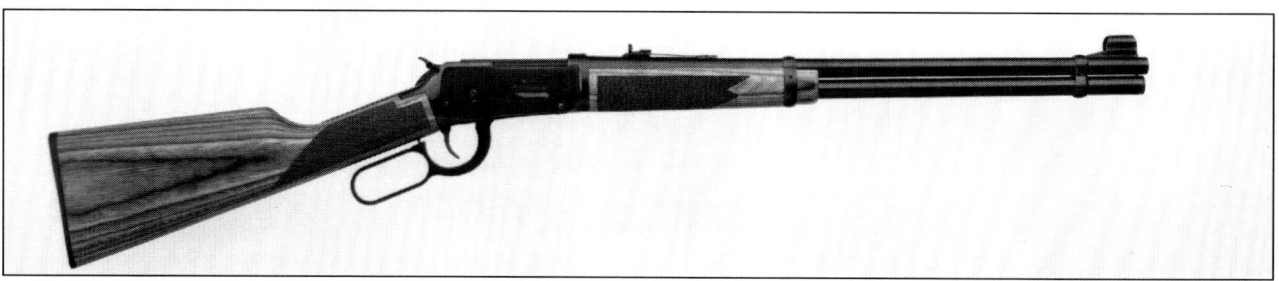

(c) Lever action (above)

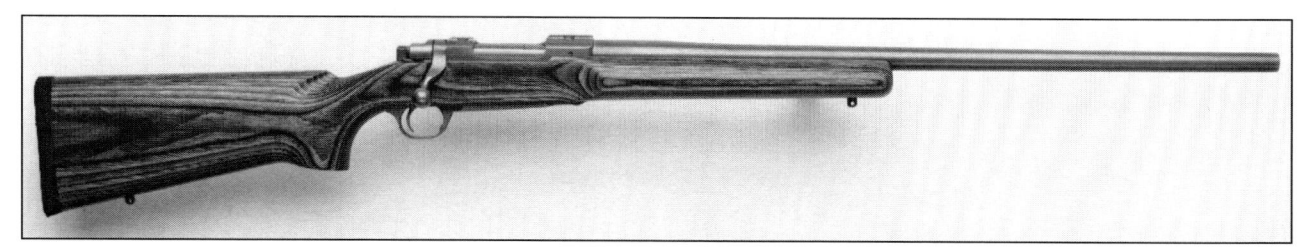

(d) Bolt action (above)

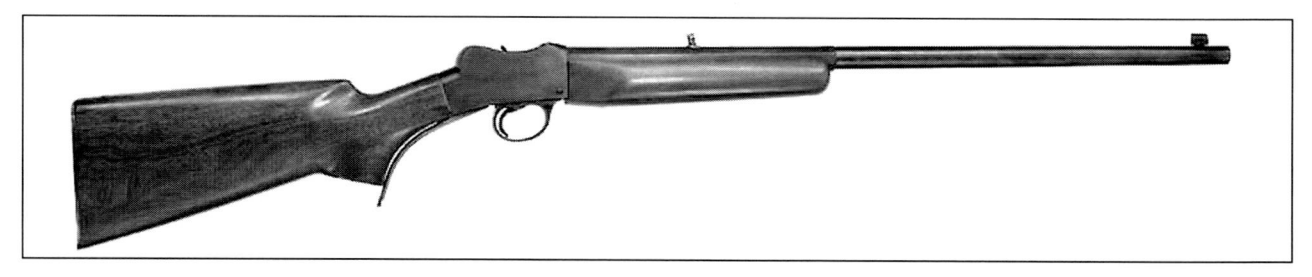

(e) Single-shot action (above)

(3) Rifle ammunition can be military (doesn't break apart in the body) or hunting (breaks up, or fragments, in the body) in origin. In anX-ray, if a snowstorm effect is present, the ammunition is probably civilian ammunition. If an incredible amount of damage is present to the internal organs, yet the

bullet passed through and through, it probably is a good indication that military ammunition was used. Due to the high velocity, visible evidence of cavitation, with huge internal injuries and disintegration of internal organs is seen with the use of these weapons. Ammunition for rifled weapons includes:
- (a) Lead bullets
- (b) Semijacketed bullets
- (c) Full-metal-jacketed bullets

2) Smooth-bore weapons
- a) Shotguns
    - i) Shotguns are classified the same way rifles are, by the way a weapon is loaded.
        - (1) Semiautomatic action
        - (2) Pump or slide action
        - (3) Lever action
        - (4) Bolt action
        - (5) Single-shot action
            - (a) Top-break action
            - (b) Double barrel
                - (i) Side by side
                - (ii) Over and under
    - ii) Shotguns may have a tapering of the barrel end called a choke. A choke concentrates the shot as it comes out of the barrel allowing for a tighter pattern of shot to travel over a longer distance.
    - iii) Ammunition for shotguns includes these:
        - (1) Birdshot
        - (2) Buckshot
        - (3) Slugs
    - iv) Shotgun shell ammunition is encased in plastic or cardboard containers, which travel for a distance with the shot or slug. Locating the discarded items may be instrumental in establishing the muzzle from the target's distance—on average:
        - (1) A heavy plastic cup and plastic wadding may be found at distances up to 20 feet.
        - (2) Paper and filler wads may be found at distances up to 15 feet.
        - (3) Polyethylene filler granules can be found at distances between 6 1/2 and 10 feet.
        - (4) Ball powder can be found at a distance of 35 to 40 inches. Flake powder can be found at a distance of 24 inches.
        - (5) Suspected suicides should have the shotgun wadding found inside the wound unless massive destruction has taken place and the wadding has fallen out of the remains.

3) Criteria for referring to any firearm
- a) Make and manufacturer
- b) Model type
- c) Type of weapon (e.g., semiautomatic, revolver)
- d) Caliber
- e) Total number of shots possible for this particular weapon
- f) Barrel length
- g) Serial number

MECHANICS

1) Cartridge, or round of ammunition, components
   a) Primer
      i) A metal cup containing a detonable mixture used in igniting the gunpowder. It is placed inside the cartridge case.
   b) Cartridge case
      i) Contains the primer and gunpowder. The bullet is fitted into the open end, or neck, of the cartridge case.
   c) Gunpowder, usually made up of four major types:
      i) Flake
      ii) Flat ball
      iii) Cylindrical
      iv) Ball
         (1) Flies through the air much better and travels greater distances than flakes or flat-ball powder. All types of flakes will penetrate clothing; Ball powder goes through best, and flake goes through least effectively.
   d) Bullet
      i) The bullet is usually made of lead or lead core encased in a higher strength metal jacket used in keeping the lead intact. The bullet is placed into the neck of the cartridge case, and the case is crimped to make the components a single cartridge or round of ammunition.

BULLET TERMS

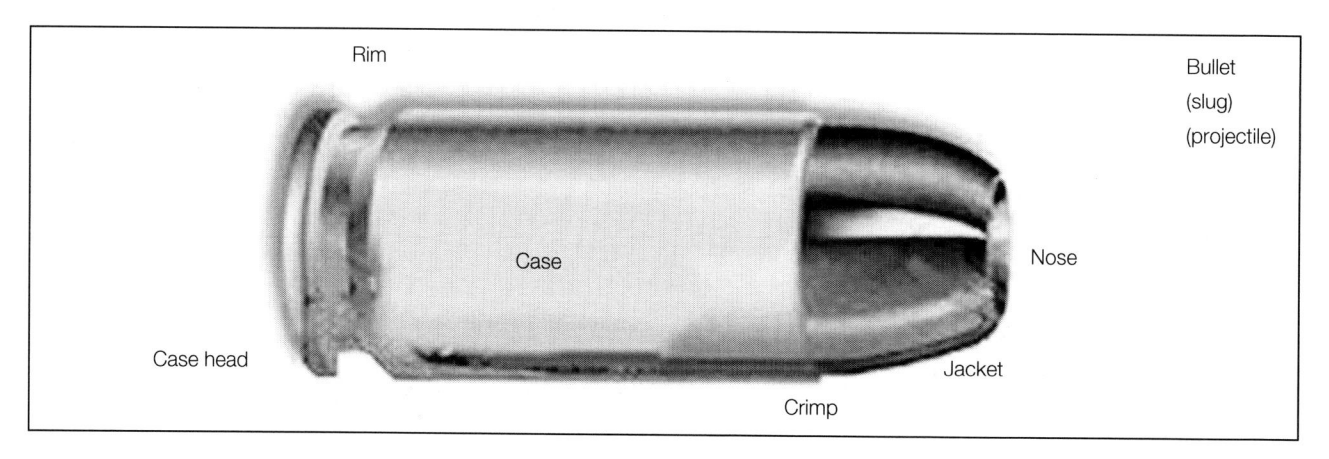

[Diagram of a cartridge with labels: Rim, Bullet (slug) (projectile), Case, Nose, Case head, Jacket, Crimp]

2) Firing the ammunition
   a) The cartridge is placed in the chamber of the firearm, immediately behind the barrel of the particular firearm. The base of the cartridge rests against the breech face or, in the case of a bolt-operated weapon, the bolt face. Pulling the trigger causes the firing pin to strike the primer of the cartridge case, resulting in a detonation of the primer mixture. The flames from the resultant explosion ignites the gunpowder, causing a rapid combustion whose force propels the bullet forward through the barrel and the cartridge case backward against the breech face of the weapon.

   b) The barrels of weapons, other than smooth-bore weapons, are rifled (i.e., spiral grooves are cut into the barrel from end to end to stabilize the bullet and prevent that bullet from tumbling as it travels through the air). This enables the bullet to spin slightly on its axis as it leaves the barrel and flies through the air. On an average, a bullet will rotate once for every foot it travels. This is why entrance wounds are a driving injuries, not corkscrew effects.

CALIBER, LANDS, AND GROOVES DETERMINATION

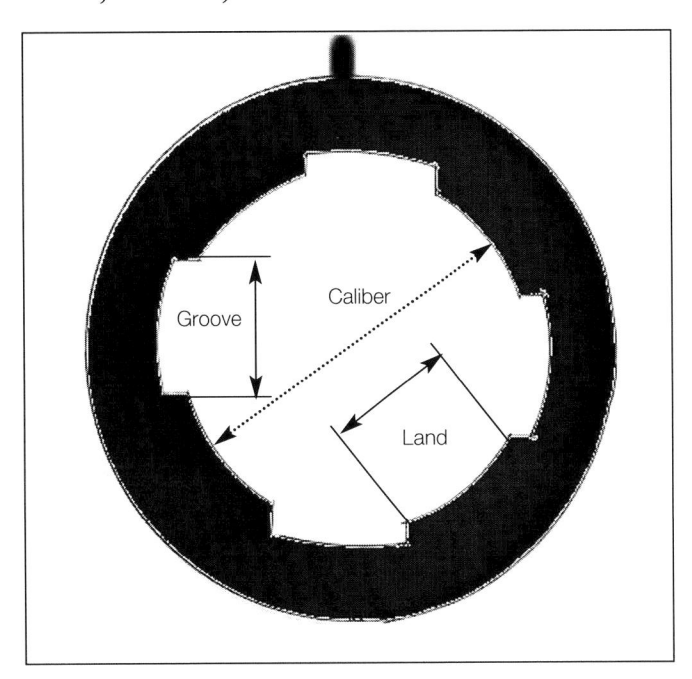

BASIS FOR IDENTIFICATION OF WEAPONS

1) The weapons of a given make and model are alike in their rifling characteristics. As the weapon is assembled, the same number of grooves and lands and the same twist of rifling are present in every similar make and model produced. When a bullet is fired through a particular make and model of weapon, the bullet is engraved with the general characteristics common to all other weapons of its make and model. This is referred to as class characteristics.

2) In addition to class characteristics, every weapon bears distinctive microscopic characteristics unique to the individual weapon and differs from those of every other weapon regardless of make and model. Such markings are initially caused during the manufacture of each weapon, since the action of manufacturing tools differs microscopically while being operated. As a weapon is used, the effects of wear, fouling, and cleaning introduce further distinctive microscopic markings. These distinctive markings are referred to as individual characteristics. They are seen in the following:
   a) Barrel markings
   b) Firing pin impressions
   c) Breech face impressions

3) When a cartridge is fired, the microscopic characteristics of the weapon's barrel are engraved into the bullet, and the microscopic characteristics of the firing pin, breech face, and in automatics and semiautomatics, the extractor and ejector markings are engraved into the cartridge case and shotgun shells.

RIGHT-HAND VERSUS LEFT-HAND TWIST DETERMINATION

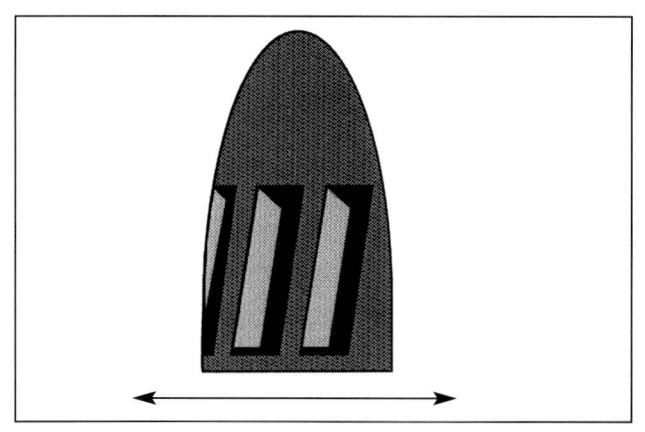

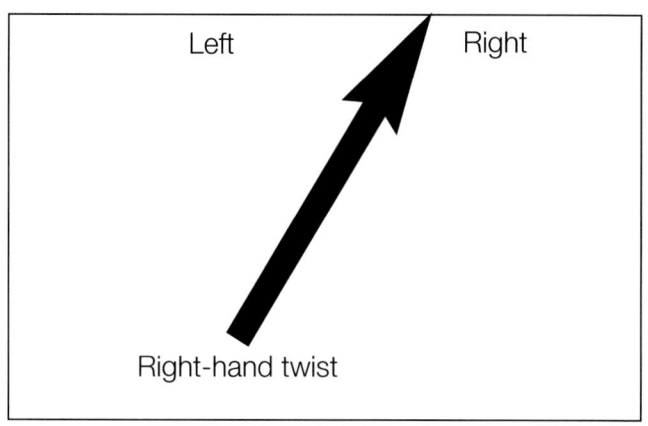

Right-hand twist

EXAMINATION OF THE SCENE

1) On gunshot cases, begin processing the scene by attempting to determine how many shots were fired and proceed by accounting for each projectile and casing involved.
   a) If many shots are involved, consider assigning a number to the recovered projectiles and a letter to all recovered shell casings.

2) If the possible involved weapon is present at the scene do the following:
   a) Be concerned for evidence linking this weapon to a particular individual. Just because the gun was registered to someone before the incident does not mean that individual had the gun at the time of the shooting. Consider other avenues for linking a particular weapon to a scene and a suspect:
      i) Blood
      ii) Hair
      iii) Fibers (e.g., the fibers recovered from the weapon match cloth fibers present in the inside pocket of the suspect)
      iv) Fingerprints
         (1) Should only be processed when all other tests for trace evidence have been completed.
   b) Never handle the weapon or attempt to lift the weapon by placing any item in the barrel of the weapon or inside the trigger guard. If possible, handle the weapon by the checkered hand grips or some other area on the weapon that is less apt to contain such evidence as fingerprints. Improper handling of the weapon may also result in the following problems:
      i) Erasing spider webs or dust present in the barrel that indicate the weapon was not fired
      ii) Eliminating fine particles of blood spatter that may be useful for reconstruction purposes
      iii) Destroying or creating rifling characteristics of the particular weapon that may affect the identification of the weapon being used in a particular death
      iv) Causing the weapon to fire

3) On revolvers, mark the position of the cylinder before opening the weapon to examine the chamber contents.

4) Note the position of each round of ammunition inside the cylinder and the status of each. Place each round in a separate bag. Mark on the bag the precise location from which the cartridge was recovered.

5) Handle casings and live rounds of ammunition with caution. Latent prints may be recovered from these items.

6) In recovering projectiles from walls and other areas where they are embedded, please use caution in digging out the bullet. Dig in an area away from where the suspected bullet is believed to be yet offers access to the projectile.

7) For trace evidence purposes, the recovered projectiles should never be cleaned or washed. Each projectile should be placed in an envelope or a cardboard box packed with tissue paper, not in soft cotton.

8) Should the firearm be recovered in water, do not attempt expose it to air. The firearm will immediately begin to rust. Place the weapon in a container and keep it submerged in the same water in which the firearm was found. Transport all immediately to the crime lab.

9) In unloading weapons, observe the following:
    a) Revolvers
        i) Before opening the weapon, mark either side of the cylinder.
        ii) Note location of each round. Record this information in a sketch drawn of the cylinder (see drawing at the bottom of p. 832).
    b) Double-barrel shotguns and double-shot derringers
        i) Note location of each round. Draw a sketch according to whether the barrel design is side by side or over/under.
    c) Semiautomatic handguns, pump-action and semiautomatic rifles, and shotguns
        i) The primary concern is an accidental discharge of the firearm. In all cases, remove the magazine and clear the live chambered round by pulling the slide to the rear. Be extremely cautious when working with some .25-caliber semiautomatics because the firing pin is used to eject the round. In all cases, work slowly and keep the weapon pointed away from any individual.
        ii) Place the chambered round in a separate container.
        iii) Place the magazine with cartridges intact in another container. Note the number of cartridges present.
        iv) Process all cartridges and the magazine for prints.
    d) Fully automatic weapons
        i) Handle these weapons in the same way you do a semiautomatic weapon. First remove the magazine. Eject the chambered round. (NOTE: On some automatic weapons, the weapon works from an open-bolt system. That is, the bolt moves forward, loads the weapon, and fires when the trigger is pressed. In these types of automatic weapons, a live round will not be found chambered).
    e) Silenced firearms
        i) Do not attempt to remove the silencer from the weapon. For ballistic purposes, removing the silencer may misalign the silencer with the bore of the weapon, eliminating the possibility of producing standards for ballistic comparison. Transport the entire weapon with silencer attached to the crime lab.

10) Always examine the hands of the victim for the presence of gunpowder residue. If present, photograph at the scene. Protect the hands when transporting the decedent. Use brown paper bags. Do not use plastic because refrigerating the body at the morgue will cause condensation to form.

11) Clothing must be retrieved in all gunshot cases. Be especially diligent in recovering the clothing of individuals who have been transported to a hospital prior to expiring. Rescue personnel, while attempting to save a life, will discard the clothing of the victim. It is the police officer's responsibility to recognize any cut-off and discarded clothing as evidence and to take the necessary precautions in preserving that evidence.
    a) Bloodied and other wet clothing should be air-dried prior to packaging. The packaging should be a brown paper bag. Do not handle the clothing excessively, thereby causing the dislodging of gunpowder residue from the item. A plain piece of brown wrapping paper may be used to cover the involved area when packaging the item being sent for analysis.

EXAMINATION OF THE BULLET

1) Examination for the class characteristics of the bullet that assist in the identification of the manufacturer of the ammunition include the following:
    a) Shape of the nose:
        i) Round, flat, pointed, hollowpoint, etc.
    b) Shape of the base:
        i) Flat, hollow, boat-tail, etc.
    c) Composition of the bullet
    d) Jacket composition, if present
        i) As weaponry advanced, the principle of kinetic energy demonstrated that heavier, slower bullets could be replaced by lighter, higher velocity projectiles and deliver the same, or greater, amount of energy. These lighter, faster bullets caused the lead bullets to become heated, resulting in high levels of lead deposits within the barrel. This necessitated the use of a stronger metal used as a jacket around the core of the lead bullet.
        ii) The jacket surrounding the lead core can be a partial jacket or a full-metal jacket.
            (1) In handgun ammunition, full-metal jacket and partial-metal jackets are normally associated with semiautomatic pistols. Although revolvers also use jacketed ammunition, lead bullets are usually associated with revolvers.
    e) Weight of the projectile
        i) Expressed in grains (1 grain = 0.06479 grams)
    f) Cannelures
        i) Location, number, size, and shape, etc.

2) Examination for the class characteristics of the bullet that assist in the identification of the make and model of the particular weapon involved include these:
    a) Caliber or gauge
        i) Developed through measurement of the diameter or weight of the projectile
    b) Rifling characteristics
        i) Distinctive patterns etched into the side of the bullet as the bullet travels through the barrel

3) Examination of shot includes the following:
    a) Size, weight, and composition of the submitted pellets are examined in developing classification.
    b) Size and shape of powder grain may identify the type of powder used in the shot.

c) Recovered wadding may be useful in identifying gauge and manufacturer of the ammunition.

d) No rifling characteristics will be present (smooth-bore weapon).

OTHER EXAMINATIONS PERFORMED BY THE BALLISTICS EXPERT

1) Possible accidental firing of the weapon
   a) The manner of some firearm-related deaths may be determined by whether a particular weapon may be predisposed to fire in an accidental fashion.
      i) Trigger pull. A firearm should not have a trigger pull (usually measured in pounds) of less than the weight of the weapon.
      ii) Firing of a weapon by dropping or striking it against some object

2) Range determinations (muzzle to target distance)
   a) As a weapon is fired, the projectile is accompanied by hot gases, soot, burning gunpowder, unburned gunpowder, flames, smoke, grease, and fine metallic particles. This residue exits the barrel and travels for a short distance in a cone-shaped formation. The subject weapon should be fired using the same type of ammunition involved in the case. Based on these tests, the ballistics expert may reach conclusions concerning muzzle-to-target distances based on similar patterns established in the test-firing of the weapon when comparison with the actual pattern involved in the clothing or wound of the victim.

3) Restoration of obliterated serial numbers
   a) The ballistics expert may take apart a weapon and locate a serial number on an interior metal part possibly overlooked by the altering individual. In addition, the examiner may treat a particular area that appears to have been altered or obliterated with a suitable acid or base, depending on the metal involved, to restore the original number.

GUNSHOT RESIDUE COLLECTION

1) The cloud or residue exiting the barrel and cylinder gap in revolvers and through the bolt action of semiautomatics when a weapon is fired may collect on the hands of the shooter. For this reason, numerous tests, through the years, have been developed in an effort to determine a positive method to determine whether an individual fired a weapon. Some of these tests have involved the following.
   a) Nitrate (paraffin) test
      i) Originally this was developed as a test used to react with nitrates used in the making of gunpowder. A paraffin cast was made of the suspect's hand. After removal of the cast, the wax was treated with a solution that would react to the presence of nitrates.
      ii) Unfortunately, the test is nonspecific for gunpowder residue, and many items in the environment can cause an individual to have nitrates on his hands. As a result, the test can be ambiguous.
   b) Fluorescence test (trace metal detection technique)
      i) In this test, a spray is applied to a hand suspected of holding a weapon and observed under fluorescent light. If the hand has held a metal gun, traces of the metal are, theoretically, left on the hand and fluoresces with the outline of the weapon.
      ii) This test has proved to be very inconsistent.

c) Scanning electron microscopy
   i) Disk lifts are used to collect specimens from the hands of an individual suspected of firing a weapon. These specimens are examined with a scanning electron microscope and analyzed by X-ray to determine whether particles of antimony, barium, copper, and lead are components of gunpowder residue.
   ii) The drawbacks to this examination are the cost and the ambiguity of the results. Gunpowder residue may be found on the hands of an individual even though he did not fire a weapon. Gunpowder residue may be present if that person's hands were in close proximity to the weapon or within the area where the soot and powder may have come from and traveled toward and eventually landing at the farthest point of travel.
d) Neutron activation analysis
   i) Once touted as the ultimate test for determining whether an individual positively did or did not fire a weapon, this test required swabbing the palms and backs of an individual's hands with a 5-percent nitric acid solution usually applied with a plastic-shaft Q-Tip. The swabbings were sent off and analyzed for the presence or absence of antimony and barium, two components of centerfire gunpowder. The presence of both compositions in equal amounts was thought to be proof positive that an individual had fired a weapon.
   ii) During the early 1990s, the FBI and many local law enforcement labs have discontinued the use of this method of gunshot residue analysis because of the ambiguous results.
      (1) A negative finding did not necessarily mean that an individual did not fire a weapon, because the results could have been eroded with the passage of any time and completely absent if the individual had washed his hands prior to the swabbings.
      (2) The presence of antimony and barium did not necessarily mean that an individual had fired a weapon. An individual whose hands were in close proximity to the weapon when it was fired could not be distinguished from those of the individual who fired a weapon.
      (3) Individuals who did not fire a weapon were found to have acquired antimony and barium on their hands from the environment.
      (4) The test was useless on most brands of .22-caliber ammunition.

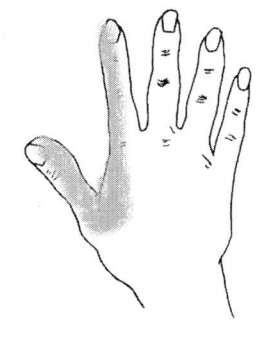

HAND SWABBING WITH A GUNSHOT RESIDUE (GSR) KIT

- Areas of the hands to swab when taking a gunshot residue swabbing.

- Both hands should always be swabbed.

- Keep in mind that, on a suicide case, the normal handling of the weapon may be altered because the weapon has to be turned unnaturally for self-infliction. Adapt accordingly.

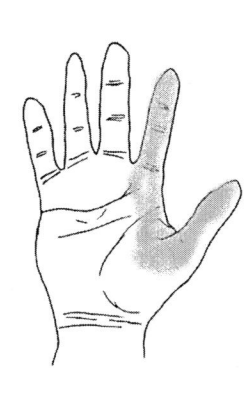

GUNSHOT-RESIDUE-COLLECTION DATA SHEET

GUNSHOT RESIDUE COLLECTION DATA SHEET

AGENCY _____ PHONE _____

CASE NUMBER _____ DATE _____

COLLECTING OFFICER _____

DATE AND TIME SWABS TAKEN _____

DATE AND TIME GUN WAS FIRED _____

NUMBER OF TIMES GUN WAS FIRED _____

TYPE AND CALIBER OF GUN _____ MAKE OF AMMO _____

SUBJECT INFORMATION [PERSON SWABBED ONLY]

NAME: _____ LIVING OR DEAD _____

OCCUPATION: _____ R OR L HANDED _____

HANDS WASHED? _____ HANDCUFFED? _____

FINGERPRINTED BEFORE COLLECTION [NOT RECOMMENDED]? _____

WEAPON IN POSSESSION OR DISCARDED _____

DESCRIPTION OF SUBJECTS ACTIVITIES PRIOR TO SHOOTING _____

_____

_____

DESCRIPTION OF SUBJECTS ACTIVITIES BETWEEN SHOOTING AND SWABBING

_____

_____

DESCRIPTION OF ENVIRONMENT WHERE SHOOTING OCCURRED (INDOORS; ROOM SIZE AND DEGREE OF VENTILATION, OUTDOORS; ATMOSPHERIC CONDITIONS, INSIDE A VEHICLE, ETC.) _____

_____

VICTIM'S NAME (IF DIFFERENT THAN SUBJECT) _____

OTHER PERTINENT INFORMATION _____

_____

COLLECTING OFFICER

_____
signature

GUNSHOT RESIDUE KIT

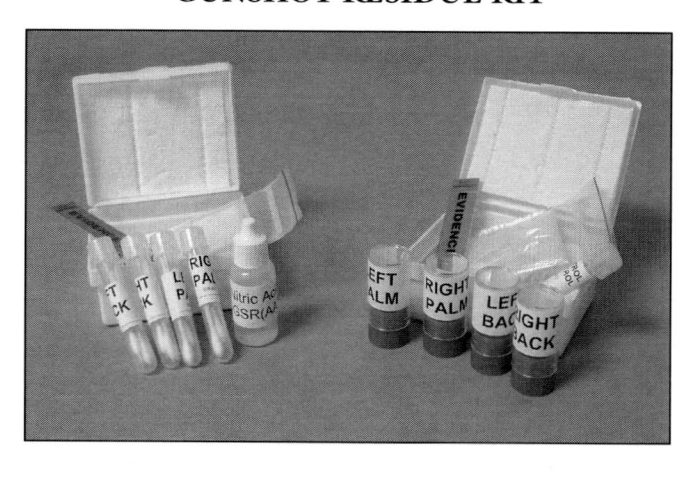

VELOCITY EXAMPLES FOR VARIOUS TYPES OF WEAPONS WITH AVERAGE WEIGHT PROJECTILES

Caliber Designation	Velocity	Grains
.22 Long Rifle	1,150 ft./sec.	40 grains
.25 ACP	760 ft./sec.	50 grains
.32 ACP	905 ft./sec.	71 grains
.38 Police Special	755 ft./sec.	158 grains
.357 Magnum	1,235 ft./sec.	158 grains
.41 Magnum	1300 ft./sec.	210 grains
.44 Magnum	1,180 ft./sec.	240 grains
.45 ACP	850 ft./sec.	230 grains
9mm (Luger)	1,160 ft./sec.	115 grains
.380 (9mm short)	955 ft./sec.	95 grains
10mm	950 ft./sec.	180 grains

NOTE: A missile velocity of 125 to 170 ft./sec. is required to penetrate naked human skin. A velocity of 200 ft./sec. is required when the skin is clothed.

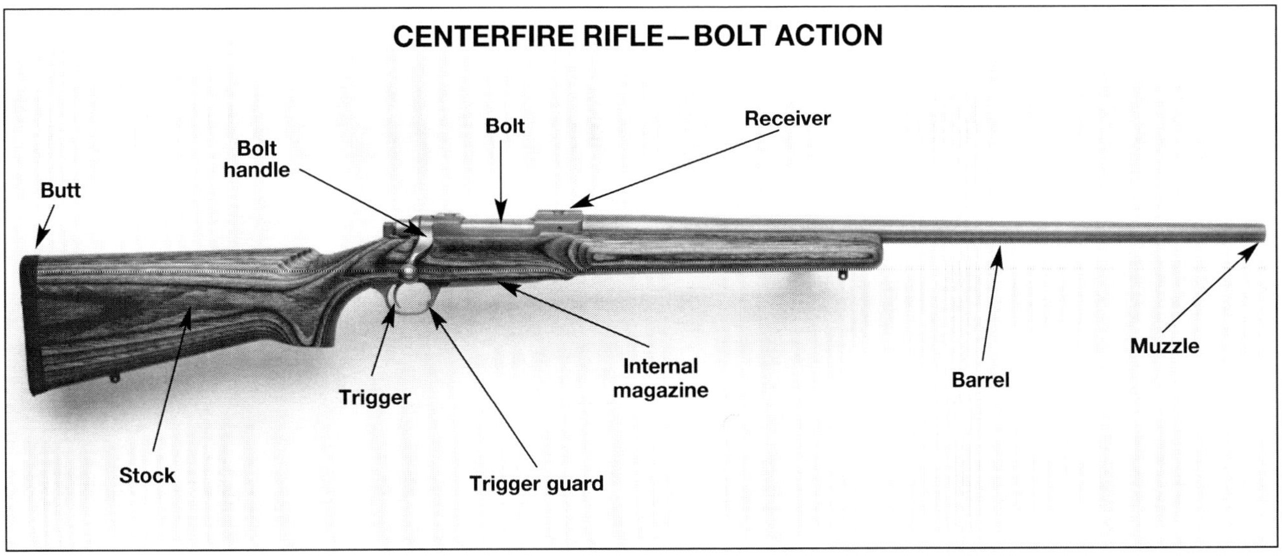
CENTERFIRE RIFLE—BOLT ACTION
Butt
Bolt handle
Bolt
Receiver
Stock
Trigger
Trigger guard
Internal magazine
Barrel
Muzzle

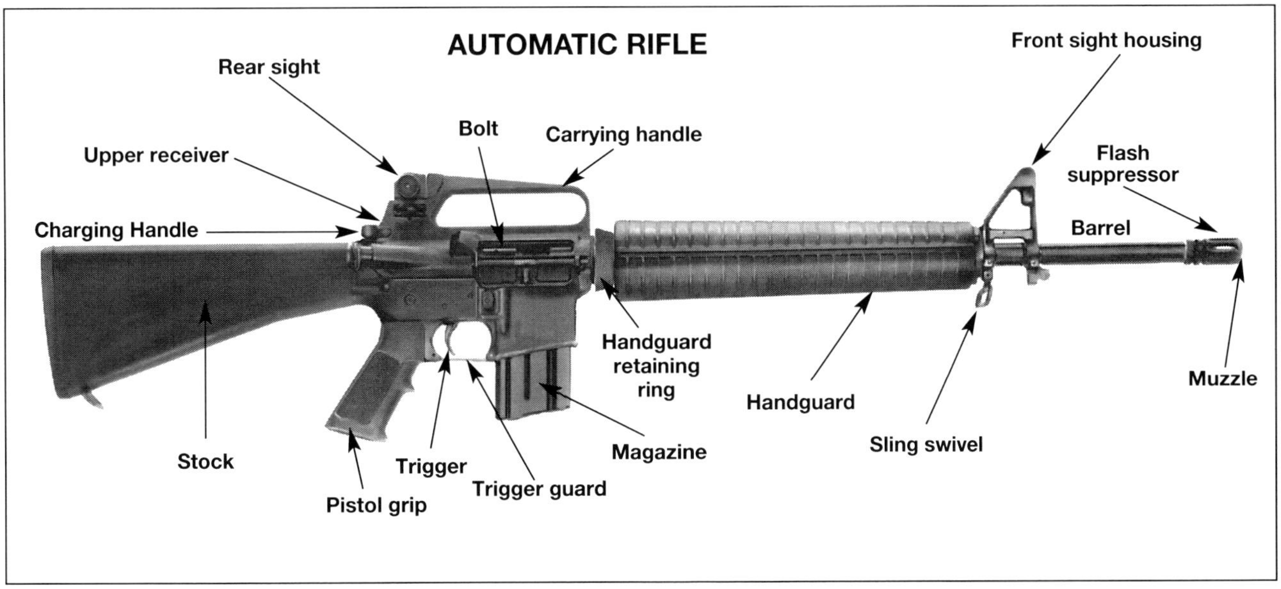
AUTOMATIC RIFLE
Rear sight
Upper receiver
Charging Handle
Bolt
Carrying handle
Front sight housing
Flash suppressor
Barrel
Stock
Pistol grip
Trigger
Trigger guard
Handguard retaining ring
Magazine
Handguard
Sling swivel
Muzzle

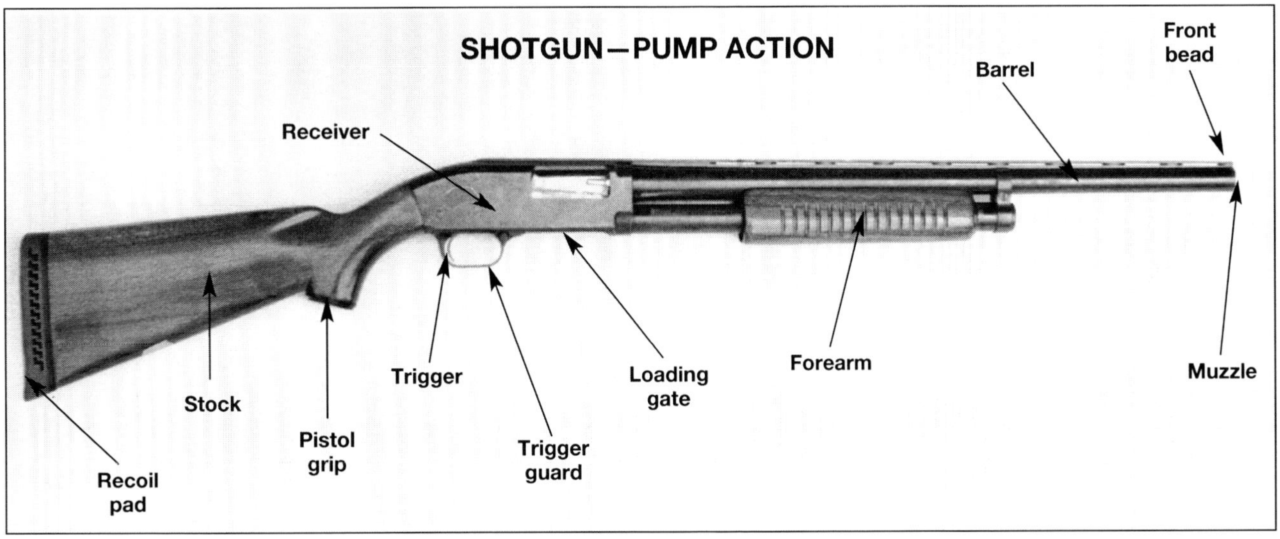
SHOTGUN—PUMP ACTION
Receiver
Barrel
Front bead
Recoil pad
Stock
Pistol grip
Trigger
Trigger guard
Loading gate
Forearm
Muzzle

REVOLVER HANDGUN

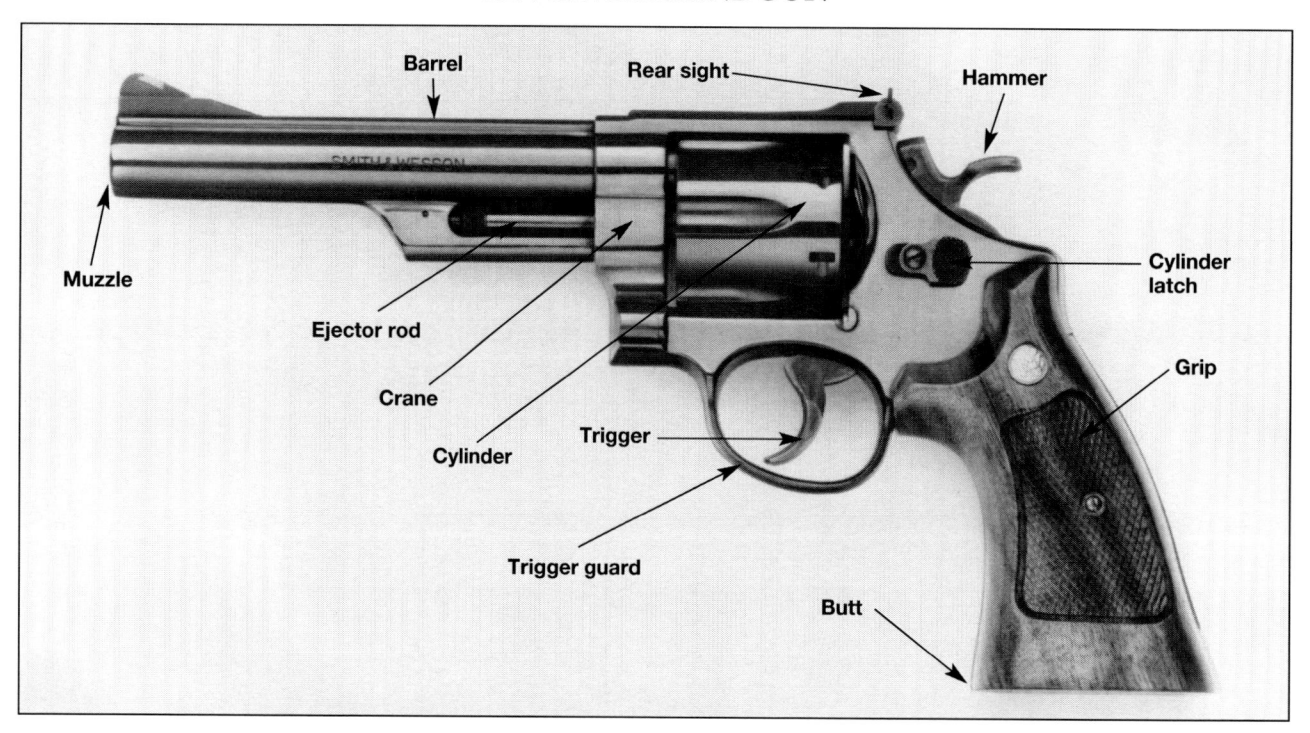

DESCRIPTION OF AMMUNITION INSIDE A REVOLVER

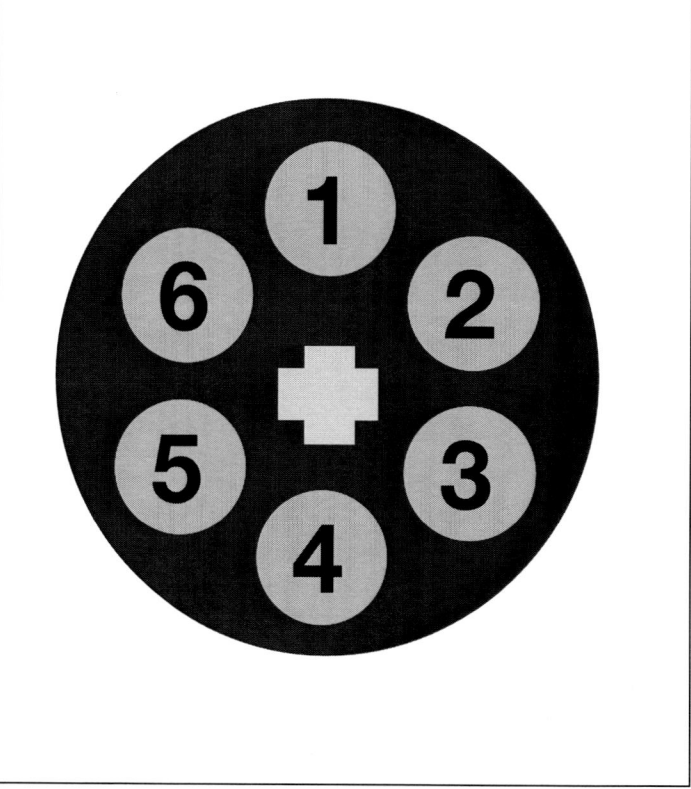

Marking the cylinder before opening the cylinder is critical for determining the location of the spent round in the suspected weapon.

The drawing on page 830 can be used as a point of reference when describing the position of live rounds, spent rounds, and misfired rounds within a revolver.

The cylinder should be referenced in the same manner as would occur when loading the weapon (from the rear of the cylinder).

The round in the 12 o'clock position (under the hammer) should be marked as number 1. Continue numbering each chamber in clockwise order. For example:

1 spent
2 misfire
3 live
4 live
5 live
6 live

SEMIAUTOMATIC HANDGUN AND MAGAZINE/"CLIP"

The magazine, sometimes erroneously called a "clip," is loaded with ammunition and placed inside of the semiautomatic's handgrip. A magazine is also used in semiautomatic and full-auto long guns.

As the magazine is inserted into the weapon, the weapon is racked to seat a live round. Sometimes, the magazine is released without the gun handler remembering or knowing that a live round is seated. In certain weapons, the weapon is still capable of firing when the trigger is engaged.

HANDGUN AMMUNITION

1) The following chart can be used as a rough guideline at the scene or during the course of an investigation when a quick estimate is needed concerning the caliber of the weapon involved.

2) The opened end of a shell casing or the base of a recovered projectile can be placed against the circular drawings. The best fit may be indicative of the caliber involved.

3) Please consider that the subtle differences in size between calibers may contribute to an error in the reading. This exercise should never be used in lieu of a thorough and competent examination conducted by a qualified firearms examiner.

HANDGUN AMMUNITION

	INCH SIZE	METRIC EQUIVALENT	AVAILABILITY	CALIBER
●	.22"	5.6 mm	Revolver or Automatic	.22
●	.25"	6.38mm	Automatic	.25
●	.31"	7.65mm	Revolver or Automatic	.32
●	.356"	9 mm	Automatic	9 mm
●	.356"	9 mm	Automatic	.380
●	.357"	9.1 mm	Revolver	.357
●	.357"	9.1 mm	Revolver	.38
●	.40"	10 mm	Automatic	.40
●	.41"	10.41 mm	Revolver	.41
●	.429"	10.91 mm	Revolver	.44
●	.451"	11.47 mm	Automatic	.45

RIMFIRE RIFLES

	CALIBER	ACTUAL SIZE	AVG WT (GRAIN)	MUZZLE VELOCITY
●	.22 Short	.22"	27-29	1095 - 1120
●	.22 Long	.22"	29	1095
●	.22 Long Rifle	.22"	36-40	1255 - 1280
●	.22 Magnum	.22"	40	1480

CENTERFIRE RIFLES

CALIBER	ACTUAL SIZE	AVG WEIGHT (Grain)	MUZZLE VELOCITY
.223 (M-16)	.223"	55	3200
.243	.243"	80-100	2960 - 3350
6mm	.243"	70-100	3300
6.5mm	.264"	100-160	3200
.270	.277"	100-150	2900 - 3480
7mm	.284"	100-175	2900
.30	.308"	110	1990
30-06	.308"	110-220	1095
30-30	.308"	150-170	2390
.308	.308"	110-200	2450 - 3180
7.62x39 (AK-47)	.310	125	2340
.303	.312"	180	2460
.32	.321"	170	2250
8mm	.323"	125-220	2360

SHOTGUN AMMUNITION - BIRDSHOT

SIZE	SHOT	DIAMETER (INCHES)	AVAILABILITY BY GAUGE	GRAIN WEIGHT
•	12	.05		.18
•	11	.06		.25
•	10	.07		.50
•	9	.08	10, 12, 16, 20, 28, 410	.75
•	8.5	.085		.88
•	8	.09	10, 12, 16, 28, 410	1.07
•	7.5	.095	10, 12, 16, 20, 28, 410	1.25
•	6	.11	10, 12, 16, 20, 28, 410	1.95
•	5	.12	10, 12, 16, 20, 410	2.58
•	4	.13	10, 12, 16, 20, 410	3.24
•	2	.15	10, 12, 16, 20	4.86
•	BB	.18	10, 12	8.75

BUCKSHOT AMMUNITION

Diameter (Inches)	Availability by Shotgun Gauge	Grain Weight	Descptn of Shot
.24	10, 12, 12 Mag	20.6	4
.25	20	23.4	3
.30	12, 16, 12Mag	40.0	1
.32	12	48.3	0
.33	12, 12 Mag	53.8	00
.36	12Mag	68.0	000

SHOTGUN AMMUNITION

Shotgun Gauge	Birdshot	Buckshot	Mag Load	Slug Type
10 Actual 0.775"	BB, 2, 4, 5 / 6, 7.5, 8, 9	4		Foster
12 Actual 0.729"	BB, 2, 4, 5 / 6, 7.5, 8, 9	1, 4, 0, 00	1, 4, 0, 00	Brenneke Sabot Foster
16 Actual 0.662"	2, 4, 5 / 7.5, 8, 9, 6	1		Brenneke Foster
20 Actual 0.615"	2, 4, 5 / 6, 7.5, 9	3		Brenneke Foster
28 Actual 0.550	6, 7.5 / 8, 9			
410 Actual 0.410	4, 5, 6 / 7.5, 8, 9			Foster

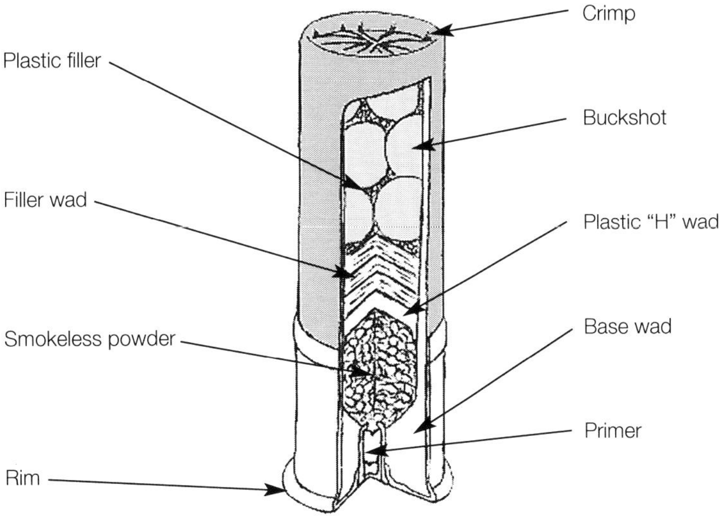
Crimp
Plastic filler
Buckshot
Filler wad
Plastic "H" wad
Base wad
Smokeless powder
Primer
Rim

SABOT SLUG	GAUGE	WEIGHT (GRAINS)
	12	440

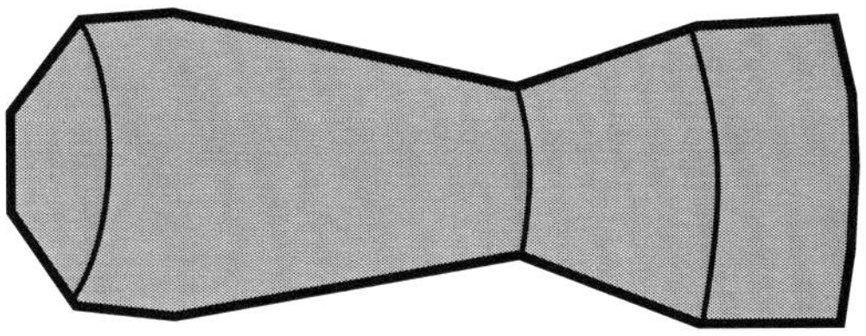

BRENNEKE SLUG	GAUGE	WEIGHT
	12	491
	16	427
	20	364

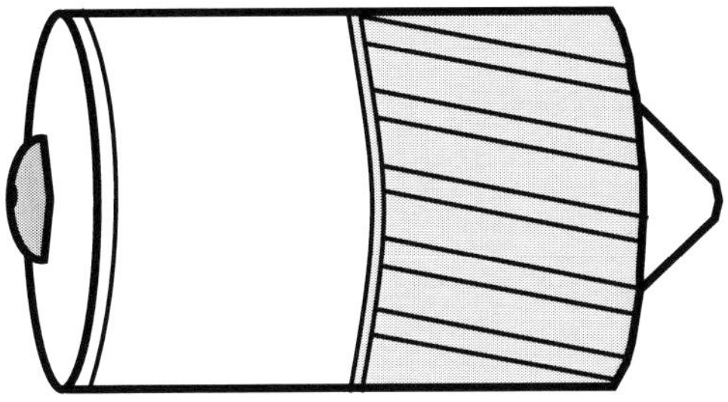

FOSTER (RIFLED) SLUG	GAUGE	WEIGHT
	10	760
	12	437
	16	350
	20	273
	410	87.5

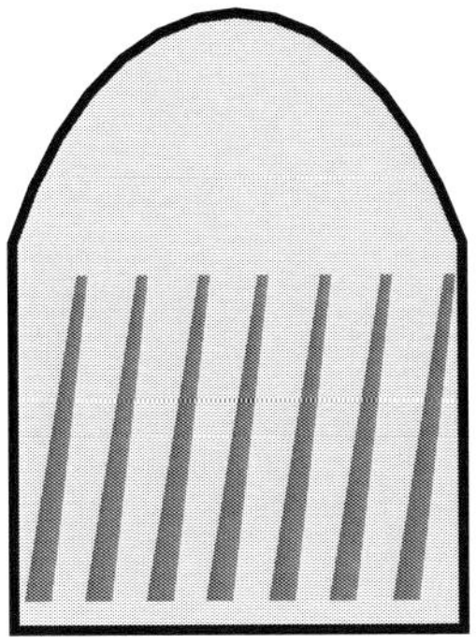

NATIONAL INTEGRATED BALLISTICS INFORMATION NETWORK (NIBIN)

1) Comparing ballistic evidence in the past was a tedious and time-consuming process.
    a) Evidence recovered at crime scenes or from recovered firearms was compared piece by piece to the vast inventory of recovered or test-fired projectiles and casings.
    b) No means of automatic comparison existed; the necessity of searching each piece manually greatly reduced the amount of evidence that could be examined, given manpower and time constraints, and made matches less likely.
    c) No comparison of ballistic evidence was made between different jurisdictions unless specifically requested by the investigator.

2) The creation of NIBIN
    a) At the same time that the Bureau of Alcohol, Tobacco, and Firearms (ATF) created its Integrated Ballistic Identification System (IBIS), the FBI created DrugFire. Unfortunately, data could not be compared between the two systems.
    b) ATF and the FBI entered into an agreement in May 1997 that created the NIBIN Board. The NIBIN Board comprises ATF, FBI, and state/local representatives. The board's goal is to unify federal efforts to deploy ballistics technology. NIBIN was created to have one system for this important forensic tool.

3) How it works?
    a) Every firearm has individual characteristics that are as unique to it as fingerprints are to human beings.
    b) When a firearm is fired, it transfers these characteristics—in the form of microscopic scratches and dents—to the projectiles and cartridge casings fired in it.
    c) The barrel of the firearm marks the projectile traveling through it, and the firearm's breech mechanism marks the ammunition's cartridge casing.

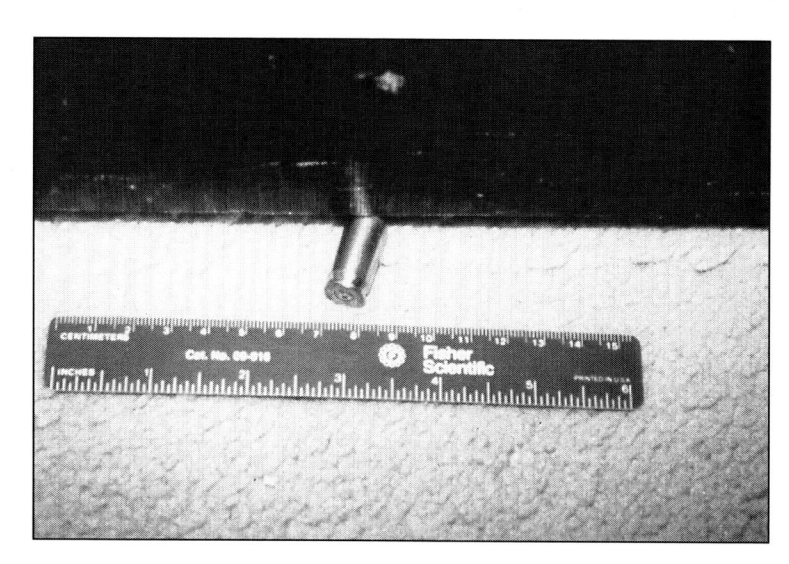

4) This information, obtained from the projectile and spent shell casings, can be placed into a searchable database system.
    a) Recovered bullets or cartridge casings found at a crime scene can be examined to identify comparison marks to determine whether or not the bullets or casings were fired or ejected from a suspect's firearm.
    b) If a firearm is recovered at the scene, test-firing the weapon creates bullets and cartridge casings for comparison.
    c) Bullets and cartridge casings found at one crime scene can also be compared with those found at another in an effort to link the crimes.

DRUGFIRE—IBIS

The striation marks on bullets are caused by the irregularities in the gun barrel as well as the larger and more distinct lands and grooves of the rifling.

The ejected cartridge case also has marks caused by the firing pin and the breech face.

The feeding, extraction, and ejection mechanisms of the firearm also leave characteristic marks.

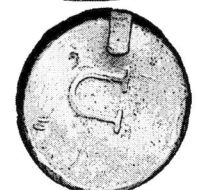

5) In developing the NIBIN, ATF recognized the benefit to law enforcement that ballistic imaging and analysis could provide.
    a) The NIBIN program includes the development and maintenance of a database of ballistic images from guns that may have been used in crimes.
    b) The database contains images of casings or bullets recovered at crime scenes, as well as casings or bullets from test-fires of recovered firearms.
    c) IBIS photographs portions of the surface (land-engraved areas) of a bullet and the primer/firing pin area of fired cartridge cases using state of the art optical and electronic technology.
    d) These images are then stored in databases, and sophisticated algorithms are used to correlate the images with each other using such filters as caliber, rifling specifications, date of crime, and date of entry.
    e) As new images are entered, the system searches the existing database, and comparisons are made for possible matches. These possible matches, or correlations, produce lists of possible matches with the highest scoring correlations at the top of the list. An examiner can then call up the images and compare them side by side on a monitor.
    f) If a possible match is found during this screening process, the actual evidence-to-test or evidence-to-evidence is then compared by a firearms examiner on a comparison microscope for final determination.
        i) The purpose of these comparisons is to link ballistic evidence from crime scenes, as well as linking one crime scene to another.
    g) When the NIBIN system discovers a likely match, firearm examiners repeat the comparison with the actual evidence to confirm the match.

CHAPTER 75: DNA PROCEDURES

DNA INFORMATION

1) Every person possesses a unique genetic code.
    a) The genetic code is contained in the chromosomes of every nucleus in every cell.
    b) This genetic code is composed of double helix strands of deoxyribonucleic acid (DNA).

UNIQUENESS OF DNA

1) With the exception of identical twins, the possibility of two people having the same DNA composition ("fingerprinting") is in the order of 1 in 10 to the 6th power.

2) DNA profiling makes positive identification virtually certain.
    a) Previous serological tests could only eliminate potential suspects or make them a part of a group of people who shared the same characteristics.

3) DNA can identify a victim through DNA from relatives, even when no body can be found.

4) When evidence from one crime scene is compared with evidence from another, those crime scenes can be linked to the same perpetrator locally, statewide, and across the nation.

DNA COMPARISON

1) In the forensic setting, the examiner does a direct comparison of samples he has obtained from a crime scene, body, or evidence, and compares them with a sample obtained from a suspect.

2) The results will indicate a match based on probability or eliminate the suspect altogether, providing that the samples are of sufficient quantity and were collected and preserved properly.
    a) If even one feature of the DNA or fingerprint is different, it is determined not to have come from that suspect.

DNA ANALYSIS—INVESTIGATIVE CONSIDERATIONS

1) Restricted fragment length polymorphism
    a) Examination considerations:
        i) When DNA is extracted from the evidence, it is cut into pieces using a restriction enzyme. The enzyme, acting like a kind of molecular pair of scissors, snips the DNA when it recognizes a specific DNA sequence (GGCC/CCGG). The resultant lengths, or fragments, depend on the location of those sequences and are called restriction fragment length polymorphisms (RFLP). Because of the wide variability, some of these fragments are short and some are long. RFLP analysis is accomplished with the "Southern blot" process.
        ii) Initially, RFLP processing was the only analysis performed by crime labs.
        iii) Limitations:
            (1) RFLP analysis require a large sample. Small biological stains may not have enough DNA present to perform DNA analysis.

(2) There may be a large enough stain, but the DNA is degraded.
(3) The time it takes to perform RFLP analysis can range between 4 weeks and 6 months.
(4) With RFLP analysis, once the sample is used up there is no way to get any more.

2) Polymerase chain reaction (PCR) DNA analysis
   a) Consideration:
      i) The hallmark of PCR is its eloquent simplicity. Conducting PCR DNA profiling on a pin-sized biological stain is accomplished by copying a designated genetic marker molecularly a million times over until enough of the specific marker is available for typing.
   b) Investigative benefits of PCR DNA analysis:
      i) With PCR, millions of copies of the DNA can be produced.
      ii) It is extremely effective on degraded DNA.

3) Polymerase chain reaction–short tandem repeat (PCR–STR)
   a) Consideration:
      i) "STR typing incorporates the concept of repeating sequences found in RFLP and the amplification powers of PCR.
      ii) Within the amplified PCR fragments are areas of junk DNA. This junk DNA exists in very small stretches of repetitive DNA sequences known as short tandem repeats (STRs). These strands are too tiny for RFLP analysis but ideal for PCR technology.
      iii) STRs are small, repeating sequences of DNA, usually three to five base pairs in length. It is the variable number of these repeats that distinguishes one profile from another and forms the basis of forensic STR analysis. The combination of profiles derived from several different STR loci (locations) can result in a genetic profile that will distinguish one person from another.
      iv) As an added bonus when using PCR to identify short DNA fragments is that many different STR sites can be copied simultaneously from the same DNA sample within the same test tube.
      v) Human DNA harbors an enormous cache of STR sites with estimates of more than 30,000 regions, making PCR STR technology a powerful tool for personal identification.
         (1) Statistical estimates suggest that typing information from 12 different STR markers will afford virtual identification of an individual.
      vi) Given their ability to obtain highly discriminatory DNA profiles from small, degraded samples both faster and less expensively, STRs are fast becoming the DNA testing method of choice of an ever-increasing number of forensic laboratories.
         (1) Combined DNA Index System (CODIS) is an FBI program supporting a network of local, state, and national databases housing DNA samples of convicted offenders and crime scene samples. These labs are required to use the 13 core STR loci technology."
            (a) The 13th marker in PCR STR DNA is a gender identifier. Therefore the male or sex nature of the contributor is identifiable.

4) Y-chromosome DNA analysis
- a) Consideration:
    - i) "The genes and nonfunctional sequences that comprise DNA are packaged on chromosomes. During fertilization, one half of the pair of chromosomes is contributed by the mother and the other half by the father. Sex chromosomes in the egg and sperm contain genes that code for sex determination. The egg always contains an 'X,' but the sperm can contain an 'X' or a 'Y.' A combination containing XX will produce a female, and an XY combination will produce a male. Therefore, the father's contribution always decides the sex of the child.
    - ii) The Y chromosome is unique for several reasons:
        - (1) It determines the sex of the child.
        - (2) The Y chromosome is passed only from father to son.
        - (3) Unlike the X chromosome, most of the information on the Y chromosome is not exchanged during cell division. Consequently, the Y chromosome generally retains its genetic makeup. As a result, when a father passes a Y chromosome to his son, it is virtually identical to his own. Then, when the son has a male child, he passes that same Y chromosome to his own son.
            - (a) When a father passes the Y chromosome to multiple sons, each son will share a Y chromosome virtually identical to their father's. As long as the biological parentage is not in question, grandfathers, fathers, sons, brothers, and uncles will have virtually identical Y chromosomes. This enables scientists to trace a Y chromosome backward through the male ancestral lineage.
- b) Forensic application:
    - i) Y chromosome DNA analysis is used for its ability to assist in deciphering mixed evidence samples often found in sexual assault cases.
        - (1) Laboratory processing endeavors to remove the female cells from the mixture, leaving only the sperm portion to be typed.
            - (a) Mixtures of cells, such as victim/suspect blood or saliva, can not be differentiated at all because they contain the same types of cells. Therefore, the technician is left with the often difficult task of subtracting the victim's type from the mixture's type to see if the suspect's type remains.
    - ii) Y chromosome testing increases the likelihood of obtaining a perpetrator's profile from male/female mixtures because:
        - (1) Y chromosome primers do not amplify X chromosome sequences. Therefore, in a rape situation where a vaginal swab contains the victim's cells and the rapist's sperm (or epithelial cells), Y chromosome testing can sift through all the female DNA to locate the male DNA, and could thus include a suspect as a possible contributor. In certain circumstances, Y chromosome testing can sometimes detect the DNA type of different male contributors to a mixture."

5) Mitochondrial DNA analysis
- a) Consideration:
    - i) Unlike regular DNA, which comes from a cell's nucleus (nuclear DNA), mitochondrial DNA (mtDNA) can be found in hair, bones, or teeth.

ii) Nuclear DNA versus mitochondrial DNA:
    (1) Nuclear DNA
        (a) It is located in the nucleus of a cell.
        (b) Half of the chromosomes are inherited from the mother, half from the father.
        (c) There are one set of chromosomes per cell.
    (2) Mitochondrial DNA
        (a) Located in the mitochondrial-cytoplasm of the cell.
        (b) Maternally inherited
        (c) 100 to 10,000 copies per cell
  b) Applications of mtDNA testing
    i) Highly degraded, limited quantities of DNA
    ii) Present in:
        (1) Skeletal material, including teeth
        (2) Telogen hairs
        (3) Fingernails
        (4) Urine

AMOUNTS REQUIRED

1) Only a small amount of specimen is usually required to perform the test, although, as a general rule, the larger the sample the better the chance of having a conclusive test.

HOW LONG DOES DNA LAST?

1) DNA is very stable and can usually be found in samples weeks, months, and sometimes even years old.

2) The younger the sample, the greater the chances for obtaining conclusive information.

3) Several factors can affect the DNA left at a crime scene, including environmental factors (e.g., heat, sunlight, moisture, bacteria, mold). Therefore, not all DNA evidence will result in a usable DNA profile.
    a) Just like fingerprints, DNA testing cannot tell officers when the suspect was at the crime scene or for how long.

WHERE CAN DNA EVIDENCE BE FOUND AT A CRIME SCENE?

1) DNA evidence can be collected from virtually anywhere.
    a) Imaginative and nontraditional methods of collection
        i) Numerous cases have been solved by DNA analysis of saliva on cigarette butts, postage stamps, and the area around the mouth opening of ski masks. DNA analysis of a single hair (without the root) found deep in the victim's throat provided a critical piece of evidence used in one capital murder conviction.
        ii) One case was solved when a suspect, after refusing to give DNA specimens, was tailed by a surveillance team that retrieved his spit from a parking lot.
    b) Evidence collection and preservation investigators and laboratory personnel should work together to determine the most probative pieces of evidence and to establish priorities.

IDENTIFYING DNA EVIDENCE

1) Since only a few cells can be enough to obtain useful DNA information to help your case, the following material identifies some common items of evidence that you may need to collect, the possible location of the DNA on the evidence, and the biological source containing the cells.

2) To avoid contamination of evidence that may contain DNA, always take the following precautions:
    a) Wear gloves and change them often.
    b) Use disposable instruments or clean them thoroughly before and after handling each sample.
    c) Avoid touching the area where you believe DNA may exist.
    d) Avoid talking, sneezing, and coughing over evidence.
    e) Avoid touching your face, nose, and mouth when collecting and packaging evidence.
    f) Air-dry evidence thoroughly before packaging.
    g) Put evidence into new paper bags or envelopes, not into plastic bags. Do not use staples.

ELIMINATION SAMPLES

1) As with fingerprints, the effective use of DNA may require the collection and analysis of elimination samples. It often is necessary to use elimination samples to determine whether the evidence comes from the suspect or from someone else. An officer must think ahead to the time of trial and possible defenses while still at the crime scene.

2) In homicide cases, collect the victim's DNA from the medical examiner at the autopsy, even if the body is badly decomposed. This may help identify an unknown victim or distinguish between the victim's DNA and other DNA found at the crime scene.

3) Other possibilities for obtaining known samples from the dead are these:
    a) Exhumation of decedent
    b) Personal effects, licked envelopes, toothbrush, hair brush, etc.
    c) Tissue blocks at medical examiner's office or from biopsy
    d) Microscopic slides from old lab work either from doctors, hospitals, crime lab, etc.
    e) Reconstructed DNA from parents, siblings.

4) When investigating a homicide case where the victim may have been raped, it may be necessary to collect and analyze the DNA of the victim's recent consensual partners, if any, to eliminate them as potential contributors of DNA suspected to be from the perpetrator.
    a) If this is necessary, it is important to approach the victim's family, husband, or boyfriend with extreme sensitivity and provide a full explanation of why the request is being made.
        i) When possible, a qualified victim advocate should be enlisted for assistance.

SUBMITTING SPECIMENS

1) Given the sensitive nature of DNA evidence, officers should always contact their laboratory personnel or evidence collection technicians when collection questions arise.
    a) It is increasingly difficult for investigators to locate a laboratory that will do ABO typing of blood. Many labs will do DNA testing only. If DNA is not successfully

extracted from a degraded sample, no other information will be supplied to the investigator.

2) Contamination
   a) Because extremely small samples of DNA can be used as evidence, greater attention to contamination issues is necessary when identifying, collecting, and preserving DNA evidence.
      i) DNA evidence can be contaminated when DNA from another source gets mixed with DNA relevant to the case.
         (1) This can happen when someone sneezes or coughs over the evidence or touches his mouth, nose, or other part of the face and then touches the area that may contain the DNA to be tested.
         (2) Because the new DNA technology PCR replicates or copies DNA in the evidence sample, the introduction of contaminants or other unintended DNA to an evidence sample can be problematic. With such minute samples of DNA being copied, extra care must be taken to prevent contamination. If a sample of DNA is submitted for testing, the PCR process will copy whatever DNA is present in the sample; it cannot distinguish between a suspect's DNA and DNA from another source.

DNA EXAMINATIONS

1) Examination considerations:
   a) DNA is analyzed in body fluids, stains, and other biological tissues recovered from evidence.
   b) The results of DNA analysis of questioned biological samples are compared with the results of DNA analysis of known samples. This analysis can associate victim(s) or suspect(s) with each other or a crime scene.

2) Collecting known samples
   a) Blood
      i) Only qualified medical personnel should collect blood samples from a person.
      ii) Collect at least two 5-milliliter tubes of blood in purple-top tubes with EDTA as an anticoagulant for DNA analysis.
      iii) Collect drug or alcohol testing samples in gray-top tubes with sodium fluoride (NaF).
      iv) Identify each tube with the date, time, subject's name, location, collector's name, case number, and evidence number.
      v) Refrigerate, do not freeze, blood samples. Use cold packs, not dry ice, during shipping.
      vi) Pack liquid blood tubes individually in Styrofoam or cylindrical tube containers with absorbent material surrounding the tubes.
      vii) Submit samples to the lab as soon as possible.
   b) Buccal swabbings
      i) Use clean cotton swabs to collect buccal swabbing samples.
      ii) Rub the inside surfaces of the cheeks and gums thoroughly.
      iii) Air-dry the swabs and place in clean paper or an envelope with sealed corners.
      iv) Do not use plastic containers.
      v) Identify each sample with the date, time, subject's name, location, collector's name, case number, and evidence number.

vi) Buccal swabbing samples do not need to be refrigerated.
vii) Submit samples to the lab as soon as possible.

3) Documenting, collecting, packaging, and preserving DNA evidence
   a) If DNA evidence is not properly documented, collected, packaged, and preserved, it will not meet the legal and scientific requirements for admissibility in a court of law.
   b) If DNA evidence is not properly documented, its origin can be questioned.
   c) If it is not properly collected, biological activity can be lost.
   d) If it is not properly packaged, contamination can occur.
   e) If it is not properly preserved, decomposition and deterioration can occur.
   f) When DNA evidence is transferred by direct or secondary (indirect) means, it remains on surfaces by absorption or adherence. In general, liquid biological evidence is absorbed into surfaces, and solid biological evidence adheres to surfaces. Collecting, packaging, and preserving DNA evidence depend on the liquid or solid state and the condition of the evidence.
   g) The more original integrity the evidence retains when it reaches the lab, the greater the possibility of conducting useful examinations.
      i) It may be necessary to use a variety of techniques to collect suspected body fluid evidence.

4) Submitting DNA evidence
   a) Blood on a person
      i) Absorb suspected liquid blood onto a clean cotton cloth or swab. Leave a portion of the cloth or swab unstained as a control. Air-dry the cloth or swab and pack in clean paper or an envelope with sealed corners. Do not use plastic containers.
      ii) Absorb suspected dried blood onto a clean cotton cloth or swab moistened with distilled water. Leave a portion of the cloth or swab unstained as a control. Air-dry the cloth or swab and pack in clean paper or an envelope with sealed corners. Do not use plastic containers.
   b) Blood on surfaces or in snow or water
      i) Absorb suspected liquid blood or blood clots onto a clean cotton cloth or swab. Leave a portion of the cloth or swab unstained as a control. Air-dry the cloth or swab and pack in clean paper or an envelope with sealed corners. Do not use plastic containers.
      ii) Collect suspected blood in snow or water immediately to avoid further dilution. Eliminate as much snow as possible. Place in a clean airtight container. Freeze the evidence and submit as soon as possible to the lab.
   c) Bloodstains
      i) Air-dry wet bloodstained garments. Wrap dried bloodstained garments in clean paper. Do not place wet or dried garments in plastic or airtight containers. Place all debris or residue from the garments in clean paper or an envelope with sealed corners.
      ii) Air-dry small, suspected wet-bloodstained objects and submit the objects to the lab. Preserve bloodstain patterns. Avoid creating additional stain patterns during drying and packaging. Pack to prevent stain removal by abrasive action or packaging materials during shipping. Pack in clean paper. Do not use plastic containers.
      iii) When possible, cut a large sample of suspected bloodstains from immovable

objects with a clean, sharp instrument. Collect an unstained control sample. Pack to prevent stain removal by abrasive action or packaging materials during shipping. Pack in clean paper. Do not use plastic containers.

    iv) Absorb suspected dried bloodstains on immovable objects onto a clean cotton cloth or swab moistened with distilled water. Leave a portion of the cloth or swab unstained as a control. Air-dry the cloth or swab and pack in clean paper or an envelope with sealed corners. Do not use plastic containers.

5) Blood examination request letter (FBI submission requirement)
   a) A blood examination request letter should contain the following:
      i) A brief statement of facts relating to the case
      ii) Claims made by the suspect(s) regarding the source of the blood
      iii) Information about whether animal blood is present or suspected
      iv) Information about whether the stains were laundered or diluted with other body fluids
      v) Information about the health of the victim(s) and suspect(s), such as AIDS, hepatitis, or tuberculosis.

6) Semen and semen stains
   a) Absorb suspected liquid semen onto a clean cotton cloth or swab. Leave a portion of the cloth or swab unstained as a control. Air-dry the cloth or swab and pack in clean paper or an envelope with sealed corners. Do not use plastic containers.
   b) Submit small, suspected dried semen–stained objects to the lab. Pack to prevent stain removal by abrasive action or packaging materials during shipping. Pack in clean paper. Do not use plastic containers.
   c) When possible, cut a large sample of suspected semen stains from immovable objects with a clean, sharp instrument. Collect an unstained control sample. Pack to prevent stain removal by abrasive action or packaging materials during shipping. Pack in clean paper. Do not use plastic containers.
   d) Absorb suspected dried-semen stains on immovable objects onto a clean cotton cloth or swab moistened with distilled water. Leave a portion of the cloth or swab unstained as a control. Air-dry the swab or cloth and place in clean paper or an envelope with sealed corners. Do not use plastic containers.

7) Semen evidence from sexual assault victim(s)
   a) Sexual assault victim(s) should be medically examined in a hospital or a physician's office using a standard sexual assault evidence kit to collect vaginal, oral, and anal evidence.
   b) Refrigerate and submit the evidence as soon as possible to the lab.

8) Saliva and urine
   a) Absorb suspected liquid saliva or urine into a clean cotton cloth or swab. Leave a portion of the cloth unstained as a control. Air-dry the cloth or swab and pack in clean paper or an envelope with sealed corners. Do not use plastic containers.
   b) Submit suspected small, dried-saliva or urine-stained objects to the lab. Pack to prevent stain removal by abrasive action or packaging materials during shipping. Pack in clean paper or an envelope with sealed corners. Do not use plastic containers.
   c) When possible, cut a large sample of suspected saliva or urine stains from immovable objects with a clean, sharp instrument. Collect an unstained control sample. Pack to prevent stain removal by abrasive action or packaging materials during shipping. Pack in clean paper. Do not use plastic containers.

9) Cigarette butts
   a) Pick up cigarette butts with gloved hands or clean forceps. Do not submit ashes. Air-dry and place the cigarette butts from the same location (ashtray) in clean paper or an envelope with sealed corners.
      i) Do not submit the ashtray unless latent print examination is requested. Package the ashtray separately.
   b) Do not use plastic containers.

10) Chewing gum
    a) Pick up chewing gum with gloved hands or clean forceps. Air-dry and place in clean paper or an envelope with sealed corners. Do not use plastic containers.

11) Envelopes and stamps
    a) Pick up envelopes and stamps with gloved hands or clean forceps and place in a clean envelope. Do not use plastic containers.

12) Hair
    a) Pick up hair carefully with clean forceps to prevent damaging the root tissue.
    b) Air-dry hair mixed with suspected body fluids.
    c) Package each group of hair separately in clean paper or an envelope with sealed corners. Do not use plastic containers.
    d) Refrigerate and submit as soon as possible to the lab.

13) Tissues, bones, and teeth
    a) Call the lab before submitting suspected tissues, bones, or teeth to ensure that the evidence will be accepted.
       i) The communication accompanying the evidence must reference the telephone conversation accepting the evidence (FBI recommendation).
    b) Pick up suspected tissues, bones, and teeth with gloved hands or clean forceps.
    c) Collect the following for DNA processing:
       i) Collect 1 to 2 cubic inches of red skeletal muscle.
       ii) Collect 3 to 5 inches of long bone, such as the fibula or femur.
       iii) Collect teeth in the following order:
            (1) Unrestored molar
            (2) Unrestored premolar
            (3) Unrestored canine
            (4) Unrestored front tooth
            (5) Restored molar
            (6) Restored premolar
            (7) Restored canine
            (8) Restored front tooth
       iv) Place tissue samples in a clean, airtight plastic container without formalin or formaldehyde.
       v) Place teeth and bone samples in clean paper or an envelope with sealed corners.
       vi) Freeze the evidence, place it in Styrofoam containers, and ship overnight on dry ice.

14) Water drinking bottles (plastic).
    a) Handle with gloved hands.

b) Poke small holes in the bottom of the bottle to drain the liquid contents.
- i) DNA from saliva (from drinking from the bottle) will collect on the inside of the container.

c) Air-dry.

d) Package in paper.

POSTMORTEM EFFECTS ON DNA

1) The success of DNA analysis in postmortem samples depends on the body's state of decomposition.
    a) How long a body has been dead and the temperature of the environment in which the body has been stored are critical in the success of DNA analysis.
        i) Postmortem blood can only be used when the body is relatively fresh.
        ii) Spleen and bone marrow are good sources of DNA.
        iii) Skeletal muscle from the thigh or upper arm is good source of DNA.
        iv) Spongy bone specimens (e.g., the ribs) are a rich source of DNA.
        v) In bodies involving advanced states of decomposition, bone becomes the best source of DNA.

PROPER TRANSPORTATION AND STORAGE OF DNA EVIDENCE

1) Evidence recovered from a crime scene should be stored properly to optimize potential DNA analysis.
    a) When transporting and storing evidence that may contain DNA, it is important to keep the evidence dry and at room temperature.
    b) Before storage, thoroughly air-dry stains, swabs, and hair root samples at room temperature to avoid the growth of mold and bacteria.
        i) The specimen should then be placed in a moisture-resistant container.
        ii) Never place evidence that may contain DNA in plastic bags because plastic bags retain damaging moisture.
        iii) Direct sunlight and warmer conditions also may be harmful to DNA, so avoid keeping evidence in places that may get hot (e.g., a room or police car without air conditioning).
    c) Once the evidence has been secured in paper bags or envelopes, it should be sealed, labeled, and transported in a way that ensures proper identification of where it was found and proper chain of custody.
    d) For long-term storage issues, contact your local laboratory.

UNIDENTIFIED DECEDENTS

1) Specimens should be collected on all unidentified decedents in anticipation of using DNA analysis to identify the remains.

2) Currently, difficult cases of identification are being identified by mitochondrial DNA, which is used extensively by the military. Cases include repatriated remains from former war areas of Vietnam, Korea, and even battlefield and airplane crash locations of World War II.

3) DNA is extracted from blood samples provided by the maternal relatives of the recovered remains of the soldier or some other unidentified subject (e.g., sister, mother, grandmother, and

two uncles in the following example). The relatives' DNA mitochondrial specimen profile is compared with the DNA retrieved from the recovered unidentified bone.

4) Locating other potential sources of DNA on unidentified decedents or missing persons includes:
    a) Toothbrush
    b) Hairbrush
    c) Stuffed toys (on missing children)
        i) These may have been collected and boxed by parents of missing child
        ii) Look through the box and find anything the child may have used and played with by placing it in its mouth.

MITROCHONDRIAL DNA

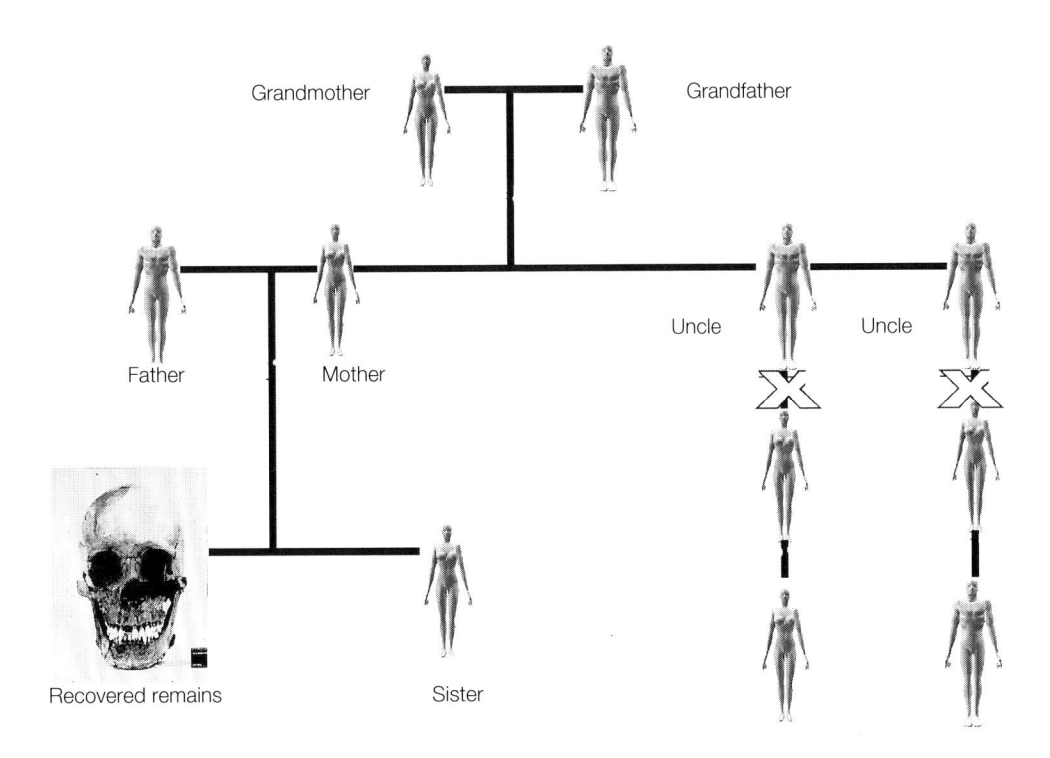

5) These are impending DNA examination advances:
    a) Gender identification from specimen
    b) Race identification
    c) Hair color
    d) Eye color
    e) Nuclear DNA extraction from tooth specimen

COMBINED DNA INDEX SYSTEM (CODIS)

1) The saliva on the stamp of a stalker's threatening letter or the skin cells shed on a ligature of a strangled victim can be compared with a suspect's blood or saliva sample. Similarly, DNA collected from the perspiration on a baseball cap discarded by a rapist at one crime scene can be compared with DNA in the saliva swabbed from the bitemark on a different rape victim.
2) CODIS is an electronic database of DNA profiles that can identify suspects.

3) It is similar to the AFIS database. Every state in the nation is in the process of implementing a DNA index of individuals convicted of certain crimes, such as rape, murder, and child abuse.
   a) Upon conviction a sample analysis of the perpetrator's DNA profile is entered into the DNA database. Just as fingerprints found at a crime scene can be run through AFIS in search of a suspect or link to another crime scene, DNA profiles from a crime scene can be entered into CODIS. Therefore, law enforcement officers have the ability to identify possible suspects when no prior suspect existed.

4) How does CODIS work?
   a) After the offender's DNA specimen is tested, the resulting DNA profile is expressed as a series of numbers much like a long SSN. These numerical profiles are entered into a computer database in an offender file. When DNA evidence is recovered from crime-scene evidence (e.g., semen from a rape victim), the evidence DNA profile is also entered into the CODIS computer. A comparison is then made by the computer to determine whether the evidence profile matches a known offender. If a "hit" is made, the investigator is promptly advised of the match. The match is used as probable cause to seek a new DNA sample from the suspect, which will be used to perform confirmation testing for subsequent use in a judicial proceeding.
   b) If a match between the evidence specimen and an offender is not found in the database, the evidence DNA profile is compared with profiles from evidence recovered from other unsolved crimes. In this way, it can be determined whether the same perpetrator is linked to other assaults even though his identity is not yet known.
   c) When case-to-case hits are made by CODIS, the investigators from the jurisdictions involved are notified of the link. Through a follow-up conference among these investigators, new leads may be developed that can help to identify the suspect and resolve several open cases.

5) CODIS began as a pilot project to help state and local laboratories. The DNA Identification Act formalized the FBI's authority to establish a national DNA index for law enforcement purposes. The FBI operates the national system, NDIS. CODIS is implemented as a distributed database with three hierarchical levels, or tiers: local, state, and national.
   a) NDIS is the highest level in the CODIS hierarchy and enables the labs participating in the CODIS program to exchange and compare DNA profiles on a national level.
   b) All DNA profiles originate at the local level (LDIS) and then flow to the state level (SDIS) and national levels (NDIS). SDIS allows laboratories in states to exchange DNA profiles.
      i) The tiered approach allows state and local agencies to operate their databases according to their specific legislative or legal requirements.
      ii) The FBI provides CODIS software, together with installation, training, and user support, free of charge to any state and local law enforcement labs performing DNA analysis.

6) CODIS blends forensic science and computer technology into an effective tool for solving violent crimes. It enables federal, state, and local crime labs to exchange and compare DNA profiles electronically, thereby linking crimes to each other and to convicted offenders.

7) CODIS generates investigative leads in crimes where biological evidence is recovered from the crime scene using two indexes: the forensic and offender indexes.
   a) The forensic index contains DNA profiles from crime-scene evidence.

THE CODIS PROCESS

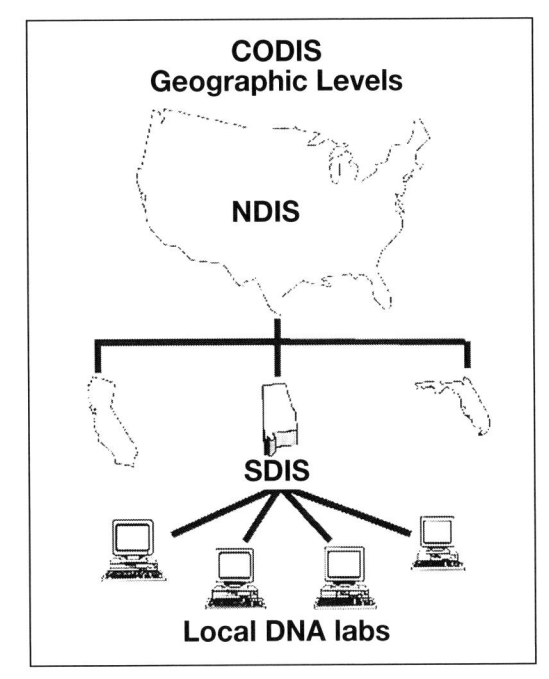

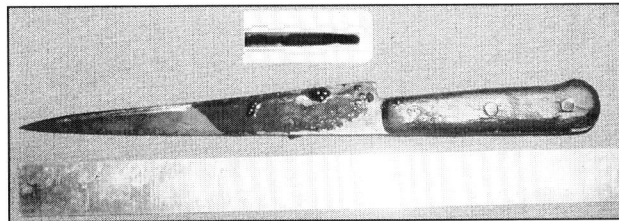

CODIS Geographic Levels

NDIS

SDIS

Local DNA labs

⬇

LDIS
Local DNA CODIS Lab

Evidence is submitted to the local lab, where a DNA (PCR-STR) specimen is extracted and a DNA profile is compiled. The profile is compared with a local database of other DNA profiles collected from local crime scenes from the particular area. The specimen from the unknown contributor is also compared to a second database of known offenders.

⬇

SDIS
State DNA CODIS Lab

The local lab then submits the DNA profile to the state lab, where the process will be repeated and compared with other crime evidence on a statewide basis, as well as for other offender evidence compiled by the state.

⬇

NDIS
National DNA CODIS Lab

Finally, the profile is entered into the national database system and compared with a national index of crimes, as well as a national collection of offenders.

i) Matches made among profiles in the forensic index can link crime scenes, possibly identifying serial offenders.

ii) Based on a match, police in multiple jurisdictions can coordinate their respective investigations and share the leads they developed independently.

b) The offender index contains DNA profiles of individuals convicted of sex offenses (and other violent crimes) with many states now expanding legislation to include other felonies.

i) Matches made between the forensic and offender indexes provide investigators with the identity of the perpetrator(s).

ii) After CODIS identifies a potential match, qualified DNA analysts in the labs responsible for the matching profiles contact each other to validate or refute the match.

CODIS CASE EXAMPLE

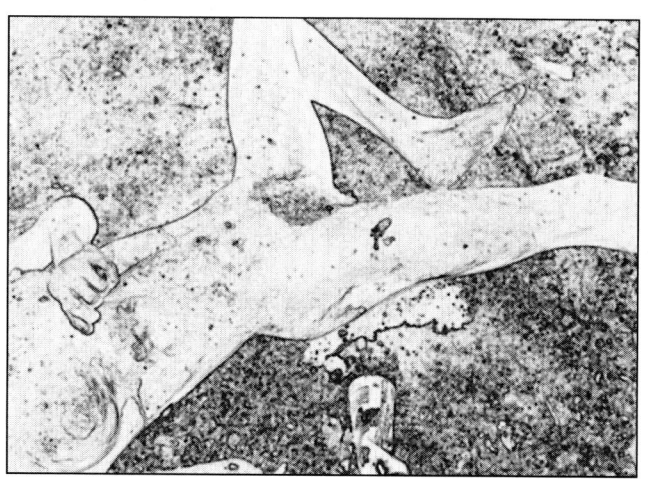

Victim is found in an abandoned house. She has apparently been strangled. A blood spatter is observed on the right thigh.

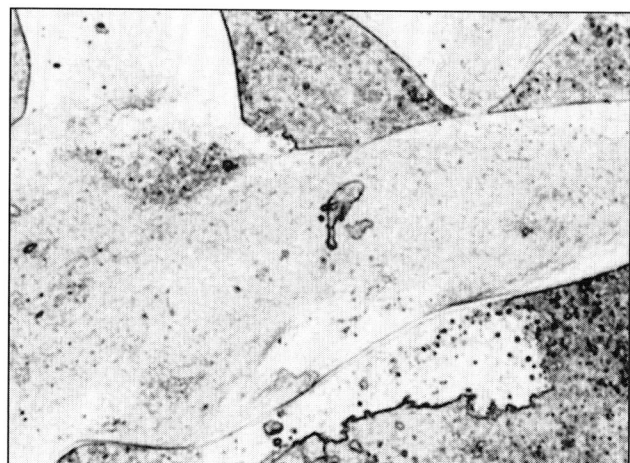

On closer inspection, the blood spatter on the victim's right thigh gives an indication of direction. The spatter would have to come from above and in front of the victim. The victim is not bleeding. She has been strangled. Investigators now work on the assumption that the blood on victim's right thigh may have originated from the perpetrator of this homicide. The blood is collected before transporting the body from the scene.

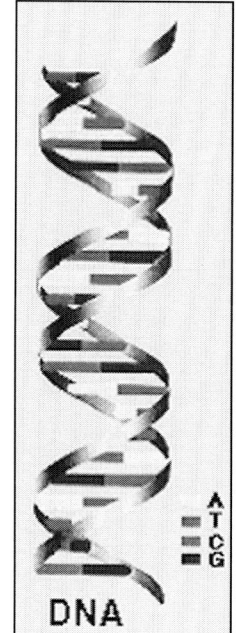

1. The blood specimen is packaged at the scene. It will then be sent to a crime lab specializing in DNA.
2. An attempt to extract DNA through PCR–STR analysis will be conducted. If the lab is successful, it will have a DNA fingerprint (profile) of the person who left the blood on the victim's leg.
3. The DNA profile will be entered locally into CODIS.
4. The profile is entered into the forensic file where the profile will be compared with other cases that have been entered into the database file. This submitted profile has the potential to identify other crimes the perpetrator has committed, although it will not identify the suspect.
5. The profile will then be entered into a convicted-offender database file. It is here that the unknown profile may be matched to a known-offender profile of someone who has been required to have his specimen on file because of state-required submission of DNA based on conviction for a specified crime.

CODIS

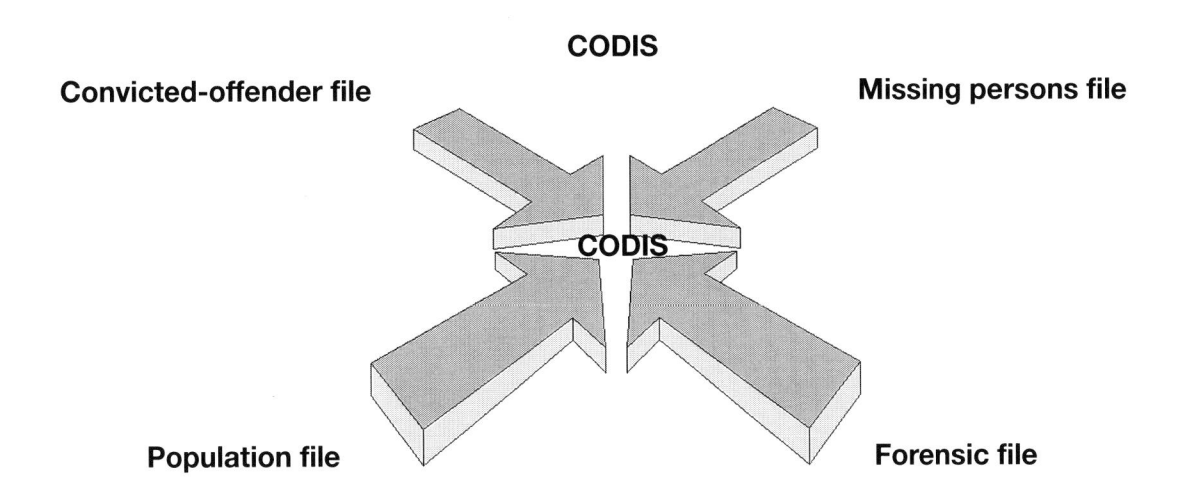

- Convicted-offender file
- Missing persons file
- CODIS
- Population file
- Forensic file

INDEXES

1) Many law enforcement officials consider forensic DNA analysis the most significant advance in forensic science since fingerprints. As a result, states are rapidly expanding the scope and size of their CODIS databases.

2) States have enacted DNA database legislation requiring the collection of blood samples from convicted offenders and the storage and analysis of such samples in state DNA databases.
   a) This legislation requires persons convicted of felony sex offenses (and other crimes, depending on each state's statute) to provide biological samples for DNA analysis. These samples are analyzed and entered into the CODIS database.

3) Studies have demonstrated that the more expansive the list of crimes to which a convicted offender must have his DNA sample submitted, the more "hits" are generated during blind searches in the forensic files of criminal cases.
   a) As the cases and offender samples are added to the database, and as more and more states get online, the number of hits will grow in proportion.
   b) Over the past 5 years about half of the states have expanded the scope of their original DNA database legislation.
      i) Six states include all felons in their database, five other states have expanded the scope of their legislation, and one state now covers all arrested persons.

4) There is currently a backlog of convicted offender samples to be analyzed simply because the analysis efforts in most states are unable to keep pace with the collection of the samples. In addition, many labs are doing retests using the new STR technology.

NDIS PARTICIPATION

1) Entities participating in NDIS as of October 2001 include these:
   a) 37 states, U.S. Army (USACIL), and the FBI

FBI

DC

US ARMY

Participating States

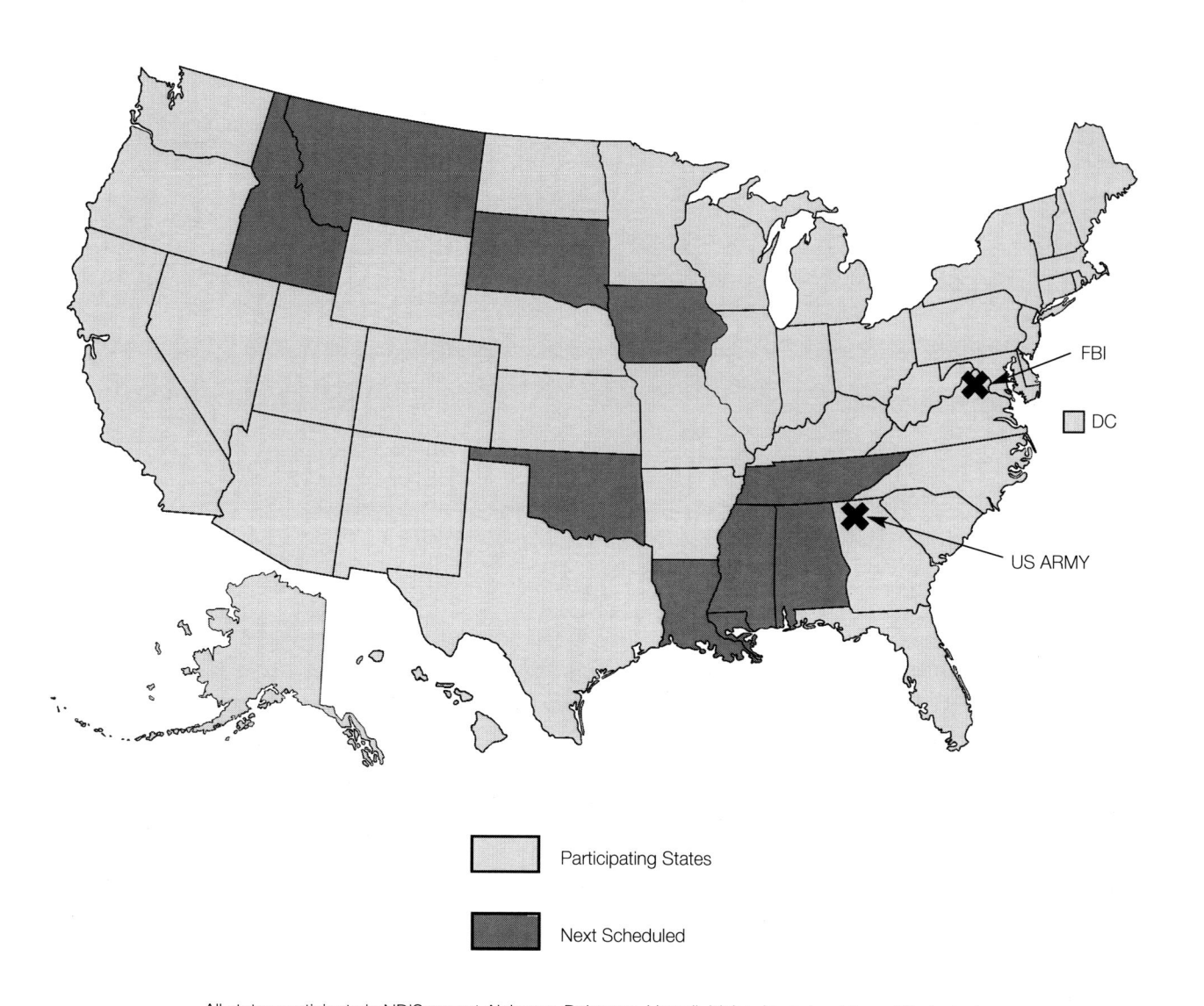

Next Scheduled

All states participate in NDIS except Alabama, Delaware, Hawaii, Idaho, Iowa, Louisiana, Mississippi, Montana, New Hampshire, Oklahoma, Rhode Island, South Dakota, and Tennessee. (Source: FBI.)

LAWS QUALIFYING OFFENSES FOR DATABASE BY STATE (SOURCE: U.S. CONGRESS)

States have enacted laws requiring convicted offenders of certain crimes to submit their DNA for placement into CODIS. The particular offenses requiring collection vary from state to state. The following chart indicates the particular criminal conviction, by state, that requires collection and submission. Studies have indicated that the more crimes included for collection purposes, the greater the success in identifying the perpetrator based on specimens from the unidentified forensic file (composed of DNA evidence from unsolved crimes).

The retroactive nature of the state statute requiring collection and submission from a convicted individual who is incarcerated or on parole or probation is also indicated.

STATE	SEX OFFENSES	CHILD CRIMES	ASSAULT/BATTERY	MURDER	ROBBERY	KIDNAPPING	BURGLARY	FELONY ATTEMPTS	JUVENILE	ALL FELONIES	INCARCERATION	RETROACTIVE PAROLE	PROBATION
Alabama	X	X	X	X	X	X	X	X		X	X		
Alaska	X	X	X	X	X	X		X	X				
Arizona	X	X					X	X					
Arkansas	X	X	X	X	X	X			X				
California	X	X	X	X				X	X				
Colorado	X	X							X			X	X
Connecticut	X	X				X					X		
Delaware	X	X						X			X		
Florida	X		X	X	X		X	X	X		X		
Georgia	X	X								X			
Hawaii	X	X	X										

STATE	SEX OFFENSES	CHILD CRIMES	ASSAULT/BATTERY	MURDER	ROBBERY	KIDNAPPING	BURGLARY	FELONY ATTEMPTS	JUVENILE	ALL FELONIES	INCARCERATION	RETROACTIVE PAROLE	RETROACTIVE PROBATION
Idaho	X	X	X	X	X			X	X		X	X	X
Indiana	X	X	X	X	X	X	X				X		
Kansas	X	X	X					X	X		X		
Louisiana	X	X	X	X		X		X	X		X		
Maryland	X		X	X	X						X		
Michigan	X												
Minnesota	X			X				X	X			X	
Mississippi	X	X									X		
Missouri	X	X	X	X		X					X	X	X
Montana	X	X	X	X	X	X		X	X				
Nebraska	X	X		X							X		

STATE	SEX OFFENSES	CHILD CRIMES	ASSAULT/BATTERY	MURDER	ROBBERY	KIDNAPPING	BURGLARY	FELONY ATTEMPTS	JUVENILE	ALL FELONIES	INCARCERATION	RETROACTIVE PAROLE	PROBATION
Nevada	X	X	X	X			X	X					
New Hampshire	X								X		X		
New Jersey	X							X	X		X		
New Mexico	X	X	X	X	X	X	X		X	X	X	X	X
New York	X		X	X							X	X	X
North Carolina	X		X	X	X	X					X		X
North Dakota	X	X						X			X		
Ohio	X	X		X		X		X	X		X		
Oklahoma	X	X	X	X							X		
Oregon	X	X		X			X	X	X		X		
Pennsylvania	X	X		X				X	X		X		
Rhode Island	X	X		X									
South Carolina	X	X	X	X			X		X		X	X	X

STATE	SEX OFFENSES	CHILD CRIMES	ASSAULT/BATTERY	MURDER	ROBBERY	KIDNAPPING	BURGLARY	FELONY ATTEMPTS	JUVENILE	ALL FELONIES	INCARCERATION	RETROACTIVE PAROLE	RETROACTIVE PROBATION
South Dakota	X	X									X	X	X
Tennessee	X	X	X	X	X	X	X	X	X	X			
Texas	X	X	X	X			X		X		X		
Utah	X	X		X		X							
Vermont	X	X	X	X	X	X	X	X			X	X	X
Washington	X	X	X	X	X	X		X	X				
Wisconsin	X	X	X	X	X	X	X	X		X	X		
FEDERAL	X	X	X	X		X	X	X			X	X	X

CHAPTER 76: SEROLOGY

CONSIDERATIONS

1) One of the most important items of evidence at a scene may be blood. It can exist in two forms:
   a) As a liquid sample
   b) As a dry stain

2) Other body fluids may be beneficial for typing purposes:
   a) Semen
   b) Saliva
   c) Vaginal secretion
   d) Perspiration

3) Urine and fecal material. Labs prefer not to analyze these because they are too unreliable. Consult with the individual laboratory for further consideration.

SCIENTIFIC BASIS FOR BODY FLUID ANALYSIS

1) People generally have blood types of A, AB, B, or O. It is also possible for the lab to find the same typing characteristics in an individual's blood common in other body fluids such as saliva, semen, tears, and perspiration. It is not possible to type all individuals through body fluids in the absence of blood because not all have specific substances in sufficient quantity to allow their other body fluids to be typed. If they do, they are considered secretors—that is, an individual whose body fluids, as well as blood, can be grouped. A nonsecretor is one whose blood can be grouped, but whose other body fluids cannot.
   a) About 65 to 80 percent of the population are secretors, while the remaining are nonsecretors.
   b) Saliva is the most suitable material for determining whether an individual is a secretor.

2) Prior to DNA development, advances in ABO serology had allowed blood typing to be further subdivided, providing for a more significant grouping of individuals with the particular blood-typing characteristics.

INVESTIGATIVE SIGNIFICANCE

1) Blood typing is available with other body fluids. Blood may have deteriorated or may not be present at a scene.
   a) Efforts to identify suspects may involve saliva sampling from cigarette butts, underarm perspiration pads, and the vinyl backing of a car seat, among others.

COLLECTING SPECIMENS

1) The evidence technician may find blood in various states during the crime-scene processing. Blood may be found in large quantities in a pooled area or be present as a small spatter on the clothing of a suspect.

a) Searching the scene
　　i) If it is believed that the suspect cut himself, search for blood in out-of-the way places. Search for tissues, towels, wash cloths, etc., that may have been discarded in out of the way places, including in trash cans, under furniture, in closets.
　　ii) If the suspect is believed to have washed off blood at a particular sink, the drain trap should be dismantled and the liquid collected and transferred to the crime lab.
　　iii) If it appears that blood has been cleaned from the floor, try to get samples from cracks or other recesses in the floor.
b) Preservation and collection
　　i) Blood is biological in nature. Once it comes out of the body, it begins to degenerate. For this reason, time is a factor and will affect the sample.
　　ii) Body fluids are best preserved when they are in a dry state.
　　iii) Do not package any serological evidence in plastic, which will make the specimen unusable by the time it gets to the serologist. Paper bags or paper envelopes should be used in all cases of dry-stain collection.
　　iv) Collect liquid blood samples for use as a control standard.
　　　　(1) Do not place liquid blood samples in a freezer.
c) Procedures for recovering a dried bloodstain on a wall or floor
　　i) It is preferable to scrape the stain onto a piece of paper for collection.
　　ii) If at all possible, reliquefying the stain should be avoided. The more concentrated a stain, the better the chances of lab personnel developing information from it.
　　　　(1) A small stain requires a small patch of gauze for recovery. Use appropriately sized gauze patches.
　　　　(2) Wet the gauze with water. Wipe up the stain and flick the gauze pad to remove excess water.
　　　　(3) Air-dry and place in a paper envelope.
　　iii) If a blood sample is being collected from the wall or a spot on the floor, the lab will want to know whether the surface area is responsible for giving a false positive. To check for this possibility:
　　　　(1) Get as close to the stain as possible without involving the original stain.
　　　　(2) Take a standard (swabbing) of the unstained wall or floor.
　　　　(3) Air-dry and place in a paper envelope.
　　　　(4) The collected items can be placed in a freezer and stored pending submission.
　　iv) Generally, a stain big enough to see is big enough to process.
　　v) Bloodstains from two different areas should never be mixed.

LABORATORY ANALYSIS

1) The lab process involving all blood associated with the case (victim and suspect) can reveal the following:
　　a) Is it blood?
　　b) If it is blood, is it human or animal in origin?
　　c) Type (A, AB, B, O) or further subgroups and isoenzymes
　　d) Alcohol content of the blood
　　e) Drugs present in the blood

f) Whether blood (human) was venous, fetal, or menstrual in origin
g) Possible method in which blood was deposited onto the surface

2) Serology isn't as definitive as DNA testing, although suspects can be eliminated on the basis of one discrepancy or mismatch involving the typing of the suspect stain.
   a) If the samples correspond along identical levels, or degrees in which the stain can be classified, then the serologist can supply the investigator with a percentage of the population in which the characteristics falls. For obvious reasons, the rarer the typing, the smaller the population group the suspect can come from. Without the use of DNA classification, the best possible serology finding will involve a characteristic classification falling within 1 percent of the population.
      i) Regardless of the type classification, the sample will never be as specifically defined as a DNA sample. Therefore, current serological examination, if it is done at all, is usually conducted as a preliminary test before the more costly and time-consuming DNA testing is performed (1 day as opposed to 6 to 8 weeks). If a match is not made through typing, DNA tests will not be performed on the sample submitted. Currently, it is extremely difficult to locate a lab in which ABO typing is offered as a test procedure.
      ii) Serologists examine for two types of identifiers:
         (1) Antigen/antibodies
            (a) This does not have any bearing on the race or sex.
         (2) Enzymes and proteins
            (a) Sickle-cell traits found in the hemoglobin may indicate race.

SEMEN STAINS

1) Semen stains are fairly resistant to chemical action, but they are very fragile when dry.

2) Never assume in an apparent sexual homicide that semen will be found in the orifices usually assumed in sexual intercourse. Semen may be absent, be found in or on other areas of the body, or be present in areas adjacent to the scene.

3) Collect the sample.
   a) For stains on garments or other easily transportable items, place them in a paper bag and send to the crime lab. Stains should not be allowed to touch one another or an unstained area.
   b) If a semen stain is found on an area not easily transportable, a clean razor blade should be used to dislodge the crust and place it in a paper envelope. The razor blade can be submitted under separate cover.

4) The best indicator that the specimen collected is semen is the identification of sperm in the specimen.

ABO BLOOD GROUPING SYSTEM			
A	**B**	**O**	**AB**
39.2%	12.7%	43.5%	4.5%

Blood grouping—frequency of occurrence.

CHAPTER 77: TRACE EVIDENCE AND OTHER CRIME LAB EXAMINATIONS

TRACE EVIDENCE

1) Trace evidence is evidence that may be present at a scene, but its minuteness necessitates special scrutiny. The particular evidence may hold some specific significance in linking a victim, a suspect, a scene, and the activities of what has occurred. An investigator, evidence technician, and other support personnel determine the significance it may play in understanding what happened and who was responsible; a crime lab technician analyzes and interprets the evidence.

2) Trace evidence is based on the philosophy that there must be an exchange of items between individuals and an environment. This exchange (Locard's principle) includes trace materials that may only be discovered through a deliberate and thorough processing procedure.

3) The clothing of the suspect is a primary source of trace material. Three possibilities exist for developing evidence:
   a) Trace materials from the victim may have collected on the suspect.
   b) Trace material from the environment, linking the particular suspect to a particular location, may be present on the suspect.
   c) Standards from the suspect must be collected and compared with items collected from the victim and the scene to link the individual to the area and the victim.

4) Trace evidence involving the victim
   a) Trace materials from the suspect may have collected on the victim.
   b) Trace material from the scene may be present on the victim.
      i) This becomes important when dealing with a body-dump case or in other cases in which another scene or scenes are involved. In the case of a body dump, red carpet fibers may link the victim not only with a transporting vehicle, but with other related cases as well. This may be the first indication to the investigative agency that several homicide cases may be related.
   c) Trace evidence from the victim must be collected to compare with trace evidence collected from the suspect and the scene.

5) The scene
   a) Evidence from the scene may be found on the suspect.
   b) If a secondary site is involved, evidence from the original death scene may be found on the body of the victim.
   c) Trace evidence from the scene must be collected for comparison should trace material be collected from the victim or suspect.

6) Clothing is a primary accumulator for trace evidence. Care and caution must be taken in the handling, collecting, and packaging of these articles.
   a) Suspect's clothing
      i) If suspect is still wearing the articles he was believed to have worn at the time of the incident, proceed as follows:

(1) Examine the clothing for any obvious signs of evidence. The item's location may be as important as what it is.
(2) The suspect should stand on a clean piece of wrapping paper. As each item of clothing is removed, it should be wrapped separately. After the suspect has removed all his clothing, the wrapping paper should be collected, folded inward, and bagged separately.
(3) Never shake or handle possible evidence any more than absolutely necessary.
(4) Never place clothing items in a plastic or an airtight container. Moisture causes bacterial growth, which makes analysis unproductive.
(5) Dry garments should be placed in a clean paper bag. If it is not possible to air-dry a garment, place it in a bag to prevent wet areas from touching.
(6) Never turn the pockets inside-out. The pockets, pants cuffs, and pants pleats often are receptacles for trace evidence.
(7) If trace evidence is removed from clothing prior to sending it off for trace analysis, note the precise location of where the item was recovered.

7) Cloth remnants, fragments, or impressions may be important to a particular incident, such as a hit-and-run traffic fatality.
   a) Note the color, pattern, general material if known, and the size and shape.
   b) Photograph the item by placing it at a 90-degree angle to the camera lens. Oblique lighting (45 degrees or less) should be used for enhancement of the fabric pattern. Package in paper.

ABRASIVES EXAMINATION

1) Lab significance
   a) Examinations can determine what type of abrasive material was used to sabotage engines or machinery.

2) Submitting abrasives evidence
   a) Submit abrasives in heat-sealed or resealable plastic bags or paint cans. Avoid using paper or glass containers.

3) Collection considerations
   a) Use personnel familiar with engine and machinery operations and mechanics to recover abrasives.
   b) Abrasives settle in oil and fuel. Submit the oil and fuel from the engine sump or filters.
   c) Abrasives embed themselves in bearings and other parts. Submit the bearings and other parts.

ADHESIVES

1) Examination considerations
   a) Identifications can be made with the torn or cut end of tape and a roll of suspect tape. Tape composition, construction, and color can be compared with known sources.
   b) Caulking, sealant, and adhesives can be compared by color and composition with known sources.

c) Fingerprint examination can be made on both sides of sticky-side tape.
   i) On tape that is stuck together, place it in a freezer for 2 hours before attempting to pull it apart slowly.
   ii) Liquid nitrogen can also be used. Dip the tape carefully into a bucket containing liquid nitrogen. Do not allow the tape to sit in the liquid nitrogen for any length of time. Upon removal, the tape can be peeled apart.
   iii) Paint a paste mixture of sticky-side powder, Photo-Flo solution, and water on to the sticky side surface of the paint.

ARSON EXAMINATION

1) Examination considerations
   a) Arson examinations can determine the presence of accelerants introduced to a fire scene.
   b) Examinations of debris recovered from scenes can identify gasoline, fuel oils, and specialty solvents.
      i) Examinations generally cannot identify specific brands.

2) Scene considerations
   a) Search for the following at questioned arson scenes:
      i) Candles, cigarettes, matchbooks, Molotov cocktails, fused chemical masses, or any electronic or mechanical devices that may have been used to assist the arsonist
      ii) Cloth or paper burn trails, burn trails on carpeted or hardwood floors, and the removal of personal property or commercial inventory

3) Submitting arson evidence
   a) Flammable liquids are volatile and easily lost through evaporation. Preserve evidence in such airtight containers as metal cans, glass jars, or heat-sealed or resealable plastic bags.
   b) Do not fill the containers to the top.
   c) Pack evidence to prevent breakage.

AUDIO ANALOG TAPE RECORDINGS

1) Audio examination considerations
   a) Authenticity
      i) Authenticity examinations are conducted to determine whether audio recordings are original, continuous, unaltered, and consistent with the stated operation of the tape recorder.
   b) Enhancement
      i) Enhancement examinations are conducted to selectively reduce interfering noise on audio recordings to improve the intelligibility and the understanding of the recordings.
   c) Voice comparisons
      i) Spectrographic examinations compare an unknown recorded voice sample with a known verbatim voice exemplar produced on a similar transmission and recording device, such as the telephone.
         (1) Decisions about voice comparisons by the spectrographic method are not conclusive. The results of voice comparisons are provided for investigative guidance only.

d) Signal analysis
- i) Signal analysis examinations are conducted to identify, compare, and interpret such signals as gunshots and telephone touch-tones.

e) Damaged media repair
- i) Audio recordings can be repaired, restored, or retrieved for playback and examination if damage is not too extensive.

2) Evidence submission considerations
   a) Label the outer container as follows:

   > **ELECTRONIC EQUIPMENT**
   > or
   > **FRAGILE, SENSITIVE**
   > **AUDIO/VIDEO MEDIA**
   > and
   > **KEEP AWAY FROM MAGNETS OR MAGNETIC FIELDS.**

   b) The FBI Laboratory does handle these types of examinations. Contact the local FBI office for guidance. Address the outer container as follows:

   > **Federal Bureau of Investigation**
   > **Engineering Research Facility**
   > **Attention: Forensic Program**
   > **Building 27958A**
   > **Quantico, VA 22135**

BANK SECURITY DYE EXAMINATION

1) Consideration
   a) Specific dyes and chemicals used in bank security devices can be identified. Items such as clothing and money can be analyzed for the presence of these dyes and chemicals.

2) Submitting bank security dye evidence
   a) Do not submit evidence without visible stains.
   b) Do not submit a large piece of stained evidence. Cut a small sample of the stained area and submit it in a heat-sealed or resealable plastic bag.
   c) Collect an unstained control sample, package separately, and submit it with the dye-stained evidence.
   d) Transfer stains by rubbing with a clean (dry or wet with alcohol) cotton swab.
   - i) Use an unstained swab as a control.
   - ii) Air-dry the swab and pack it in a heat-sealed or resealable plastic bag.

BUILDING MATERIALS EXAMINATION

1) Examination consideration
   a) Examinations can compare such building materials as brick, mortar, plaster, stucco, cement, and concrete.

2) Submitting building materials evidence
   a) When building materials are penetrated or damaged, debris can adhere to persons,

clothing, tools, bags, and other articles.
b) If possible, submit the evidence to the lab for examiners to remove the debris.
c) Package each item of evidence in separate paper bags.
d) Collect known samples from the penetrated or damaged areas.
e) Submit known and questioned debris in separate leakproof containers, such as film canisters or plastic pill bottles. Avoid using paper or glass containers.
f) Pack to keep any lumps intact.

COMPUTER EXAMINATION

1) Examination considerations
   a) Examinations can determine what type of data files are in a computer.
      i) Comparison
         (1) Examinations can compare data files with known documents and data files.
      ii) Transaction
         (1) Examinations can determine the time and sequence data files were created.
      iii) Extraction
         (1) Data files can be extracted from the computer.
      iv) Deleted data files
         (1) Deleted data files can be recovered from the computer.
      v) Format conversion
         (1) Data files can be converted from one format to another.
      vi) Keyword searching
         (1) Data files can be searched for a word or phrase, and all occurrences recorded.
      vii) Passwords
         (1) Passwords can be recovered and decrypted.
      viii) Limited source code
         (1) Source code can be analyzed and compared.
      ix) Storage media
         (1) Storage media used with stand-alone word processors (typewriters) can be examined.

2) Requesting a search or field examination with the crime lab (FBI recommendation)
   a) Submit requests for a search or field examination at least 1 week in advance.
   b) Obtain as much of the following information as possible before submitting a request:
      i) Determine the type of computers and operating systems.
      ii) If applicable, determine the type of network software, the location of the network servers, and the number of computers on the network.
      iii) Determine whether encryption or password protection is used.
      iv) Specify whether seizure of computers and media or on-site examination is required.

3) Submitting computer evidence
   a) For most examinations, submit only the central processing units and the internal and external storage media.
   b) Use a sturdy cardboard container when shipping computer components.
      i) If possible, use the original packing case with the fitted padding.

ii) Use large, plastic bubble wrap or foam-rubber pads as packing.
iii) Do not use loose Styrofoam because it lodges inside computers or components and creates static charges that can cause data loss or damage to circuit boards.
iv) Seal the container with a strong packing tape.
c) Pack and ship central processing units in the upright position. Label the outside container as follows:

THIS END UP!

d) Disks, cartridges, tapes, and hard drives should be packed to avoid movement during shipping.
e) Label the outer container as follows:

**FRAGILE, SENSITIVE ELECTRONIC EQUIPMENT
and
KEEP AWAY FROM MAGNETS OR MAGNETIC FIELDS**

CONTROLLED-SUBSTANCE EXAMINATION

1) Examination considerations
   a) Controlled-substances examinations can establish trace drug presence, identity, and quantity.

CORD, STRING, AND ROPE

1) Examinations
   a) Microscopic materials adhering to the string or rope may be analyzed for possible linkage with a particular environment.
   b) A piece of rope or cord can be compared with a questioned rope or cord. The composition, construction, color, and diameter can be determined.
   c) Fracture matches from cord found on the victim and a sample found in possession of the suspect that matches the ends of both ropes or cords
   d) Knots may be identified as particularly common among a specific group.
   e) String can be identified by its fibers and particular method of manufacturer. The rarer the qualities of the string or rope, the more valuable it is from an investigative standpoint.
   f) If a tracer is present, the manufacturer can be determined.

2) Collection
   a) Never cut through any knots. Pack any in an appropriate clean container.
      i) If the rope or cord must be cut, specify which end was cut during evidence collection.
   b) Label the known and questioned samples.
   c) Submit the entire rope or cord.
   d) Handle the sections of rope or cord carefully to prevent contamination or loss of trace material.
   e) Submit in heat-sealed or resealable plastic or paper bags.

CONTAINERS

1) Any containers left at a scene by a possible suspect should be collected and processed for evidence. An obvious consideration is processing for latent prints. In addition, trace evidence analysts can obtain other information, including:
    a) Form and construction of the container
    b) Any information written on the surface is potentially traceable.

DNA EXAMINATION

1) Examination considerations
    a) DNA is analyzed in body fluids, stains, and other biological tissues recovered from evidence.
    b) The results of DNA analysis of questioned biological samples are compared with those of known samples. This analysis can associate victim(s) or suspect(s) with each other or with a crime scene.

2) Blood examinations
    a) Examinations can determine the presence or absence of blood in stains.
    b) Examinations can also determine whether blood is human or nonhuman and can determine the animal species.
    c) Blood examinations cannot determine the age or race of a person. Conventional serological techniques are not adequately informative to positively identify a person as the source of a stain.

3) Collecting known samples
    a) Blood
        i) Only qualified medical personnel should collect blood samples from a person.
        ii) Collect at least two 5-milliliter tubes of blood in purple-top tubes with EDTA as an anticoagulant for DNA analysis.
        iii) Collect drug or alcohol testing samples in gray-top tubes with sodium fluoride.
        iv) Identify each tube with the date, time, subject's name, location, collector's name, case number, and evidence number.
        v) Refrigerate, do not freeze, blood samples. Use cold packs, not dry ice, during shipping.
        vi) Pack liquid blood tubes individually in Styrofoam or cylindrical tube containers with absorbent material surrounding the tubes.
        vii) Submit to the lab as soon as possible.
    b) Saliva
        i) Use clean cotton swabs to collect saliva samples.
        ii) Rub the inside surfaces of the cheeks and gums thoroughly.
        iii) Air-dry the swabs and place in clean paper or an envelope with sealed corners.
        iv) Do not use plastic containers.
        v) Identify each sample with the date, time, subject's name, location, collector's name, case number, and evidence number.
        vi) Saliva samples do not need to be refrigerated.
        vii) Submit to the lab as soon as possible.

4) Documenting, collecting, packaging, and preserving DNA evidence

a) If DNA evidence is not properly documented, collected, packaged, and preserved, it will not meet the legal and scientific requirements for admissibility in a court of law.
b) If DNA evidence is not properly documented, its origin can be questioned.
c) If it is not properly collected, biological activity can be lost.
d) If it is not properly packaged, contamination can occur.
e) If it is not properly preserved, decomposition and deterioration can occur.
f) When DNA evidence is transferred by direct or secondary (indirect) means, it remains on surfaces by absorption or adherence. In general, liquid biological evidence is absorbed into surfaces, and solid biological evidence adheres to surfaces. Collecting, packaging, and preserving DNA evidence depends on the liquid or solid state and the condition of the evidence.
g) The more original integrity the evidence retained when it reaches the lab, the greater the possibility of conducting useful examinations.
   i) It may be necessary to use a variety of techniques to collect suspected body fluid evidence.

5) Submitting DNA evidence
   a) Blood on a person
      i) Absorb suspected liquid blood onto a clean cotton cloth or swab. Leave a portion of the cloth or swab unstained as a control. Air-dry the cloth or swab and pack in clean paper or an envelope with sealed corners. Do not use plastic containers.
      ii) Absorb suspected dried blood onto a clean cotton cloth or swab moistened with distilled water. Leave a portion of the cloth or swab unstained as a control. Air-dry the cloth or swab and pack in clean paper or an envelope with sealed corners. Do not use plastic containers.
   b) Blood on surfaces or in snow or water
      i) Absorb suspected liquid blood or blood clots onto a clean cotton cloth or swab. Leave a portion of the cloth or swab unstained as a control. Air-dry the cloth or swab and pack in clean paper or an envelope with sealed corners. Do not use plastic containers.
      ii) Collect suspected blood in snow or water immediately to avoid further dilution. Eliminate as much snow as possible. Place in a clean, airtight container. Freeze the evidence and submit as soon as possible to the lab.
   c) Bloodstains
      i) Air-dry wet bloodstained garments. Wrap dried bloodstained garments in clean paper. Do not place wet or dried garments in plastic or airtight containers. Place all debris or residue from the garments in clean paper or an envelope with sealed corners.
      ii) Air-dry small suspected wet bloodstained objects and submit the objects to the lab. Preserve bloodstain patterns. Avoid creating additional stain patterns during drying and packaging. Pack to prevent stain removal by abrasive action or packaging materials during shipping. Pack in clean paper. Do not use plastic containers.
      iii) When possible, cut a large sample of suspected bloodstains from immovable objects with a clean, sharp instrument. Collect an unstained control sample. Pack to prevent stain removal by abrasive action or packaging materials during shipping. Pack in clean paper. Do not use plastic containers.
      iv) Absorb suspected dried bloodstains on immovable objects onto a clean cotton cloth or swab moistened with distilled water. Leave a portion of the cloth or

swab unstained as a control. Air-dry the cloth or swab and pack in clean paper or an envelope with sealed corners. Do not use plastic containers.

6) Blood examination request letter (FBI submission)
   a) A blood examination request letter should contain the following:
      i) A brief statement of facts relating to the case
      ii) Claims made by the suspect(s) regarding the source of the blood
      iii) Information about whether animal blood is present or suspected
      iv) Information about whether the stains were laundered or diluted with other body fluids
      v) Information about the health of the victim(s) and suspect(s), such as AIDS, hepatitis, or tuberculosis.

7) Semen and semen stains
   a) Absorb suspected liquid semen onto a clean cotton cloth or swab. Leave a portion of the cloth or swab unstained as a control. Air-dry the cloth or swab and pack in clean paper or an envelope with sealed corners. Do not use plastic containers.
   b) Submit small suspected dried semen–stained objects to the lab. Pack to prevent stain removal by abrasive action or packaging materials during shipping. Pack in clean paper. Do not use plastic containers.
   c) When possible, cut a large sample of suspected semen stains from immovable objects with a clean sharp instrument. Collect an unstained control sample. Pack to prevent stain removal by abrasive action or packaging materials during shipping. Pack in clean paper. Do not use plastic containers.
   d) Absorb suspected dried-semen stains on immovable objects onto a clean cotton cloth or swab moistened with distilled water. Leave a portion of the cloth or swab unstained as a control. Air-dry the swab or cloth and place in clean paper or an envelope with sealed corners. Do not use plastic containers.

8) Semen evidence from sexual assault victim(s)
   a) Sexual assault victim(s) should be medically examined in a hospital or a physician's office using a standard sexual assault evidence kit to collect vaginal, oral, and anal evidence.
   b) Refrigerate and submit the evidence as soon as possible to the lab.

9) Saliva and urine
   a) Absorb suspected liquid saliva or urine into a clean cotton cloth or swab. Leave a portion of the cloth unstained as a control. Air-dry the cloth or swab and pack in clean paper or an envelope with sealed corners. Do not use plastic containers.
   b) Submit suspected small, dry saliva- or urine-stained objects to the lab. Pack to prevent stain removal by abrasive action or packaging materials during shipping. Pack in clean paper or an envelope with sealed corners. Do not use plastic containers.
   c) When possible, cut a large sample of suspected saliva or urine stains from immovable objects with a clean, sharp instrument. Collect an unstained control sample. Pack to prevent stain removal by abrasive action or packaging materials during shipping. Pack in clean paper. Do not use plastic containers.

10) Cigarette butts
    a) Pick up cigarette butts with gloved hands or clean forceps. Do not submit ashes. Air-dry and place the cigarette butts from the same location (ashtray) in clean paper or an envelope with sealed corners.

i) Do not submit the ashtray unless latent print examination is requested. Package the ashtray separately.
    b) Do not use plastic containers.

11) Chewing gum
    a) Pick up chewing gum with gloved hands or clean forceps. Air-dry and place in clean paper or an envelope with sealed corners. Do not use plastic containers.

12) Envelopes and stamps
    a) Pick up envelopes and stamps with gloved hands or clean forceps and place in a clean envelope. Do not use plastic containers.

13) Tissues, bones, and teeth
    a) Call the lab before submitting suspected tissues, bones, or teeth to ensure that it will accept the evidence.
        i) The communication accompanying the evidence must reference the telephone conversation accepting the evidence (FBI recommendation).
    b) Pick up suspected tissues, bones, and teeth with gloved hands or clean forceps.
    c) Collect the following for DNA processing:
        i) 1 to 2 cubic inches of red skeletal muscle
        ii) 3 to 5 inches of long bone, such as the fibula or femur.
        iii) Teeth in the following order:
            (1) Unrestored molar
            (2) Unrestored premolar
            (3) Unrestored canine
            (4) Unrestored front tooth
            (5) Restored molar
            (6) Restored premolar
            (7) Restored canine
            (8) Restored front tooth
        iv) Place tissue samples in a clean, airtight plastic container without formalin or formaldehyde.
        v) Place teeth and bone samples in clean paper or an envelope with sealed corners.
        vi) Freeze the evidence, place in Styrofoam containers, and ship overnight on dry ice.

ELECTRONIC DEVICE EXAMINATION

1) Examination considerations
    a) Personal digital assistants
        i) Examinations of personal digital assistants (PDAs) provide printouts of user-entered information.
            (1) In some cases, it is necessary to disassemble the PDAs during examination.
    b) Interception of communication services
        i) Interception of communication (IOC) devices are used to unlawfully intercept oral or wire communications.
        ii) IOC devices consist of radio frequency transmitters and receivers.
        iii) IOC examinations are conducted to identify operating characteristics.

(1) In some cases, it is necessary to disassemble the IOC devices during examination.
c) Other electronic devices
i) Examinations are conducted on devices containing electronic circuitry such as cellular telephones, pagers, bomb detonators, and stun guns.
ii) The examinations can identify operating characteristics and modifications.
(1) In some cases, it is necessary to disassemble the devices during examination.

2) Submitting personal digital assistants, interception of communication devices, and electronic devices evidence (FBI submission requirements).
a) Label the outer container:

**FRAGILE, SENSITIVE ELECTRONIC EQUIPMENT
and
KEEP AWAY FROM MAGNETS OR MAGNETIC FIELDS**

b) Address the outer container as follows:

Federal Bureau of Investigation
Engineering Research Facility
Attention: Forensic Program
Building 27958A
Quantico, VA 22135

ELEMENT ANALYSIS EXAMINATION

1) Examination considerations
a) Element analysis examinations can identify and compare the chemical element composition of evidence, including firearm projectile lead, bullet jacket alloys, other metals, and unknown substances.
i) Firearm projectile lead
(1) Element analysis of the lead component of a firearm projectile is valuable when the projectile is too mutilated or lacks sufficient microscopic marks for identification with a firearm, when no firearm is recovered, or when the firearm cannot be associated with the suspect or suspects.
(2) The concentrations of selected elements in the lead portion of bullets, shot pellets, and other firearm projectiles can chemically characterize the source of the lead.
(a) Some chemical elements present in leads are intentionally specified or added by the ammunition manufacturer. Other chemical elements found in leads are unspecified contaminants. Differences in the concentrations of manufacturer-controlled elements and uncontrolled trace elements provide a means of differentiating among the leads of manufacturers, among the leads in an individual manufacturer's production lines, and among specific batches of lead in the same production line of a manufacturer.

ii) Bullet jacket (copper-zinc) alloys
- (1) Elemental analysis of the jacket component of firearm projectiles is valuable when the projectile has fragmented so that jacket fragments cannot physically be associated with specific bullets.
- (2) This analysis is helpful in situations when there are multiple shooters and multiple types of jacketed ammunition fired.
- (3) The concentrations of copper and zinc making up the bullet jacket serve to characterize the alloy class of the metal.
  - (a) Although there is a limited number of copper-zinc alloys used in the manufacture of bullet jackets, alloy classification can provide a means of differentiating among bullet jacket alloys of different manufacturers and among the bullet jacket alloys in individual manufacturer's production lines.

iii) Other metals
- (1) Element analysis and comparison of such metals as copper wire, steel, and aluminum can determine whether two metals or metallic objects came from the same source or from each other.
  - (a) The concentrations of selected elements in objects made of these metals can chemically characterize the source of the metal.
  - (b) The concentrations of several elements are controlled by the manufacturers to impart specific end-use properties to products. These manufacturer-controlled elements help to chemically characterize a metal object by placing it in an alloy class.
  - (c) The manufacturers generally do not control the concentrations of trace elements. Differences in the concentrations of manufacturer-controlled elements and uncontrolled trace elements provide a means of differentiating among metals made by different manufacturers, among metals from different product lines of a single manufacturer, and among specific production runs of the metal from a single manufacturer.

iv) Gunshot residue
- (1) When a firearm is discharged, vaporous and particulate materials, called gunshot residue (GSR), are expelled.
- (2) Collecting GSR from a suspected shooter's hands and analyzing it for the presence of barium, antimony, and lead may provide data to associate a suspect with the recent discharge of a firearm. It could also mean the subject may have handled a contaminated firearm or ammunition component. Antimony, barium, and lead are major element components of most cartridge primer mixtures
- (3) Because of the ambiguous nature of test results, the FBI Laboratory does not currently provide GSR examinations; however, a revised program is being field-tested.

2) Submitting element analysis evidence (FBI submission guidelines)
  a) Such ammunition components as bullets, cartridge cases, and shotshell casings can be sent via registered mail through the U.S. Postal Service.
    i) Evidence should be packaged separately and identified by date, time, location, collector's name, case number, and evidence number.

b) Live ammunition must be shipped by Federal Express.
  i) The following guidelines must be followed to comply with U.S. Department of Transportation regulations.
    (1) Pack ammunition in a cardboard container.
    (2) Label invoices FEDERAL EXPRESS.
    (3) The shipper's certification for restricted articles must be included.
    (4) The outside of the container must be labeled ORM-D AIR, CARTRIDGES SMALL ARMS.
    (5) The shipping papers must also include the weight in grams.
c) Do not mark bullets, cartridges and cartridge cases, and shotshells and shotshell casings.
  i) The date, time, location, collector's name, case number, and evidence number should be on the container.

EXPLOSIVES EXAMINATION

1) Examination considerations
   a) Remains of improvised explosive devices, improvised incendiary devices, and hoax bombs are examined to identify the main charge and components such as switches, batteries, detonators, tapes, wires, and timing mechanisms.
   b) Fabrication techniques, unconsumed explosives, and the construction of bombs are also identified.
   c) Examinations can determine whether the device functioned as designed.

2) Submitting explosives evidence (FBI submission requirements)
   a) Explosives are hazardous materials and should only be handled by qualified police or bomb disposal personnel.
   b) Special packaging is required, and the amount to be shipped is regulated.
     i) An FD-861 form is required for shipping bomb components.
   c) Call the lab each time an explosive device or a related explosive item needs to be shipped.

3) Evidence examinations
   a) Conduct explosives residue examinations, including these:
     i) Instrumental analyses of explosives residue can determine whether substances are high explosive, low explosive, or explosive or incendiary mixtures.
     ii) Determine whether the composition of the substances is consistent with known explosive products.
     iii) Determine the type of explosives.
       (1) Explosives residue can be deposited on metal, plastic, wood, paper, or glass.
         (a) Residue may be deposited after handling, storing, or initiating an explosive.

4) Submitting explosives residue evidence
   a) Some explosives residue is water soluble and must be protected from moisture.
   b) Other residue evaporates quickly and must be collected as soon as possible in airtight containers (e.g., metal cans, glass jars, or heat-sealed or resealable plastic bags).
     i) Do not fill the containers to the top.
     ii) Pack to prevent breakage.

c) Collect and preserve control samples from the blast site.
d) Extreme care should taken to avoid contamination of explosives residue evidence.

FBI DISASTER SQUAD

1) Examination considerations
   a) Prints the deceased at disaster scenes
   b) Assists in identifying the deceased

2) Request considerations
   a) Requires consent from the ranking law enforcement official at the scene or from a representative of the National Transportation Safety Board or Federal Aviation Administration, a coroner or medical examiner, or other ranking official (e.g., a mayor or governor).
   b) Requests from other sources submitted through official channels and from the U.S. Department of State are also considered.

FIBER EVIDENCE

1) Examination considerations
   a) Fiber examinations can identify the type of fiber, such as animal (e.g., wool), vegetable (e.g., cotton), mineral (e.g., glass), and synthetic (manufactured).
   b) Questioned fibers can be compared with fibers from the clothing of the victim(s) and suspect(s), carpeting, and other textiles.
   c) A questioned piece of fabric can be physically matched to known fabric.
      i) Fabric composition, construction, and color can be analyzed, and impressions on fabric and from fabric can be examined.
   d) Clothing manufacturers' information can be determined by label searches.

2) Fiber is generally classified as follows:
   a) Mineral
      i) Glass, asbestos, etc.
   b) Animal
      i) Wool, silk, furs
   c) Vegetable
      i) Cotton, linen, hemp, and jute
   d) Synthetic
      i) Rayon, nylon, dacron, etc.

3) Collection of samples
   a) When possible, submit the entire garment or textile.
   b) Other fibers are usually collected through vacuumed sweepings.
      i) Vacuum separate areas individually. Collect specimens. Wipe the sweeper completely clean and begin a new area. Repeat the process until the scene has been completed.

4) Packaging of evidence
   a) Submit fibers in clean paper or an envelope with sealed corners.

5) Laboratory findings

a) The crime lab will identify fibers according to these:
   i) Type
   ii) Color
   iii) Matching characteristics
b) In most cases, the laboratory conclusions are not positive evidence. The findings may directly related to how rare or how common the specimen is.

FIREARMS EXAMINATION

1) Examination considerations
   a) Firearms
      i) Firearm examinations can determine the general condition of a firearm and whether the firearm is mechanically functional.
      ii) Trigger-pull examinations can determine the amount of pressure necessary to release the hammer or firing pin of a firearm.
      iii) Examinations can determine whether a firearm was altered to fire in the full-auto mode.
      iv) Obliterated or altered firearm serial numbers can sometimes be restored.
      v) Firearms can be test-fired to obtain known specimens for comparison with such evidence ammunition components as bullets, cartridge cases, and shotshell casings.
   b) Bullets
      i) Fired bullets can be examined to determine the general rifling characteristics, such as caliber and physical features of the rifling impressions and the manufacturer of the bullets.
      ii) The microscopic characteristics of evidence bullets can be compared with test-fired bullets from a suspect firearm to determine whether the evidence bullet was fired from that firearm.
   c) Cartridge cases or shotshell casings
      i) Examinations of cartridge cases or shotshell casings can determine the caliber or gauge, the manufacturer, and whether there are marks of value for comparison.
      ii) The images of questioned cartridge cases and shotshell casings can be scanned into DrugFire or IBIS (NIBIS) to compare with evidence from other shooting incidents.
      iii) The microscopic characteristics of evidence cartridge cases and shotshell casings can be examined to determine whether they were fired in a specific firearm.
   d) Shot pellets, buckshot, or slugs
      i) Examinations of shot pellets, buckshot, or slugs can determine the size of the shot, the gauge of the slug, and the manufacturer.
   e) Wadding
      i) Examinations of wadding components can determine the gauge and the manufacturer.
   f) Unfired cartridges or shotshells
      i) Examinations of unfired cartridges or shotshells can determine the caliber or gauge and whether there are marks of value for comparison.
      ii) Examinations can also determine whether the ammunition was loaded into and extracted from a specific firearm.
         (1) Unfired and fired cartridges or shotshells can be associated through manufacturing marks.

g) Gunshot residue
　i) The deposit of gunshot residue on such evidence as clothing varies with the distance from the muzzle of the firearm to the target.
　　(1) Patterns of gunshot residue can be duplicated using a questioned firearm and ammunition combination fired into test materials at known distances. These patterns serve as a basis for estimating muzzle-to-garment distances.
h) Shot pattern
　i) Shot pattern examinations can determine the approximate distance at which a shotgun was fired by testing a specific firearm and ammunition combination at known distances.
i) Silencers
　i) Muzzle attachments can reduce the noise of a firearm by suppressing sound during firing. Testing can determine whether a muzzle attachment can be classified as a silencer based on its measurable sound reduction capability.
j) Gun parts
　i) Gun parts examinations can determine the caliber and model of gun from which the parts originated.

2) Submitting firearms evidence
a) Firearms must be packaged and shipped separately from live ammunition.
　i) All firearms must be unloaded.
　ii) The firearm should be submitted.
　iii) The firearm should be minimally handled to avoid loss or destruction of evidence.
　iv) Do not allow objects to enter or contact the firearm's barrel, chamber, or other operating surface.
b) Firearms and such ammunition components as bullets, cartridge cases, and shotshell casings can be sent by registered mail through the U.S. Postal Service.
　i) Evidence must be packaged separately and identified by date, time, location, collector's name, case number, and evidence number.
c) Live ammunition must be shipped via Federal Express. The following guidelines must be followed to comply with U.S. Department of Transportation regulations.
　i) Pack ammunition in a cardboard container.
　ii) Label invoices FEDERAL EXPRESS.
　iii) The shipper's certification for restricted articles must be included.
　iv) The outside of the container must be labeled ORM-D AIR, CARTRIDGES SMALL ARMS.
　v) The shipping papers must also include the weight in grams.
d) Do not mark the firearm.
　i) Firearms should be identified with a tag containing the caliber, make, model, and serial number.
　ii) The date, time, owner name(s), location, collector's name, case number, and evidence number should be on the container.
e) Do not mark bullets, cartridges and cartridge cases, shotshells and shotshell casings, and other firearms-related evidence.
　i) The date, time, location, collector's name, case number, and evidence number should be on the container.
f) Clothing submitted for gunshot residue examination should be carefully handled, air-dried, and wrapped separately in paper.

i) Clothing with blood must be air-dried and labeled BIOHAZARD on the inner and outer containers.
ii) The date, time, location, collector's name, case number, and evidence number should be on the container.

GLASS EXAMINATION

1) Glass composition
   a) The components of glass constitute a mixture of sand, soda, lime, and other materials. The mixture is placed in a furnace until it reaches a temperature in which the glass can be placed into molds and made into various shapes.
   b) Common types of glass
      i) Soda-lime
         (1) This is used in plate and window glass, glass containers, and electric light bulbs.
      ii) Soda-lead
         (1) More expensive than soda-lime glass, soda-lead glass is used for fine tableware and art objects.
      iii) Borosilicate glass
         (1) Commonly known as Pyrex, borosilicate glass is heat resistant.
      iv) Silica
         (1) This is used in chemical wares.
      v) Colored
   c) Kinds of glass
      i) Flat
         (1) Used in windows, mirrors, etc.
      ii) Containers
      iii) Ceramic
      iv) Specialty
      v) Laminated safety
         (1) Sandwiched layers
      vi) Bullet-resistant
         (1) Multiple layers.
      vii) Tempered safety
         (1) Specially treated with heat to produce glass that will break into small dice-like pieces, used in rear and side windows of cars
      viii) Colored structural
         (1) Used in exterior facings of building constructed with glass.
      ix) Opal
         (1) Opaque glass used in lightning fixtures
      x) Foam
         (1) Used in insulation
      xi) Building blocks
         (1) Used in insulation
      xii) Heat-resistant
         (1) Used in making cookware
      xiii) Laboratory glassware
         (1) Specially treated to resist heat and shock
      xiv) Electrical
      xv) Heat-conducting

xvi) Tubing
    (1) Used to make fluorescent lamp fixtures, neon signs, glass piping, etc.
xvii) Radiation-absorbing and radiation-transmitting
xviii) Optical
    (1) Used in manufacturing lenses for various items
xix) Invisible
    (1) Used to coat lenses
xx) Photosensitive
xxi) Photochemical
xxii) Photochromic
    (1) Used in sunglasses, windows, etc.

2) Investigative significance of glass examination
    a) Corroborating circumstantial evidence
        i) Glass fragments found on the suspect may match the composition of the glass broken at the scene. This may help the investigation in putting the suspect at the scene.
        ii) Positive identification can be made with a fracture match. If a fragment found on the suspect matches like a "jigsaw" piece with the fragments collected at the scene, this information can place the suspect at the scene.

3) Examination of glass at the crime lab
    a) If glass is broken, the side from which the force was exerted
        i) Important in certain cases in which it appears a burglary may have been faked
    b) Height at which force entered causing the glass to break
    c) Angle at which projectile entered the glass
    d) Whether gunpowder residue is present on the fragments
    e) The sequence of separate penetrations
        i) Sequence of the bullets
    f) Sometimes the type of weapon used to break the glass
    g) Information about common origin of the samples based on an elemental analysis of the glass using instrument techniques

4) Collecting and submitting glass evidence
    a) Submit samples of glass from each broken window or source in leakproof containers (e.g., film canisters, plastic pill bottles).
        i) Avoid using paper or glass containers. Package the glass in such a way to prevent leakage or contamination in to or out of the evidence.
    b) When removing fragments that are still intact, indicate the inside and outside of the glass.
    c) Submit samples of laminated glass (e.g., windshield) from each side of the laminate.
        i) Label the samples INSIDE and OUTSIDE and package separately in leakproof containers (e.g., film canisters, plastic pill bottles).
        ii) Avoid using paper or glass containers. Package the glass to prevent leakage or contamination in to or out of the evidence.
    d) For examination purposes, separately bag any tools in the suspect's possession that may contain pieces of glass.
    e) If suspect clothes are collected, do not attempt a visual identification and collection of glass fragments. Package the item and send it to the crime lab. The location of the glass fragment may become an important feature of the examiner's expert testimony.

i) Submit the victim(s)' and suspect(s)' air-dried clothing. Each clothing item should be packaged separately in a paper bag.
- f) Search for particles in the hair, skin, and wounds of victim(s) and suspect(s). Submit particles in leakproof containers (e.g., film canisters, plastic pill bottles). Avoid using paper or glass containers.
- g) Search for particles in vehicles by vacuuming each section of the vehicle separately. Do not use tape for recovering glass particles. Submit vacuum sweepings in leakproof containers. Avoid using paper or glass containers.
- h) Do not process evidence for latent prints.

GRAPHIC ARTS (PRINTING)

1) Examination consideration
   - a) Printed documents can sometimes be identified as originating from a common source or being associated with known printing paraphernalia, such as art work, negatives, and plates.

HAIR EXAMINATION

1) Examination consideration
   - a) Examinations can associate a hair with a person on the basis of microscopic characteristics of the hair but cannot provide absolute personal identification.

2) Hair description
   - a) Hair is an appendage of skin consisting of the following:
     - i) Bulb
       - (1) Pulled or plucked hair roots, including the cell, are necessary for submission for DNA profiling (PCR–STR analysis). A hair shaft that has fallen out naturally or been cut does not contain enough DNA for PCR–STE analysis.
     - ii) Shaft
       - (1) The shaft grows out away from the root end and comprises these:
         - (a) Cuticle (outside cover), which is composed of overlapping scales that always point toward the tip
         - (b) Cortex (walls), which is made up of long, flat cells that give the hair its pliability
         - (c) Medulla (core), which contains the coloring agent (pigment) of the hair

3) Investigative significance. In crimes involving physical contact or bodies that have been dumped away from the original scene, hair and fibers are often transferred among the victim, suspect, and scene. From recovered hair specimens from scenes the following information can be derived:
   - a) Whether hairs are animal or human.
     - i) The animal species and family can be determined from hair analysis.
   - b) The possible identification of the owner, based on a mathematical probability through DNA techniques (PCR). Pulled or plucked hair containing hair roots can be submitted for DNA profiling. Hair may also be used for mitochondrial DNA.
   - c) The race of the individual, subject to biological overlap and variation
   - d) The part of the body from which the hair originated.
     - i) Head, including scalp, eyebrow, nose, eyelid, ear, mustache, and beard

ii) Trunk hairs
iii) Limb hairs
iv) Pubic hairs
v) Axillary hairs
e) Whether the hair was forcibly removed
f) Whether the hair had been cut with a dull or sharp instrument
g) Whether the hair had undergone chemical treatment (e.g., dye, bleach)
h) Whether the hair had been crushed or burned

4) Possible lab conclusions
   a) The hairs match based on PCR DNA or mitochondrial DNA analysis.
      i) PCR gives a much lower probability of exclusion but requires a much smaller sample (e.g., 1 person in 100). Mitochondrial DNA may be used in a degraded specimen. The probabilities are much less than PCR analysis.
   b) The hairs match based on microscopic characteristics, and they originated from the same individual or another individual whose hair exhibits the same microscopic characteristics.
   c) The hairs are not similar and did not originate from the individual whose hair specimens were submitted for comparison.
   d) No conclusion can be reached.

5) Collection of samples
   a) Comb and pull out the hairs. Collect hair standards (approximately 25 to 40) from the following locations:
      i) Head hair
         (1) Collect from sides, top, and back of head. Collect beard, mustache, and eyebrows. At least 40 specimens should be collected by plucking. Do not use tweezers, which may damage the specimens.
      ii) Pubic hair
         (1) Before obtaining specimens, comb pubic hairs to obtain loose specimens that may not be the subject's.
         (2) Pluck at least 40 specimens of hair.
         (3) Other locations as deemed necessary, including arm, underarms, chest, and leg areas. Remove hair surrounding any wounds on the body.

6) Preservation of specimens
   a) Submit hairs in clean paper or an envelope with sealed corners.
      i) Separately bag, according to the region from which the sample hair was plucked, before placing in an envelope.
   b) From object or garment possibly containing hair:
      i) Air-dry garment if the garment is wet
      ii) Individually package each item in a paper bag. It may be necessary to protect the area suspected of containing hair by placing cellophane or taping paper over the area before placing the article in a bag.

INK EXAMINATION

1) Examination consideration:
   a) Examinations can compare the formulation of known and questioned ink, including

typewriter ribbon ink and stamp pad ink.
: i) When ink formulations are the same, it is not possible to determine whether the ink originated from the same source to the exclusion of other sources.
: b) Examinations cannot determine how long ink has been on a document.

2) Submitting ink evidence
: a) Pack ink evidence separately from any document or surface with ink marks.

LAMP BULBS

1) Examination consideration
: a) Examinations can determine whether a lamp bulb was incandescent at the time the glass was broken and whether an unbroken lamp bulb was incandescent at the time it was subjected to an impact force, such as a vehicular collision.

LATENT PRINT EXAMINATION

1) Developing latent prints at crime scenes
: a) The lab is the best place to develop latent prints; however, it is sometimes necessary to develop latent prints at crime scenes.
: b) Be careful not to destroy latent prints.
: c) Examine all evidence for visible latent prints before using any latent-print development processes.
: d) Photograph visible latent prints first.
: e) Examine evidence with an ALS to find latent prints.
: f) CYVAC vacuum chamber processing (cyanoacrylate superglue) is a method for obtaining fingerprints on such nonporous surfaces as weapons and plastic (drug) bags.
: : i) Cyanoacrylate glue fumes should not be applied on wet surfaces.
: g) Print powders are used extensively in developing prints. Black and gray powders are used most often because other colors are difficult to photograph.
: : i) Black powder is used on evidence with a light background. Gray powder is used on dark or reflective evidence.
: : ii) Do not apply powders to greasy, bloody, dusty, or putty-covered evidence.
: : iii) Allow wet evidence to dry before applying powders.

2) Photographing and lifting latent prints
: a) Photograph latent prints separately.
: b) Photograph latent prints developed with fingerprint powders before lifting.
: : i) Use transparent, black, or white rubber lifting tape to lift latent prints. When transparent tape is used, the color of the backing card should contrast with the color of the powders.
: c) Use a medium-format camera with adaptability to one-to-one photography.
: d) Photograph prints with a scale and an identification label that includes the reference number, date, collector's initials, and the location of prints. The scale and label should be placed on the same plane as the prints.
: e) Fill the frame completely.
: f) Photograph latent prints close to each other in one frame.
: g) Use T-Max 400J film.
: : i) Set the f-stop to f/8.
: : ii) Adjust the shutter speed setting until the green light appears.

iii) Take three exposures of each latent print by bracketing:
    (1) Original exposure
    (2) Underexposed image
    (3) Overexposed image
iv) Maintain a photographic log that includes the reference number, date, collector's initials, the location of prints, and other pertinent information.

3) Submitting latent print evidence
    a) Place nonporous evidence in separate protective coverings, such as thick transparent envelopes, or suspend in a container so that there is minimal surface contact.
    b) Place porous evidence in separate protective coverings, such as paper envelopes. Stabilize the evidence to avoid movement or friction during shipment.
    c) Fingerprint card
        i) When fingerprint cards or major case prints are submitted for comparison with evidence, the criminal/suspect or noncriminal/elimination nature of the prints should be stated in the communication.
        ii) Submit the fingerprints and palm prints of all personnel who handled the evidence and of all individuals who are suspects in the investigation with the evidence. All fingerprint cards must include pertinent information.
            (1) Palm prints should be taken on a separate card, not on the reverse side of a fingerprint card.
        iii) When inked prints are submitted separately, a communication should be sent with the prints referencing previous communications and pertinent numbers.
    d) Fingerprints from decomposed bodies are often not classifiable, which precludes a search of the FBI's fingerprint files. An individual fingerprint may, however, be suitable for identification purposes. If fewer than 10 legible fingerprints are obtained, submit the available fingerprints and a complete physical description of the unknown deceased.
    e) Legible, unknown-deceased, 10-print fingerprint cards should be submitted for identification purposes to the FBI's Criminal Justice Information Services Division at the following address:

Federal Bureau of Investigation
Criminal Justice Information Services Division
1000 Custer Hollow Road
Clarksburg, WV 26306

f) Telephone inquiries about 10-print fingerprint card submissions should be directed to 304-625-2360.

METAL EXAMINATION

1) Examination considerations
    a) Comparison
        i) Comparison examinations can determine whether two metals or metallic objects came from the same source or from each other.
        ii) Metal comparisons can identify surface and microstructural characteristics (e.g., fractured areas and accidental, damage, and fabrication marks) to determine whether the object was cast, forged, hot- or cold-rolled, extruded, drawn, swaged, milled, spun, or blanked.

            iii) Examinations can determine mechanical properties (e.g., the response of a
                metal to an applied force or load).
            iv) Examinations can also determine chemical composition, including alloying
                and trace elements.
        b) Broken or mechanically damaged metal
            i) The causes of failure or damage (e.g., stress exceeding the strength or yield
                limit of the metal, a material or manufacturing defect, corrosion, cracking,
                excessive service use [fatigue]) can be determined.
            ii) The magnitude of the force or load that caused the failure, how the force or
                load was transmitted to the metal, and the direction it was transmitted can also
                be determined.
        c) Burned, heated, or melted metal
            i) Examinations can determine the temperature at which a metal was exposed, the
                nature of the heat source, and whether a metal was in an electrical short-circuit
                situation.
        d) Cut or severed metal
            i) Examinations can determine the method by which a metal was severed
                (e.g., sawing, shearing, milling, turning, arc cutting, flame cutting).
            ii) The skill of the person who made the cut and the length of time it took to
                make the cut can also be determined.
        e) Metal fragments
            i) Examinations can determine how fragments were formed.
                (1) If fragments were formed by high-velocity forces, it can be
                    determined whether an explosive was detonated and the magnitude of
                    the detonation velocity.
                (2) The identification of the object that was the source of the fragments
                    can also be determined.
        f) Objects unidentified as to use or source
            i) Examinations can determine the possible use for which an object was designed,
                formed, or manufactured on the basis of the construction and the type of
                metal.
            ii) It is also possible to determine the identification of the manufacturer and
                specific fabricating equipment used to form the object.
            iii) If an unusual metal or alloy is involved, the source of the object can be
                determined.

2) Submitting metallurgy evidence
        a) Different metals and alloys require specific methods of restoration. Objects can be too
            large or heavy to submit. Call the lab for specific instructions.
        b) Submit information about environmental conditions when the metal was recovered.

PAINT EXAMINATION

1) Examination considerations and investigative significance of paint comparison:
        a) The color, year, make, and model of an automobile can be determined by comparing
            questioned paint with known sources.
        b) Paint on safes, vaults, window sills, and door frames can be transferred to and from
            tools. A comparison can be made between the paint on an object and that on a tool.
        c) Paint chips that match along a fracture line are very conclusive about the known and
            questioned specimen being of the same origin.

d) Paint chips that match according to composition tend to indicate origination from the same source.

2) Paint evidence can be in the form of a liquid, chip, or smear.

3) Examination of paint evidence will determine and compare the following:
    a) Color
        i) Known and questioned samples and submerged in mineral oil. The two chips are then overlapped to observe common or uncommon color characteristics.
    b) Type
    c) Texture, including:
        i) Glossiness
        ii) Granularity
        iii) Hardness
        iv) Wrinkling property
        v) Cracking property
        vi) Blistering property
        vii) Chalking property
    d) Layer structure
        i) Chemicals in paint dry at different thicknesses in different levels. In specimens involving known or questioned evidence, each layer is examined for its thickness, the position of the layer within the layers, and texture.
    e) Composition
        i) Particular paint dye and other compositions in the paint may be developed through chemical testing.
    f) Occasionally, fracture line comparisons can be made of the known and questioned paint specimens.
        i) Microscopic examination may allow for the matching of two surfaces along their fracture lines.

4) The National Paint File maintained by the FBI Laboratory is a collection of paint panels furnished by automobile manufacturers. The finish on the panel corresponds to the finish originally used on one or more makes and models of an automobile.

5) Collection of paint evidence
    a) When collecting a known sample, do the following:
        i) Collect an adequate amount for testing purposes.
        ii) Collect a representative sample from the approximate area where the paint transfer occurred.
    b) The most important consideration is to collect the paint in its appropriate layered sequence by chipping away at the paint surface.
        i) Paint should never be scraped or shaved from a surface.
        ii) Chip paint from the surface to the foundation or substrate rather than scraping it off. When paint is chipped, its layer structure remains intact, so each layer can be a point of comparison.
            (1) If the paint surface won't allow chipping, cut out a sample of the surface and submit this to the lab.
    c) Search the accident or crime scene and the personal effects of the victim(s) and suspect(s) to locate paint fragments.

i) Paint fragments are often found in the clothing of hit-and-run victims. Submit the clothing.
ii) Paints can be transferred from one car to another, from car to object, or from object to car during an accident or a crime.
iii) Submit an entire component, such as a fender or bumper, if paint transfer is minimal. Car or car parts dealers may have appropriate containers to ship car components.
iv) Pack particles of paint in leakproof containers (e.g., pillboxes or envelopes with sealed corners). Do not stick particles on adhesive tape or put particles in cotton.

PAPER EXAMINATION

1) Examination consideration
   a) Altered or obliterated writing
      i) The presence of alterations or obliterated writing can sometimes be determined, and the writing can sometimes be deciphered.
   b) Paper
      i) Torn edges can sometimes be positively matched.
      ii) The manufacturer can sometimes be determined if a watermark is present.
      iii) Paper can be examined for indented writing.
         (1) An electrostatic detection apparatus (ESDA) is used to pick up indented writing off paper. Writing on a tablet may be developed from a page as far as 14 pages down from the page written on.
            (a) Do not rub the indentations with a pencil.
            (b) Do not add indentations by writing on top of the evidence.
         (2) If the suspect stepped on a newspaper or other paper while at the scene, ESDA processing may be able to bring up a footprint.
   c) Burned or charred paper
      i) Information on burned or charred documents can sometimes be deciphered.
         (1) Handling of the document should be minimal.
         (2) The document should be shipped in the container in which it was burned, in polyester film encapsulation, or between layers of cotton in a rigid container.
   d) Age of a document
      i) The earliest date that a document could have been prepared may be determined by examining watermarks, indented writing, printing, and typewriting.
   e) Carbon paper or carbon-film ribbon
      i) Examination of used carbon paper or carbon-film ribbon can sometimes disclose the content of the text.
   f) Check writers
      i) A check writer impression can sometimes be identified with the check writer that produced it.
      ii) Examination of a check writer impression can sometimes determine the brand of the check writer.
   g) Embossings and seals
      i) An embossed or seal impression can sometimes be identified with the instrument that produced it.
   h) Rubber stamps
      i) A rubber stamp impression can sometimes be identified with the rubber stamp that produced it.

(1) Submit the rubber stamp to the lab uncleaned.

2) Submitting questioned-documents evidence
    a) Preserve documentary evidence in the condition in which it was found.
    b) It should not be folded, torn, marked, soiled, stamped, written on, or handled unnecessarily.
    c) Protect the evidence from inadvertent indented writing.
    d) Mark documents unobtrusively by writing the collector's initials, the date, and other information with a pencil.
    e) Whenever possible, submit the original evidence to the lab.
        i) The lack of detail in photocopies makes examinations difficult.
        ii) Copies are acceptable for reference file searches.
    f) Flash paper is a hazardous material.
        i) Do not store flash paper near combustible materials.
        ii) Seal flash paper in polyethylene envelopes and refrigerate.
    g) Do not store or ship photocopies in plastic envelopes.

PHOTOCOPY EXAMINATION

1) Examination consideration
    a) Photocopies can sometimes be identified with the machine producing them if the exemplars and questioned copies are relatively contemporaneous. The possible make and model of the photocopying machine can sometimes be determined by comparison with the reference file.

2) Procedures for obtaining known photocopy exemplars
    a) Obtain at least 10 exemplars with no document on the glass plate, with the cover down.
    b) Obtain at least 10 exemplars with no document on the glass plate, with the cover up.
    c) Obtain at least 10 exemplars with a document on the glass plate, with the cover down.
    d) Record on each exemplar the date it was obtained, the name of the person who directed the exemplar, and the conditions under which it was made.
    e) Record the make, model, and serial number of the photocopying machine, information about the toner supplies and components, whether the paper supply is sheet- or roll-fed, and such options as color, reduction, enlargement, zoom, mask, trim, and editor board.
    f) Do not store or ship photocopies in plastic envelopes.

PHOTOGRAPHIC EXAMINATION

1) Examination considerations in bank robbery and other surveillance films and videotapes
    a) Photographic comparisons
        i) Examinations of bank surveillance films, videotapes, and photographs involve comparisons of subject(s) depicted in the surveillance images with known photographs of suspect(s).
        ii) Similar comparisons can be conducted of the subject(s)' clothing and clothing seized from suspect(s).
        iii) Comparisons can also be conducted of firearms, vehicles, and other objects depicted in surveillance images.

2) Photogrammetry
    a) Dimensions can be derived from photographic images through the use of geometric formulae or on-site comparison.
        i) Examples of photogrammetry include determining the height of bank robbery subject(s) and the length of the weapon(s) used by the subject(s) depicted in the surveillance films.
        ii) For more information about FBI Laboratory photogrammetry, contact 202-324-0491, 202-324-0492, or 202-324-4339.
            (1) Photogrammetric analysis (height determination) of a bank robber can be conducted analytically using vanishing points.
    b) Location, time, and date
        i) Examinations of photographic evidence can determine the location, time, and date that an image was taken.
    c) Authenticity
        i) Photographic evidence, including film, video, and digital images, can be examined to determine whether the image is the result of a composite, an alteration, or a copy.
    d) Source and age
        i) Photographic products, including film and prints, can be dated, and the source can be established by examining manufacturing characteristics.
            (1) This can establish the time frame during which a photograph was taken.
    e) Cameras
        i) Cameras can be examined and compared with negatives to determine whether a specific camera exposed a specific image.
    f) Videos
        i) Black-and-white and color photographic images can be produced from video images for enlargement and used in courtroom presentations.
    g) Automobile make and model identification
        i) Vehicles depicted in surveillance images can be compared with the National Automotive Image File to determine make and model.
    h) Child pornography examinations
    i) The seized images of child pornography can be compared against images in the Child Exploitation and Obscenity Reference File to identify the original source of the images.

3) Submitting photographic evidence
    a) Submit original evidence (film or videotape) whenever possible because it contains the greatest level of detail.
        i) If the originals are unavailable, submit first-generation photographic prints or videotapes.
    b) Process all film, including bank surveillance film, before submission.
    c) When requesting forensic examinations based on video images, queue the original videotape to the approximate time of the questioned sequence.
        i) State in a communication the date and time of the relevant sequence and use the date-time stamp on the images or the counter indicator (set from the beginning of the tape at 000).
        ii) If prints from the relevant frames are available, submit them to the lab.
        iii) Always remove the record tab on the back edge of the videocassette.
            (1) Never use the pause operation when viewing original videotapes. If a videotape must be viewed, use a copy.

d) Arrest or known photographs of suspect(s) for comparison with questioned images should depict the suspect(s) from many angles, specifically angles similar to the questioned images.
    i) If a facial comparison is requested, ensure that the face or head of a suspect fills more than half of the frame.
    ii) If questioned images show tattoos or marks on a suspect's body, include photographs depicting them on the known body.
        (1) When taking known photographs for comparison with questioned images, use 35mm black-and-white film.
            (a) If color film is used, include a color chart in the photographs.
e) When submitting clothing, firearms, or other items for comparison, do not mark the exteriors of the items or parts that may be visible in the questioned images.
f) If photogrammetry is requested, include the dimensions of the scene to the nearest 1/8 inch and include a diagram or print from the surveillance film indicating the location of the measurements.
    i) Include one diagram or print for every angle used in the scene.
    ii) Do not touch or move surveillance cameras except to remove the film.
g) Submissions for comparison with the Child Exploitation and Obscenity Reference File should not exceed 30 images.
    i) Call 202-324-6997 for specific instructions.
    ii) Address the outer container as follows:

> **Federal Bureau of Investigation**
> **Engineering Research Facility**
> **Attention: Forensic Program**
> **Building 27958A**
> **Quantico, VA 22135**

POLYMERS EXAMINATION

1) Examination considerations
    a) The source, use, or manufacturer of plastic evidence usually cannot be identified by composition analysis.
    b) Automobile trim can be compared with plastic remaining on the property struck in a hit-and-run case.
        i) The year, make, and model of an automobile can be determined if a manufacturer's part number is on the trim.
    c) Plastics in wire insulation and miscellaneous plastics (e.g., buttons) can be compared with known sources.

QUESTIONED-DOCUMENT EXAMINATION

1) Examination consideration
    a) Handwriting and hand printing
        i) Although not all handwriting can be matched to a specific writer, the examination of handwriting characteristics can sometimes determine the origin or authenticity of questioned writing.
            (1) Traits such as age, sex, and or personality, or intent cannot be determined from handwriting examinations.
        ii) Some reasons for inconclusive results include the following:

(1) Limited questioned or known writing
(2) Lack of contemporaneous writing or lapse of time between execution of questioned and known writing
(3) Distortion or disguise in the questioned or known writing
(4) Lack of sufficient identifying characteristics
(5) Submission of photocopied evidence instead of original evidence
b) Various handwriting and hand printing analysis techniques are used to examine different forms of obliterated writing.

2) Procedures for obtaining known writing exemplars
a) The text, size of paper, space available for writing, writing instrument, and writing style (i.e., handwriting or hand printing) should be as close to the original writing as possible.
b) Give verbal or typewritten instructions about the text to be written.
i) Do not give instructions on spelling, punctuation, or arrangement of writing.
c) All exemplars should be on separate pieces of paper.
d) The writer and witness should initial and date each page of writing.
e) Do not allow the writer to see the previous exemplars or the questioned writing. Remove exemplars from the writer's sight as soon as completed.
f) Obtain exemplars from dictation until normal writing has been produced.
i) Normal handwriting is assessed by determining whether the writing is too quickly or slowly executed and whether the handwriting is consistent.
g) Obtain exemplars from the right and left hands.
h) Obtain hand-printing exemplars in upper- and lower-case letters.
i) Obtain exemplars written rapidly, slowly, and at varied slants.
j) Obtain enough exemplars to account for natural variation in the writing.
k) Obtain such writing samples as business records, personal correspondence, and canceled checks.

3) Common types of nongenuine signatures
a) Traced signatures are prepared by using a genuine signature as a template or pattern.
b) Simulated signatures are prepared by copying or drawing a genuine signature.
c) Freehand signatures are written in the forger's normal handwriting with no attempt to copy another's writing style.

4) Typewriting
a) Questioned typewriting can occasionally be identified with the typewriter that produced it.
i) This is most common when the typewriter is a typebar machine.
ii) The identification can sometimes be based on individual characteristics that develop during the manufacturing process and through use and abuse of the typewriter.
iii) Typewriters with interchangeable elements (e.g., ball, printwheel, thimble) are less likely to be associated with questioned typewriting.
(1) However, these elements and carbon film or correction ribbons can sometimes be associated with specific texts by examining individual characteristics of the elements and correlating the text and ribbons.
b) Comparison of questioned typewriting with reference standards can sometimes determine a possible make and model of the typewriter or typewriter elements.
i) Carbon-film typewriter ribbons can sometimes be read for content or specific wording of questioned material.

ii) Carbon-film ribbons can sometimes be identified with questioned typewritten impressions.
iii) Fabric ribbons cannot be read.
c) Paper examination
   i) Paper is composed of numerous fibers. The randomness of the paper fibers is an identifying characteristic that makes fiber designs unique to a paper sample.
   ii) The transfer of fiber designs can link a typewriter ribbon to typed text, which enables examiners to positively link a ribbon to text on a document.
d) Procedures for obtaining known typewriting exemplars
   i) If the typewriter has a carbon-film ribbon, remove it from the typewriter and submit it to the lab.
      (1) Also submit the correction tape.
      (2) Insert a new ribbon in the typewriter before obtaining exemplars.
   ii) If the typewriter has a fabric ribbon, remove it from the typewriter and put the typewriter in the stencil position.
      (1) Place a sheet of carbon paper over a sheet of blank paper and insert both into the typewriter.
      (2) Allow the typeface to strike the carbon paper.
      (3) Submit the fabric ribbon strike and the carbon paper strike exemplars to the lab.
   iii) Obtain two full word-for-word texts of the questioned text and type the entire keyboard (all symbols, numbers, and upper and lowercase letters) two times.
   iv) Record the make, model, and serial number of the typewriter on the exemplars.
      (1) Also record the date the exemplars were obtained and the name of the person who directed the exemplars.
   v) Obtain the typewriter service or repair history.
   vi) It is not normally necessary to send the typewriter to the lab, but in some cases, the examiner will request it.
      (1) It should be packed securely to prevent damage during shipment.
      (2) Typewriter elements (e.g., ball, printwheel, thimble) should also be submitted to the lab.

RACKETEERING RECORDS EXAMINATION

1) Examination consideration of the following types of records
   a) Cryptanalysis
      i) Cryptanalysis examinations involve the analysis of encrypted clandestine drug and racketeering documents.
   b) Drug records
      i) Drug records are examined to determine the overall scope of the businesses, including the hierarchy, type of drugs distributed, gross sales, gross or net weights or quantities, price structures, and other pertinent information.
   c) Gambling
      i) Gambling examinations include the interpretation of records from sports and racing bookmaking businesses, numbers or lottery operations, and other gambling businesses.
   d) Loan-sharking
      i) Loan-sharking records are examined to determine the amounts of the loans, amounts paid in interest and principal, number of loans, and interest rates.

c) Money laundering
- i) Money-laundering records are examined to determine the scope of the operations, the amounts laundered, how the funds were laundered, and any other illegal activities.

f) Prostitution
- i) Prostitution records are examined to determine the scope of the businesses, including the number of employees, their roles, gross and net revenues, and other financial and organizational information.

g) Racketeering
- i) Racketeering records are examined to determine the roles of the suspect(s); salaries, commissions, or shares of the operation's profit; dates and amounts of wagers, loans, and percentage rates; and income from video gambling operations.

2) Submitting racketeering records evidence
- a) Documentary evidence should be preserved in the same condition it was found.
    - i) It should not be folded, torn, marked, soiled, stamped, written on, or handled unnecessarily.
    - ii) Documents should be marked unobtrusively by placing the collector's initials, the date, and other information with a pencil.
- b) Flash paper is a hazardous material.
    - i) Do not store flash papers near combustible materials.
    - ii) Seal flash paper in polyethylene envelopes and refrigerate.

SAFE-INSULATION EXAMINATION

1) Examination considerations
- a) Safe insulation can be compared with a known source.
- b) Examinations of safe insulation can sometimes determine the manufacturer.

2) Submitting safe-insulation evidence
- a) Safe insulation exposed by peeling a safe door
    - i) Collect safe-insulation samples from damaged areas.
- b) Safe insulation can adhere to persons, clothing, tools, bags, and loot, and can be transferred to vehicles.
    - i) If possible, submit the evidence to the lab for examiners to remove the debris.
    - ii) Package each item of evidence in a separate paper bag.
    - iii) Do not process tools for latent prints.
    - iv) Submit known and questioned debris in leakproof containers (e.g., film canisters, plastic pill bottles).
        - (1) Avoid using paper or glass containers.
        - (2) Pack to keep any lumps intact.

SERIAL NUMBER EXAMINATION

1) Examination consideration
- a) Obliterated serial or identification numbers are often restorable, including markings on metal, wood, plastic, and fiberglass.

2) Casting stamped numbers
    a) Make a cast before number restoration.
    b) Use an acrylic surface-replica cast kit.
        i) Different formulas are used in different temperatures. If possible, move the evidence to a warm area.
    c) Casts will duplicate foreign material in the stamped characters.
        i) Clean the area before proceeding.
        ii) Remove paint and dirt with a solvent, such as acetone, gasoline, or paint remover.
        iii) Use a soft brush, not a wire brush. Use naval jelly to remove rust.

3) Preparation for casting stamped numbers
    a) Build a dam around the stamped characters to retain the acrylic liquid while it hardens. The dam material should be soft and pliable (e,g., modeling clay). Ensure that there are no voids in the dam.
    b) Following instructions in the kit, mix the liquid and powder for 1 minute and pour it into the dam.
    c) The acrylic liquid takes 30 minutes to harden.
        i) Remove the cast when it is hard.
        ii) If paint and rust are on the cast, make additional casts and submit the cleanest cast to the lab.

4) Submitting serial number evidence
    a) If possible, remove the piece of frame rail containing the serial number, indicate where on the vehicle the cut was taken, and submit it to the lab.
    b) Pack the cast to prevent breakage.

SHOEPRINT AND TIRE TREAD FILES

1) Examination consideration
    a) A file of shoe manufacturers' designs and a file of tire treads and other reference material can be searched to determine brand names and manufacturers.

2) Submitting shoeprint and tire tread evidence
    a) For shoeprint and tire tread comparisons, submit original evidence whenever possible (e.g., shoes, tires, photographic negatives, casts, lifts).
    b) For shoeprint and tire tread file searches, submit quality photographs of the impressions.
        i) If photographs are not available, submit casts, lifts, or the original evidence.
        ii) Detailed sketches or photocopies are acceptable.
    c) Unobtrusively write the collector's initials, the dates, and other relevant information on the evidence.
    d) Air-dry and package evidence separately in bubble wrap; clean, smooth-quality paper or laminated folders; or paper bags.

SOIL EXAMINATION

1) Examination considerations
    a) Soil is usually considered the top surface of earth most likely to contain footprints and tire marks.

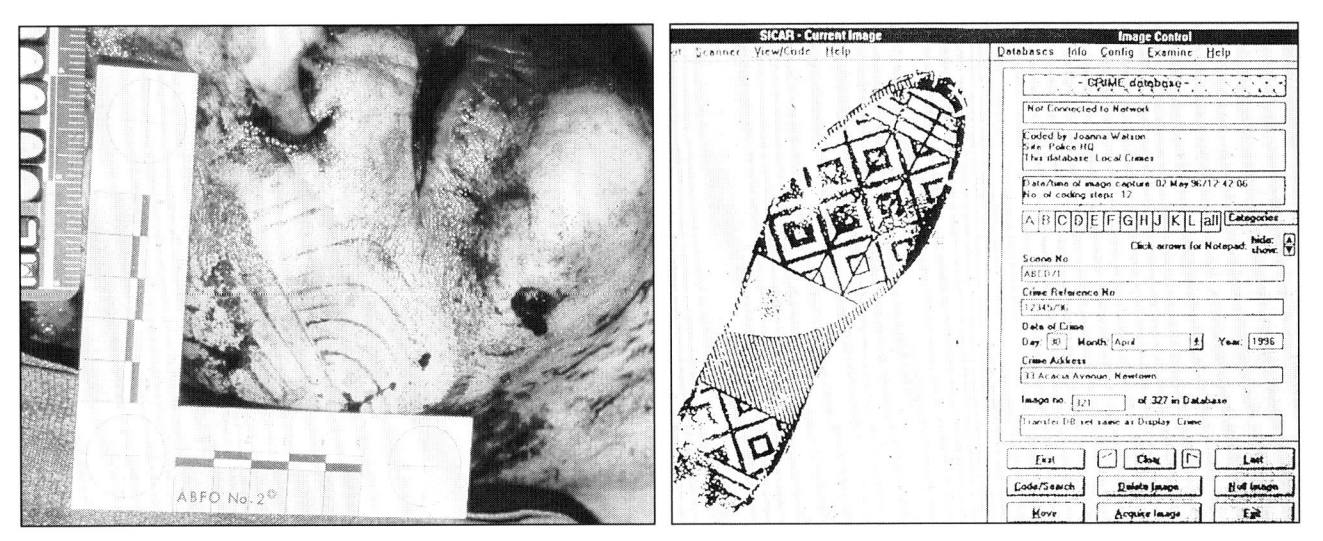

A database system can be extremely helpful in identifying the type of shoe used to kick the decedent in the face.

The British developed a software program (SICAR) whereby a footwear pattern taken from a crime scene, either whole or in part, can be entered into the computer and the database program will identify the shoe. In Britain, the program actually serves to identify the wearer of the suspect shoe. In the United States, the program is used for the identification of the shoe types.

TIRE TREAD DATABASE

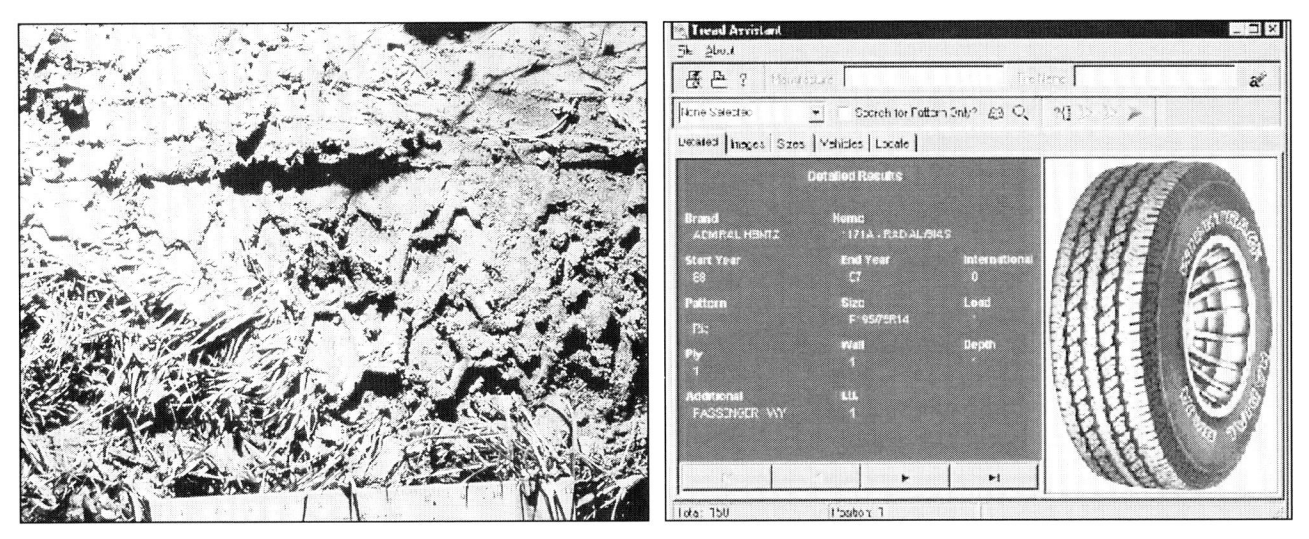

Database programs to identify tires from tread-designs discovered at crime scenes are available to investigators, usually through the crime lab. This type of database usually contains thousands of tread patterns dating back to 1990. The tire lines include passenger cars, light trucks, off-road, agricultural, motorcycle, and retreads. The database includes the United States, Canada, and other major countries around the world. The information includes an up-to-date listing of all major tire manufacturers and their brand names.

Tire tracks present at the scene could lead to the identification of the suspect vehicle for the investigator. If one or more of the following measurements are available—inside to inside, outside to outside, or outside to inside—the database will identify all vehicles matching the submitted measurements.

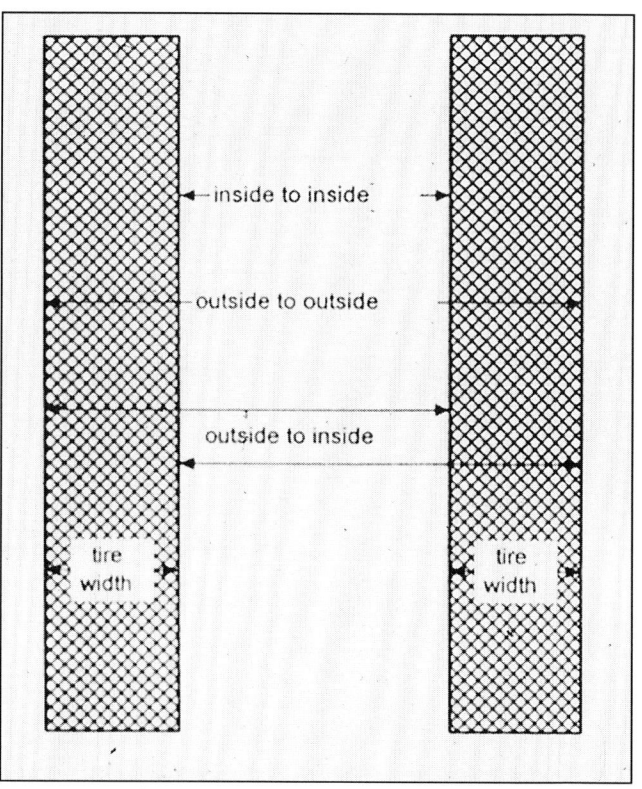

   b) Soil is the natural accumulation of weathering rocks, minerals, and decomposing plants.
   c) Soil may contain such man-made materials as brick, roof shingle stones, concrete, glass, and paint.
   d) Soil development is influenced by geologic parent material, relief, climate, biological activity, man, and time.
   e) Soil examinations can determine whether soils share a common origin by comparing color, texture, and composition.

2) Investigative potential
   a) Soil may be found on the suspect's shoes, clothing, or other personal items, such as vehicles. It may be consistent enough to link a potential suspect or property in the possession of the suspect to an environment similar to the one in which the body was recovered and/or killed.
   b) Soil from the undercarriage of a vehicle involved in a hit-and-run may be found on the victim. This soil may be compared with the soil found on the bottom of the undercarriage of a suspect vehicle.
   c) On any footprint or tire-tread case in which castings were completed, a representative soil sample should be collected from an area immediately adjacent to the area where the casting occurred. The recommended procedure is to take seven such samples from an area immediate adjacent up to a point of 20 feet.

3) Submitting soil evidence
   a) Collect soil samples as soon as possible because the soil at the crime scene can change dramatically.
   b) Collect soil samples from the immediate crime-scene area and from the logical access or escape route(s).

c) Collect soil samples that exhibit noticeable changes in color, texture, and composition.
d) Collect soil samples at a depth that is consistent with the depth from which the questioned soil may have originated.
e) If possible, collect soil samples from alibi areas, such as the yard or work area of the suspect(s).
f) Submit a map identifying soil sample locations.
g) Do not remove soil adhering to shoes, clothing, and tools.
h) Do not process tools for latent prints.
  i) Air-dry the soil and the clothing, and package separately in paper bags.
i) Carefully remove soil adhering to vehicles.
  i) Air-dry the soil and package separately in paper bags.
j) Submit known and questioned soil in separate leakproof containers (e.g., film canisters, plastic pill bottles).
  i) Avoid using paper envelopes or glass containers.
  ii) Pack to keep lumps intact.

TOOL MARK EXAMINATION

1) Examination considerations
   a) Tool marks
      i) Tools can bear unique microscopic characteristics because of manufacturing processes and use. These characteristics can be transferred to surfaces that contact the tools.
      ii) Evidence tool marks can be compared with recovered tools.
         (1) In the absence of a questioned tool, tool mark examinations can determine the type of tool(s) that produced the tool mark and whether the tool mark is of value for comparison.
   b) Fractures
      i) Fracture examinations can determine whether evidence was joined together and subsequently broken apart.

2) Submitting tool mark evidence
   a) If possible, submit the tool marked evidence. The lab will make a cast of the tool mark, if needed.
      i) If it is not possible to submit the tool-marked evidence, submit a cast of the tool mark.
   b) Photographs locate tool marks but are of no value for identification purposes.
   c) Obtain samples of any material deposited on the tools.
   d) To avoid contamination, do not place the tool against the tool-marked evidence.
   e) Submit the tool rather than making test cuts or impressions.
   f) Mark the ends of the evidence and specify which end was cut during evidence collection.

TOXICOLOGY EXAMINATION

1) Examination considerations
   a) Toxicology examinations can disclose the presence of drugs or poisons in biological specimens. The examinations can determine the circumstances surrounding drug- or poison-related homicides, suicides, or accidents.

b) Because of the large number of potentially toxic substances, it may be necessary to screen for classes of poisons, for example:
- i) Volatile compounds (e.g., ethanol, methanol, isopropanol)
- ii) Heavy metals (e.g., arsenic)
- iii) Nonvolatile organic compounds (e.g., drugs of abuse, pharmaceuticals)
- iv) Miscellaneous (e.g., strychnine, cyanide)

2) Submitting toxicology evidence
- a) The quantity of biological specimens submitted depends on whether the identity of a toxic substance is known, the route of administration, the time after exposure that biological specimens are collected, and whether subjects(s) or victim(s) are living or deceased.
- b) Each biological specimen must be placed in separate, labeled, sealed glass tubes, plastic cups, or heat-sealed or resealable plastic bags. Affix BIOHAZARD labels to the inside and outside containers.
- c) To avoid deterioration, biological specimens must be refrigerated or frozen during storage and shipping.
    - i) Pack so that no breakage, leakage, or contamination occurs.
- d) Submit a copy of the autopsy or incident report.
- e) Describe the symptoms of the suspect(s) or victim(s) at the time of the crime or prior to the death.
- f) List any known or questioned drugs consumed by or prescribed for the suspect(s) or victim(s).
- g) Describe any known or questioned environmental exposure to toxic substances by the suspect(s) or victim(s).

VIDEO EXAMINATION

1) Examination consideration
- a) Authenticity
    - i) Authenticity examinations are conducted to determine whether analog video recordings are original, continuous, and unaltered.
- b) Enhancement
    - i) Video processors and time-base correctors can be used to maximize the clarity of videotapes.
- c) Video image processing
    - i) Enhanced prints can be produced from images depicted on videotapes.
- d) Standards conversion
    - i) Videotapes can be converted from one standard to another, such as from PAL to NTSC or SECAM.
- e) Format conversion
    - i) Videotapes can be converted from one format to another, such as from Beta to VHS.
- f) Synchronization
    - i) Audio and video signals can be combined to produce one composite recording.
- g) Special effects
    - i) Special effects, such as a mosaic, can be added to videotapes to protect a person's identity.
- h) Damaged media repair
    - i) Videotapes can be repaired, restored, or retrieved for playback and examination if the damage is not too extensive.

2) Submitting video evidence
    a) Submit original video recordings.
        i) Identify the location(s) of the image(s) on the video recordings and describe the image(s).
    b) Label the outer container as follows:

FRAGILE, SENSITIVE ELECTRONIC EQUIPMENT
or
FRAGILE, SENSITIVE AUDIO/VIDEO MEDIA
and
KEEP AWAY FROM MAGNETS OR MAGNETIC FIELDS.

    c) Address the outer container as follows:

> **Federal Bureau of Investigation**
> **Engineering Research Facility**
> **Attention: Forensic Program**
> **Building 27958A**
> **Quantico, VA 22135**

WATCHES, CLOCKS, AND TIMERS

1) Examination consideration
    a) The conditions causing a watch, clock, timer, or other mechanism to stop or malfunction, and whether the time displayed represents A.M. or P.M. (calendar-type timing mechanisms only) can be determined.

WOOD EXAMINATION

1) Examination considerations
    a) A wood examination can match sides, ends, and fractures.
    b) It can determine wood species.
    c) It can compare wood particles found on clothing, vehicles, and other objects with wood from the crime scene.

2) Submitting wood evidence
    a) Submit wood in heat-sealed or resealable plastic or paper bags.

CONVERSION CHARTS

VELOCITY

To Obtain	Centimeters per second	Meters per second	Kilometers per hour	Feet per second	Feet per minute	Miles per hour
Multiply # of	By	By	By	By	By	By
Centimeters per second	1	0.01	0.036	0.0328	1.968	0.02237
Meters per second	100	1	3.6	3.281	196.85	2.237
Kilometers per hour	27.78	0.2778	1	0.9113	54.68	0.6214
Feet per second	30.48	0.3048	18.29	1	60	0.6818
Feet per minute	0.5080	0.00508	0.0183	0.0166	1	0.01136
Miles per hour	44.70	0.4470	1.609	1.467	88	1

PRESSURE

To Obtain	Pounds per square inch	Atmospheres	Inches (Hg)	Millimeters (Hg)	Kilopascals	Feet (H_2O) (15°C)	Inches (H_2O)	Pounds per square foot
Multiply # of	By	By	By	By	By	By	By	By
Pounds per square inch	1	0.068	2.036	51.71	6.895	2.309	27.71	144
Atmospheres	14.696	1	29.92	760.0	101.32	33.93	407.2	2,116
Inches (Hg)	0.4912	0.033	1	25.40	3.386	1.134	13.61	70.73
Millimeters (Hg)	0.01934	0.0013	0.039	1	0.1333	0.04464	0.5357	2.785
Kilopascals	0.1450	9.87x10-3	0.2953	7.502	1	0.3460*	4.019	20.89
Feet (H_2O) (15°C)	0.4332	0.0294	0.8819	22.40	2.989*	1	12.00	62.37
Inches (H_2O)	0.03609	0.0024	0.073	1.867	0.2488	0.0833	1	5.197
Pounds per square foot	0.0069	4.72x10-4	0.014	0.359	0.04788	0.016	0.193	1

*At 40°C

HEAT, ENERGY, OR WORK

To Obtain	Joules	Foot-pounds	Kilowatt hours	HP-hours	Kilopascals	Calories	BTUs
Multiply # of	By	By	By	By	By	By	By
Joules	1	0.737	2.773x10-7	3.725x10-7	2.39x10-4	0.2390	9.478x10-4
Foot-pounds	1,356	1	3.766x10-7	5.05x10-7	3.24x10-4	0.3241	1.285x10-3
Kilowatt hours	3.6x106	2.66x106	1	1.341	860.57	860,565	3,412
HP-hours	2.68x106	1.98x106	0.7455	1	641.62	641,615	2,545
Kilocalories	4,184	3,086	1.162x10-3	1.558x10-3	1	1,000	3.9657
Calories	4.184	3.086	1.162x10-6	1.558x10-6	0.001	1	0.00397
BTUs	1,055	778.16	2.930x10-4	3.93x10-4	0.252	252	1

DENSITY

To Obtain	Grams per cubic centimeter	Pounds per cubic foot	Pounds per gallon (U.S.)
Multiply # of	BY	BY	BY
Grams per cubic centimeter	1	62.43	8.345
Pounds per cubic foot	0.01602	1	0.1337
Pounds per gallon (U.S.)	0.1198	7.481	1

FORCE

To Obtain	Dynes	Newtons	Kilogram-force	Pound-force
Multiply # of	By	By	By	By
Dynes	1	1.0×10^{-5}	1.02×10^{-4}	2.248×10^{4}
Newtons	1.0×10^{5}	1	0.1020	0.2248
Kilogram-force	9.807×10^{-5}	9.807	1	2.205
Pound-force	4.448×10^{-5}	4.448	0.4563	1

AREA

To Obtain	Square meter	Square inch	Square foot	Square centimeter	Square millimeter
Multiply # of	By	By	By	By	By
Square meter	1	1,550	10.76	10,000	10^{6}
Square inch	6.452×10^{-3}	1	6.94×10^{-3}	6.452	645.2
Square foot	0.0929	144	1	929.0	92,903
Square centimeter	0.0001	0.155	0.001	1	100
Square millimeter	10^{-6}	0.00155	0.00001	0.01	1

LENGTH

To Obtain Multiply # of	Meters By	Centimeters By	Millimeters By	Microns By	Angstroms By	Unit inches By	Feet By
Meters	1	100	1,000	106	1,010	39.37	3.28
Centimeters	0.01	1	10	104	108	0.394	0.0328
Millimeters	0.001	0.1	1	103	107	0.0394	0.00328
Microns	10-6	10-4	10-3	1	10	3.94x10-5	3.28x10-6
Angstroms	10-10	10-8	10-7	10-4	1	3.94x10-9	3.28x10-10
Inches	0.0254	2.540	25.40	2.54x104	2.54x108	1	0.0833
Feet	0.305	30.48	304.8	304,800	3.048x109	12	1

VOLUME

To Obtain Multiply # of	Cubic feet By	Gallons (U.S. liquid) By	Liters By	Cubic centimeters By	Cubic meters By
Cubic feet	1	7.481	28.32	28,320	0.0283
Gallons (U.S. liquid)	0.1337	1	3.785	3,785	3.79x10-3
Liters	0.03531	0.2642	1	1,000	1x10-3
Cubic centimeters	3.531x10-5	2.64x10-4	0.001	1	10-6
Cubic meters	35.31	264.2	1,000	106	1

FLOW RATES

To Obtain	Liters per minute	Cubic meters per second	Cubic meters per hour	Gallons (U.S.) per minute	Cubic feet per minute	Cubic feet per second
Multiply # of	By	By	By	By	By	By
Liters per minute	1	1.67×10^{-5}	0.06	0.2640	0.0353	5.89×10^{-4}
Cubic meters per second	4.63×10^{-3}	1	2.77×10^{-4}	1.22×10^{-3}	1.63×10^{-4}	2.7×10^{-6}
Gallons (U.S.) per minute	3.78	6.3×10^{-5}	0.227	1	0.1338	2.23×10^{-3}
Cubic feet per minute	28.32	4.71×10^{-4}	1.699	7.50	1	0.01667
Cubic feet	1.69×10^{3}	2.83×10^{-3}	1.02×10^{2}	448.8	60	1

MASS

To Obtain	Grams	Kilograms	Grains	Ounces	Pounds
Multiply # of	By	By	By	By	By
Grams	1	0.001	15.432	0.03527	0.00220
Kilograms	1,000	1	15,432	35.27	2.205
Grains	0.0648	6.480×10^{-5}	1	2.286×10^{-3}	1.429×10^{-4}
Ounces	28.35	0.02835	437.5	1	0.0625
Pounds	453.59	0.4536	7,000	16	1

CONTRIBUTORS

I gratefully acknowledge the contribution of the following individuals in the creation of this book:

- Alford, Steve, Florida Department of Law Enforcement, Jacksonville, Florida
- Arruza, Margarita, MD, chief medical examiner, Medical Examiner's Office, Jacksonville, Florida
- Austin, Ed, former mayor, Jacksonville, Florida
- Baker, Andrew, MD, assistant medical examiner, Milwaukee, Wisconsin
- Barker, Donnie, training specialist, Institute of Police Technology and Management, Jacksonville, Florida
- Blanton, Sheri, ("my partner"), Medical Examiner's Office, Orlando, Florida
- Blincoe, Ralph, special agent, Naval Criminal Investigative Service, Washington, D.C.
- Breton, Damon, forensic investigator, Office of the Medical Examiner, Largo, Florida
- Bunney, William G., officer, Alexandria Police Department, Alexandria, Virginia
- Burns, Arthur Dr., forensic odontologist, Jacksonville, Florida
- Carbone, Laura S., MD, assistant medical examiner, Bergen County Medical Examiner's Office, Paramus, New Jersey
- Carlyle, Billy, Sgt., Jacksonville Beach Police Department, Jacksonville Beach, Florida
- Carne, Linda P., director of education and research, Virginia Institute of Forensic Science and Medicine, Richmond, Virginia
- Carson, Dale, Jr., consultant, Jacksonville, Florida
- Carter, R. Bruce, U.S. Customs, Jacksonville, Florida
- Chester, Albert D., SAC, Naval Investigative Service, Mayport, Florida
- Coman, Bret, Detective Sergeant, Homicide and Serial Violent Crime Agency, Sydney, Australia
- Cordle, David H., chief investigator, State Attorney's Office, Annapolis, Maryland
- Corey, Angela, assistant state attorney, State Attorney's Office, Fourth Judicial Circuit, Jacksonville, Florida
- Darnell, Sadie Capt., commander, Gainesville Police Department, Gainesville, Florida
- Dean, Carol, (ME-12) forensic investigator, retired, Medical Examiner's Office, Jacksonville, Florida

- Delaney, John, mayor of Jacksonville, Florida

- Dorsey, Charles K., supervisory special agent, Behavioral Analysis Unit, FBI, Quantico, Virginia

- Downes, Gerald F., supervisory special agent, Behavioral Analysis Unit, FBI, Quantico, Virginia

- Eliopulos, Anthony C., consultant, Orlando, Florida

- Eliopulos, Gisele, consultant, Jacksonville, Florida

- Eliopulos, Jason K., consultant, Jacksonville, Florida

- Eliopulos, Lindsay M., consultant, Jacksonville, Florida

- Eliopulos, Nicholas R., consultant, Jacksonville, Florida

- Falsetti, Anthony B., Ph.D, director, C.A. Pound Human Identification Laboratory, Gainesville, Florida

- Floro, Bonifacio Dr., chief medical examiner (retired), Medical Examiner's Office, Jacksonville, Florida

- Fox, Mark, special agent, Naval Criminal Investigative Service, Naples, Italy

- Freeman, Michael D., special agent, FBI, Norfolk, Virginia

- Frigo, Kathy M., U.S. Postal Service, Jacksonville, Florida

- Frost, Louis O., public defender, Florida Office of the Public Defender, Jacksonville, Florida

- Garavaglia, Jan Dr., associate medical examiner, San Antonio, Texas

- Gelles, Michael, Dr., Naval Criminal Investigative Service, Washington, D.C.

- Gilbreath, Dale, homicide detective, Jacksonville Sheriff's Office, Jacksonville, Florida

- Grebas, James, special agent, Naval Criminal Investigative Service, Washington, D.C.

- Greenwood, John, insurance claims specialist, Jacksonville, Florida

- Greffen, Kirk, special agent, Naval Criminal Investigative Service, Washington, D.C.

- Groves, Larry and Babette, consultants, Kansas City, Missouri

- Hagerty, Bill, FBI (retired), educator, Institute of Police Technology and Management, Jacksonville, Florida

- Halil, Don, chief investigator, Florida Office of the Public Defender, Jacksonville, Florida

- Hall, David W. Ph.D forensic botanist, Gainesville, Florida

- Halyard, Morris, forensic investigator (retired), Medical Examiner's Office, Jacksonville, Florida
- Hammond, Randy, Jacksonville Sheriff's Office, Jacksonville, Florida
- Hanson, Steven R., OSI Forensics (retired), chief medical investigator, Bexar County, San Antonio, Texas
- Healy, John J., Insurance Investigator, New York, New York.
- Herring, Bruce, OSI (Retired), Criminal Investigations Training Chief, Institute of Police Technology and Management, Jacksonville, Florida
- Hickson, A.W., homicide detective (retired), Jacksonville Sheriff's Office, Jacksonville, Florida
- Hinman, Dayle, special agent (retired), criminal investigative analyst, Florida Department of Law Enforcement, Tallahassee, Florida
- Hinson, Robbie, detective, Jacksonville Sheriff's Office, Jacksonville, Florida
- Housend, Roger, homicide detective (retired), Jacksonville Sheriff's Office, Jacksonville, Florida
- Hughes, Pete, special agent, Naval Criminal Investigative Service, Washington, D.C.
- Japour, Frank, Sgt., Jacksonville Sheriff's Office, Jacksonville, Florida
- Jenkins, Bob and Stathia, consultants, Reidsville, Virginia
- Jesonek, Jerry Dr., Jacksonville Sheriff's Office, Jacksonville, Florida
- Johnson, Debra, special agent (retired), Florida Department of Law Enforcement, Pensacola, Florida
- Killacky, Brian Investigator, Cold Case Homicide/Organized Crime, State Attorney's Office, Chicago, Illinois
- Klopfer, Micheline, consultant, Jacksonville, Florida
- Kuzniar, Frank G., Medical Examiner's Office, Ft. Lauderdale, Florida
- Lassiter, Robert W., Jacksonville, Florida
- Leary, Steve, crime laboratory analyst, Florida Department of Law Enforcement, Jacksonville, Florida
- Leroux, Denny, musician extraordinaire, Atlantic Beach, Florida
- Leroux , Judith Williamson, consultant/writer, Atlantic Beach, Florida
- Levine, Philip J., DDS, forensic odontologist, Pensacola, Florida

- Link, Robert J., attorney, Jacksonville, Florida

- Lipkovic, Peter, MD, chief medical examiner (retired), Medical Examiner's Office, Jacksonville, Florida

- Lord, Wayne D. Dr., unit chief, Child Abduction and Serial Murder Investigative Resources Center, FBI, Quantico, Virginia

- Maples, William R. Dr., forensic anthropologist, University of Florida, Gainesville, Florida

- Marzouk, Abu Bakr A. Col., U.S. Air Force, MC, FS, chief medical examiner, Office of the Armed Forces Medical Examiner, Rockville, Maryland

- McGuinness, Brian, private investigator, Miami, Florida

- McGuinness, Patrick, assistant public defender, Florida Office of the Public Defender, Jacksonville, Florida

- McLeod, Scott, Det. Sgt., Jacksonville Sheriff's Office, Jacksonville, Florida

- McMillan, James, Jr., forensic artist, Jacksonville Sheriff's Office, Jacksonville, Florida

- McMillan, Jim, Sheriff (retired), Jacksonville Sheriff's Office, Jacksonville, Florida

- Mellecker, Kirk, major case specialist, FBI, Quantico, Virginia

- Miller, T. Allen, senior crime scene laboratory analyst (retired), Florida Department of Law Enforcement, Jacksonville, Florida

- Mittleman, Pete, Lt., Ed.D., Jacksonville Sheriff's Office, Jacksonville, Florida

- Mobley, Leonard T., forensic investigator, Medical Examiner's Office, Jacksonville, Florida

- Moore, Kenneth N., chief forensic investigator, Medical Examiner's Office, St. Augustine, Florida

- Mullaney, Rick, general counsel, General Counsel's Office, Jacksonville, Florida

- Nance, Gerald, National Center for Missing and Exploited Children, Alexandria, Virginia

- Nelson, John, chief of police, Orange Park Police Department, Orange Park, Florida

- Ondina, Michael and Janine, consultants, West Palm Beach, Florida

- O'Steen, T.C., detective, Intelligence Section, Jacksonville Sheriff's Office, Jacksonville, Florida

- Owens, Charles, Dr., Criminal Justice Department, University of North Florida

- Parker, James Det. Sgt., Cold Case Homicide, Jacksonville, Sheriff's Office, Jacksonville, Florida

- Platt, Steve, crime lab chief, Florida Department of Law Enforcement, Jacksonville, Florida

CONTRIBUTORS

- Pollock, James M., Jr, Dr., serologist/DNA, Florida Department of Law Enforcement, Jacksonville, Florida

- Pulley, Thomas J., firearms examiner, Florida Department of Law Enforcement, Jacksonville, Florida

- Raybon, Don W., chairman, Law Enforcement Department, N.C. Justice Academy, State of North Carolina, Salemburg, North Carolina

- Rasche, Chris Dr., Criminal Justice Department, University of North Florida, Jacksonville, Florida

- Redmond, Jimm, Capt., Clay County Sheriff's Office, Green Cove Springs, Florida

- Roach, Kenneth, (retired homicide detective), priest, Jacksonville, Florida

- Ruby, Larry, special agent, Florida Department of Law Enforcement, Jacksonville, Florida

- Sands, Michael, forensic investigator, Medical Examiner's Office, Jacksonville, Florida

- Schoettler, Jim, reporter, *Florida Times Union*, Jacksonville, Florida

- Scott, H.L., homicide detective, St. Marys, Georgia

- Seibler, Richard H., chief of patrol, Jacksonville Sheriff's Office, Jacksonville, Florida

- Silvestro, Yvette and Tom, consultants, Jacksonville, Florida

- Smith, Greg, detective, Cold Case Squad, Miami, Florida

- Sopp, Teresa, attorney, Jacksonville, Florida

- Spano, Vito R., deputy inspector, Cold Case and Apprehension Squad, New York Police Department, Brooklyn, New York

- Stetson, Brad, judge, State of Florida, 4th Judicial Circuit, Jacksonville, Florida

- Stewart, Larry, director, Criminal Laboratory, U.S. Secret Service, Washington, D.C.

- Sullivan, Michael, Homicide (retired), Metropolitan Police Department, Washington, D.C.

- Swear, D'Wayne, special agent, EPA, New Orleans, Louisiana

- Takacs, Zsolt and Ruth, consultants, Jacksonville, Florida

- Tewes, Warren D., DDS, MS, assistant professor, Baltimore College of Dental Surgery, University of Maryland, Baltimore, Maryland

- Thorwart, R.C., Jacksonville Sheriff's Office, Jacksonville, Florida

- Tucker, James R., detective, Bureau of Investigative Services, Portsmouth, New Hampshire

- Vorpagel, Russell E., consultant, Loomis, California

- Walker, Homer, consultant, Lake Butler, Florida

- Warniment, David, firearms examiner/expert, Florida Department of Law Enforcement, Jacksonville, Florida

- Warren, Michael W., Ph.D, deputy director, C.A. Pound Human Identification Laboratory, Gainesville, Florida

- Whitcomb, Carrie M., MSFS, director, National Center for Forensic Science, University of Central Florida, Orlando, Florida

- White, William, Chief Assistant Public Defender, Florida Office of the Public Defender, Jacksonville, Florida

- Williams, Deborah (Debi) A., FBI, Norfolk, Virginia

- Williams, T.L., assistant branch chief, Department of the Army, Criminal Investigation Command, Ft. Belvoir, Virginia

- Zoller, Beth, chief investigator, Medical Examiner's Office, Jacksonville, Florida

BIBLIOGRAPHY

CRIME SCENES

Crime-Scene Investigation

Basic Training Manual for Crime Scene Procedures and Explosive Technology. Miami, Fla.: Dade County Public Safety Department, Crime Laboratory Bureau.

Chisum, W. Jerry. "Crime Scene Reconstruction." Presentation at the International Symposium on the Forensic Aspects of Mass Disasters and Crime Scene Reconstruction, FBI Training Academy, Quantico, Virginia, June 23–29, 1990.

Department of the Treasury Forensic Handbook. Washington, D.C.: Government Printing Office, 1975.

Fisher, Barry, Arne Svensson, and Otto Wendel. *Techniques of Crime Scene Investigation.* New York: Elsevier Science Publishing Co., 1987.

Fox, Richard H., and Carl L. Cunningham. *Crime Scene Search and Physical Evidence Handbook.* Washington, D.C.: U.S. Department of Justice, 1973.

Gilbert, James N. *Criminal Investigation,* Columbus, Oh.: Charles E. Merrill Publishing Co., 1986.

Goddard, Kenneth W. *Crime Scene Investigation,* Reston, Va.: Reston Publishing Co., 1977.

Kirk, Paul L. *Crime Investigation.* New York: John Willey and Sons, Inc., 1974.

McCullers, Dale et al. *The Field Guide for Crime Scene Investigators.* Naval Criminal Investigative Service (n.d.).

McFeely, Patricia, MD. "Crime Scene/Evidence Collection." Presentation at the Medicolegal Investigation of Death Conference, Albuquerque, New Mexico, September 11–13, 1991.

Miller, T. Allen. "Crime Scene Processing." Presentation at the Death Investigation Seminar, Jacksonville Police Academy, November, 1990.

Petty, Charles S., MD, and Vincent J.M. Di Maio, MD. "Scene Investigation for Medical-Legal Investigators." *The Forensic Science Gazette,* 6, no. 2, April 1975.

Rynearson, Joseph M., and William J. Chisum. *Evidence and Crime Scene Reconstruction.* Redding, Calif., 1991.

Westveer, Arthur E. *Death Investigation* Washington, D.C.: U.S. Department of Justice, Federal Bureau of Investigation.

Dead Body Processing

German, Ed. *Latent Print Examination of Skin.* Internet articles. KLS Forensics, Inc., 1997.

Photographing a Death Scene

Basic Training Manual for Crime Scene Procedures and Explosive Technology. Miami, Fla.: Dade County Public Safety Department, Crime Laboratory Bureau.

Miller, T. Allen. "Photographing a Crime Scene." Presentation at the Death Investigation Seminar, Jacksonville Police Academy, November, 1990.

Staggs, Steven B. "The Admissibility of Digital Photographs in Court." Internet article, May 2, 2001.

Videotaping a Death Scene

Miller, T. Allen. "Videotaping a Crime Scene." Presentation at the Death Investigation Seminar, Jacksonville Police Academy, November, 1990.

Thomas, Peter William. "Video Guidelines for Evidence Scenes." Internet article (not dated).

Evidence Collection

Basic Training Manual for Crime Scene Procedures and Explosive Technology. Miami, Fla.: Dade County Public Safety Department, Crime Laboratory Bureau.

Blackledge, Robert D. "Condom Trace Evidence: A New Factor in Sexual Assault Investigations." Internet article, http://www.fbi.gov/leb/may964.txt. May 1996.

Department of the Treasury Forensic Handbook. Washington, D.C.: Government Printing Office, 1975.

"Evidence Collection Guidelines." California Commission on Peace Officer Standards and Training's Workbook for the Forensic Technology for Law Enforcement telecourse, May 13, 1993.

Fisher, Barry, Arne Svensson, and Otto Wendel. *Techniques of Crime Scene Investigation.* New York: Elsevier, 1987.

Fox, Richard H., and Carl L. Cunningham. *Crime Scene Search and Physical Evidence Handbook.* Washington, D.C.: U.S. Department of Justice, 1973.

Rynearson, Joseph M., and William J. Chisum. *Evidence and Crime Scene Reconstruction.* Redding, Calif.: 1991.

Springer, Faye. *Processing of Nude Bodies for Physical Evidence.* State of California, Department of Justice: 1-2.

Wade, Colleen, ed. *Handbook of Forensic Sciences.* U.S. Department of Justice, Federal Bureau of Investigation, www.fbi.gov, revised, 1999.

Toolmark Evidence Collection. Physical Evidence Bulletin. California Department of Justice, Bureau of Forensic Services, February 1984.

Westveer, Arthur E. *Death Investigation.* Washington, D.C.: U.S. Department of Justice, Federal Bureau of Investigation.

Electronic Evidence

Clede, Bill. "Phone Companies Can Assist Local Police." *Law and Order*, February 1997.

International Association of Chiefs of Police and The Secret Service. *Best Practices for Seizing Electronic Evidence*, 1999.

Northeast Florida Violent Crime Regional Coordination Meeting. Violent Crime Council and Homicide Cold Case Meeting. May 26, 1999.

Body-Dumped Cases

Springer, Faye. *Processing of Nude Bodies for Physical Evidence*. State of California, Department of Justice: 1–2.

Westveer, Arthur E. *Death Investigation*. Washington, D.C.: U.S. Department of Justice, Federal Bureau of Investigation.

Buried-Body Cases

Boyd, Robert M. "Buried Body Cases." *FBI Law Enforcement Bulletin*, February 1979.

Davenport, Clarke. "Necro Search in Death Investigation—Techniques in Locating Buried Bodies." Lecture presented at Florida Department of Law Enforcement, Violent Crime Level 1 Course, Palatka, Fla., August 21, 1996.

Killan, Edward W. *The Detection of Human Remains*. Springfield, Ill.: Charles C. Thomas Publishing Co. 1990.

Rynearson, Joseph M., and William J. Chisum. *Evidence and Crime Scene Reconstruction* Redding, Calif., 1991.

Decomposed Remains

Byrd, Jason H., and James L. Castner, eds. *Forensic Entomology: The Utility of Arthropods in Legal Investigations*. New York: CRC Press.

Catts, Paul E., and Neal H. Haskell, eds. *Entomology and Death: A Procedural Guide*. Clemson, S.C.: Joyce's Print Shop, Inc., 1990.

"Entomology Guidelines for Police Crime Scene Investigators." www.Insectinvestigations@sympatico.ca. September, 2002.

Goff, M. Lee. "Forensic Entomology: Determination of Time Since Death." Presentation at the American Academy of Forensic Sciences, Las Vegas, Nev., February 13, 1989.

Haglund, William D. "Scene Investigation and Recovery of Decomposed Bodies." Presentation at the American Academy of Forensic Sciences, Las Vegas, Nev., February 13, 1989.

———. "Tooth Mark Artifacts and Survival of Bones in Animal Scavenged Human Skeletons." *Journal of Forensic Sciences*, 33, no. 4 (July 1988): 985–97.

———. "Carnivore-Assisted Disarticulation/Dismemberment of Human Remains." Presentation at the 57th Annual Meeting of the American Association of Physical Anthropologists, Kansas City, Mo., March 22–26, 1988.

Killan, Edward W. *The Detection of Human Remains.* Springfield, Ill.: Charles C. Thomas Publishing Co., 1990.

Lord, Wayne D. "Collection and Identification of Forensically Important Insects." Presentation at the American Academy of Forensic Sciences, Las Vegas, Nev., February 13, 1989.

———. "Entomology." Presentation at the Medicolegal Investigation of Death Conference, Albuquerque, N.M., September 11–13, 1991.

———. "Forensic Entomology." Presentation at the International Symposium on the Forensic Aspects of Mass Disasters and Crime Scene Reconstruction, FBI Training Academy, Quantico, Va., June 23–29, 1990.

Rodriguez, William C. III, MD. "Human Decomposition: Post Mortem Changes and Decompositional Rates." Presentation at the American Academy of Forensic Sciences, Las Vegas, Nev., February 13, 1989.

———. "Irregular Decomposition and Postmortem Pathologies." Presentation at the American Academy of Forensic Sciences, Las Vegas, Nev., February 13, 1989.

Smith, Kenneth G.V. *A Manual of Forensic Entomology.* London: British Museum of Natural History, 1986.

Tate, Larry R., MD. "Examination and Autopsy of Decomposed Bodies." Presentation at the American Academy of Forensic Sciences, Las Vegas, Nev., February 13, 1989.

Zumwalt, Ross E., MD. "Postmortem Artifact." Presentation at the Medicolegal Investigation of Death Conference, Albuquerque, N.M., September 11–13, 1991.

Blood Spatter Interpretation

Bodziak, William J. "The Use of Leuco Crystal Violet to Enhance Shoe Prints in Blood." Presentation for the European Meeting for Shoe Print and Tool Mark Examiners, Helsinki, May 8-11, 1995.

Bunker, Judy. "Bloodstain Spatter Analysis." Presentation at the Blood Workshop, St. Petersburg, Fla., April 26–28, 1982.

DeForest, P.R. "A Review of Bloodstain Evidence at Crime Scenes." *Journal of Forensic Sciences*, vol. 35: 1491–1495.

Eckert, William G., MD, and Stuart H. James. *Interpretation of Bloodstain Evidence at Crime Scenes.* New York: Elsevier, 1989.

Edell, Chuck. "Blood Spatter Interpretation." Presentation at the Florida Medicolegal Investigators Association, Ft. Lauderdale, Fla., February 9, 1991.

Englert, Rodney Dale. "Homicide, Suicide, or Accident? Solving the Puzzles, Old and New." *The Practical Prosecutor.*

MacDonell, Herbert Leon. "Bloodstain Pattern Interpretation." *Forensic Sciences.* New York: Matthew Bender Publisher, 1991.

MacDonnell, Herbert Leon, and Lorraine Fiske Bialousz. *Flight Characteristics and Stain Patterns of Human Blood.* New York: LEAA, 1980.

Wecht, Cyril, ed. *Forensic Sciences.* New York: Matthew Bender, 1991.

Westveer, Arthur E. *Death Investigation.* Washington, D.C.: U.S. Department of Justice, Federal Bureau of Investigation.

Wolson, Toby L. *Bloodstains.* Metro-Dade Police Department, Crime Laboratory Department.

Time Frame of Death

McFeeley, Patricia J., MD. "Standards Currently Employed to Determine Time of Death." *Recovery, Examination, and Evidence of Decomposed Bodies.* Collection of papers presented at the American Academy of Forensic Sciences, Las Vegas, Nev., February 13, 1989.

Rodriguez, William C. III, MD. "Human Decomposition: Post Mortem Changes and Decompositional Rates." Presentation at the American Academy of Forensic Sciences, Las Vegas, Nev., February 13, 1989.

Simson, Laurence R. Jr., MD. "Death Investigation." Presentation at the Sixth Annual Forensic Pathology: The Investigation of Violent Death Seminar, Lansing, Mich., September 10–14, 1984.

Westveer, Arthur E. *Death Investigation.* Washington, D.C.: U.S. Department of Justice, Federal Bureau of Investigation.

INVESTIGATIONS

Interview and Interrogation

Aubry, Arthur S., Jr., and Rudolph R. Caputo. *Criminal Interrogation.* Springfield, Ill.: Charles C. Thomas Publishers, 1980.

Buckley, David M., and Mark D. Reid. "The Reid Technique of Interview and Interrogation." Presentaion at the Reid Technique Seminar, Baltimore, Md., September 1992.

Grau, Joseph J., Ph.D. *Criminal and Civil Investigation Handbook.* New York: McGraw-Hill Book Co., 1981.

Kurz, Dylan. "Dominance and Submission: How the Police Use Psychological Manipulation to Interrogate Citizens." <www.grayarea.com/police8.htm> January 29, 1997.

Porter, Wayne D. "Kinesic Interview Techniques." Lecture notes.

Raybon, Don. *Interviewing and Interrogation.* Durham, N.C.: Carolina Academic Press, 1992.

———. "Kinesic Interview Techniques." Presentaiton at I.P.T.M., Jacksonville, Fla., August 1987.

———. "Kinesic Interview Techniques." Presentation at the Death Investigation Seminar, Jacksonville Police Academy, November, 1990.

Reid, John E. *The Reid Technique, Interview and Interrogation Workbook.* Chicago: John E. Reid and Associates, 1991.

Royal, Robert F., and Steven R. Schutt. *The General Art of Interviewing and Interrogation.* Englewood, N.J.: Prentice-Hall, Inc., 1976.

Ryals, James R. "Successful Interviewing." *FBI Law Enforcement Bulletin.* March 1991.

Wakefield, Hollida, MA, and Ralph Underwager, Ph.D. *Coerced or Nonvoluntary Confessions.* John Wiley & Sons, Ltd., 1998.

White, William P. III. "Interviewing Skills for Legal Services Workers." Lecture notes (February 24, 1984).

Homicides

Douglas, John E., Ann W. Burgess, Allen G. Burgess, and Robert K. Ressler. *Crime Classification Manual.* New York: Lexington Books, 1992.

Fisher, Barry, Arne Svensson, and Otto Wendel. *Techniques of Crime Scene Investigation.* New York: Elsevier, 1987.

Grau, Joseph J., Ph.D. *Criminal and Civil Investigation Handbook.* New York: McGraw-Hill Book Co., 1981.

Lee, Henry, Dr. "Analytical Approaches for Homicide Investigation." Presentation at the Florida Homicide Investigators Association, Tampa, Fla., November 1991.

MacLeod, Scott. "Homicide Investigation." Presentation at the Death Investigation Seminar, Jacksonville Police Academy, November 1990.

Westveer, Arthur E. *Death Investigation.* Washington, D.C.: U.S. Department of Justice, Federal Bureau of Investigation.

Altercation Homicides/Contract Murder

Westveer, Arthur E. *Death Investigation.* Washington, D.C.: U.S. Department of Justice, Federal Bureau of Investigation.

Drug-Related Murders/Robbery-Related Homicides/Sexually Related Homicides

Egger, Steven A. "A Working Definition of Serial Murder and the Reduction of Linkage Blindness." *Journal of Police Science and Administration,* 12 (no. 3) (1984): 348–57.

———. *Serial Murder: An Elusive Phenomenon.* New York: Praeger, 1990.

Enter, Jack, Ph.D. "Serial Killers." Presentation at the Naval Criminal Investigative Service at the Naval Air Station, Jacksonville, Fla., May 20, 1992.

Hazelwood, Robert R. "Criminal Profiling—VICAP." Presentation at the International Symposium on the Forensic Aspects of Mass Disasters and Crime Scene Reconstruction, FBI Training Academy, Quantico, Va., June 23–29, 1990.

Hazelwood, Robert R., and Ann W. Burgess. *Practical Aspects of Rape Investigation: A Multidisciplinary Approach.* New York: Elsevier, 1987.

Hinman, Dayle. "Criteria for Criminal Personality Profile." Lecture notes (January 29, 1987).

———. "Psychological Profiling." Presentaion at the Death Investigation Seminar, Jacksonville Police Academy, November, 1990.

Holmes, Ronald M. *Profiling Violent Crimes.* Newbury Park, Calif.: Sage Publications, 1989.

O'Reilly-Fleming, Thomas. "Serial Murder Investigation: Prospects for Police Networking." *Contemporary Perspectives on Serial Murder* (Edited by Ronald M. Holmes and Stephen T. Holmes.) Thousand Oaks, Calif: Sage Publications, 1996.

Ressler, Robert K. "Psychological profiling in Homicide Investigations." Presentation at the Sixth Annual Forensic Pathology: The Investigation of Violent Death Seminar, Lansing, Mich., September 10–14, 1984.

Ressler, Robert K., Anne W. Burgess, and John E. Douglas. *Sexual Homicides: Pattern and Motives.* Lexington, Mass.: D.C. Heath and Company, 1988.

Westveer, Arthur E. *Death Investigation.* Washington, D.C.: U.S. Department of Justice, Federal Bureau of Investigation.

Wetli, Charles V., MD, and Roger E. Mittleman, MD. "Forensic Pathology for the Hospital Pathologist." *Laboratory Medicine*, May 1989: 299–304.

Cold-Case Investigation

NCIS Cold Case Homicide Unit. *Cold Case Protocol.* March 2000.

Suicide Investigation

Norman, Winston C. "Suicide Investigation." *Death Investigation.* FBI Training Academy.

Retail Credit Company. "Violent Death Qestionnaire." Form 1459.

Rosenberg, M.L., MD, et al. "Operational Criteria for the Determination of Suicide." *JFSCA*, 33, no. 6, (November 1988).

Westveer, Arthur E. *Death Investigation.* Washington, D.C.: U.S. Department of Justice, Federal Bureau of Investigation.

Psychological Autopsy

Berman, A.L. "Forensic Suicidology and the Psychological Autopsy in Suicidology: Essay in Honor of Edwin S. Schneidman." *Forensic Suicidology and the Psychological Autopsy*. (Edited by A.A. Leenaars.) Northvale, NJ: Aronson, 1993: 248-67.

Berman, A.L., and R.E. Litman. "Psychological Autopsy." 1993.

Costa, P., and R. McCrae. *Revised NEO Personality Inventory*. Odessa, Fla.: Psychological Assessment Resources, 1989.

Ebert, B.W. "Guide to Conducting a Psychological Autopsy." *Professional Psychological Research and Practice* 18 (1987): 52–56.

Findley, Jerry. "Reconstruction." 1995.

Hazelwood, R.R., P.E. Dietz, and A.W. Burgess. "The Investigation of Autoerotic Fatalities." *Journal of Police Science and Administration*, 9 (1981): 404–11.

Humphrey, D. *Final Exit*. New York: Bantam Doubleday, 1991.

Jobes, D.A., J.O. Casey, A.L. Berman, and D.G. Wright. "Empirical Criteria for Determination of Suicide Manner of Death." *Journal of Forensic Sciences*, 36 (1991): 244–56.

Petty, C.S., and V.J.M. DiMaio. "Scene Examinations for Medico-legal Investigators." *The Forensic Science Gazette*, vol. 6, no. 2 (1975).

Poythress, N., R. Otto, J. Darkes, and L. Staw. "APA's Expert Panel in the Congressional Review of the USS Iowa Incident." *American Psychologist*, 48 (1993): 8–15.

Rosenberg, M.L., L.E. Davidson, and J.C. Smith. "Operational Criteria for the Determination of Suicide." *Journal of Forensic Sciences*, 33 (1988): 1,445–56.

Rynearson, J.M., and W.J. Chisum. *Evidence and Crime Scene Reconstruction*. California Crime Investigation Training, 1991.

Schneidman, E. *The Definition of Suicide*. New York: Wiley, 1985.

Schneidman, E. *Suicide as Psychache: A Clinical Approach to Self-Destructive Behavior*. Northvale, N.J.: Aronson, 1993.

Wellford, C., and J. Cronin. *An Analysis of Variables Affecting the Clearance of Homicides: A Multistate Study*.

OTHER DEATHS

Aircraft (Small)

Medical Examiner's Handbook. Richmond, Va.: Virginia Depatment of Health, Office of the Chief Medical Examiner, 1982.

Simson, Laurence R. Jr., MD. "Death Investigation." Presentation at the Sixth Annual Forensic Pathology: The Investigation of Violent Death Seminar, Lansing, Mich., September 10–14, 1984.

Alcohol

Wecht, Cyril, ed. *Forensic Sciences.* New York: Matthew Bender, 1991.

Asphyxia Related

Bell, Michael D., MD. "Postural Asphyxiation in Adults." Presentation at the Florida Medicolegal Investigators Association Conference, Ft. Lauderdale, Fla., February 1991.

Simson, Laurence R. Jr., MD. "Death Investigation." Presentation at the Sixth Annual Forensic Pathology: The Investigation of Violent Death Seminar, Lansing, Mich., September 10–14, 1984.

Westveer, Arthur E. *Death Investigation.* Washington, D.C.: U.S. Department of Justice, Federal Bureau of Investigation.

Wetli, Charles V., MD, and Roger E. Mittleman, MD. "Forensic Pathology for the Hospital Pathologist." *Laboratory Medicine* (May 1989): 299–304.

Bioterrorism Considerations

Los Angeles County Department of Public Health. *Bioterrorism Syndromes.* October 2001.

U.S. Postal Service, <http://www.usps.com/news/2001/press/pr01_1010tips.htm> 2001.

Blunt Trauma

Campbell, Homer, DDS. "Pattern Injuries." Presentation at the Medicolegal Investigation of Death Conference, Albuquerque, N.M., September 11–13, 1991.

Chicago Police Department. "Homicide Part III." *Training Bulletin*, vol. XI, no. 8 (February 23, 1970).

Clack, W. Pearson, MD. "Injuries from Blunt Head Trauma." *Florida Association of Medical Examiners Newsletter.*

Lipkovic, Peter, MD. "Causes of Death." Presentation at the Death Investigation Seminar, Jacksonville Police Academy, November, 1990.

Schultz, Randall R., MD. "The Basics Of Head Trauma with a Grain Of Salt." Internet article.

Simson, Laurence R. Jr., MD. "Death Investigation." Presentaion at the Sixth Annual Forensic Pathology: The Investigation of Violent Death Seminar, Lansing, Mich., September 10–14, 1984.

Vilas, Raul, MD. "Natural Deaths." Presentation at the second annual meeting of the Florida Medicolegal Investigator's Association, Ft. Lauderdale, Fla., February 7–9, 1991.

Westveer, Arthur E. *Death Investigation*. Washington, D.C.: U.S. Department of Justice, Federal Bureau of Investigation.

Carbon Monoxide

Retail Credit Company. "Violent Death Qestionnaire." Form 1459.

Children-Related Deaths

Lipkovic, Peter, MD. "Causes of Death." Presentation at the Death Investigation Seminar, Jacksonville Police Academy, November 1990.

"Quick Reference Guide, Infancy, Ages Birth Through Two." BarCharts.com, July 1999.

Simson, Laurence R. Jr., MD. "Death Investigation." Presentation at the Sixth Annual Forensic Pathology: The Investigation of Violent Death Seminar, Lansing, Mich., September 10–14, 1984.

Valdes-Dapena, Marie A., MD. *Sudden Unexplained Infant Death 1970 Through 1975*. Rockville, Md.: U.S. Department of Health, Education and Welfare, 1980.

Virginia Department of Health. *Medical Examiner's Handbook*. Richmond, Va.: Virginia Depatment of Health, Office of the Chief Medical Examiner, 1982.

Westveer, Arthur E. *Death Investigation*. Washington, D.C.: U.S. Department of Justice, Federal Bureau of Investigation.

Wetli, Charles V., MD, and Roger E. Mittleman, MD. "Forensic Pathology for the Hospital Pathologist." *Laboratory Medicine* (May 1989): 299–304.

Delayed Fatal—Hospital Cases

Virginia Department of Health. *Medical Examiner's Handbook* Richmond, Va.: Virginia Depatment of Health, Office of the Chief Medical Examiner, 1982.

Wetli, Charles V., MD, and Roger E. Mittleman, MD. "Forensic Pathology for the Hospital Pathologist." *Laboratory Medicine* (May 1989) :299-304.

Drowning

Davis, J H. "Bodies Found in Water." *American Journal of Forensic Medicine and Pathology,* 7 (1986): 291-97.

Pounder, Derrick J. *Bodies Recovered from Water*. University of Dundee Publication, <///uodscan.htm/uodscan.htm/news//news//weblink.htm> (1992).

Mant A.K, Churchill Livingstone. *Diatoms in Taylor's Principles and Practice of Medical Jurisprudence.* Edinburgh (1984): 297–299.

Retail Credit Company. "Violent Death Qestionnaire." Form 1459.

Teather, Robert G. *Encyclopedia of Underwater Investigation.* Best Publishing Company, 1994.

Simson, Laurence R. Jr., MD. "Death Investigation." Presentation at the Sixth Annual Forensic Pathology: The Investigation of Violent Death Seminar, Lansing, Mich., September 10–14, 1984.

Virginia Department of Health. *Medical Examiner's Handbook.* Richmond, Va.: Virginia Depatment of Health, Office of the Chief Medical Examiner, 1982.

Wetli, Charles V., MD, and Roger E. Mittleman, MD. "Forensic Pathology for the Hospital Pathologist." *Laboratory Medicine* (May 1989): 299–304.

Drug Overdose

Gleason, M.N., R.E. Goselin, H.C. Hodge, and R.P. Smith. *Clinical Toxicology of Commercial Products.* 3rd ed. Baltimore, Md.: Williams and Wilkins Co., 1969.

"Methamphetamine."< www.lec.org/DrugSearch/Documents/Meth.html>. June 2001.

"Methamphetamine: Abuse and Addiction." National Institute of Drug Abuse, Research Report Series. <www.nida.nih.gov/ResearchReports/Methamph/methamph4.html>. May 1999.

Mittleman, Roger E., MD, and Charles V. Wetli, MD. "Death Caused by Recreational Cocaine Use, an Update." *Journal of the American Medical Asociation*, vol. 252, no. 14 (October 12, 1984).

Retail Credit Company. "Violent Death Qestionnaire." Form 1459.

Rivers, David W. "Cocaine Psychosis." Presentation to the 96th I.A.C.P. Conference, Louisville, Ky., October 13, 1989.

Westveer, Arthur E. *Death Investigation.* Washington, D.C.: U.S. Department of Justice, Federal Bureau of Investigation.

Wetli, Charles V., MD. "Investigation of Drug-Related Deaths." *The American Journal of Forensic Medicine and Pathology*, vol. 5, no. 2 (June 1984).

Wetli, Charles V., MD, and Roger E. Mittleman, MD. "Forensic Pathology for the Hospital Pathologist." *Laboratory Medicine* (May 1989): 299–304.

Electrocution

Frankel, William, ed. *Basic Wiring.* Chicago: Time-Life Books, Inc., 1980.

Simson, Laurence R. Jr., MD. "Death Investigation." Presentation at the Sixth Annual Forensic Pathology: The Investigation of Violent Death Seminar, Lansing, Mich., September 10–14, 1984.

Wetli, Charles V., MD, Roger E. Mittleman, MD, and Valerie J. Rao, MD. *Practical Forensic Pathology.* New York: Igaku-Shoin Medical Publishers, Inc., 1988.

Wright, Ronald K., MD. "Death by Electrocution." Presentation at the National Association of Medical Examiner's Conference at Sannibel Island, Fla., October 1990.

———. "Medical Legal Investigation, Electrocution Deaths, A Marriage of Engineering and Medical Science." Presentation at the George Ganter Memorial Lecture, April 25, 1991.

Wright, Ronald K., MD, and Joseph H. Davis, MD. "The Investigation of Electrical Deaths: A Report of 220 Fatalities." *Journal of Forensic Sciences*, vol. 25, no. 3 (July 1980).

Explosion Deaths

Anonymous, Basic Training Manual for Crime Scene Procedures and Explosive Technology, Dade County Public Safety Department, Crime Laboratory Bureau, Miami, Fl.

Brodie, Thomas G. "Investigation of Explosions." *Forensic Sciences.* Matthew Bender, 1991.

Department of the Treasury Forensic Handbook. Washington, D.C.: Government Printing Office, 1975.

Fisher, Barry, Arne Svensson, and Otto Wendel. *Techniques of Crime Scene Investigation.* New York: Elsevier Science Publishing Co., Inc. 1987.

Fox, Richard H., and Carl L. Cunningham. *Crime Scene Search and Physical Evidence Handbook.* Washington, D.C.: U.S. Department of Justice, 1973.

Midkiff, Charles R. "Arson and Explosive Investigation."

Saferstein, Richard. *Forensic Science Handbook.* Englewood Cliffs, N.J.: Prentice-Hall, 1982.

Falls from Heights

Besant-Matthews, P.E., MD. "Falls and Falling—A Brief Review." October 1986.

Retail Credit Company. "Violent Death Qestionnaire." Form 1459.

Fire-Associated Deaths

Basic Training Manual for Crime Scene Procedures and Explosive Technology. Miami, Fla.: Dade County Public Safety Department, Crime Laboratory Bureau.

Department of the Treasury Forensic Handbook. Washington, D.C.: Government Printing Office, 1975.

Factory Mutual System. *A Pocket Guide to Arson Investigation.* Norwood, Mass.: Factory Mutual Engineering and Research, 1979.

O'Conner, John J. *Practical Fire and Arson Investigation.* New York: Elsevier, 1987.

Simson, Laurence R. Jr., MD. "Death Investigation." Presentation at the Sixth Annual Forensic Pathology: The Investigation of Violent Death Seminar, Lansing, Mich., September 10–14, 1984.

Virginia Department of Health. Medical Examiner's Handbook. Richmond, Va.: Virginia Depatment of Health, Office of the Chief Medical Examiner, 1982.

Westveer, Arthur E. *Death Investigation.* Washington, D.C.: U.S. Department of Justice, Federal Bureau of Investigation.

Wetli, Charles V., MD, and Roger E. Mittleman, MD. "Forensic Pathology for the Hospital Pathologist." *Laboratory Medicine* (May 1989): 299–304.

Gunshot Wounds

Besant-Matthews, Patrick E., MD. "Gunshot Wounds." Presentation at the Sixth Annual Forensic Pathology: The Investigation of Violent Death Seminar, Lansing, Mich., September 10–14, 1984.

Chicago Police Department. "Homicide—Part I." *Training Bulletin*, vol. XI, no. 6 (February 9, 1970).

Lipkovic, Peter, MD. "Causes of Death." Presentation at the Death Investigation Seminar, Jacksonville Police Academy, November 1990.

Retail Credit Company, "Violent Death Qestionnaire", Form 1459.

Virginia Department of Health. *Medical Examiner's Handbook.* Richmond, Va.: Virginia Depatment of Health, Office of the Chief Medical Examiner, 1982.

Westveer, Arthur E. *Death Investigation.* Washington, D.C.: U.S. Department of Justice, Federal Bureau of Investigation.

Wetli, Charles V., MD, and Roger E. Mittleman, MD. "Forensic Pathology for the Hospital Pathologist." *Laboratory Medicine* (May 1989): 299–304.

Natural (Apparent)

Davis, Joseph H., MD. "Apparent Natural Deaths." Paper presented at the Florida Association of Medical Examiners Conference (n.d.).

———. "The Hazardous Environment." Paper presented at the Florida Association of Medical Examiners Conference (n.d.).

———. "The Scene Investigation of a Natural Death." Paper presented at the Florida Association of Medical Examiners Conference (n.d.).

Irvine, Rebecca A., MD. "Sudden Natural Deaths in Adult." Paper presented at the Forensic Science Seminar, Albuquerque, N.M., September 1995.

Simson, Laurence R. Jr., MD. "Death Investigation." Presentation at the Sixth Annual Forensic Pathology: The Investigation of Violent Death Seminar, Lansing, Mich., September 10–14, 1984.

Vilas, Raul, MD. "Natural Deaths." Presentation at the second annual meeting of the Florida Medicolegal Investigator's Association, Ft. Lauderdale, Fla., February 7–9, 1991.

Virginia Department of Health. *Medical Examiner's Handbook*. Richmond, Va.: Virginia Depatment of Health, Office of the Chief Medical Examiner, 1982.

Poison-Related Deaths

Department of the Treasury Forensic Handbook. Washington, D.C.: Government Printing Office, 1975.

Fox, Richard H., and Carl L. Cunningham. *Crime Scene Search and Physical Evidence Handbook*. Washington, D.C.: U.S. Department of Justice, 1973: 126.

Kirk, Paul L. *Crime Investigation*. New York: Interscience Publishers, Inc., 1953.

O'Hara, Charles E., and Gregory L. O'Hara. *Fundamentals of Criminal Investigation*. Springfield, Ill.: Charles C. Thomas Publishers, 1980.

Retail Credit Company. "Violent Death Qestionnaire." Form 1459.

Stevens, Serita Deborah, and Anne Klarner. *Deadly Doses*. Cincinnati: Writer's Digest Books, 1990.

Trestall, John H. "Criminal Poisoning, Forensic Toxicology." Handout (n.d.).

Virginia Department of Health. *Medical Examiner's Handbook*. Richmond, Va.: Virginia Depatment of Health, Office of the Chief Medical Examiner, 1982.

Westveer, Arthur E. *Death Investigation*. Washington, D.C.: U.S. Department of Justice, Federal Bureau of Investigation.

Police/Correctional Custody Deaths

Davis, Joseph H., MD. "Police Custody Deaths."

―――. "Medical Examiner Procedures for Police Shooting/Custody Deaths." Dade County Medical Examiner's Office, 1962.

Dean, Dennis. "Police Shooting Policy Undergoing Changes." *PBA HEAT*, vol. 7, no. 14.

Donoghue, Edmund R., MD. "Checklist for Suicide in Custody." *American Society of Clinical Pathologists*.

Rivers, David W. "Officers Involved Shootings."

Virginia Department of Health. *Medical Examiner's Handbook*. Richmond, Va.: Virginia Depatment of Health, Office of the Chief Medical Examiner, 1982.

Scuba-Related Deaths

Davis, Joseph H., MD. "The Autopsy in Diving Fatalities."

Exley, Sheck. "Florida Cave Diving." *Underwater Florida*.

Divers Alert Network. "DAN Fatality Worksheet." Duke University Medical Center.

McAniff, John J., director, National Underwater Accident Data Center. Interview, August 1990.

Nicholson, Henry, Captain, Jacksonville Sheriff's Office. "Dive Recovery Operations, Hazards of Cave Diving." Interview, August 1990.

Voboril, Mary. "Why Divers Die." *Miami Herald* (July 25, 1990): 1D-2D.

Sharp-Force Injuries

Chicago Police Department. "Homicide, Part II." *Training Bulletin*, vol. XI, no. 7 (February 16, 1970).

Grey, Todd C., MD. "Sharp Force Injuries." Presentation at the State of New Mexico, Medical Examiner's Conference, Albuquerque, N.M., September 1991.

Lipkovic, Peter, MD. "Causes of Death." Presentation at the Death Investigation Seminar, Jacksonville Police Academy, November 1990.

Virginia Department of Health. *Medical Examiner's Handbook*. Richmond, Va.: Virginia Depatment of Health, Office of the Chief Medical Examiner, 1982.

Westveer, Arthur E. *Death Investigation*. Washington, D.C.: U.S. Department of Justice, Federal Bureau of Investigation.

Traffic Related/Railroad Related

Retail Credit Company. "Violent Death Qestionnaire." Form 1459.

Vehicle Versus Vehicle

Lawrence, Christopher, MD, "Motor Vehicle Accidents." Presentation at the Medicolegal Investigation of Death Conference, Albuquerque, N.M., September 11–13, 1991.

Malone, Richard. "Motor Vehicle Accidents." Presentation at the Medicolegal Investigation of Death conference, Albuquerque, Ne.M., September 11–13, 1991.

Retail Credit Company. "Violent Death Qestionnaire." Form 1459.

Van Kirk, Donald J. "A Scientific Approach to Documenting Evidence for Accident Reconstruction." *Journal of Forensic Science*, vol. 29, no. 3 (July 1984): 806-815.

Virginia Department of Health. *Medical Examiner's Handbook*. Richmond, Va.:, Virginia Depatment of Health, Office of the Chief Medical Examiner, 1982.

Zumwalt, Ross, MD. "Issues in Forensic Pathology: Airbags." Presentation at the Medicolegal Investigation of Death Conference, Albuquerque, N.M., September 11–13, 1991.

Vehicle Versus Pedestrian

Lawrence, Christopher, MD. "Motor Vehicle Accidents." Presentation at the Medicolegal Investigation of Death Conference, Albuquerque, N.M., September 11–13, 1991.

Malone, Richard. "Motor Vehicle Accidents." Presentation at the Medicolegal Investigation of Death Conference, Albuquerque, N.M., September 11–13, 1991.

Retail Credit Company. "Violent Death Qestionnaire." Form 1459.

Van Kirk, Donald J. "A Scientific Approach to Documenting Evidence for Accident Reconstruction." *Journal of Forensic Sciences*, vol. 29, no. 3 (July 1984): 806–15.

Virginia Department of Health. *Medical Examiner's Handbook*. Richmond, Va.: Virginia Depatment of Health, Office of the Chief Medical Examiner, 1982.

Mass Disaster Cases

Armentrout, Terry. "Reconstructive Analysis of the Space Shuttle Challenger." Presentation at the International Symposium on the Forensic Aspects of Mass Disasters and Crime Scene Reconstruction, FBI Training Academy, Quantico, Va., June 23–29, 1990.

Baechtel, F. Samuel. "The Potential of DNA Typing in Disaster Situations." Presentation at the International Symposium on the Forensic Aspects of Mass Disasters and Crime Scene Reconstruction, FBI Training Academy, Quantico, Va., June 23–29, 1990.

Bigbee, Paul D. "Physical and Biological Hazards." Presentation at the International Symposium on the Forensic Aspects of Mass Disasters and Crime Scene Reconstruction, FBI Training Academy, Quantico, Va,, June 23–29, 1990.

Davidson, Oliver. "International Emergency Plans." Presentation at the International Symposium on the Forensic Aspects of Mass Disasters and Crime Scene Reconstruction, FBI Training Academy, Quantico, Va., June 23–29, 1990.

Fisher, Barry, Arne Svensson, and Otto Wendel. *Techniques of Crime Scene Investigation*. New York: Elsevier, Inc., 1987.

Goode, Col Robert K. "Dentistry's Role in Mass Disaster Victim Identification—A Military Dentist's Perspective." Presentation at the International Symposium on the Forensic Aspects of Mass Disasters and Crime Scene Reconstruction, FBI Training Academy, Quantico, Va., June 23–29, 1990.

Greenberg, Reuben. "Crisis Situations and the Media," Presentation at the International Symposium on the Forensic Aspects of Mass Disasters and Crime Scene Reconstruction, FBI Training Academy, Quantico, Va., June 23–29, 1990.

Hamilton, Harry A. "Identification of Victims, Northwest Flight 255." Presentation at the International Symposium on the Forensic Aspects of Mass Disasters and Crime Scene Reconstruction, FBI Training Academy, Quantico, Va., June 23–29, 1990.

Hazen, Robert J., and Clarence E. Phillips. *FBI Disater Identification Preparation—Organization Procedures*. Quantico, Va.: FBI Academy, 1982.

Henderson, Stuart. "Lockerbie Air Disaster, Presentation at the International Symposium on the Forensic Aspects of Mass Disasters and Crime Scene Reconstruction, FBI Training Academy, Quantico, Va., June 23–29, 1990.

Luke, James, MD. "Investigation of the Crash of Air Florida Flight 90, Mass Disaster Planning." Presentation at the International Symposium on the Forensic Aspects of Mass Disasters and Crime Scene Reconstruction, FBI Training Academy, Quantico, Va., June 23–29, 1990.

Monserrate, Robert, and Dennis Chapman. "The Crash of United Flight 232: The Use of Forensic Personnel in the Collection and Identification of the Victims, the Psychological Aftermath, and Recommendations." Presentation at the International Symposium on the Forensic Aspects of Mass Disasters and Crime Scene Reconstruction, FBI Training Academy, Quantico, Va., June 23–29, 1990.

Peterson, Grant. "Federal Emergency Plans." Presentation at the International Symposium on the Forensic Aspects of Mass Disasters and Crime Scene Reconstruction, FBI Training Academy, Quantico, Va., June 23–29, 1990.

Raulin, Leslie A. "Computer-Assisted Postmortem Identification System—Dental." Presentation at the International Symposium on the Forensic Aspects of Mass Disasters and Crime Scene Reconstruction, FBI Training Academy, Quantico, Va., June 23–29, 1990.

Reese, James T. "Psychology of Stress." Presentation at the International Symposium on the Forensic Aspects of Mass Disasters and Crime Scene Reconstruction, FBI Training Academy, Quantico, Va., June 23–29, 1990.

Slayton, Addison E. Jr. "State Emergency Plans." Presentation at the International Symposium on the Forensic Aspects of Mass Disasters and Crime Scene Reconstruction, FBI Training Academy, Quantico, Va., June 23–29, 1990.

Smith, Brion C. "United States Army Central Identification Laboratory—Hawaii." Presentation at the International Symposium on the Forensic Aspects of Mass Disasters and Crime Scene Reconstruction, FBI Training Academy, Quantico, Va., June 23–29, 1990.

U.S. Postal Inspection Service. "Bombs by Mail." Notice 71, <http://www.usps.gov/cpim/ftp/notices/not71.pdf> February 1998.

U.S. Postal Service <http://www.usps.com/news/2001/press/pr01_1010tips.htm>, USPS Message to Customers, October 17, 2001.

Vessey, Robert D. "Volunteer Organizations in Emergency Situations." Presentation at the International Symposium on the Forensic Aspects of Mass Disasters and Crime Scene Reconstruction, FBI Training Academy, Quantico, Va., June 23–29, 1990.

Identifying Human Remains

Fisher, Barry, Arne Svensson, and Otto Wendel. *Techniques of Crime Scene Investigation*. New York: Elsevier, 1987.

Simson, Laurence R. Jr., MD. "Death Investigation." Presentation at the Sixth Annual Forensic Pathology: The Investigation of Violent Death Seminar, Lansing, Mich., September 10–14, 1984.

Forensic Art

Eliopulos, Louis N. "Forensic Art in Identification." January 1990.

Gatliff, Betty. "Facial Sculpture on the Skull for Identification." Presentation at the International Symposium on the Forensic Aspects of Mass Disasters and Crime Scene Reconstruction, FBI Training Academy, Quantico, Va., June 23–29, 1990.

Next-of-Kin Handling

Chadeayne, Catherine. "Dealing with Victims Through the Grief Process." Presentation at the Death Investigation Course, Jacksonville Police Academy, November 1990.

Understanding Grief. Oakbrook, Ill.: The Compassionate Friends, Inc, 1980.

White, Beverly. "Grief Intervention." Presentation at the Medicolegal Investigation of Death Conference, Albuquerque, N.M., September 11–13, 1991.

Media Management

Darnell, Sadie. "Media Management." Presentation at the Florida Association of Medical Examiners Conference, Gainesville, Fla., October 1991.

Gerberth, Vernon. *Practical Homicide Investigation.* New York: Elsevier, 1983.

Greenberg, Reuben. "Crisis Situations and the Media." Presentation at the International Symposium on the Forensic Aspects of Mass Disasters and Crime Scene Reconstruction, FBI Training Academy, Quantico, Va., June 23–29, 1990.

Information Sources

Dolan, John P. "Use of Public Records State, County, and Local Levels."

Equifax Services. "Sources of Information, Federal."

———. "Availabilty of State Records."

———. "Records Available From Other Sources."

McGuinness, Brian P. "Accessing Electronic Information Intelligently." *National Defenders Investigators Association Newsletter*, May 1, 1992.

Pankau, Edmund J. "Tracking Down the Global Criminal." *Security Management* magazine (March, 1992).

Schultz, Donald O. *Crime Scene Investigation.* Englewood Cliffs, N.J.: Prentice-Hall, Inc., 1977.

Department of Defense. "Military Grades and Rank." Internet site (March 26, 2002).

Prosecution

Chicago Police Department. "Homicide—Part I." *Training Bulletin*, vol. XI, no. 6 (February 9, 1970).

Corey, Angela. "Prosecuting Homicides." Presentation at the Death Investigation Seminar, Jacksonville Police Academy, November 1990.

Delaney, John. "Prosecuting Homicides." Presentation at the Death Investigation Seminar, Jacksonville Police Academy, November 1990.

Greenfield, Lawrence A. "Capital Punishment 1990." *Bureau of Justice Statistics Bulletin*, September 1991.

O'Hara, Charles E., and Gregory L. O'Hara. *Fundamentals of Criminal Investigation*, Springfield, Il., Charles C. Thomas Publishers, 1980.

Rionda, Bernie de la. "Prosecuting Homicides." Presentation at the Death Investigation Seminar, Jacksonville Police Academy, November 1990.

Zera, Paula. "Expert Testimony." Presentation at the Sixth Annual Forensic Pathology: The Investigation of Violent Death seminar, Lansing, Mich., September 10–14, 1984.

SCIENTIFIC SECTION

Medical Examiner/Coroner Systems

Center for Disease Control. Medical Examiner and Coroner Information Sharing Program Contents, <http://www.cdc.gov/epo/dphsi/mecisp/death_investigation.htm>, last updated August 1995, November 15, 2001

Combs, D.L., R. Gibson Parrish, MD, and Roy Ing, MD. *Death Investigation in the United States and Canada, 1990.* Atlanta, Ga.: U.S. Department of Health and Human Services (August 1995).

Autopsy

Blackbourne, Brian D., MD. "Anatomy for Investigators." March 2, 1978.

Francisco, J.T., MD. "Law Enforcement and the Forensic Pathologist." *FBI Law Enforcement Bulletin* (February 1973).

Rynearson, Joseph M., and William J. Chisum. *Evidence and Crime Scene Reconstruction*. Redding, Calif., 1991.

Westveer, Arthur E. *Death Investigation*. Washington, MD, U.S. Department of Justice, Federal Bureau of Investigation.

Forensic Anthropology

Fitzpatrick, John J. "Forensic Radiology." Presentation at the International Symposium on the Forensic Aspects of Mass Disasters and Crime Scene Reconstruction, FBI Training Academy, Quantico, Va., June 23–29, 1990.

Maples, William, Ph.D. "Forensic Anthropology." Presentation at the Death Investigation Seminar, Jacksonville Police Academy, November 1990.

Rhine, Stanley, Ph.D., and Wayne Granger. "Examination of Skeletal Remains." Presentation at the Medicolegal Investigation of Death Conference, Albuquerque, N.M., September 11–13, 1991.

Sauer, Norman, Ph.D. "Physical Anthropology." Presentation at the Sixth Annual Forensic Pathology: The Investigation of Violent Death seminar, Lansing, Mich., September 10–14, 1984.

Snow, Clyde C. "Forensic Anthropology—Reconstruction." Presentation at the International Symposium on the Forensic Aspects of Mass Disasters and Crime Scene Reconstruction, FBI Training Academy, Quantico, Va., June 23–29, 1990.

Stewart, T.D. "What the Bones Tell—Today." FBI Law Enforcement Bulletin (February 1972).

Forensic Odontology

Burns, Arthur, DDS. "Dental Records Acquisition."

———. "Bite Mark Protocol."

Goode, Col. Robert K. "Dentistry's Role in Mass Disaster Victim Identification—A Military Dentist's Perspective." Presentation at the International Symposium on the Forensic Aspects of Mass Disasters and Crime Scene Reconstruction, FBI Training Academy, Quantico, Va., June 23–29, 1990.

Levine, Lowell J., DDS. "Forensic Odontology Today—A New Forensic Science." *FBI Law Enforcement Bulletin* (August 1972).

Mittleman, Roger E., MD. Willard Carl Stuver, and Richard Souviron, DDS. "Obtaining Saliva Samples from Bite Mark Evidence." *FBI Law Enforcement Bulletin* (November 198).

Raulin, Leslie A. "Computer-Assisted Postmortem Identification System–Dental." Presentation at the International Symposium on the Forensic Aspects of Mass Disasters and Crime Scene Reconstruction, FBI Training Academy, Quantico, Va., June 23–29, 1990.

Sperber, Norman D., DDS. "Bite Mark Evidence in Crimes Against Persons." *FBI Law Enforcement Bulletin* (July 1981).

Toxicology

Backer, Ronald C. "Unraveling the Secrets of Toxicology or Making the System More User Friendly." Presentation at the Medicolegal Investigation of Death Conference, Albuquerque, N.M., September 11–13, 1991.

Nolte, Kurt B. "The Pathology of Drug Abuse."

Nuernberger, Barbara M. "Toxicology in Death Investigations." Presentation at the Death Investigation class, Jacksonville Police Academy, November 14, 1990.

Thomas, Clayton, MD, ed. *Tabers Cyclopedic Medical Dictionary*. Philadelphia: F.A. Davis Company, 1985.

Prescriptive Medication Listing

Barnhart, Edward R., publisher. *Physicians' Desk Reference*. Oradell, N.J.: Medical Economics Data, 1991.

Fingerprints

Arima, Takashi. "Development of Latent Fingerprints on Sticky Surfaces by Dye Staining or Fluorescent Brightening." *Identification News*, February, 1981.

Basic Training Manual for Crime Scene Procedures and Explosive Technology. Miami, Fla.: Dade County Public Safety Department, Crime Laboratory Bureau.

Department of the Treasury Forensic Handbook. Washington, D.C.: Government Printing Office, 1975.

International Association for Identification, Chesapeake Bay Division. "Latent Fingerprint Processing Techniques—Selection and Sequencing Guide." Internet article, <www.cbdiai.org/Reagents/main.html. 9/07/2002>.

Dalrymple, B.E., J.M. Duff, and E.R. Menzel, Ph.D. "Inherent Luminescence of Fingerprints by Laser." *Identification News* (May 1977).

Everse, K.E., and E.R. Menzel."Blood Print Detection by Fluorescence." *Fluorescence Detection* (Edited by E.R. Menzel.) SPIE Proc. 743 (1987): 184–9.

Fischer, John F. "An Aqueous Leucocrystal Violet Enhancing Reagent for Blood Impressions" (undated).

Fisher, Barry, Arne Svensson, and Otto Wendel. *Techniques of Crime Scene Investigation*. New York: Elsevier Science Publishing Co., Inc., 1987.

Fox, Richard H., and Carl L. Cunningham. *Crime Scene Search and Physical Evidence Handbook*. Washington, D.C.: U.S. Department of Justice, 1973.

Hamm, Ernest. "Fingerprints and Footprints at Death Scenes." Presentation at the Death Investigation Seminar, Jacksonville Police Academy, November 1990.

Institute of Police Technology and Management. Crime Scene Processing Course: "TMB Formula," 1995.

Kendall, Frank G., and Burton W. Rehn. "Rapid Method of Super Glue Fuming for the Development of Latent Prints." *Identification News* (June, 1982).

Menzel, E. Roland. "Laser Detection of Latent Fingerprints." *CIS Newsletter* (January 1984).

Nutt, J. "Chemically Enhanced Bloody Fingerprints." *FBI Law Enforcement Bulletin*, 54 (1985): 22–15.

"Proper Procedures for Taking Major Case Prints." *FBI Law Enforcement Bulletin* (July 1976).

Rynearson, Joseph M., and William J. Chisum. *Evidence and Crime Scene Reconstruction*. Redding, Calif., 1991.

Sahs, P.T. "DAB: An Advancement in Blood Print Detection." *Journal of Forensic Identification*, 42 (1992): 412–20.

Tario, Allan. "Restoring Identifiable Ridge Detail on Badly Decomposed Fingers." *RCMP Gazette*, vol. 53, no. 3 (1991).

Thornton, John E., and Buster W. Emmons. "Development of Latent Prints in Arson Cases." *Identification News* (March 1982).

Firearms

Basic Training Manual for Crime Scene Procedures and Explosive Technology. Miami, Fla.: Dade County Public Safety Department, Crime Laboratory Bureau.

Carr, James. "Gunshot Residue Test."

Department of the Treasury Forensic Handbook. Washington, D.C.: Government Printing Office, 1975.

DiMaio, Vincent J.M., MD. *Gunshot Wounds*. New York: Elsevier, 1985.

Fisher, Barry, Arne Svensson, and Otto Wendel. *Techniques of Crime Scene Investigation*. New York: Elsevier Science Publishing Co., Inc., 1987.

Fox, Richard H., and Carl L. Cunningham. *Crime Scene Search and Physical Evidence Handbook*. Washington, D.C.: U.S. Department of Justice, 1973.

"Gunshot Residues and Shot Pattern Tests." *FBI Law Enforcement Bulletin* (February 1979).

Jarrett, William S., ed. *Shooter's Bible*. South Hackensack, N.J.: Stoeger Publishing Co., 1992.

Matthews, J. Howard. *Firearms Identification, Volumes 1, 2, and 3*. Springfield, Ill.: Charles C. Thomas Publisher, 1962.

Rynearson, Joseph M., and William J. Chisum. *Evidence and Crime Scene Reconstruction*. Redding, Calif., 1991.

Saferstein, Richard. *Forensic Science Handbook II*. Englewood Cliffs, N.J.: Prentice-Hall, 1988.

Warniment, David. "Firearms Examination." Presentation at the Death Investigation Seminar, Jacksonville Police Academy, November 1990.

Wilber, Charles G. *Ballistic Science for the Law Enforcement Officer.* Springfield, Ill.: Charles C. Thomas, 1977.

DNA

Clack, W. Pearson, MD. "DNA Profiling." *Florida Association of Medical Examiners Newsletter*, vol. III, issue II (June 1989): 1–3.

Collins, K.A., MD, et al. "Identification of Sperm and Non-Sperm Male Cells in Cervicovaginal Smears using Fluorescence in Situ Hybridization: Applications in Alleged Sexual Assault Cases." *Journal of Forensic Sciences*: 1,347–55.

Herd, Kim, and Adrianne Day. "A Short Primer on STRs." *The Silent Witness*, vol. 4, no. 5 (Fall 1999).

———. "Y Chromosome DNA Typing—A New Forensic Tool on the Horizon." *The Silent Witness*, vol. 4, no. 3 (Spring 1999).

Hicks, John W. "DNA Profiling: A Tool for Law Enforcement." *FBI Law Enforcement Bulletin* (August 1988).

Lewis, Ricki. "DNA Fingerprints, Witness for the Prosecution." *Discover* Magazine (June 1988).

National Institute of Justice. *What Every Law Enforcement Officer Should Know About DNA Evidence.* 1999.

Rao, P. Nagesh, Ph.D. "Identification of Male Epithelial Cells in Routine Postcoital Cervicovaginal Smears using Fluorescence in Situ Hybridization." *Anatomic Pathology* vol. 104, no. 1: 32–35.

Pollock, James, Ph.D. "DNA Profiling." Presentation at the Death Investigation Seminar, Jacksonville Police Academy, November 1990.

Serology

Department of the Treasury Forensic Handbook. Washington, D.C.: Government Printing Office, 1975.

Fox, Richard H., and Carl L. Cunningham. *Crime Scene Search and Physical Evidence Handbook.* Washington, D.C.: U.S. Department of Justice, 1973.

Garner, Daniel D., Ph.D. "Evidentiary Value of Cigarette Butts." *Identification News* (December 1977).

Hamm, Ernest D. "Enhancement of Bloody Footwear Prints."

Pollock, James, Ph.D. "Serology." Presentation at the Death Investigation Seminar, Jacksonville Police Academy, November 1990.

Saferstein, Richard. *Forensic Science Handbook.* Englewood Cliffs, N.J.: Prentice-Hall, 1982.

———. *Forensic Science Handbook II.* Englewood Cliffs, N.J.: Prentice-Hall, 1988.

Trace Evidence

Basic Training Manual for Crime Scene Procedures and Explosive Technology. Miami, Fla.: Dade County Public Safety Department, Crime Laboratory Bureau.

Deadman, Harold A., Jr. "Atlanta Child Murders." Presentation at the International Symposium on the Forensic Aspects of Mass Disasters and Crime Scene Reconstruction, FBI Training Academy, Quantico, Va., June 23–29, 1990.

Doleman, Paul. "Trace Evidence Collection and Processing." Presentation at the Death Investigation Course, Jacksonville Police Academy, November 1990.

Fisher, Barry, Arne Svensson, and Otto Wendel. *Techniques of Crime Scene Investigation.* New York: Elsevier Science Publishing Co., Inc., 1987.

Fox, Richard H., and Carl L. Cunningham. *Crime Scene Search and Physical Evidence Handbook.* Washington, D.C.: U.S. Department of Justice, 1973.

O'Brien, Kevin P., and Robert C. Sullivan. *Criminalistics.* Boston: Holbrook Press, Inc., 1976.

Saferstein, Richard. *Forensic Science Handbook.* Englewood Cliffs, N.J.: Prentice-Hall, 1982.

———. *Forensic Science Handbook II.* Englewood Cliffs, NJ, Prentice-Hall, 1988.

Wade, Colleen, ed. *Handbook of Forensic Sciences.* Washington, D.C.: U.S. Department of Justice, Federal Bureau of Investigation <www.fbi.gov>, revised 1999.

INDEX

NOTE: This index is found in the back of all three volumes. Pages 1–132 appear in Volume 1; pages 133–648 in Volume 2; pages 649–976 in Volume 3.

1, 2 Indanedione, 765–767, 779
14 point photographing of crash vehicle, 464
Fifth Amendment right against self-incrimination, 424
5-MTN, 765–767, 785, 800–801

A

Abandoned newborn, 322
Abnormal grief process, 515
Abnormal heart rhythm, 401
ABO blood grouping system, 861
ABO serology, 859
Abrasions, 53, 55, 93, 180, 187, 198, 272–274, 283, 290, 322, 342, 393, 462, 466, 479–480, 482, 682
Abrasives examinations, 864
Absorbed light, 787, 800
Abusive behavior, 254, 314
    Triggers, 314
Accelerants introduced to a fire scene, 865
Accidental (fatal) cutting or stabbings,
Accidental firing of a weapon, 825
Accidental whorl, 813
Acidic and neutral drug screen, 713
Acne, 731, 733–736, 739–743, 746, 755–756, 758, 760
Acute rash with fever, 287
Acute respiratory distress with fever, 286
Adam, 271, 727
Adrenals, 675
    Average weight, 675
Adhesive, 70–71, 122, 125, 766, 782–783, 796, 803–804, 806, 887
Adhesive tape surfaces for fingerprinting, 766, 783
Adhesives, 778, 864
Adipocere, 110, 343
Admissibility of a confession, 152–153
Aerial infrared photography, 91
Aerial photography, 37, 91–92, 95, 378

AFIP, 666
    Jurisdiction of, 666
AFIS, 22, 174, 220, 222, 802, 815, 850
Age of a document, 887
Air bag, 463, 466, 469–470
    Dangers associated with use of, 469–470
Air bags in traffic fatalities, 469–470
Air embolism, 431, 438
Air Force, 535, 545, 550–551, 564
Aircraft crash, 263, 266
Airline reporting corporation, 540
Alcohol, 5, 19, 48, 103–104, 110, 122–123, 145, 175, 179, 185, 210–212, 225, 255, 267–269, 277, 309, 311, 314, 318, 328, 333, 345–346, 350, 358–359, 366, 373–374, 379, 401, 403, 405, 410, 412, 419, 422, 427, 434, 436, 457–458, 462–463, 465, 468, 480, 482, 484, 529, 542, 557–558, 583, 654, 662, 711–712, 715, 727–728, 732, 788, 836, 844, 860, 866, 869
Alcohol–related death, 267
Alcoholism, 254, 267, 270, 334, 403, 656, 659, 664, 721, 731, 735, 741, 753, 759
Alcoholism and its manifestations, 267, 403
Algor mortis, 109, 173
Alien registration, 530
Alloy, 874, 885
Alphanumeric pagers, 83, 602
Altercation homicides, 159–160, 177, 179, 181
Altered or obliterated writing, 66, 887
Alternate light source, 16, 21
Amido black methanol based, 767–768
Amido black 10b, 803
Amino acid techniques, 765
Ammunition, 46, 60–61, 181, 199, 246, 259, 392–393, 395, 426, 428, 643, 817–820, 822–826, 830–832, 836, 873–875, 877–878
    Firing process, 820–821
Ammunition for rifled weapons, 819
Ammunition for shotguns, 819

Ammunition mechanics, 820
Amniotic fluid embolism, 403
Amperes, 355–356
Amyl nitrite, 717
Analgesic, 731, 733
Anatomy, 459, 677
　　Anterior, 677
　　Posterior, 677
Angina, 399–400
Angle of impact, 112, 116
Anorexiant, 731, 734–736, 738, 740–741, 743–744, 747–749, 751–754, 756–760, 762
ANS screen, 713
Antacid, 731, 734–744, 746, 748–750, 752–758, 760–762
Antemortem data, 684
　　Sources for, 684
Antemortem team, 265, 491, 496–498
　　In mass disasters, 496–498
　　Purposes of, 496–498
Anterior skull view, 707
Anthrax infection, 283
Anthrax procedures, 284
Anthrax protocol, 284
Anthrax symptoms, 284
Anthrax treatment, 284
Anthropologic characteristics, 502
Antibiotic, 731, 733–763
Antibody, 333, 714
Anticoagulant, 731, 735, 737, 739–741, 752, 754, 757, 762, 844, 869
Antidepressant, 725, 731, 734–735, 737–743, 745–758, 760–763
Antidiarrheal, 731, 739–740, 742, 745, 747, 751–752
Antiemetic, 711, 731, 736, 738–741, 748–749, 753, 756, 760, 762
Antiepileptics, 731
Antigen, 861
Antihistamines and decongestants, 731
Antihypertensive medication, 732
Anti-inflammatory, 731, 733–743, 745–756, 758, 760, 762
Antipsychotics, 731
Antispasmodic, 731, 735–736, 738–741, 744–747, 749, 751–752, 755, 762
Antivertigo, 731, 735–736, 741, 760, 762
Apocrine glands, 15

Arch, 293–294, 422, 681, 699–700, 707, 812, 814–815
Arcing burns, 357
Ardrox, 765–769, 776, 782, 790–791, 799
Area, 903
　　Conversion chart, 903
Argon-ion laser technique, 810
Armed Forces Institute of Pathology (AFIP), 666
　　Jurisdiction of, 666
Arrhythmia, 400
Arsenic, 409, 419–420, 711–712, 898
Arsenic, 409, 419–420, 711–712, 898
Arson evidence submission,
Arson examination, 865
Arson material, 45, 57
Arterial bleeding, 117–118, 132, 296
　　Sources of, 132
Arteriosclerotic heart disease, 399
Artery, 117–118, 132, 296, 333, 399–400, 448, 676, 678, 712, 732
　　Cross section of, 399
Arthritis, 731–743, 745–756, 758, 760, 762
Artifacts, 377, 667, 670
　　Third party, 670
Artifacts of the environment, 670
ASCVD, 333, 399
Asphyxia, 271, 273, 275–277, 279, 281, 324, 461
Asphyxiating gases, 277
Asthma/respiratory aids,
ATF, 366, 542, 583, 836–837
Atherosclerosis, 399
Atypical actions involving vehicles versus pedestrians, 480
Audio analog tape recordings, 865
Audio tape, 865
　　Authenticity of, 865
　　Damaged media repair, 866, 898
　　Enhancement of, 865
　　Signal analysis, 866
　　Voice comparisons, 865
Autoerotic death, 277, 279–280
Automated Fingerprint Identification System (AFIS), 22, 174, 220, 222, 802, 815, 850
Automatic rifle, 829
Automobile make and model identification, 889
Autopsy blood samples, 49
Autopsy in a homicide, 673
　　Purpose of, 673
Autopsy procedure, 669

Autopsy protocol, 211, 224, 495, 670
Autopsy references, 675–678
Average beats per minutes, 407

B

Background investigation, 225, 523–551
    Nontraditional methods, 538–841
Ballistics expert, 825
    Other examinations performed, 825
Bank Secrecy Act, 538
Bank security dyes evidence, 866
    Submission of, 866
Bank security dyes examination, 866
Bankruptcy courts, 531, 554, 556
Barbiturate, 639, 715–716
Barrel markings, 821
Barrels of weapons, 820
Basic drug screen, 713
Basic red, 28, 766, 769–770, 791
Basic yellow, 40, 765–767, 770, 777, 786, 791, 799
Basilar skull fracture, 294
Battered-child syndrome, 311–313
Battle's sign, 294, 300
BDS, 713
Behavior symptom analysis in interrogation, 146
Benzedrine, 726, 736
Benzidine, 803
Bereaved family of a decedent, 514
    Handling of, 513–515
Berry aneurysm, 403
Bioterrorism, 283–287
Bioterrorism syndromes, 285–286
Bird's-eye view, 30
Birth and death records, 524, 634
Bite site, 695–696
    Impression of, 695–696
    Photographic documentation of, 695
Bitemark, 203, 695–704
    Collecting evidence from the suspect, 699–700
    Collecting evidence from the victim, 698–699
    Investigative significance, 704
    Terms indicating degree of certainty, 700–701
Bitemark analysis guidelines, 697–698
Bitemark analytical methods, 697

Bitemark evidence, 695–704
    Methods of comparison, 697
    Photography of, 703–704
    Preservation of, 695–697
    Standards for, 697
Bitemark linking to a suspect, 701–702
    Terms describing, 701–702
Bitemark methodology guidelines, 695, 697, 699, 701, 703
Bitemarks on decedent protocol, 702–703
Black powder, 24, 363, 390, 783, 797, 809, 883
Blade thickness, 447
Blasting agents, 364
Bloating, 110
Blood, 4–6, 20, 31–32, 37–39, 42, 44–45, 47–49, 51, 53, 59, 68, 77, 90, 93–94, 101, 109–118, 120–124, 126–127, 164–165, 168, 171–174, 177–180, 184–187, 190–192, 196–198, 204, 209, 221, 245–247, 251, 270, 272, 275, 277, 279–281, 283–284, 286, 290, 292, 294–295, 297, 300, 302–304, 313, 321, 325, 327–328, 330, 333, 337, 341, 343, 345, 350, 352, 357, 367, 387, 394–396, 398–403, 408, 420–422, 426–429, 431, 440, 442, 448–449, 452–454, 462, 465, 469, 484–485, 495, 498, 519, 642–643, 670, 703, 711–713, 717, 720–721, 725–727, 729, 731–732, 748, 765, 767–768, 771–772, 774, 776, 778, 781, 783, 788, 797, 799, 801–802, 807, 810, 822, 841, 843–846, 848–849, 852–853, 859–861, 869–871, 879
    Collecting known samples, 859–860
    Laboratory analysis, 860–861
    Liquid standards, 49
Blood (air-dried), 45, 47–48
Blood (liquid), 45, 48–49
Blood (scraping), 45
Blood at scene, 6, 185, 191, 197, 440, 448–449
    Preservation and collection, 47–48, 859
Blood collection supplies, 77
Blood drying, 109
Blood ethanol level, 270
Blood examination request letter for FBI lab submission, 846, 871
Blood examinations, 869
Blood on a person, 845, 870
    Collection of,

Blood on surfaces or in snow or water, 845, 870
    Collection of, 845, 870
Blood pressure rates, 408
Blood samples from live individuals, 49
Blood spatter, 31–32, 37, 39, 44, 111–114,
    117–118, 122, 164, 168, 177–180,
    184–186, 190–191, 196–198, 221,
    245–247, 251, 279–280, 303–303, 387,
    395–396, 398, 426, 428–429, 448, 452,
    462, 465, 670, 822, 842
Blood spatter impact chart, 129–131
Blood spatter interpretation, 111–131
    Establishing direction, 114–115
Blood techniques, 765, 781
Blood typing, 122, 281, 304, 396, 429, 453,
    843, 859
Bloodied and other wet clothing, 824
    Handling of, 824
Bloodstain, 47–48, 53, 111–115, 117–118,
    120–122, 845, 860, 870
    Collection of, 47–48, 845, 860, 870
Bloodstain as a timing mechanism, 121
Bloodstain photography, 113
Bloodstain sequence, 122
Bloodstain terminology, 111
Bloodstain transfer, 112, 121
Bloody prints, 324, 803
Blow-back spatter, 112, 120
Blue-green discoloration of skin, 110
Blunt head trauma, 297
    Types of injuries, 297
Blunt trauma, 172, 289–293, 295, 297–299, 301,
    303, 305, 443, 495, 520
    Types of injuries, 297–300
Blunt trauma, head injury, 297
    Signs of, 300–301
Body-dumped case, 87–90
Body examination at the crime scene, 4–5, 15–19,
    180, 269, 351–352, 359, 406, 413
Body fluid analysis, 859
    Scientific basis for, 859
Body identification, 686
    Categories and terminology, 686
Body selection target for suicide victims, 442
Body temperature, 105, 173, 318, 343, 729
    In drowning deaths, 343
Bomb, 363–370, 875
Bomb crater, 363–364, 366–367
Bomb experts, 366
Bombing deaths, 363–370

Bolt-action rifle, 818
Bones, 45, 51, 74, 102, 110, 273, 290, 293–294,
    322, 371, 377, 420, 479, 667, 686,
    705–709, 841, 847, 872
Botany, 99
Bottleneck case, 163, 175
Botulism, 287
Brain, 120, 124, 267, 272, 275, 284, 292–297,
    299–301, 304–305, 336, 343, 356, 377,
    400, 403, 431, 495, 671, 675, 678, 711,
    715, 717–718, 727–729, 731
    Average weight, 675
    Injuries to, 296–297
    Layers of, 294–295
Brain contusions, 299
Brain injury, 292–297, 731
Breech face impressions, 821
Bruise, 290, 300, 345
Buccal swabbings, 469, 844
Buckshot or pellets, 833
Buckshot ammunition, 833–834
Building materials examinations, 866–867
Bulb, 124–125, 305, 381, 384, 881, 883
Bullet, 32, 45, 61, 173–174, 179, 185, 189, 365,
    387, 389, 391, 393, 396, 426, 428, 498,
    519, 817, 819–821, 823–824, 837,
    873–874, 877
Bullet casing, 45
Bullet examination, 824
Bullet jacket, 824, 873–874
Bullet jacket (copper/zinc) alloys, 874
Bullet wipe, 393
Bullets, 59, 102, 164, 391, 669, 817, 819, 824,
    837, 873–875, 877–878, 880
Buoyancy compensator, 434, 438
Bureau of Alcohol, Tobacco, and Firearms (ATF),
    366, 542, 583, 836–837
Buried bodies cases, 91–100
    Sunken areas, 91
    Vegetation considerations, 91
Buried body grave site, 97
Burned or charred paper, 887

C

Cadaver dogs, 99
Cafe coronary, 277
Caliber, 51, 59, 186, 192, 197, 393, 395, 643,
    819, 821, 824, 828, 832, 837, 877–878

Caller id devices, 83
Camouflaged victim in poisoning deaths, 416
Cancer, 254, 261, 333, 731, 735, 737–740, 742–744, 746–751, 754, 756, 758–759, 763
Cannabis, 722, 724
Cannelures, 824
Canvass, 3, 8, 135, 170, 189, 199
Canvassing detectives, 3
CAPMI dental codes, 688
Capturing latent prints on human skin, 22
Carbon monoxide, 246, 277, 287, 307–309, 377, 390, 404, 409, 418, 434, 711–712
    Sources of, 307
Carbon monoxide deaths, 307–309
Carbon monoxide toxicity in fire deaths, 377
Carbon paper or carbon film ribbon, 891–892
Carbon paper strike, 892
Cardiac rhythm disturbances, 267, 403
Cardiomyopathy, 402–403
Cartridge case, 60, 817, 820–821, 837
Cartridge cases or shotshell casings, 877
Case preparation, 162–163, 176
Cases in which the media may be helpful to the investigation, 521
Casting an impression, 72
Casting equipment, 75
Casting in snow, 74
Casting in water, 74
Casting stamped numbers, 894
Cast-off bloodstain, 112, 120
Cast-off bloodstain spatters, 120
Cause of death, 20, 87, 92, 94, 103–104, 163, 172, 246, 251, 277, 284, 311, 341, 360, 377, 404, 415, 425, 427, 451, 462, 492, 494, 520–521, 652, 654–655, 657–658, 660, 662–663, 665, 670, 673, 711, 714
Cause of the crash, 266, 462
Cause of the fire, 377, 379–380, 382
Caustic poison, 418
Cave ceiling, 431
Cave diving, 431–433
    5 major rules, 432–433
Cavern dive, 432
Cellular intercept, 82
Cellular portable phones, 518
Cellular telephone, 82–83
Census records, 532, 535
Centerfire rifle, 817, 829
    Sample sizes, 832

Central pocket loop, 813
Chain of custody, 6, 8, 40, 670, 848
    Challenging the detective, 151, 154
Charred documents, 45, 66, 887
CHD, 399
Check writers, 887
Chewing gum, 847, 872
    Collection of, 847, 872
Child abuse, 221, 254, 291, 311, 314, 318, 321, 323, 555, 655, 665, 850
Child death, 311–312, 314, 316, 655, 665
    Scene investigation, 315–319
Child exploitation and obscenity reference file, 889–890
Child pornography examinations, 889
Children's teeth, eruption and shedding, 693
Chloral hydrate, 715
Choke, 392, 819
Chokehold, 273
Choking, 276–277, 317
Cholesterol, 399–400, 731, 735, 738–739, 743–744, 746–747, 749, 754–755, 757, 760, 762–763
Cholesterol reducer, 731, 735, 738–739, 743–744, 746–747, 749, 754–755, 757, 760, 762–763
Chopping wounds, 444
Chromotography, 714
Cigarette butt, 45
    Collection and submission, 52
Clandestine graves, 95, 97
Class characteristics of firearms, 821, 824
Class characteristics of the bullet, 824
Close range, 196, 390
Clothing, 4, 9, 12, 20, 37–39, 42–45, 48, 50–51, 53–54, 56–58, 60–61, 78, 88–90, 92–95, 103–104, 109, 113, 118, 121, 123, 125, 140–141, 149, 165, 167, 169–170, 172, 179–180, 185–187, 190–192, 196–198, 201–204, 210, 247, 264–265, 269, 276, 278–281, 285, 302–304, 309, 311, 315, 318–319, 324, 328, 342, 345–346, 351, 358–359, 368–369, 373–374, 379–380, 385, 392–394, 396, 398, 406, 413, 426–427, 429, 442, 448–449, 451–453, 458, 466, 469, 482, 485, 492–498, 503, 505, 668–670, 707, 711, 820, 824–825, 859, 863–864, 866–867, 876, 878–879, 881, 887–888, 890, 893, 896–897, 899
    On gunshot victims, 824

Clothing of the suspect, 53, 859, 863–864
    Regarding trace evidence, 863–864
Club drug, 727
Coast Guard, 533, 535–536, 545, 550, 569
Cocaine, 219, 349, 351, 401, 403, 410, 711–713, 726–728
Cocaine-related deaths, 349
Codeine, 410, 713, 718, 739, 744, 749, 753, 756–757, 761
CODIS (Combined DNA Index System), 174, 220, 222, 840, 849–853, 855
CODIS case example, 852
CODIS indexes, 853
CODIS process, 851
Coerced confessions, 151, 155
Coerced confessions and false confessions, 155
Coercive tactics, 151, 154–155
Coffee, 24, 38, 43, 419, 488, 725, 732
Cola, 725
Color of smoke, 380
Color of the flame, 381
Colorimetric screening test, 713
Combined DNA Index System (see CODIS), 174, 220, 222, 840, 849–853, 855
Command post, 167, 488
Comparison of antemortem and postmortem evidence, 684
Computer assistance, 163, 175
Computer evidence, 81, 867
    Submission of, 81–82, 867–868
Computer examinations, 867–868
Concealment of the remains, 209
Condom evidence, 52
Confessions, 133, 151–156, 161, 176
Contact burns, 356
Contact wounds on clothing, 398
Container examination, 75
Contaminated package emergency procedures, 285
Contamination, 3, 47–48, 55, 57, 63, 122, 165, 170, 343–344, 369, 415, 669, 698, 703, 843–845, 868, 870, 876, 880, 897–898
Contraceptive, 731, 734, 736, 740, 742, 744, 747, 749–752, 760–762
Contract murders, 183–188, 370
    Scene investigation, 185–186
Contre-coup, 299–300
Controlled substances, 45, 64
Controlled substances and medical preparations, 64–65

Contusions, 290–292, 299–300, 322, 444, 459, 461–462
Conversion charts, 901–905
Cookie cutter, 392
Coomassie blue, 765, 771–772
Copper sulfate, 418
Cord, string, and rope examination, 868
Cornea drying, 110
Corneal cloudiness, 110
Coronary heart disease, 399
Coroner/medical examiner systems in the United States, 651–666
Cortex, 881
Cough and cold medications, 731–763
County medical examiner/coroner, 528
County offices, 527
County or property assessor's, 527
County/state boards of health, 528
Coup, contre-coup, 299–300
Court clerk offices, 525
CPR efforts, 321, 345
    In child death cases, 321
Cranial vault, 292–297, 300
Cranium, 294, 296, 706
Crashworthiness of the involved vehicle, 459
Crashes, 34, 263, 265, 459, 463, 469, 487
    Types of, 459–462
Creating a blood kit, 122
Credit card accounts, 539
Crime scene, 3–4, 6, 8, 19, 30, 33, 40–41, 47, 54, 57, 61–62, 68–69, 73, 81, 87, 95, 125, 161–170, 173–174, 178, 191, 201, 203, 209, 211–212, 220, 224–225, 250, 261, 411, 558, 802, 837, 839–840, 842–844, 848–850, 869, 886, 895–896, 899
    Establishing perimeters, 3
Crime scene control procedures, 3–4, 166–167
Crime-scene drawings, 29–36
    Coordinate method, 29
    Information included, 30
    Legal aspects, 29
    Measurements, 29
    Preparation of, 29
    Triangulation, 29–30
    Types of, 30–33
Crime-scene integrity, 4
Crime-scene perimeter, 3
Crime-scene photographs, 37–40
Crime-scene processing, 47, 174

Crime-scene search, 25–27, 169
    Circle search, 26
    Sector or zone search, 25
Crime-scene sketch, 63, 168–169
Crime theory, 163, 174, 176
    Updated, 163, 174
Crimes that can be profiled, 207
Crimes that cannot be profiled, 208
Criminal and traffic records, 524
Criminal investigative analysis, 205, 207, 211
    Requesting assistance, 211
Cross transfer of evidence, 484
    Vehicle vs. pedestrian, 485
Crowle's double stain, 765, 772
Crowle's double stain formula, 772
Crush asphyxia, 277
Cryptanalysis, 892
Crystal, 70, 126, 728, 773
Crystal violet, 70, 126, 773
CSF and/or bleeding from nose or ears, 287, 293, 295, 300, 334
Currents, 110, 345, 431, 434
Cut or incised wounds, 442
Cuticle, 881
Cyanide, 419–420, 641, 712, 898
Cyanoacrylate (superglue) fuming of the decedent, 22–24
Cyanoacrylate ester, 765–767, 773, 778, 805
Cyanoacrylate ester formula, 773
Cystic fibrosis, 731, 739, 752, 761

D

D.A.B., 126–128, 765, 774
DFO, 765–767, 775, 777, 800
DAS screen, 713
Data files, 85, 867
Date rape drug, 728
Dead body examinations, 15–24
Death penalty, 588–589, 637, 639, 641, 643, 654
Deceased print kit, 77
Decedent identification, 163, 174, 267, 350, 405, 411, 502, 508, 810
Decomposed remains, 101–107, 451, 507, 656
    Bloated stage, 101
    Decayed stage, 101
    Fresh stage, 101
    Mummified or dry stage, 101
    Post-decay stage, 101
    Remains stage, 101
Decomposed, incinerated, or fragmented bodies, 680
    Jaw resection, 680–681
Delayed fatal hospital cases, 327–339
Demerol, 718, 740, 748
Dendritic burns, 357
Density, 97, 295, 371, 392, 686, 811
    Conversion chart, 902
Dental comparisons, 500
Dental examination procedures,
Dental evidence, 679
    Photographing of, 71, 315, 488, 508
Dental features useful in identification, 684
Dental impressions, 679, 683, 695–696
Dental radiology, 683
Dental records acquisition, 687
Dental stone, 73–74, 683
Dental supplies and equipment, 75, 681
Dental surfaces of the teeth, 687
    Drawing of, 30, 35, 168, 323, 507–508, 510
Dentition type, 682
Depressants, 728
Depressed skull fracture, 294, 298–299, 479
Depression, 91, 97, 210, 254, 260, 349, 417, 514–515, 686, 715, 722, 724–727, 729, 731, 733
Description of the deceased, 172, 258, 884
Determination of who was driving vehicle, 462
Dexedrine, 726, 740
DFO, 765–767, 775, 777, 800
Diabetes, 334, 400, 403, 732–735, 738, 740, 742, 744–746, 748–752, 754–756, 758, 760–761
Diaminobenzidine (D.A.B.) formula, 126–128, 765, 774
Diastatic skull fracture, 299
Diastolic pressure, 408
Diatoms, 343–344
Digital photography, 39
    Admissability in court, 39–40
Direct superglue fuming, 22–24
Directed light, 800
Directional microphones, 518
Directory search, 523, 599
Displaying of the remains,
Disposal of body, 209
Dissection/resection, 679–681
    Techniques, 680

Diuretic, 732–735, 737–738, 740–747, 749–751, 753, 757–762
Diver's equipment, 434–435, 437–438
    Examination of, 434–435
Diver's gear in cave-diving deaths, 432–433
    Examination of, 434
Diver's network, 434, 438
DMT, 722
DNA, 47, 50–52, 104, 152, 174, 222, 266, 325, 365, 367–368, 498, 502–503, 505, 571, 839–845, 847–853, 855, 857, 859, 861, 869–870, 872, 881–882
    Amounts required, 842
    Collecting known samples, 843–844
    Contamination, 843
    Durability of, 842
    Elimination samples, 843
    PCR, 840, 844, 881–882
    PCR-STR, 851
    Postmortem effects, 848
    RFLP, 839–840
    Submission of, 843–845
    Uniqueness of, 839
DNA analysis—investigative considerations, 839–842
DNA collection from unidentified decedents, 508, 848–849
DNA comparison, 502, 839
DNA database laws by state, 855–858
DNA database legislation, 853
DNA evidence, 47, 571, 842–845, 848, 850, 855, 869–870
    At crime scenes, 842
    Documenting, collecting, and preserving, 845
    Proper transportation and storage, 848
DNA examination advances, 849
DNA examinations, 844
DNA information, 839, 843
DNA on unidentified decedents, 849
    Locating potential sources, 849
DNA procedures, 839, 841, 843, 845, 847, 849, 851, 853, 855, 857
Doriden, 715, 741
Dose equivalent in household measures, 729
Double-action revolver, 817
Double-edged blade, 446
Double loop, 813–814
Draw back, 112
Dried bloodstains, 48, 860

Dried-out digits, 811
Driver, 50, 65, 160, 371, 387, 431, 457, 459–463, 466–468, 471–475, 480, 483–484, 496, 524–525, 534
    Type of injuries, 459–462
Driver behavior, 468, 484
Drones, 96
Drowning, 256, 277, 341–347, 352, 403, 495, 654–656, 659, 662, 664
Drowning process, 341
Drowning victim recovery, 342
Drug death, 349, 351, 353, 750, 752, 756
Drug records, 892
Drug-related homicides, 189, 191–193
DrugFire, 59, 222, 836, 877
Drugs of abuse, 713, 715, 717, 719, 721, 723, 725, 727, 729, 898
Drugs of abuse screen, 713
Dura mater, 295
Dye-staining, 769, 771, 777, 805–807

E

Ebola, 287
Eccrine glands, 15
Eccrine techniques, 765
Ecstasy, 727–728
Ectopic pregnancy, 403
Ejection of occupant, 462
El Paso Intelligence Center, 538
Elasticity of the victim's skin, 21
Elavil, 725, 734, 742
Elder abuse, 557, 604
    National Center on, 604
Electric and water company, 529
Electrical burns, 356, 358–359
    Appearance of, 356–357
Electrical outlet, 360
    Common household, 360
Electrical principles, 355
Electrostatic detection apparatus, 887
Electrocution, 355–361, 404, 637–642, 656, 664
Electrocution deaths, 355–358
Electromagnetic surveying tool, 98
Electronic devices examinations, 873
Electronic evidence, 81–8, 873
    Seizing of, 81–86
Electronic paging devices, 83
Electrostatic lifting, 70, 765, 776

Elemental analysis evidence,
    Submission guidelines, 75, 874
Elemental analysis examinations, 873–875
Embossings and seals, 887
Encephalitis, 287
Endocarditis, 402
Entomology, 95, 99, 104, 106, 580
    Collecting living insects, 105
    Collection equipment, 104
    Kill and preserve, 105
    Temperature collection, 105
Entomology scene report–sample sheet,
Envelopes and stamps, 847, 872
    Collection of, 847, 872
Environmental conditions affecting the skin's
    temperature, 109–110
Enzymes and proteins, 861
EPIC, 538
Epidermolysis, 110
Epidural hematoma, 296, 299
Epilepsy, 345, 402–403, 731
Equanil, 721, 742
Equivocal death analysis, 249
ESDA (electrostatic detection apparatus), 887
Establishing a perimeter for the scene, 519
Ethanol concentrations, 270
Euthanasia, 161
Events leading to the death, 261, 396, 667
Evidence at the crime scene, 6, 173
Evidence collection, 40, 45–47, 49–51, 53, 55,
    57, 59, 61, 63, 65, 67, 69, 71, 73, 75, 77,
    79, 163–164, 251, 481, 488, 696, 698–699,
    842–843, 868, 897
Evidence collection equipment, 75–79
Evidence collection guidelines, 45–79
Evidence collection of suspected dentition, 696
Evidence definition, 250
Evidence packaging supplies, 76–77
Evidence processing, 40, 47, 58, 163, 173, 251,
    668, 785, 804
Evidence processing, 40, 47, 58, 163, 173, 251,
    668, 785, 804
Examination of the body at the scene, 16–17
Examination of the body for physical evidence, 15
Exclusion, 245, 341, 503, 686,
    In dental comparison, 503, 686
    In identification cases, 503, 686
Exophthalmoses, 110
Expired blood, 120–121
Exploded view, 31

Explosion, 363–364, 367, 369, 383, 655, 820
    Effects of, 112, 144, 247, 267, 342,
    355–356, 371, 403, 415, 480, 501, 508,
    716–725, 728–729, 731, 821, 886
Explosion and bombing deaths,
Explosions, 118, 289, 363, 365, 367, 369, 383,
    487
    Concentrated, 363
    Diffuse, 363
Explosives, 363–365, 367, 875–876
    High, 363–364
    Low, 364–365
Explosives evidence, 875–876
    Submission considerations, 866
Explosives examinations, 875
Explosives residue examinations, 875
Expressions of farewell, 259
Exsanguination, 447
Extra-alveolar air syndrome, 431
Eyeball changes, 110

F

Fabric, 45, 50, 53–54, 70, 95, 121, 126, 398,
    465, 482, 485, 496–497, 806, 864, 876,
    892
Fabric (air-dried), 45
Fabric ribbon strike, 892
Face and head descriptions, 676
Facsimile machines, 83
Fall from heights, 371–
False confessions, 155–156
    Types of, 156
Fatty metamorphosis of the liver, 334, 403
FBI disaster squad, 876
FDI numbering system, 682
Federal and state codes, statutes, and legislation,
    593
Federal Anti–Tampering Act, 415
Federal Communications Commission (FCC),
    532, 556, 565
Federal government employment records, 532
Federal sources of information, 530
Felonious homicide, 645
Female hormone, 732, 734, 738–740, 743, 748,
    751–752, 754–755, 757–758, 762
Fiber evidence, 367, 876
    Collection of samples, 876
Fibers, 38, 42–43, 45, 52–54, 89, 95, 168, 172,

203, 295, 426, 429, 445, 448, 462, 519,
  810, 822, 863, 868, 876–877, 881, 892
Fibers and threads, 52–53
Financial Crimes Enforcement Network, 538,
  542, 565, 585
Financial statements, 524
FinCen, 225, 538–539, 542, 565, 585
Finger wipes, 18, 20
Fingernail scrapings, 45, 51, 89, 180, 187, 198,
  204, 281, 304, 346, 374, 396, 429, 453,
  458
Fingerprint(s), 15, 18-19, 21, 23, 42, 57, 59, 62,
  67-68, 81, 89, 94, 153, 168-169, 174, 178,
  202, 324-325, 364, 366-368, 380, 410,
  488, 496, 498, 500-501, 505, 510, 525,
  528, 530, 765–815, 822, 836, 842-843,
  850, 853, 883-884
  As physical evidence, 801
  At indoor scenes, 807–808
  Cards, 45, 75, 811, 884
  Cards involving decedents, 811
  Chemicals used for developing and
    enhancing, 767–801
  Classification, 812
  Comparisons, 499
  Definition, 801
  Dusting for at a homicide scene, 803–805
  Equipment, 75
  Formation, 15
  Identification, 22, 47, 501, 802, 812,
    814–815
  Identification by, 499–500, 812–815
  In vehicles, 808–809
  Limitations of, 812
  Locating at scenes, 807–810
  On glossy paper surfaces, 767
  On the decedent's body, 18–24, 809–810
  Precautions, 810
  Processing chemistry, 802
  Residue, 19, 22, 776, 789, 805
  Quick reference guide, 765–767
  Types, 802–803
Fingerprinting, 810–812
  A decomposing body, 810–811
  The decedent, 810
Fire deaths, 377–386
  Cause and origin investigation, 378–379
  Fire-induced fractures, 377
  Locating the point of origin, 381
  Fire pattern, 382

Firearm(s), 45, 58–61, 67, 90, 94, 112, 118, 159,
  164, 173–174, 177–178, 184, 204,
  221–222, 247, 259, 366, 387–398, 425,
  520, 528, 542, 583, 586–587, 665, 773,
  817–837, 873–874, 877–878, 888, 890
  Definition of, 817
  Evidence, 58, 878
  Submission of, 852, 891
  Examinations, 877–879
  Firearm recovered in water, 823
  Types of, 817–819
Firing pin impressions, 821
Firing squad, 637–639, 643
Flammable fluids/arson material, 45, 57–58
Flammable liquids, 382, 384, 865
Flammable material, 45, 57
FLIR, 97
Floor plan, 30–31
Flow rates, 905
  Conversion chart, 905
Fluorescence examination, 776
Fluorescence test, 825
Fluorescent light, 765, 784, 786, 790–793, 799,
  825
Fluorescent techniques, 765
FML, 334, 403, 743–744
Food bolus, 277
Force, 903
  Conversion chart, 903
Foreign asset identification investigations, 538
Forensic anthropologist, 87, 92, 167, 204, 281,
  301, 304, 366, 379, 394, 397, 450–451,
  454, 502, 507–508, 705
  In forensic art cases, 508
Forensic anthropology, 451, 705, 707, 709
Forensic art, 507–509, 511
  General dispersal, 510
  Preparing for a response, 510–511
  Targeted dispersal, 510
  Forensic art in identification, 507
Forensic autopsies, 669–671
  Procedures, 669
  Reasons for performing, 669
Forensic botanist, 74, 99, 104
Forensic examination, 47, 669–670
  Cross–examination, 47
  Contamination, 47
  Major concerns, 47
Forensic investigative analysis, 249
Forensic odontology, 23, 679, 681, 683, 685,

687–689, 691, 693, 695
Forward spatter, 112
Fractures, 272, 277, 279, 291–292, 294, 297–299, 302, 313, 323, 377, 395, 452, 459–462, 479, 495, 498, 669, 682, 897, 899
Frankfort plane, 508–509
Frenulum, 313, 321
Freon, 276, 717
Front passenger injuries in vehicle crash, 461, 469
Full-metal jacket (FMJ), 824

G

Gambling, 248, 257, 892–893
Gamma–hydroxybutyric acid, 727
Gas chromatography/mass spectrometry,
Gas liquid chromatography,
Gastrointestinal, 267, 283, 286, 338, 403, 732–733, 735–744, 746, 748–749, 751–756, 758, 761–762
Gauge , 60, 445, 824–825, 835, 877
GC/MS, 714
GDS, 713
Gender estimation n skeletal remains, 706
General description of the body, 4
General drug screen, 713
Gentian violet, 765–766, 777, 783, 796
Geographic profiling, 214
Geophysics, 97
Gestures, 146, 148–149, 247, 255, 646
    Indicating suicide, 247
Getting through grief, 515
GHB, 727
Glasgow coma scale, 297, 330
Glass, 54–55, 879–881
    Common types, 879
    Composition of, 879
    Fragments, 880
    Kinds of, 879–880
    Surfaces, 766
Glass evidence, 54–55, 880
    Submission of, 880–881
Glass examination, 879–880
    Investigative significance, 880
GLC, 714
Glossy paper surfaces, 767

Fingerprints, 767
Glove formation, 110, 810
Glove formation of hands and feet, 110
Gout, 732, 736, 739, 747, 754, 758, 763
Graphic arts (printing), 881
Grid search (see crime-scene searches), 27
Grief counselors, 425, 488, 491, 514
    At mass disasters, 496
Grief process, 514–515
Ground–penetrating radar, 95, 98, 100, 562
Ground radar enhancement, 91
Grouping of wounds, 441
    Sharp force injuries, 442–443
Gun bluing, 767, 778
Gun cleaning incident, 387
Gun parts, 878
Gunpowder, 53, 61, 179, 185, 245, 380, 388–389, 820, 823–826, 880
Gunpowder residue, 53, 61, 179, 185, 245, 823–826, 880
Gunshot residue, 45, 61, 79, 173, 246, 387, 825–826, 828, 874, 878
    Collection, 826–827
    Collection data sheet, 827
    Kit, 826, 828
Gunshot wound mortality rate, 398
Gunshot wounds, 94, 112, 120, 178, 193, 196, 387–390, 396–397, 656, 664
    Homicide versus suicides, 397

H

Hair, 10, 12, 22–23, 38, 43, 45, 50–51, 75, 78, 89, 94, 102, 110, 121, 139, 148, 172, 203–205, 264, 281, 283, 304, 321, 346, 357–358, 364, 367, 374, 384, 396, 419–420, 426, 429, 448, 453, 458, 462, 465, 468, 482, 485, 495, 497–498, 503, 505, 507–508, 510, 669–670, 700, 775, 782–783, 796, 822, 841–843, 847–849, 881–882
    Collection of, 45, 50–51, 882
    Description, 881
    Examinations, 881–882
Hair swipe patterns, 121
Hallucinogens, (also see psychedelic), 728
Hand tools, 77
Handgun, 45, 97, 387, 393, 397, 520, 817, 824, 830–832

Handgun ammunition, 824, 832
    Sample sizes, 832–834
Handwriting and hand printing, 890–891
Hanging, 271–272, 275, 280, 428, 637–639,
    642–643, 656, 659, 664
    Judicial, 272
Hashish, 410, 724
Hate crime murder, 161
Head hair, 12, 89, 94, 204, 346, 374, 458, 468,
    485, 882
    Collection of, 882
Heart, 49, 132, 190, 267, 272, 276–277, 292,
    332, 334–335, 337, 341, 343, 345, 356,
    399–403, 408, 420–421, 431, 442, 448,
    458, 641, 643, 675–676, 678, 712, 725,
    727, 729, 731–732
    Average weight, 675
Heart attacks, 431, 458
Heart drugs (cardiac), 733–737, 739–741,
    744–746. 749–762
Heat sources, 97, 383
Heat, energy, or work, 902
    Conversion chart, 902
Heavy machinery in searching for the remains,
Heavy metals (arsenic), 711
Heroin, 410, 719, 728
Hesitation marks, 441–442
High blood pressure (antihypertensive), 345, 401,
    403, 732–762
High-force impact, 121, 124
High-force spatter, 112, 118–120, 398
High voltage, 356–357
Hilt mark, 447
Hit-and-run cases, 54–56
    Paint, 56
Hit-and-run traffic fatality, 864
    Trace evidence, 864
Homicide, 1, 7, 19, 24–25, 35, 56, 81, 87–88,
    95, 102, 104, 151, 154, 157–165, 167,
    169–171, 173, 175, 177–178, 181,
    183–184, 187–190, 192–193, 195–196,
    201, 205, 208, 213–214, 219–223,
    226–228, 245–246, 249, 253, 263,
    273–275, 280–281, 289, 303–304,
    314–315, 320, 322, 324, 327, 343–344,
    346–347, 358, 372, 374–375, 377–378,
    387, 394, 396–397, 410, 414–416, 419,
    426, 439–441, 450, 453–454, 457–459,
    462, 464, 480–481, 485, 521, 535, 622,
    645–647, 652, 655–656, 658–659,
    661–662, 664–667, 673, 680, 702, 808,
    811, 843, 852, 861, 863
Homicide death scene, 102
    Arrival at, 69, 165, 327, 427, 659
    Discovery of, 162–164
Homicide investigation, 24, 161–162, 205, 221,
    228
Homicide scenes, 164–166, 315
    Types of, 159–161
Homicide statistics, 157–159
Homicide victimization, 158
Human error, 462
Hungarian red, 778
Hunting, 161, 256, 396, 818
Hunting ammunition, 818
Hydrochloric acid, 380, 418, 777
Hydrogen sulfide, 110, 404, 409
Hyoid, 271–273
Hyperthermia, 349, 351, 729
    Drug induced, 349, 351, 729
Hypertrophic (enlarged) heart, 401, 403, 743,
    758
Hypoglycemic, 732
Hypothermia, 341

I

IBIS, 59, 222, 836–837, 877
Ice, 5, 102, 351, 444, 466, 483, 728, 844, 847,
    869, 872
Identity (basis for degree of certainty), 498
Identification and arrest, 162–163, 175
Identification by fingerprints, 801, 814–815
Immersion effects, 342
Immigration and Naturalization, 530, 533, 542,
    567
Immunization, 284, 317, 528
Immunization for disaster team, 489
Immunoassays, 714
Immunosuppressant, 732, 739
Impression-type (plastic) prints, 803
In-custody deaths, 423–430
Incendiary devices, 384, 875
Indented writing, 66, 887–888
Indoor scene searches, 5
Infarct, 400
Information available through vital statistics,
    623–635

Information released to media, 489–490, 520–1
Inhalation anthrax, 283–284, 286
Injuries associated with child abuse, 321
Ink examinations, 882–883
Inorganic poisons, 409
Insufficient evidence in dental comparison, 686
Integrated Ballistic Identification System (IBIS), 59, 222, 836–837, 877
Interception of communication devices, 872–873
Intermediate range, 389
Internal affairs, 424–425, 528
Internal Revenue Service (IRS), 533, 566
International Air Transport Corporation, 540
International Criminal Police Organization, 541
Internet, 81–82, 85, 415–416, 471, 553, 555, 557, 559, 561, 563–567, 569, 571, 573, 575–577, 579, 581, 583–589, 591–595, 597–605, 607, 609, 611, 613, 615, 617, 619, 621
    Law enforcement sites, 553–622
Internet fraud resources, 577
Internet sources by state, 604–621
Interpol, 541–543, 568
Interpol member countries, 543
Interrogation, 143–149, 151, 153–156, 171, 192, 208, 220, 225, 227
    Evaluating the subject, 144
    Legal considerations, 143–144
    Preparation for, 144
    Promises, 144
    Purposes of, 144
    Trickery by the investigator, 143
Interrogative suggestibility, 155
Interstate Commerce Commission (ICC), 533
Interview versus interrogation, 143
Interviewing, 137–138, 144, 146, 220, 222, 225–226, 320, 490, 539, 586, 668
Intracranial bleeding, 297, 299
Intraoral entrance wound, 391
Inverted
Investigation of homicides, 159, 251
Investigation resources for conducting location and background investigations, 523–551
Investigative liaisons for law enforcement agencies, 546–550
Investigative sources on the Internet, 553–622
Investigative stage, 162–163, 174
Involuntary manslaughter, 646
Iodide fuming, 75, 805
Iodine fuming, 765–767, 780, 805

Irregular decomposition, 101
Isopropanol (2-propanol), 769, 784, 786, 790–792, 898

J

Jail walk–over, 521
Jaw resection, 680–681
Jewelry, 4, 9, 13, 38, 43, 45, 88, 93, 103, 141, 172, 179, 185–186, 191, 197–198, 202–203, 215, 263–264, 268, 276, 278, 302, 351, 368, 385, 394, 405, 413, 426, 451, 492–498, 503
Justifiable homicide, 645

K

K hole, 728
Ketamine, 727–728
Keyhole entrance wound, 391
Keyword searching of computer data files, 867
Kidneys, 335-336, 398, 448, 495, 711-712, 717-718, 732
    Average weight, 675
Kinetic energy, 824
Knots, 868
Kromekote cards, 23

L

Lacerations, 291–292, 352, 371, 391, 459–460, 462, 479
Lamp bulbs, 883
Langer's lines, 445
LASER processing of evidence, 804–805
Last–hour activities of decedent, 175
Latent fingerprint lifting techniques, 803–807
Latent fingerprints, 15, 19, 21, 59, 62, 67–68, 769, 805, 809
Latent print, 15, 20–22, 24, 62, 69, 169, 220, 775–776, 795, 801–802, 804, 809, 812, 814, 847, 872, 883–884
Latent print evidence, 169, 884
    Photographing and lifting, 22–24, 883
    Submission of, 852, 891
Latent print examination of skin, 20–22

Latent print examinations, 883–884
Latent print identification on human skin,
Lateral skull view, 707
Laxative, 732, 734, 736–742, 744–746, 753–758
LDIS, 850–851
Lead bullets, 819, 824
Lead component of a firearm projectile, 873
Legal aspects of homicide, 645
Legal Internet sites, 553–622
Length, 904
    Conversion chart, 904
Lethal gas, 637, 639, 641–642
Lethal injection, 637–644
Lethality of injuries, 447
Leucocrystal violet, 126, 765, 781
Leuconalachite green, 803
Library of Congress, 533, 567, 600–601
Librium, 720, 738, 747
Lift transfer method, 22–23
Lifting materials, 71
Ligature strangulation, 273–274, 277, 520
Light amplification through stimulated emission of radiation (LASER) processing of evidence, 804–805
Lightning, 41, 356, 358, 380, 656, 664, 879
Line of demarcation, 382
Linear skull fracture, 298
Lines of cleavage, 445
Liquid nitrogen, 865
Liqui–Drox, 765–767, 777, 782–783
Liqui-Nox, 783
Liquids (standards), 49–50
Liqui–Nox, 766, 782–783
Litigation support services on the Internet, 591–592
Liver, 49, 104–105, 267, 292, 317, 322, 334–336, 343, 398, 403, 421, 460, 462, 495, 670, 675, 678, 711–712, 715, 717–718, 725, 727, 732
    Average weight, 675
Local, county, and state police agencies, 528
Local/state law enforcement Web sites, 592
Locard principle, 47, 863
Locating fingerprints on bodies, 18–21, 809–810
Location investigation, 309
Long guns, 817, 831
    Examples of, 817–818
Long range, 387
Looking for buried bodies, 95
Loop, 812–815
Loss of consciousness, 255, 300, 341, 345, 733

Low–force spatter, 112, 116–117
Low voltage, 356–357
    Alternating current, 356
    Direct current, 356
LSD, 722, 727, 729
Luminol, 123–128, 169, 783, 799, 803
Luminol photography, 124–126
Luminol use, 123–124
Lungs, 283–284, 321, 341, 343, 403–404, 431, 639, 643, 675, 731–732
    Average weight, 675
Lust murder, 160, 208
Lye, 418

M

M.B.D., 765–767, 784, 790
MRM, 765–766, 786–787
Magna Brush technique, 809
Magnetic powder, 23–24
Magnetometer, 98
Mail cover, 86, 224
Major case prints, 90, 94, 180, 187, 192, 198, 204, 247, 281, 304, 320, 374, 396, 414, 429, 453, 811, 884
Major case squad call–out, 425
Malaria, 287, 732, 745, 754–755
Male hormone, 732, 735, 743–744, 748, 752, 759, 762
Mallet and chisel method for jaw resection, 681
Mania (drug induced), 349
Man–made disasters, 487
Manslaughter, 645–647, 665
Manual strangulation, 273
Maps, 223, 227, 472, 563, 566, 568, 593, 597, 622, 809
    On the Internet, 563, 566, 568, 593, 597, 622
Marbling, 110
Marijuana, 64, 713, 724, 728
Marine Corps, 535–536, 545, 549, 564, 581
Marine hospitals, 536
Mass, 905
    Conversion chart, 905
Mass disaster, 487–498
    Types of, 487
Mass disaster investigation, 487–498
Mass disaster scene, 488
    Communication facility, 490

Establishing a staging area,
Morgue facility considerations,
Processing the scene,
Securing the scene,
Specialized equipment necessary,
Mass murders, 161, 487
Maxillary fractures, 294
M.B.D., 765–767, 784, 790
    M.B.D. dye, 766–767
MDMA, 727
Media briefing sites, 518
Media considerations, 222, 425, 517
    In police–involved deaths, 424
Media management, 517
Media relations, 489
    At mass disaster scenes,
Media release, 425, 427, 505, 517
    Officer–involved death, 427
Medical abbreviations, 333
Medical examiner at the scene, 172, 184
Medical examiners, 24, 221
Medium–force spatter, 118
Medulla, 296, 304–305, 881
Melting points, 386
Merchant Marine personnel, 533
Mercury, 409, 419, 711–712
Mescaline, 723
Metal, 4, 6, 45–46, 49, 51, 53, 56, 58, 61–62, 67, 70, 75, 77–78, 94, 97–98, 121, 281, 364, 367, 386, 419–420, 443, 465, 468, 484, 489, 497–498, 640–642, 683, 685, 766, 780, 805–806, 820, 824–825, 865, 874–875, 884–885, 893
    Broken or damaged, 885
    Burned, heated, or melted, 885
    Cut or severed, 885
    Comparisons, 884
    Detectors, 6, 97–98, 378
    Fragments, 880, 885–887
    Surfaces, 884
    Fingerprints, 766
Metallurgy evidence, 885
    Submission of, 885
Metallurgy examinations, 885
Methamphetamine, 728
Methadone, 713, 719, 748
Methamphetamine, 712, 727–729, 748
Methamphetamine hydrochloride, 728
Methedrine, 726
Methyl (wood) alcohol,

Microscopic characteristics, 73, 821, 877, 881–882, 897
    Firearms, 821
Military ammunition, 819
Military dependents, 545, 666
Military discharge records, 544
Military explosives, 364
Military grade and rank, 550
Military information sources, 544
Military personnel and medical records, 544–545, 581
Military records, 535–536, 544–546, 593, 684
Military sites, 593
Miltown, 721, 749
Mineral supplement, 732, 734, 736–737, 739, 743–744, 746, 748–750, 752, 754–758, 762
Miranda warnings, 143–144
    Oral waivers, 143
Miscellaneous equipment, 78
Missed call redial, 84
Mitochondrial DNA chart, 502
Mitochondrial DNA analysis (MTDNA), 841–842
Mitral valve prolapse, 402
Model airplanes, 96
Model glue, 717
Modus operandi, 192, 195, 198, 202, 210, 213, 368, 520
    Changes in, 210
Money, 4, 12, 38, 43, 46, 148, 171, 180, 183, 186, 189, 191, 193, 197, 246, 248, 372, 418, 497–498, 518, 538–539, 562, 574, 581, 584, 866, 893
Money laundering, 538–539, 574, 584, 893
Morphine, 410, 719, 749, 756
Motive, 95, 135, 154, 159, 163, 171, 174–178, 183, 205, 207, 212, 226, 245, 251, 281, 304, 309, 320, 346, 375, 377, 384, 386, 396–397, 418, 441, 453–454, 458, 485, 520, 673
    Development, 171, 175, 207, 251
Motive investigation for arson, 384
Motor vehicle records, 530, 533
Motorist and vehicle services available through the Internet, 471
Moving dead bodies, 4
M.R.M., 765–766, 786–787
MTDNA, 841–842
Mummification, 110

Murder, 153, 157, 159, 161, 175, 183, 185, 187, 207, 214, 219, 370, 416, 487, 521
Muscle relaxants, 713, 732
Muzzle impression, 390
Muzzle-to-target distance, 825
Myocarditis, 402

N

Narcotic withdrawal, 733, 741, 748, 750, 756, 760
Narcotics, 46, 585, 664, 712, 733
National Central Bureau, 542–543, 568
National Integrated Ballistics Information Network (NIBIN), 836–837
National paint file, 886
Natural death, 268, 311, 323, 350, 399–408, 411
    Scene indicators, 402–403
Natural disasters, 487
Navy, 85, 535–536, 546, 549–551, 564, 581
NCB, 542
NDIS, 850–851, 853–854
NDIS participation, 853
    By state, 854
Near-drowning deaths, 341
Near contact, 390
Necro Search, 95
Necrotizing pancreatitis, 403
Negative evidence, 163, 175
Nembutal, 716, 750, 753
Neurologic syndromes, 287
Neutron activation analysis, 826
News sources, 562–563, 595–596
News sources on the Internet, 562–563, 595–596
Newspapers, 70, 103, 180, 185, 268, 351, 385, 406, 412–413, 424, 563, 576, 594–595
Next-of-kin handling, 513–515
Next-of-kin relationship, 513
    Legal heirarchy, 513
NIBIN, 836–837
NIBIS, 877
Nickel nitrate, 767, 787
Nile red, 787
Ninhydrin, 75, 169, 765–767, 774–775, 780, 785, 787–789, 794, 800, 803–805
Ninhydrin method, 805
Nitrate (paraffin) test, 825
Nitroglycerin, 364, 750
Nitrous oxide, 336, 718

No-Doz, 726
Nonvolatile materials (plant origin), 898
Nondestructive fingerprint techniques, 67, 810
Nonporous surfaces, 70, 766–767, 771–777, 780, 784–786, 788, 790–793, 795, 798, 806, 808–810, 883
Nonsecretor, 859
Nontraditional methods for locating and/or conducting a background investigation, 538–541
Nontransparent lifting mediums, 23
Nonverbal expressions, 259
Nonvisible (latent) prints, 5, 20–22, 24, 62, 69, 169, 220, 775–776, 795, 801–802, 804, 809, 812, 814, 847, 872, 883–884
Nonvolatile organic compounds, 898
Notification of next of kin, 513, 515, 491
    Mass disaster scenes, 489, 491
Nuclear DNA, 841–842, 849
Number of respirations per minute, 407
Numeric pagers, 83
Nutmeg, 723

O

Oblique light, 776, 800
    Fingerprints, 776, 800
Obliterated writing, 887, 891
Occupant kinematics, 459
Ocular injuries, 313
Offender index, 610, 852
    CODIS, 174, 220, 222, 840, 849–853, 855
Office supplies, 78
Official records clerk or the county recorder, 529
Ohms, 355–356, 360–361
Ohms law, 355
On-off rule, 82
    Electronic evidence, 81–83
Open-water diving, 431–432
Opium, 711–712, 718–720
Opportunity, 175
Organic poisons, 410
Organs, average weight, 675–676
Ortho tolidine, 803
Outdoor scene searches, 7
Outdoor scenes, 26, 29, 34, 95, 105, 168

P

Painkillers (analgesics), 731, 733–737, 739–763
Paint, 20, 45–46, 55–57, 62–63, 72, 276, 281, 318, 380, 410, 484–485, 783, 802–803, 864–865, 885–887, 894, 896
    Layer structure, 886
Paint chips, 46, 56, 885–886
Paint composition, 485
Paint evidence, 55, 380, 885–886
    Collection of, 886–887
    Examination of, 886
Pancreas, 675, 731–732
    Average weight, 675
Paper burn trails, 865
Paper examination, 864, 887, 892
Paraffin test, 825
Parkinson's disease, 276, 727–728, 733–737, 739, 741–742, 746–747, 749, 752, 754–758, 760
Partial-metal jackets, 824
Passports, 534, 539
Passwords, 867
Patent prints, 112, 281, 303, 396, 453, 802
Pathologist at the death scene, 267, 667–668
    Call-out protocol, 668
Patient's medical chart, 328
PCR, 840, 844, 881–882
PCR–STR, 851
PDA, 872
Pedestrian versus high vehicle, 479
Percodan, 720, 752–753
Perimeters for the scene, 166
Perpetual calendar, 229
Persistent vomiting, 300
Personal digital assistants, 872–873
Personality assessment, 211, 261
Phenobarbital, 410, 716, 741, 753
Phenolphthalein, 122–123, 803
Phloxine B, 789
Phone company services, 84
Phosphorous, 419
Photocopies examination, 888
Photocopy exemplars, 888
    Obtaining, 888
Photo-flo solution, 865
Photograhic equipment, 76
Photogrammetry, 889–890
Photographic authenticity, 889
Photographic comparisons, 888
Photographic documentation of a bite site, 695–696
Photographic evidence, 889
    Submission of, 889–890
Photographic examinations, 888–889
Photographing a body, 38–39
Photographing a death scene, 37–40, 378
    Exterior shots, 37
    Interior shots, 37–38
Photographing of decedent for forensic art purposes, 508
Photographing the skull, 508–509
Physical developer, 765–767, 775, 780, 788–789, 795, 797
Physical neglect in children, 313–314
Pilots and aircraft records, 534
Pituitary, 305, 675
    Average weight, 675
Placenta previa, 404
Plain arch, 812
Plain whorl, 813
Planning and zoning offices, 528
Plant material, 46, 92, 343
Plants, 74, 420, 490, 896
Plastic prints, 68, 803, 806
Plastic surfaces, 766
Playing with the victim's body after death, 20
Pneumonic plague, 286
Point of impact, 54, 56, 457–458, 465, 468, 477, 481, 484
    Pedestrian vs. vehicle, 477–480
Poison, 172, 267, 403, 409–416, 418–422, 652–656, 727, 897–89
    Identification of, 409, 411
    Metals, 409
    Nonmetals, 409
    Physical manifestations, 418–419
    Symptoms, 418–419
    Types of, 409
Poison procurement, 415
Poisoners, 415–417
    Identifying types of, 415
    Profile of, 416–418
Poisoning, 48, 246, 287, 307, 409, 411, 413–421, 652, 656, 661, 664–665, 731
    Chronic, 409
    Acute, 409
Poisoning death, 409, 419

    Highly planned crime, 416
    Spontaneous crime, 416
Poisonous gases, 277, 404
Police and correctional custody deaths, 423, 427
Police radios as a form of communication, 518
Police shooting deaths, 423
Police-assisted suicide, 423
Policy for crime-scene integrity, 3, 164–165
Polymerase chain reaction (PCR) DNA analysis, 840, 882
Polymerase chain reaction–short tandem repeat (PCR–STR), 851
Polymers examination, 890
Porous surfaces, 766–767, 772, 775, 785, 787–789, 794, 796–797, 800, 805
Posing of the decedent, 201
Positive identification, 47, 67, 496, 498–499, 686, 814, 839, 880
    In dental comparisons, 500, 686
Positive identification techniques, 499
Possible identification, 48, 54, 62, 449, 686, 881
    In dental comparison, 686
Postmortem injuries, 180, 186, 341–342, 378
    Drowning deaths, 341, 659
Post Office, 523, 534, 568
Postal mail cover, 86
Postcyanoacrylate, 766, 782
Postmortem artifacts, 377, 670
Postmortem decomposition, 110
    Stages of, 110
Postmortem dental evidence, 679–680
    Collection and preservation of,
Postmortem dental record, 681
Postmortem lividity, 109
Postmortem mutilation, 20, 441
Postmortem team, 495, 498
    In mass disasters, 27
Post-ninhydrin, 787, 800
Postoffense behavior, 210
Postpartum hemorrhage, 404
Post-scene investigation, 172
Postural asphyxia, 277
Powder and shot pattern, 61
Powder processing involving dry surfaces, 803
Precautions to avoid rescue, 246, 260
Pregnancy, 316, 322, 336–337, 403, 657, 675, 731
    Complications, 403–404
Preliminary steps in obtaining latent prints from human skin, 22

Preludin, 726, 754
Prescriptive medications, 269, 352, 406
Pressure, 901
    Conversion chart, 901
Pressure and depth gauges, 438
Presumptive blood testing, 122
Previous suicide attempt, 260
Previous suicide threat, 260
Primary explosives, 364
Primer, 74, 817, 820, 835, 837, 874
Printers' spray powder, 285
Prison and parole records, 530
Prisoner in custody, 428, 657
Prisons, 534, 565, 582, 584, 588
    Bureau of, 534, 565, 584
Private investigator, 592, 596
Probes, 99, 104
Processing of a body–dump site, 87–90
Processing the body for latent print development, 19–24
Product tampering, 415
Profiling (see criminal investigative analysis), 205–211
Projectile weight, 824
Promises, 144, 152
Prosecution, 87, 151, 161, 176, 208, 223, 227–228, 538, 581, 645, 647, 669
Prostitution, 161, 893
Protective clothing at a homicide scene, 51, 78, 125, 165
Protective clothing and biohazard kit, 78
Proving arson, 386
Pruning shears method for jaw resection, 681
Psilocybin, 723
Psychedelic, 722–724
Psychological autopsy, 249–252, 261
Psychological profile, 202, 212, 214
    The report, 212
Pubic hair, 51, 89, 94, 203–204, 670, 882
    Collection of, 51, 670, 882
Public records, 525, 530, 556, 582
Public utilities, 523
Pugilist position, 377
Pulmonary embolism, 286, 404
Pulmonary thromboemboli, 402
Pulse rates, 407
Puncture wounds, 444
Purging, 110
Pyramid investigative technique of homicide investigation, 162

Q

Questioned documents, 46, 65–66
Questioned–documents evidence, 888
    Submission of, 888
Questioned documents examinations, 890–892

R

Racketeering, 892–893
Racketeering records evidence, 893
    Submission of, 893
Radial loop, 812–813
Radiating lacerations, 391
Radioimmunoassays, 714
Railroad death involving a pedestrian, 456–457
Railway retirement board, 534
RAM, 765–766, 790, 792–793
RAM mixture, 790
Random victim, 369, 416–418
    Poisoning deaths, 416–418
Range determination, 59
Rape, 25, 49–52, 160, 645, 655–656, 665, 727–728, 841, 849–850
Raw wood surfaces (fingerprints), 767
R.A.Y., 765–766
R.A.Y. mixture, 791
Rear impact to vehicle, 461
Rear passenger injuries in vehicle crash, 461
Reconciliation in identification, 494, 498
Reconstruction, 48, 57, 59, 64, 163, 174, 177–179, 185, 195, 211, 224, 249–251, 262–263, 368, 387, 448, 459, 464, 481, 507, 667, 687, 822
Reconstruction components of the crime scene, 174
Recovering latent fingerprints on the body, 15
Recovering projectiles from walls, 823
Recovery divers, 432
Recovery teams at mass disaster sites, 493
Red flags, 251, 314, 384–385
    Fire death investigation, 384–385
    Of child abuse, 314, 318, 323, 555, 657
Red-yellow mixture, 791
Reference sources on the Internet, 553–622
Reflected light, 800
Regulator, 434, 438

Releasing information, 192, 518, 520
Respiration rates, 407
Restricted Fragment Length Polymorphism (RFLP), 839–840
Revolver, 59, 173, 393–394. 398, 817, 819, 822–825, 830–831
RFLP, 839–840
Rheumatic heart disease, 337, 402
Rhodamine, 765–766, 786, 790–792, 802
Rhodamine 6g, 765–766, 786, 790–792
RIA, 714
Ricin, 286, 410
Ridge details, 809, 814–815
Rifle, 46, 59, 387, 393, 397, 588, 643, 817–818, 828–829
Rifle ammunition, 393, 818
Rifling characteristics, 821–822, 824–825, 877
Rigor mortis, 4, 109, 172-173, 268-269, 279, 302, 350-351, 357, 359, 394, 405–406, 412-413, 426, 452, 669-670, 811
Rimfire rifles, 832
    Sample sizes, 832
Ritalin, 725, 739, 748–749, 756
Robbery–related homicides, 195–199
Rock, 46, 433, 531, 536, 547, 624, 726
Rohypnol, 727–728
Roll-over of vehicle, 461
Roofies, 728
Rope, 46, 54, 78, 183, 190, 259, 271–272, 278, 280, 426, 493, 642, 728, 868
Rope examination, 54
Rubber stamps, 66, 887

S

Sigh process, 514
Safe insulation examinations, 893
Safety line, 432
Safranin O, 765, 793
Saliva, 46, 49, 90, 124, 202, 204, 276, 695–696, 700, 703, 841–842, 846, 848–849, 859, 869, 871
    Liquid standards, 49–50
Saliva and urine, 846, 871
    Collection of, 846, 871
    Submission of, 846, 871
Saliva samples, 696, 869
    Of suspected bitemark areas, 695–697
Saliva swabs, 46, 695

Saliva swabs of bite site, 695
Saponification, 110
Satellite spatter, 112
Scanning electron microscopy, 697, 826
Scavenger patterns, 99
Scavengers, 95
Scene examination, 3–13
    In firearm cases, 395–396
Schleral discoloration, 110
School census records, 535
Scopolamine, 724, 756
Scuba–related deaths, 431, 433, 435, 437
SDIS, 850–851
Search engines/tools, 597–603
Search for people/businesses, 603–604
Search locations, 8, 414
Searching dead bodies, 4
Sebaceous glands, 15, 19
Sebaceous techniques, 765
Seconal, 410, 716, 756
Secondary explosive, 364
Secretary of State, 530, 604–621, 632
Secretors, 859
Sector or zone search, 25
Securities and Exchange Commission (SEC), 535, 565
Semen (air-dried),
Semen and semen stains, 89, 203, 846, 861, 871
    Collection of, 861, 871
    Submission of, 871
Semen evidence from sexual assault victim, 861, 871
Senile/mental changes, 247, 257, 260, 276–277, 416
Senility, 276–277, 403
Sepsis, 284, 403, 448
Serial killers, 208
    Hedonistic, 208
    Mission oriented, 208
    Power/control oriented, 208
    Visionary, 208
Serial murder, 208
Serial murderers, 208
Serial number examinations, 893–894
Serial number restoration, 61
Serologic analysis, 503
Serology, 50–52, 54, 211, 703, 859–861
Serrated knife blade, 447
Service deaths, 535
Sexual homicide investigation, 201–217

Sex-related homicides, 201–217
Sexual questionnaire, 215
Shaft, 383, 881
Sharp-force injuries, 439–456
    Classification of, 442–444
    Depth of the wound, 445
    Evidence considerations, 448–449
    Examination of clothing, 448–449
    Width of the wound, 445
Shoe cast, 46
Shoe prints in blood, 126
    Enhancements of, 126–128
Shoeprint and tire tread evidence, 67–74, 894
    Submission of, 894
Shoeprint and tire tread examinations, 67–74
Shoeprint and tire tread files, 894
Shoeprint and tire tread impressions, 67–74
    Photography of, 71–72
Shoes, 13, 46, 54, 97, 113, 141, 167, 279, 302, 329, 345, 359, 373–374, 394, 428, 452, 466, 497, 894, 896–897
Shored exit wound, 393
Shot examination, 824
Shot pattern, 61, 392, 819, 878
Shot pellets, buckshot, or slugs, 877
Shotgun, 46, 59–60, 118–119, 251, 391–393, 397, 819, 821, 823, 829, 878
    Pump action, 818–819, 823, 829
Shotgun ammunition, 46, 819
    Birdshot, 819
Shotgun shell, 60, 819
Shotgun wadding, 46, 819
Shotgun wounds, 391
Shoulder arm, 817
SICAR, 895
Sickle-cell traits, 861
Side impact, 461
Side-Scan Sonar, 99
SIDS profile, 311
Signatures, 65, 891
    Common types of nongenuine, 891
Silenced firearms, 823
Silencers, 878
Silent M.I., 400
Silt, 343, 431–434, 438
Silver nitrate, 765, 767, 794, 805
Silver nitrate treatment, 805
Silver salts, 418
Single-action revolver, 817
Single-edged blade, 446–447

Skeletal injuries, 313
    Child abuse, 313
Skeletonization, 110
Skeletonized remains, 281, 304, 397, 679–680
    Jaw resection requirement, 680–681
Sketch, 29
Skin blistering, 110, 268, 350, 405, 412
Skin slippage, 110, 268, 312, 350, 405, 412
Skull, 102, 292-300, 391-392, 459, 462, 479, 503, 507-509, 680, 684, 705–709
Skull fractures, 297–298, 459, 462
    Types of, 298–300
Slurries, 364
Small–particle reagent, 765–767, 795, 807
Smallpox, 287
Smart card, 84–85
Smokeless powder, 363, 835
Smooth-bore weapons, 819–820
Smothering, 276–277, 280, 656, 664
Smudging, 390
Social Security number (SSN), 522–523. 560
Social Security records, 535
Sodium fluoroacetate, 421
Soil, 46, 54, 58, 73, 91–94, 96–99, 105, 171, 367, 894, 896–897
    Investigative potential, 896
Soil evidence, 896
    Submission of, 896
Soil examination, 894–896
Soiling, 246, 390
Soot, 378, 382, 387–390, 393, 398, 495, 825–826
Specialized personnel at the crime scene, 4, 488
Specific procedures in handling the notification, 513
Specific victim in poisoning deaths, 416–418
Spectacle hemorrhages, 299
Spectrographic examinations, 865
Spectroscopy, 714
Speed, 64, 82, 96, 372, 457, 459, 466–467, 477–478, 483, 728, 780, 883
Spleen, 336, 398, 460, 462, 675, 678, 711, 848
    Average weight, 675
Spontaneous combustion, 383–384
Spree, 161
Stab wound, 172, 444–448, 455
    V-shaped, 445–446
Stab wounds, 440–441, 444, 446–450
Stabbing, 439–440, 442, 445–449, 452–453, 659

Depth of wound, 445–447, 455
Standard blood specimens, 48
Staphylococcal enterotoxin, 286
State census records, 535
State Highway Patrol, 535
State/county engineering department,
Stellate contact wound, 390
Steroid, 733, 735–736, 738–741, 743, 745–746, 748–749, 752, 754, 758, 761
Sticky–side powder, 766, 796, 865
Sticky–side tape, 865
Stimulants, 403, 711, 725, 733–734, 736, 739–740, 742–743, 745, 748–749, 753, 755–757
Stomach contents, 5, 110, 276–277, 495
STP, 724
Straight–line search, 26
Stranger–to–stranger homicide, 205
Strip search (see crime–scene searches)
Strychnine, 410, 422, 898
Stryker autopsy, 681
Subarachnoid hemorrhage, 299, 459
Subdural hematoma, 299, 313, 321
Sudan black, 766, 795, 797
Sudden infant death syndrome (SIDS),
Suffocation, 172, 276, 311, 654, 656, 664
Suicidal intent, 252
Suicide by cop, 423
Suicide investigation, 245–248
Suicides by sharp-force injuries, 442
Sulfuric acid, 365, 384, 418, 641
Superglue, 21–24, 47, 802, 807, 883
Superglue fuming, 21–24, 802
Superheated air, 377
Surgical incisions and hospital-produced wounds, 328
Surveillance films and videotapes, 888
Suspect at the scene, 68, 170, 842, 880
Suspect clothes, 369, 880
    In glass examinations, 880–881
Suspect description, 139–141, 192, 213
Suspect development, 170–171, 175
Suspect's clothing, 53, 57, 113, 118, 167, 369, 863, 881, 896
    Trace evidence, 863–864
Suspension of the body, 271
Suspicious suicides, 397
Swipe (blood), 112, 121, 123
Systolic pressure, 117–118, 330, 408, 732

T

Tache noire, 110
Tagging remains at mass disaster scenes, 494
Tardieu spots, 272
Target, 34, 111–112, 118, 125–126, 192, 195, 201, 207, 210, 370, 387, 392, 397, 572, 819, 825, 878
Target to muzzle, 387, 825
Teeth numbering system, 682
Telephones, 3, 8, 81–82, 169, 518, 873
    Wireless, 82
Telephoto lenses, 518
    Media considerations, 518
Temporary morgue facilities, 490
Tentative identification techniques, 502
Tented arch, 812
Test bite media, 697
Test trenching/archaeology, 100
Tetramethylbenzidine (TMB), 797–798
THC, 722
Thenoyl europium chelate (TEC), 798–799
Thermal infrared imagery, 97
Thin-layer chromatography, 714
Thorazine, 640, 721, 738, 760
Three-dimensional drawings, 32–33
Thrombus, 400
Thymus, 675
    Average weight, 675
Thyroid, 675, 733, 735, 737, 740, 742–743, 745, 747–749, 754, 758–761
    Average weight, 675
Time-delay devices, 364
Time frame of death, 4, 87, 92, 102–103, 109, 173, 202, 246, 251, 279, 302, 315, 350, 358, 394, 427, 435, 452, 520
Time line, 96, 257, 259, 261
    Psychological autopsy, 249–252, 261
Tire treads, 46, 64, 174, 190, 894
Tissues, bones, and teeth, 847, 872
    Collection of, 847, 872
    Submission of, 847, 872
TLC, 714
TMB, 797–798
Tofranil, 725, 745, 760
Tool mark, 57, 61–64, 449, 897
Tool mark evidence, 61–62, 897
    Submission of, 897
Tool mark examinations, 897

Tooth surfaces, 682
Total station, 34–35
Toxemia, 404
Toxicological substances in postmortem cases, frequently encountered, 712
Toxicological substances screened, 711
Toxicology, 211, 252, 424, 495, 711, 713, 897–898
Toxicology evidence, 897–898
    Submission of,
Toxicology examinations, 897
Trace evidence, 3, 7, 38–39, 43–44, 47, 52, 59, 62–63, 172–173, 205, 250, 280–281, 302–303, 320, 368, 374, 394, 396, 426, 448, 452–453, 462, 699, 822–823, 863–865, 867, 869, 871, 873, 875, 877, 879, 881, 883, 885, 887, 889, 891, 893, 895, 897, 899
    Clothing, 863–864
    Definition, 863
    Involving the scene, 863
    Involving the victim, 863
Trace metal detection technique, 825
Tracing an Internet e-mail, 85
Traffic fatality, 459, 461, 463, 465, 467, 469, 471, 473, 475, 477, 479, 481, 483, 485, 864
    Vehicle versus stationary object, 460
    Vehicle versus vehicle, 459–475
Trajectory of the projectile, 387
Tranquilizer, 720–721, 728, 734–763
Tranquilizers, sedatives, and hypnotics, 733
Transfer bloodstain patterns, 121
Transmitted light, 776, 800
Trash pulls, 541
Trauma score codes, 329
Traumatic, 271, 273, 275–277, 279, 281, 324, 461
Trigger pull, 246, 825
Trigger-pull examinations, 877
Truthful versus deceptive behavior, 147
Tuberculosis, 733, 743, 745–746, 749, 751–752, 755–757, 846, 871
Types of homicides, 159, 177, 645
Typewriting examinations, 891–892
Typewriting exemplars, 892
    Procedures for obtaining, 892

U

U.S. National Central Bureau, 542–543, 568
U.S. Public Health Service Hospitals, 536
Ulnar loop, 812–813
Ultraviolet examination, 799
Ultraviolet induced, 767, 770, 798
Ultraviolet lamp, 765, 771, 782, 798
Unemployment benefits, 535
Unfired cartridges or shotshells, 877
Unidentifed remains protocol, 505
Universal tooth numbering system, 682–683
Using luminol, 123–126
USNCB, 542–543, 568
    Contacting, 542–543
Uterine rupture, 404

V

Vacuum metal deposition (VMD), 806
Vegetation, 74, 88, 91, 93, 95, 99, 102–103, 705
    Buried body remains,
Vehicle crash with a stationary object, 459
    Mechanics of, 459
Vehicle malfunction, 463, 467, 480, 483
Vehicle versus child, 479
Vehicle versus pedestrian, 477, 479, 481, 483, 485
Velocity, 371, 392, 817, 819, 824, 828, 885
    Conversion chart, 901
Ventricular fibrillation, 267, 355–357, 403
Verbal expressions, 259
Veterans Administration hospital, 536
VICAP, 175
    Crimes reported, 213
    Missing person cases, 213
    Purpose, 214
    Unidentified dead bodies, 213
VICLAS, 213–214
    Other countries using,
Victim, 7, 15, 18–22, 37–38, 42–43, 49–52, 54, 56, 61, 81, 86–87, 93, 104–105, 111, 113, 116, 120–121, 135, 152–153, 157, 159–160, 164–165, 167, 169–170, 172, 174–175, 177–181, 183–186, 189–191, 193, 195–198, 201–207, 209–215, 225–226, 249, 251–252, 254–255, 257–258, 264–265, 273–275, 291–292, 298, 301, 328, 341–344, 346–347, 357, 363, 367, 369–370, 374, 377, 379, 387, 389, 391, 397–398, 410–411, 415–419, 421–422, 428, 433, 439–442, 446, 448–450, 454, 458, 465, 469, 478–480, 482, 484, 491–494, 496, 499, 501, 503, 519–521, 526, 558, 612, 622, 645–647, 656, 663, 667, 680, 695, 697–700, 704, 728, 807, 823–825, 839, 841–844, 846, 849–850, 852, 860, 863, 868–869, 871, 876, 881, 886, 896, 898
Victim identification, 205, 298, 499–501, 503
Victim procurement, 209
Victim typology, 209–210
Video authenticity, 898
Video damaged media repair, 898
Video enhancement, 898
Video evidence, 899
    Submission of, 899
Video examinations, 898–899
Video format conversion, 898
Video image processing, 898
Video special effects, 898
Video synchronization, 898
Videos, 889
Videotaping, 41, 43, 151, 503, 521
    Body shots, 44
    Exterior shots, 42
    Interior shots, 42–43
    Vehicle shots, 43–44
Videotaping a death scene, 41, 43
    Camera techniques, 41
Violence-related Web sites, 622
Violent crime linkage analysis system, 213
Violent criminal apprehension program, 175, 212
Violent criminal apprehension program, 175, 212
Viral Hemorrhagic Fever (Ebola), 287
Visible (patent) prints, 112, 281, 303, 396, 453, 802
Visual examination for fingerprints, 680, 683, 765, 767–775, 777, 779–798, 800
Visual identification, 368, 499–500, 880
Vital statistics, 537, 611, 623–635
    Federal Bureau of, 537, 542, 565, 578, 584, 866, 873, 884, 890, 899
Vital statistics availability for Canada, 633–635
Vitamins, 733
VMD, 806–807

Voice pagers, 83
Volatile compounds, 898
Volatile screen, 898
Volatile substances, 410
Volts, 355–356, 360, 640
Volume, 904
    Conversion chart, 904
Voluntary manslaughter, 645–646

W

Wadding, 46, 60, 392, 819, 825, 877
Watches, clocks, and timers, 899
    Examination of, 899
Water drinking bottles (plastic), collection of, 847–848
Wave cast-off, 112, 115
Weapon identification, 51, 163, 173, 667
    Basis for, 821
Weapon identification, 51, 163, 173, 667
Weapon velocity, 828
Weapons, 6, 39, 44, 59, 121, 151, 159, 168–169, 171, 174, 178, 184, 247, 289, 391, 398, 428, 450, 528, 571, 643, 667, 817, 819–821, 823, 828, 831, 883
    Unloading of, 387
Weather conditions, 68, 91, 138, 165, 168, 263–264, 345, 380, 436, 458, 463, 467, 480–481, 483, 538
    Traffic crash, 463, 467, 480–481
Weather Internet sites, 622
Weather records, 538
Weathering of bones, 110
Weight belt, 434, 436, 438
Weight percentiles for boys, 316
Weight percentiles for girls, 316
Wet surfaces, 766, 883
Where to look for latent prints on the decedent's body, 18–24, 809–810
Whorl, 812–813, 815
WINID antemortem dental record form, 691
WINID codes, 688–689
WINID examples, 690
WINID postmortem chart, 691
WINID3, 688
Wipe, 22, 48, 52, 56, 67–68, 112, 324, 393, 860, 876
Witness development, 163, 170
Witness interviewing, 137–138
    Court requirements, 137–138
Witnesses, 3, 8, 32, 57–58, 135, 137, 151, 153, 164–165, 167, 170–171, 175, 185, 189, 197, 199, 211, 220, 222–223, 225–227, 247, 252, 325, 346, 367, 385, 414, 425, 427, 429, 468, 484–485, 519–521, 527, 578, 581, 592–594, 663, 668
Wood examination, 899
Wrapping up the crime scene, 8
Writing exemplars, 891
    Procedures for obtaining, 891
Written report, 261, 669, 683

X

X-ray comparisons, 502, 707
X-ray examination at autopsy, 669
X–rays in gunshot wounds, 396, 669
XTC, 727

Y

Y-chromosome DNA analysis, 841

Z

Zinc chloride, 766–767, 777, 779, 785, 788, 800

ABOUT THE AUTHOR

Louis N. Eliopulos has 25 years of experience in death investigations. Currently, he is a senior homicide investigations analyst with the Naval Criminal Investigative Service (NCIS), where he reviews, consults, and suggests investigative analysis and strategy on active and cold-case homicide investigations from all over the world. He also consults on homicide investigations for other criminal justice agencies. Before being employed by NCIS, Eliopulos was chief forensic investigator for the Medical Examiner's Office in Jacksonville, Florida, where he created, hired and trained the investigative staff, as well as serving as the special investigator in the Capital Crimes Division for the Florida Public Defender's Office. He also was a forensic consultant for the teams responsible for recovering the remains from the Pentagon after the September 11, 2001, terrorist attack.

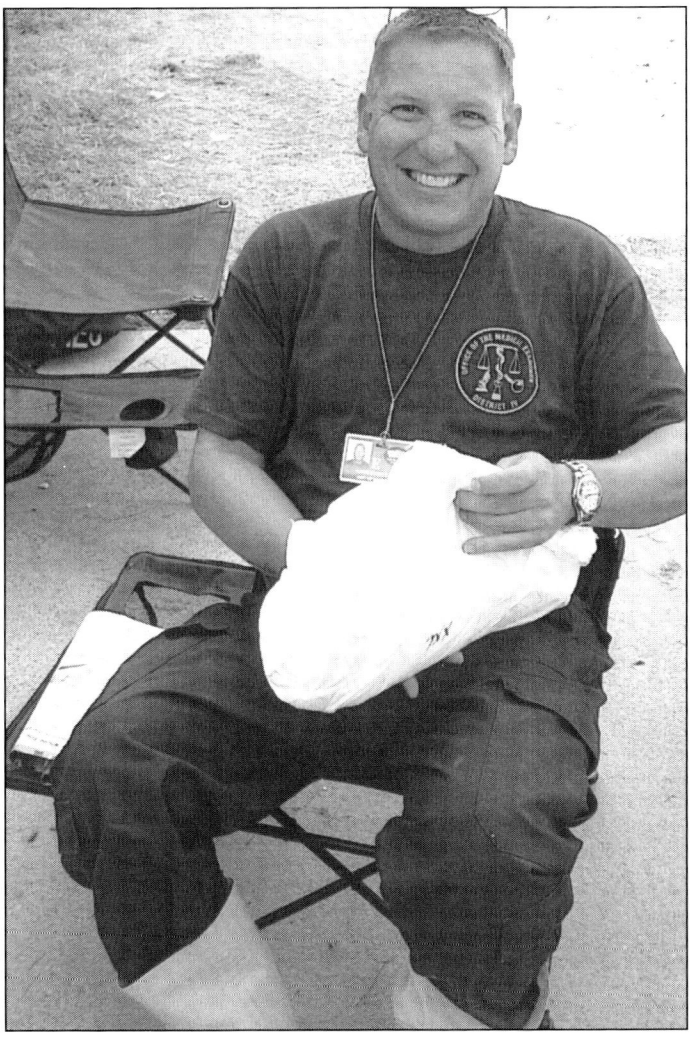